"I have tracked the work that lies behind this book for more than five years. It has greatly influenced my thinking on corporate strategy in multi-sector businesses."

Guy Jillings
Head of Strategic Planning
Shell International

"Most corporate managers rightly expect their business unit managers to be clear how they will achieve competitive advantage. Yet they themselves would be hard pressed to state clearly how the corporate level will add value to each of those businesses. One of the reasons is the lack of sound concepts and tools to examine corporate level strategy. The Ashridge team starts to fill this gap admirably. Their concept of parenting advantage and the clear treatment of it in this book is the basis for a simple but demanding reflection on what the corporate center is for. It is there for the businesses."

Philippe Haspeslagh
Professor of Corporate Strategy
INSEAD

"How corporations add value across the range of their business units is an important but seldom discussed topic. *Corporate-Level Strategy* clearly exposes the difficulties in succeeding at this and the misconceptions many have about it. The analytical and company examples offer a substantive discussion for both managers and business analysts on not only the development of these skills, but also their choices about which businesses corporations should and should not pursue."

Charles A. Peters
Vice President, Development & Technology
Emerson Electric

"An absolutely first class book. Should be made compulsory reading for any executive operating at the center. It's powerful ammunition . . . Shows clearly how we can look at the role of the corporate parent to understand how it can bring out the best in its businesses."

Robin Buchanan
Managing Partner
Bain & Company

"At last a book that cuts through all the corporate jargon and academic generalizations to answer the question 'Does the corporate parent create or destroy value for the organization?' The authors suggest a simple yet compelling framework for making this determination. Must reading for students and practitioners alike."

Robert Cizik
Chairman and Chief Executive Officer
Cooper Industries

"In an era when the role of corporate level management is quite justifiably being questioned and challenged, it is refreshing to find a book that clearly shows how parent companies can add rather than destroy value in their businesses. As we would expect of these world class authorities, Goold, Campbell, and Alexander have leveraged their fascinating research findings into an eminently readable and highly practical book."

Chris Bartlett
Professor
Harvard Business School

"A vital and deeply researched contribution to thinking about corporate strategy."

Gary Hamel
London Business School

"I am very impressed by the extensive work on which this book is based, and by the concept of parenting advantage that it puts forward."

Yasutaka Obayashi
Senior General Manager, Corporate Strategy
Canon

"Great companies grow, they don't just cut. With breakups and restructuring done, corporate parenting is coming back. Goold, Campbell, and Alexander have produced a comprehensive and intelligent book which should become a standard guide on the subject."

Tom Hout
Vice President
The Boston Consulting Group

"A perceptive and valuable insight into an often underestimated area of strategy. This book clearly demonstrates the importance of parenting to the longer term development and prosperity of multi-business companies."

Alan R. Jackson
Chief Executive, BTR

"I am glad someone has so well and so fully shed light on this important body of thinking."

Sigurd Reinton
Director, McKinsey & Company, 1981–1988

Corporate-Level Strategy

Creating Value in the Multibusiness Company

Michael Goold

Andrew Campbell

Marcus Alexander

John Wiley & Sons, Inc.

New York · Chichester · Brisbane · Toronto · Singapore

Since so much of this book is about "parenting," it seems appropriate to dedicate it to our children:

Rupert, Toby, and Edward Goold
Alastair, Lucy, Duncan, and Flora Campbell
Victoria, Gaius, and Torsten Alexander

This text is printed on acid-free paper.

Copyright © 1994 by Michael Goold, Andrew Campbell, and Marcus Alexander.
Published by John Wiley & Sons, Inc.

All rights reserved. Published simultaneously in Canada.

This publication is designed to provide accurate and
authoritative information in regard to the subject
matter covered. It is sold with the understanding that
the publisher is not engaged in rendering legal, accounting,
or other professional services. If legal advice or other
expert assistance is required, the services of a competent
professional person should be sought.

Library of Congress Cataloging in Publication Data:

Goold, Michael.
    Corporate-level strategy: creating value in the multibusiness
company / Michael Goold, Andrew Campbell, Marcus Alexander.
        p.   cm.
    Includes bibliographical references and index.
    ISBN 0-471-04716-3 (cloth)
    1. Conglomerate corporations—Management. 2. Subsidiary
corporations—Management. 3. Conglomerate corporations—Planning.
I. Campbell, Andrew. II. Alexander, Marcus. III. Title.
HD2756.G658   1994
658'.046—dc20   94-8805

Printed in the United States of America

10 9 8 7 6 5 4 3 2 1

Acknowledgments

The roots of this book go back as far as 1983 at the London Business School's Centre for Business Strategy. It was there that Michael Goold launched a research project into the decision-making processes of large multibusiness companies. Many people have contributed to our work since then and all can claim some credit for what follows.

An event of particular importance in the early years was a presentation in 1986 of the findings of the initial research project. The project had ended up by focusing on the value added to decisions by the top layers of management, particularly the corporate center, and the presentation described how good companies succeed in adding value. At the presentation, Sigurd Reinton, then a director of McKinsey & Company, pointed out that adding value was a necessary but insufficient requirement for corporate centers. The more demanding challenge, he believed, was to add more value than other corporate centers. This remark, and the work McKinsey had been doing on which it was based, led to a 1987 project run by Sigurd, in which we attempted to define the parenting skills of successful corporate centers. This project, and our subsequent work with Nathaniel Foote at McKinsey, had an important influence on our thinking.

Around the same time, the Ashridge Strategic Management Centre was launched with the intention of pursuing a research agenda dedicated to corporate strategy and the management of multibusiness companies. We owe a particular debt to Philip Sadler, then chief executive of Ashridge, who sponsored the initiative, and to the founding six member companies of the Centre. Four of these companies, BP, Courtaulds, ICI, and Shell, have continued to support our work ever since those early days.

The Ashridge Strategic Management Centre's Research Committee is made up of representatives from each of our member companies, and this book was conceived in 1990, when the Research Committee approved a research proposal on the topic of corporate-level strategy. The continuing interest, support, and constructive criticism of all our member companies have been invaluable. This is very much their book as well as ours.

We would like particularly to thank the companies who agreed to participate in the research. They gave generously of their management time in explaining their corporate strategies, in allowing us to test their explanations, and in criticizing and approving our interview notes and case write-ups. Our understanding of the issues of corporate strategy, and our development of the parenting advantage concept, depended heavily on the insights that these companies shared with us.

We also want to acknowledge the valuable contributions to the research made by our colleagues at the Ashridge Strategic Management Centre. David Sadtler has helped with much of the field research and has actively participated in the development of our thinking. Kathleen Luchs has made numerous contributions, based particularly on her extensive knowledge of the literature on corporate strategy. David Young has been involved in much of the conceptual development and has worked on several related projects, most notably leading the Centre's research into the size and activities of corporate headquarters staffs.

Outside the Centre, Professor Tadao Kagono of Kobe University and Nigel Campbell of Manchester Business School helped with introductions and research in Japan. Tadao Kagono's understanding of Japanese corporate strategies was specially valuable to us. Tom Lewis and other members of the Boston Consulting Group's European offices helped with research in Sweden, Germany, and France. Many other managers, academics, and consultants have helped to shape the book through innumerable discussions around presentations, consulting projects, and informal meetings.

Our remaining debt is to those who have helped with the writing and production of the book. David Collis of the Harvard Business School provided us with a thorough and influential review. David's parallel work, based around his Harvard course "Corporate Strategy," has influenced our thinking and deepened our understanding of the resource-based approach to strategy. Many others have read and commented on drafts of the manuscript and we hope they will recognize the influence they have had. In particular, we would like to mention Charlie Peters, Vice President of Development and Technology of Emerson Electric, and David Guyton, Planning Manager of ICI

Chemicals and Polymers, who both provided specially detailed and helpful comments. Lastly, we would like to thank John Mahaney of John Wiley & Sons, who has been an enthusiastic and supportive editor, and Nancy Marcus Land of Publications Development Company, who has taken the book through the production process with efficiency and helpfulness.

Undoubtedly, the most arduous task has fallen on Elaine Johnson, Sue Little, Stephanie Maggin, Juliet Venter, and Sally Yeung. They have helped us to edit and transcribe dozens of drafts and redrafts of every chapter. The book has been a constant, if not always welcome, companion for them for more than a year. Their efficiency, accuracy, and lack of complaint deserves special mention and their efforts have helped to make what follows more readable.

MICHAEL GOOLD
ANDREW CAMPBELL
MARCUS ALEXANDER

April 1994

Reader's Guide

Few readers of business books sit down and read them from cover to cover. We have therefore tried, at the cost of some repetition, to make each chapter and each Part of the book largely self-contained. Readers can then use the book in different ways.

Part One introduces the parenting advantage concept and outlines our framework for corporate strategy analysis and development. It then answers some basic questions about the parenting advantage concept and shows how the concept relates to other approaches to corporate strategy.

Part Two explores the ways in which parent organizations create value and achieve parenting advantage in more depth. The main ideas and conclusions are contained in Chapter 5, which introduces the concepts, and Chapter 11, which summarizes the findings. Chapters 6 through 10 provide detailed discussions of different sorts of value creation and of the main companies that we have researched.

Part Three provides practical guidance on developing a corporate strategy around parenting advantage. The approach builds on the framework put forward in Parts One and Two. Chapter 12 gives an overview of the approach, and Chapters 13 through 15 provide examples and guidance on specific issues. Chapter 16 concludes with practical tips for putting the principles into practice.

The Appendixes take up specific topics in some detail. They are intended to give a fuller treatment of these topics for readers with special interest in them.

Readers who wish to gain a rapid overview of the main points should start with Chapters 1, 2, 4, 5, 11, and 12. They can then dip into other chapters to pursue topics or companies in which they have particular interest. Readers such as consultants or corporate development executives, who are confronted with an immediate task of reviewing and improving companies' corporate strategies, may be particularly interested in Part Three. Finally, readers who want to examine the underpinnings of our argument in detail will find the bulk of the research findings in Part Two and will find detailed discussion of specific conceptual issues in Chapters 3, 4, and the Appendixes.

Contents

APPENDIXES 387

PART ONE

CORPORATE STRATEGY AND PARENTING ADVANTAGE

1 CORPORATE STRATEGY: THE ISSUES

The justification for multibusiness companies is under question. "Value gaps"—gaps between a quoted company's total market capitalization and the apparent breakup value of its individual businesses—are widespread. Management buyouts frequently flourish once they are released from corporate influence. Business unit managers tend to disparage the contributions made by their corporate-level bosses. Grandiose acquisitions all too often end in ignominious divestments. The research on which this book is based suggests that, while a few multibusiness companies have corporate strategies that create substantial value, the large majority do not; they are value destroyers. This disturbing conclusion, which applies to multibusiness companies in many different countries and cultures, and of varied size and complexity, casts serious doubt on whether multibusiness companies should continue to play a leading role in the world economy.

Recent developments in the market for corporate control and changes in corporate governance have increased the focus on the value created by multibusiness companies. In the past, there were few effective ways of bringing pressure to bear on incumbent managements that destroyed value. But, during the 1980s and 1990s, hostile takeover bids, MBOs, leveraged partnerships, and corporate breakups have shown the massive potential for improving performance by changing the nature, role, and objectives of multibusiness companies. The growing awareness of this potential amongst investors and boards of directors has also led to a train of corporate upheavals. Reversals of corporate strategy and management changes at famous companies such as IBM, General Motors, Eastman Kodak, Sears Roebuck,

3

British Aerospace, or American Express are dramatic proof of the change in climate.

The upheavals at these famous companies are symptomatic of a wider questioning of the validity of multibusiness companies' strategies. Across the globe, multibusiness managements are under increasing pressure, as they struggle with decisions about what businesses they should be in and how they should structure and influence these businesses.

In the United States and the United Kingdom, multibusiness companies have been under unprecedented attack. For years, size and diversity appeared to ensure safety from predators; suddenly, the opposite seemed to become true. Past diversification was seen by corporate raiders and buyout specialists as present opportunity. In 1979, the Fortune 500 accounted for nearly 60% of U.S. Gross National Product. By 1991, this share had dropped to only 40%. Successful predators multiplied the stock market value of many companies by eliminating corporate-level structures and staffs, and by splitting up diversified groups. Was this just a short-term phenomenon? Did the predators gain at the expense of the long-term health of the businesses involved? Or were they releasing value that had previously been suppressed by ineffective corporate managements?

In Germany, supporters of the "Mittelstand" companies argue that focus and simplicity outweigh scope and scale.[1] They would prefer the dismemberment of large, diversified companies, and the travail of multibusiness organizations such as Daimler Benz and Metallgesellschaft seems to give weight to their arguments. Many large groups in Germany are now setting up holding company structures to act as parent organizations to which their different businesses report. Will this prove to be a solution that improves their performance? Or is it an attempt to paper over deeper problems in managing diverse businesses that will require a more radical response?

Others believe that without large, multibusiness companies, Western economies cannot invest enough to compete: Fragmentation undermines investment in core technologies and core competences.[2] Such commentators point to the many successes of Japanese corporations as evidence that a different sort of multibusiness company will succeed in the future. But in Japan itself, there is increasing concern over poor corporate profitability and bureaucratic decision making—referred to as "big company disease." Questions are being raised about Japanese companies that, until recently, enjoyed the same kudos reserved for U.S. champions in the 1950s and 1960s. Will the diversifications of Japanese steel corporations into businesses ranging from electronics to theme parks lead to corporate renewal or disaster? Will the huge acquisitions of Matsushita and Sony in Hollywood lead to valuable new business streams or costly failures? Will the large corporate centers of most Japanese companies provide a source of advantage over delayered Western competitors or become bureaucratic millstones?

Many of the old certainties have been undermined by sharper competition and economic adversity. The large diversified corporations that were once so dominant now face major challenge. The reason for this challenge is that many, if not most, do not have clear and convincing corporate strategies.

CORPORATE STRATEGY

Corporate strategy should guide corporate-level decisions, just as business strategy should guide business-level decisions. Corporate-level decisions relate to two primary questions:

1. In what businesses should the company invest its resources, either through ownership, minority holdings, joint ventures, or alliances?
2. How should the parent company influence and relate to the businesses under its control?

The first type of corporate-level decision is easily illustrated. Consider Westinghouse's ill-fated decision in the late 1980s to enter the financial services business, paralleling a successful move by its old rival, General Electric. The decision cost Paul Lego his job and his reputation as one of the United States' better managers. Consider the 1993 decision at Imperial Chemical Industries (ICI), one of the world's top chemical groups, to split in two, forming Zeneca, in pharmaceuticals and speciality chemicals, and ICI, in bulk chemicals. Consider the acquisition battle for Paramount, won in 1994 by Viacom. Alliances headed by Viacom and QVC brought together complex groupings of companies that sought to shape and build on the fast-evolving convergence between the entertainment, telecommunications, and cable industries. These examples of large and highly public decisions are no different, in principle, from a decision by a small shoe retailer to set up a separate business selling luggage. They are all "portfolio decisions": decisions about the range of businesses in which the company should invest its money and management effort.

Now consider Jack Welch's decision in the early 1980s to cut out much of GE's highly regarded planning process, and to change the way the parent company was structured. It helped earn him the title of "Neutron Jack"—he left the buildings standing but removed the people. Consider the decision by Bob Horton, chairman of British Petroleum between 1990 and 1992, to revitalize the head office by eliminating committees, decentralizing powers, outsourcing activities like tax management, and championing a new set of corporate values. Horton's personal style may have alienated his colleagues and led to his departure, but the changes he initiated appear to have helped the company. Consider Nestlé's decision in 1992 to eliminate central functions and set up a matrix of product divisions and regional managers. Hailed by Nestlé's managers as the biggest revolution in the company's history, it was described by the *Financial Times* as "tiptoeing into the 1980s." These are examples of high-profile and public decisions, but they do not differ in principle from a decision by a small group of manufacturing businesses to change the budgeting process and establish a specialist planning team. All are examples of the second type of corporate-level decision. They are decisions about how the central organization should influence and relate to its businesses.

Corporate strategy should guide both types of decision. But few multibusiness companies today have a clear and convincing answer to the basic question: What is your corporate strategy? For most companies, the corporate strategy is the sum of the division strategies, together with some broad objectives and, perhaps, a companywide statement of mission, much the same as that of a hundred other companies. Senior managers who are responsible for defining the overall corporate strategy often recognize that something is missing. They may offer some financial guidelines, and they may be able to articulate a list of which businesses are "core." Beyond that, the question about corporate strategy usually makes them uncomfortable. This book is designed to fill the void; to help companies develop corporate strategies that are clearer, more powerful, and harder to challenge.

THE ROLE OF THE PARENT

Multibusiness companies consist of businesses, many of which could exist independently, and a corporate hierarchy of line managers, functions, and staffs outside these businesses. It is this corporate hierarchy, which we refer to as the corporate parent, that is responsible for making corporate strategy decisions. It is the parent that decides what new businesses to support, what acquisitions to make, and whether to form joint ventures or alliances. It is the parent that determines the structure of the corporation, defines budgeting and capital expenditure processes, and sets the tone for corporate values and attitudes. It is the parent that comes under intense scrutiny during hostile takeover bids, or when large shareholders are dissatisfied with their returns. The parent is at the heart of corporate strategy decisions. Our approach to corporate strategy therefore places the role of the parent in centre stage. Corporate strategy concerns what the parent will do, and across what businesses it will operate, just as business strategy concerns the role of business managers and the scope of business activities in which they will operate.

The parent has the potential both to create and to destroy significant amounts of value. At the simplest level, the parent organization incurs costs. If its activities do not justify its costs, value is destroyed.

Our research, however, has highlighted the significance of the parent's influence on decisions much more than its basic cost. A misguided acquisition, for example, can destroy more value in six months than the cost of running the parent organization for many years. In contrast, an inspired parental appointment of a particularly talented business unit general manager can create more value in one business than the total annual cost of the parent. The parent's influence on business-level plans, aspirations, and investments can provide vital stretch, specialist understanding, and tough discipline; alternatively, it can promote choking constraints, crucial delays, or suicidal ambitions.

The role of the parent is clearly important. Yet advice about how this role should be played is confusing and contradictory. Parents are exhorted to downsize and delayer, but also to intensify the search for synergy and to foster core competences. They are told to stick to the knitting, but to ensure corporate growth and renewal. They are urged to manage strategic alliances and global networks, while empowering individual businesses. They are pressed to balance their portfolios, while increasing their focus. Demergers, acquisitions, and divestments are portrayed at one moment as the central opportunity to unlock true shareholder value, at the next as shoddy accounting tricks. While layer upon layer of thinking has been introduced, the parenting task has generally been performed poorly.

The issue of determining a valid role for the parent organization is now firmly on the agenda of most companies. It has become a topic of central importance to chief executives who are eager to improve the performance of their groups of businesses. It is a matter of increasing debate among shareholders, who are no longer prepared to remain purely passive owners. It is a topic of lively gossip among business unit managers within multibusiness companies. It is also, most significantly, a major determinant in the Darwinian evolution of the corporate world. Corporations that lack a convincing corporate-level strategy are gradually being weeded out. If performance is unsatisfactory, corrective steps are now being taken more rapidly. To forestall the crises and management changes referred to at the start of this chapter, parent organizations must focus on how they can create value: Why will a group of potentially independent businesses benefit from being owned by a common parent?

THE QUEST FOR PARENTING ADVANTAGE

So far, we have focused on the fundamental question of why the parent organization should exist at all. This question lies behind most of the challenge to multibusiness companies. The only satisfactory answer is that the businesses perform better in aggregate under the parent's ownership than they would if they were independent entities, and that the parent creates sufficient value to more than offset its cost.

But we propose a more ambitious aspiration for the parent. Rather than simply creating some net value, it should strive to gain "parenting advantage"; it should aim to be the best possible parent for its businesses. In aggregate, the businesses under its stewardship should perform not only better than they would as stand-alone entities but also better than they would under the stewardship of any other parent. Otherwise, more value could be created by a change in ownership for some, or all, of the businesses in the portfolio. Parenting advantage, as a principle, should guide decisions about the nature of the businesses in the portfolio and about the structure of the parent, its activities, and relationships. Corporate strategy should clarify how and where the company can achieve parenting advantage.

The link between parenting advantage and corporate strategy therefore closely parallels the link between competitive advantage and business strategy. Competitive advantage has become the touchstone for successful business strategies, guiding strategic analysis and providing a basis for assessing alternative action plans. We see the concept of parenting advantage playing a similar role at the corporate level. It should be the fundamental test for judging corporate strategies and the guiding principle in corporate-level decisions.

This book contains abundant evidence that the quest for parenting advantage underlies the decisions of successful multibusiness companies and distinguishes them from their less successful rivals. We also show that a corporate strategy development process can be designed around the concept, and that a focus on parenting advantage can, and does, lead to corporate strategies and corporate decisions that run counter to popular logic. We believe that parenting advantage is a practical and vitally useful principle for parent managers, just as competitive advantage has proved to be vitally useful for business managers.

RESEARCH APPROACH

Our research has been grounded in contacts with many different multibusiness companies over several years. As academics, we have carried out a number of research projects focused on the problems of multibusiness companies. These projects started ten years ago at the London Business School. For the past 6 years, they have formed the prime focus of our work at the Ashridge Strategic Management Centre. Furthermore, as consultants, we have been drawn into the practical questions and concerns of corporate-level management in both large and small companies. For this book, we have focused particularly on 15 corporate parents, with annual company sales ranging from $2 billion

EXHIBIT 1–1 Primary companies researched

Company	1993 Sales[1] ($US million)	1993 Profits[2] ($US million)	1993 Employees (thousand)
Asea Brown Boveri	28315	2181	206.5
Banc One	7227	1699	45.3
BTR[4]	14658	2159	128.5
Canon	16394	880	64.5
Cooper	6274	725	49.5
Dover	2484	268	20.4
Emerson Electric[3]	8174	1231	71.6
General Electric	60652	13564	222.0
Grand Metropolitan[3, 4]	11870	1529	102.4
Hanson[3, 4]	14640	1524	71.0
3M	14020	1956	86.2
RTZ[4]	7233	684	60.0
Shell[4]	95025	8916	117.0
TI Group[4]	2090	207	24.0
Unilever[4]	41794	3135	294.0

[1] *Sales for year ending December 31, 1993.*
[2] *Profit before interest and tax for year ending December 31, 1993.*
[3] *For year ending September 30, 1993.*
[4] *Results reported in pounds sterling; stated here in U.S. dollars at exchange rate £1 = $1.50.*

to $95 billion (see Exhibit 1–1). These companies were selected because each can claim success in major parts of its corporate strategy. We neither assume nor argue that all their decisions have been faultless; but we do believe that these parents have pursued fundamentally successful corporate strategies, and illustrate the variety of approaches among today's leading companies. Although the companies chosen are relatively large, mainly to aid readers' recognition and familiarity, we use them to illustrate approaches that are equally appropriate for much smaller organizations. Our consulting work has spanned a broad range of company size and complexity, and confirms the relevance of the same underlying concepts.

In these companies, we conducted interviews with management both in the parent and in the businesses.[3] We supplemented our interviews by consulting published material—books, articles, and case studies on the companies. We thus developed an impression of each company's parenting approach and its corporate strategy, which is described in detail in these pages. We assessed the impact of these corporate strategies, both by analyzing overall corporate results and by following through the parent's influence on specific decisions and situations. We have conducted similar, but less extensive, research with a further two dozen companies, many referred to in the book, but without detailed description of their corporate strategies.

The book is divided into three parts. Part One examines the concept of parenting advantage, outlines a basic framework for assessing and developing corporate strategy, and sets this framework in the context of historical thinking. Part Two explores the ways in which parent organizations create, or destroy, value. It brings out the underlying paradoxes that confront parents and make it difficult for them to avoid destroying value. The chapters focus on the conditions under which parents are able to overcome these paradoxes, and succeed in creating value. Part Three describes a process for developing corporate strategy built around parenting advantage. It provides tools, checklists, and a worked example that will help corporate strategists in applying the concepts discussed in the earlier parts. Each part starts with an overview chapter. Subsequent chapters develop the framework in more detail, providing examples and illustrations.

SUMMARY

Our observation as academics and consultants is that corporate-level strategy is currently underserved. The implication of research on unsuccessful diversification, corporate breakups, and value gaps is that billions of dollars of value are destroyed or suppressed by bad corporate-level decisions each year.[4] There has been a shortage of convincing corporate-level strategies, and of practical guidance in creating them.

We aim to put forward a sounder, more fundamental way of thinking about corporate-level strategy than has previously been developed. We provide a principle—parenting advantage—to guide corporate-level decisions, and a framework built around this principle to help managers develop better corporate strategies. We believe that analysing and understanding the essence of parenting advantage can significantly enhance the chances of creating, rather than destroying, value.

Parenting advantage is simple in concept, but it challenges many management beliefs when worked through in detail. We hope that reading this book will stimulate corporate managers to challenge their own company's performance: How does the parent create value—and does it create more than would be created by other rivals?

NOTES

1. See e.g., T. Peters, "Rethinking Scale," *California Management Review,* Fall 1992.

2. See, e.g., C. K. Prahalad, and Gary Hamel, "The Core Competence of the Corporation," *Harvard Business Review.* May–June 1990. (The plural of "core competence" is spelled variously. We adopt the spelling without an "i" before the final "e.")

3. In most of these companies, we carried out a total of 10 to 15 in-depth interviews, each lasting between one and three hours. By interviewing managers at different levels and in different parts of the company, we were able to cross-check and validate the information we received.

4. See, for example, Michael Jensen, "The Eclipse of the Public Corporation," *Harvard Business Review,* September–October 1989, pp. 61–74 and "Corporate Control and the Politics of Finance," *Journal of Applied Corporate Finance,* vol. 4, no. 2, Summer 1991; S. Bhagat, A. Shleifer, and R. Vishny, "Hostile Takeovers in the 1980s: The Return to Corporate Specialization," *Brookings Papers on Economic Activity: Microeconomics 1990;* James P. Walsh and Rita D. Kosnik, "Corporate Raiders and Their Disciplinary Role in the Market for Corporate Control," *Academy of Management Journal,* vol. 36, no. 4, 1993, pp. 671–700; Michael E. Porter, "From Competitive Advantage to Corporate Strategy," *Harvard Business Review,* May–June 1987, pp. 43–59.

2 PARENTING ADVANTAGE: THE FRAMEWORK

Parenting advantage is the central concept that should drive thinking about corporate-level strategy. This chapter shows why parenting advantage should play this role. It then presents a framework for analyzing corporate strategies and shows how successful companies embody the principles of parenting advantage in their corporate-level decisions. Whether they use the terminology or not, their behavior displays consistent patterns. We summarize these patterns and structure them in a common format called a "parenting advantage statement." We then consider the dynamics of corporate strategy by looking at two cases: One shows the evolution of parenting advantage in a company, the other highlights the challenge posed by different types of rival. Finally, we draw out the implications of parenting advantage for formulating and assessing corporate strategy.

PARENTING ADVANTAGE AS A GOAL

The business units of multibusiness companies create value through direct contact with customers.[1] They compete in their markets to satisfy customer needs and to generate revenues and profits. These businesses report to the parent, which includes the corporate headquarters and, perhaps, group and division managements.[2] In contrast to the businesses, the parent does not have external customers and generates costs but no revenues. It acts as an intermediary, influencing the decisions and strategies pursued by the businesses, and standing between the businesses and those who provide capital for their use (see Exhibit 2–1).

12

EXHIBIT 2–1   The corporate parent is an intermediary

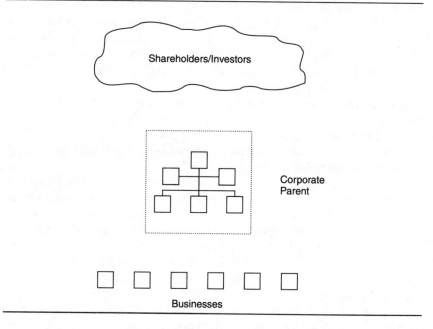

It follows that primary wealth creation takes place only at the business level, and that the parent must work through its businesses to create value. The first test of a parent is therefore whether it creates any value in its businesses. Would they perform better or worse in aggregate if they were stand-alone entities?[3] For the parent to destroy value,[4] either through damaging influence on the businesses or through imposing unjustified costs, cannot be acceptable. It should either find a way of creating value or else set up the businesses independently and dissolve itself.[5]

This basic test is an excellent challenge for most parents. It nearly always leads to a worthwhile clarification of the parent's role and the basis of its corporate-level strategy. Unfortunately, many companies have still not seriously addressed themselves to the challenge. They cannot make any convincing argument to show that they enhance the collective performance of their businesses.

Failure to meet this challenge has been highlighted by studies of acquisitions. In a widely read article,[6] Michael Porter reported the results of his research on acquisitions made by 33 large American companies between 1950 and 1986. More than half of these acquisitions were subsequently resold, usually within 5 or 6 years. This did not always indicate problems, but Porter inferred that the new parents frequently decided that they had made a mistake and were unsuitable owners of the businesses. To help parent companies make better acquisition decisions, he proposed three tests. One of these, the "better-off test," required that the new unit should gain competitive advantage from its link with the corporation, or vice versa. In other words, the combination should result in value creation.

Porter's research highlights one aspect of corporate decision making. It points up the need for parents to create value with new acquisitions. But the implications of the better-off test are much wider and relate to all areas of corporate decision making. The better-off test should be applied to the existing portfolio as well as to new acquisitions. The essential role of the corporate parent is to influence the businesses in its portfolio in ways that enhance their collective performance, net of the full costs of the parent. If the parent cannot demonstrate that businesses are indeed better off in its ownership, the corporate strategy must be fundamentally flawed.

Creating some net value is therefore a minimum objective for corporate strategy. But the corporate parent should be more ambitious and set a more demanding goal. The appropriate benchmark for value creation is not what would happen without a parent, but what the best available parent would achieve. Ideally, each parent should aim to create more value from its businesses than could be attained by any alternative owner. Otherwise, the corporate strategy is suboptimal, and the company is failing to maximize value creation for its stakeholders.

"Parenting advantage," the ability to create more value than rival parents, has implications for portfolio composition. For example, a parent may add value by helping a business improve its planning disciplines. It may even add more value through this process than it adds cost. The business is better off as part of the parent than it would be as an independent company. But what if another parent can not only improve planning disciplines, but also make better senior management appointments and exert more powerful financial controls? The business will perform better if owned by the second parent. The second parent may be able to acquire the business at a premium—yet still create value out of the deal. If many of its businesses fall into this category, the first parent is—at least in theory—vulnerable to predators, since other, "better" parents should be willing to pay a premium to gain corporate control.

In practice, hostile changes in ownership only occur in extreme cases. Companies in many countries are largely immune from predatory action. Even in the United States and United Kingdom, the predator has to anticipate a return in excess of a large takeover premium (typically 30%–50%). Parents can therefore survive without achieving parenting advantage. But motivation should not spring simply from the fear of takeover. The ambitious parent will seek to maximize the value it creates and to make the best possible use of its parenting skills. To reject this goal is to accept a second-best situation in which shareholders, employees, and customers are underrewarded. This is certainly economically inefficient: Arguably, it is morally wrong. Increasing pressure from all stakeholders is making it more and more difficult for the parent to accept such a situation knowingly. The parent's duty must be to maximize the value it creates from its businesses and thus the benefits it can provide to stakeholders.

To create more value than other parents, it is necessary to have some advantage over them. This can come either from seeing more or better opportunities for performance enhancement, or from being better qualified to realize these opportunities. If a business creates more value than its competitors, it is achieving competitive advantage through its business strategy. By analyzing the sources of competitive advantage, it is possible to identify how the business strategy enables the business to outperform its competitors. Similarly, if a corporate parent creates more value than rival parents, it is achieving parenting advantage. By analyzing the sources of parenting advantage, it is possible to identify how the corporate strategy enables the parent to outperform its rivals. Parenting advantage is the fundamental test and basis for a sound corporate strategy, just as competitive advantage is for business strategy. It provides a goal to guide decisions about the parent and the portfolio, and a benchmark against which to assess these decisions.

A FRAMEWORK FOR CORPORATE STRATEGY

The Basic Framework

Successful parents create significant value. They do so by realizing specific performance improvement opportunities that exist in their businesses. But the nature of these opportunities varies from one business to another. In one business, there may be an opportunity to improve performance through applying tighter controls than would exist if the business was independent. In another business, there may be an opportunity to facilitate the sharing of complex know-how that would not occur between stand-alone entities. Different opportunities can only be realized by applying different parenting skills or characteristics.

The essence of successful parenting is to create a fit between the way the parent operates—the parent's characteristics—and the improvement opportunities that the parent addresses.[7] A parent that is well suited to address certain opportunities may be ill suited to address others. For example, a parent whose systems and staff are well suited to squeezing cash out of mature businesses and to resisting unprofitable growth strategies that may destabilize the market, will not be well suited to facilitating complex linkages across emergent high-growth applications of new technology.

To be particularly good at creating value, the parent must focus on some opportunities to the exclusion of others. It must have distinctive characteristics that are specially relevant to its businesses. The characteristics of the parent and of its businesses must fit. Conversely, an obvious misfit between the parent and its businesses will cause the parent to destroy value. The very characteristics that help in one situation will be damaging in some others. The foundation for a successful parenting relationship is therefore the achievement of a high degree of fit between the characteristics of the parent and those of the businesses it owns.[8] This is illustrated in Exhibit 2–2.

In pursuit of parenting advantage, it is not enough simply to have some level of fit, or merely to avoid major misfits. The parent must seek to achieve a closer fit with its businesses than would be achieved by rivals. In adopting the goal of parenting advantage, corporate strategy must therefore consider rival parents.

Furthermore, fit today does not ensure fit tomorrow. The environment is not stable, so achieving fit is a dynamic, not a one-time, task. Corporate strategy must address the changes and trends that are taking place: Improvement opportunities that existed at one point in time may diminish or disappear altogether. Upgrading general management skills to professional levels may have been a major opportunity that parents could exploit in the 1950s. It is a much more confined opportunity in the 1990s. In contrast, new parenting opportunities may arise. Changes in technology and customer preference may create valuable benefits from linkages between previously stand-alone businesses. If these linkages are complex for individual businesses to achieve, they provide an improvement opportunity for parents with the right skills and characteristics. In developing corporate strategy based on parenting advantage, it is important to take a dynamic view, in which the impact of trends and scenarios is considered, as well as the current state of play.

Our model must therefore be expanded to take account of rival parents and future trends and scenarios. The outcome of fit between a parent and its businesses can then be judged in terms of current and potential parenting advantage, rather than merely historical value creation.

Corporate strategy guides the parent's decisions. Decisions about the portfolio, covering acquisitions, divestments, alliances, business redefinitions, and new ventures determine what businesses will be in the

EXHIBIT 2–2   The need for fit

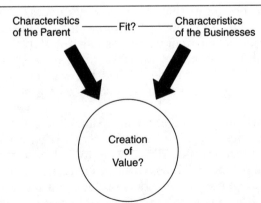

Characteristics of the Parent ———— Fit? ———— Characteristics of the Businesses

Creation of Value?

portfolio and hence, what characteristics and opportunities they will present. Decisions about the parent, including how to structure corporate management levels, who to employ at the center, what planning and control systems to use, and so on, determine the parent's characteristics and the degree to which they fit with the businesses. These two outputs of corporate strategy therefore feed back into the original inputs. Exhibit 2–3 draws the various elements together into a general framework for assessing and developing corporate strategy and parenting advantage.

Understanding Current Fit

The framework in Exhibit 2–3 gives a dynamic view of parenting advantage. At any time, however, the fit between the parent and its businesses will provide the basis for value creation. Understanding the nature of this fit is a crucial task in assessing and developing corporate strategy.

In an earlier book, *Strategies and Styles*, [9] two of us examined the issue of fit between the parent and its businesses in terms of the parent's overall behavior. We found it possible to discern some broad patterns in parenting, which represent basically different parenting philosophies. We refer to these as parenting styles. [10] The book identified three main parenting styles; Strategic Planning, Strategic Control, and Financial Control. Strategic Planning parents are closely involved with their businesses in developing plans and strategies, and emphasize long-term goals and underlying competitive developments in the control process. Financial Control parents decentralize responsibility for the development of plans and strategies to the managements of each business, and

EXHIBIT 2–3   Corporate strategy framework

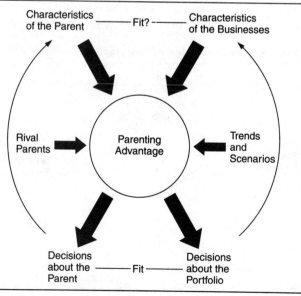

operate a tight control process that stresses short-term profitability goals. Strategic Control parents seek a balance between the extremes of the other two styles.[11]

The three parenting styles were broadly drawn, but they illustrated how differences in parental role or philosophy can impact value creation across the whole portfolio. The research showed that successful companies enjoyed a fit between their parenting style and the needs of their businesses. In contrast, a misfit between the business units and the parenting style damaged company performance.

While endorsing these broad observations, our subsequent research has focused on much finer-grained aspects of fit. Fit at the level of overall style is a necessary condition for successful corporate strategy, but by no means a sufficient one. Companies with a portfolio of businesses that fit their parenting style may nevertheless fail to create value, let alone achieve parenting advantage. Consideration of the fit between the parent and its businesses must go beyond the issue of overall style and explore in more detail specific characteristics of the parent and its businesses.

Characteristics of the Parent

In developing a deeper understanding of the parent's characteristics, we have found it helpful to examine five groups of related characteristics.[12] These are depicted in Exhibit 2–4 and are described in the following sections.

The Parent's Mental Maps.   Parent company managers have rules of thumb and mental models that help them to interpret and synthesize information. These rules and models, which we refer to as the parent's mental maps, largely stem from their management experience and often

EXHIBIT 2–4   Characteristics of the parent

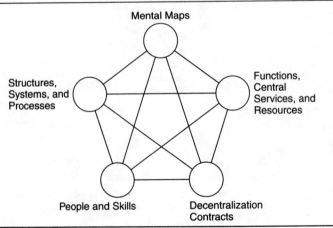

appear to outsiders as biases and predispositions. They shape the parent's perception of business improvement opportunities. They embody its understanding and feel for different types of business. They underlie the knee-jerk reactions and intuitive assumptions of the parent. They reflect deeply held values and objectives. Some are general precepts, such as might be included in an MBA course. Others are business specific, outlining ways to approach particular situations. Yet others relate to elements of the manager's personal experience. A manager with 20 years' experience in commodity chemicals will have very different maps from one who has spent 20 years in fashion retailing. Although each manager's mental maps are therefore unique, the parent can be characterized and differentiated with regard to its dominant maps. These may be the maps of dominant individuals, or the maps that are widely shared by managers in the parent.

The Parenting Structures, Systems, and Processes.   These are the mechanisms through which the parent creates value. The number of layers in the hierarchy, the existence or not of a matrix, the appointment processes, human resource systems, budgeting and planning processes, capital approval systems, decision-making structures, transfer pricing systems, and other coordination or linkage mechanisms are all relevant aspects of parenting. The formal design of these structures and processes can be important, but more often it is how the managers interact within the structure or process that is particular to one company rather than another. It is important, therefore, to understand the influences and behaviors that these structures and processes encourage.

Functions, Central Services, and Resources.   These are the corporate staff departments and central assets that support line management's efforts to create value. Some parents have large central functions; some as few as possible. Resources, such as patents held by the parent, the corporate brand, special government relationships, or access to scarce property or financial assets, can also be important characteristics.

People and Skills.   Parents often create value because they contain people with unique expertise. There is overlap here with the concept of the parent's mental maps and with the skills in functions and services. Yet neither of those categories captures sufficiently the special individuals we have met in parent companies. Because of the small size of most parent organizations, they are frequently dominated by a handful of individuals whose personalities and individual skills make a critical difference. Jack Welch at General Electric or Allen Sheppard at Grand Metropolitan are both exceptional individuals. Yet, individuals at the very top are not the only ones who matter. A parent may have a unique division head or a particularly skilled technical director. These individuals can be the parent's most valuable characteristic.

Decentralization Contracts. The "decentralization contract" between the parent and a business defines the issues on which the parent normally provides influence and those that it normally decentralizes to business managers. It is partly captured in authorization limits, job descriptions, and formal statements of due process. However, it is typically embedded in the culture of the company and is not fully explicit. It involves both principles and precedents, and is continuously tested in specific cases. It represents an implicit "franchise agreement" between the parent and the head of each business. It also covers changes in parental involvement that are likely to accompany changing circumstances, such as deterioration in business performance.

Scrutiny through each of the five lenses can reveal a much fuller view of a parent's individual characteristics than is captured in its generic parenting style.

Characteristics of the Businesses

To understand the extent of fit between a parent and its businesses, business characteristics also need examination in some detail.[13] First, the businesses themselves must be defined. The starting point is whatever definitions are currently employed within the company. If these organizational definitions are not appropriate, changing them represents a potential opportunity to improve performance.[14] After defining the businesses, two sets of characteristics should be analyzed: (1) parenting opportunities and (2) critical success factors.

Parenting Opportunities. Businesses contain various opportunities for a parent to create value. The specific situation in each business determines the nature and extent of these opportunities. Factors that give rise to opportunities include weaknesses in the business management team, conflicts between business managers' interests and those of other stakeholders, the need for specialist expertise not possessed by the business, and the existence of potentially useful, unrealized linkages with other businesses. Opportunities that are significant to one business may be largely irrelevant to another. For example, complex cross-fertilization of different technology streams may offer benefits to a business addressing rapidly evolving customer needs with successive generations of new products. On the other hand, fine-tuning product profitability may be more important in a relatively mature, niche business. The mix of opportunities is unique to each business. It determines the extent of the potential for a parent to add value. In assessing fit, it is important to determine whether the opportunities that are significant for the business in question are likely to be well addressed by a particular parent.

Critical Success Factors.   In each business, certain factors play a major role in business-level success. These factors are different in different types of business. In one business, the ability to attract and motivate exceptionally creative individuals may be critical. In another, the ability to manage labor costs very tightly may be more important. In one business, understanding and developing new technological solutions may be critical. In another, technology may be far less critical than site location. To create value, and avoid value destruction, the parent's characteristics must be compatible with the critical success factors in the business. For example, the parent's mental maps may highlight the importance of technological superiority. If technological leadership is a critical success factor, this will be appropriate. In businesses where technology is less vital, however, such a parent may well apply pressure to indulge in costly and wasteful technical investments. Without an understanding of the relevant critical success factors, the parent risks inadvertently causing damage. Misfits between parental characteristics and the critical success factors in the business will lead to value destruction.

EXHIBIT 2–5   Corporate strategy framework

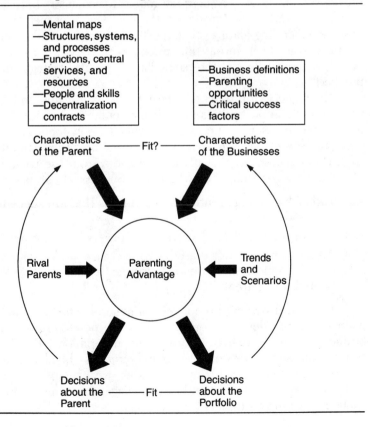

—Mental maps
—Structures, systems, and processes
—Functions, central services, and resources
—People and skills
—Decentralization contracts

—Business definitions
—Parenting opportunities
—Critical success factors

Characteristics of the Parent —— Fit? —— Characteristics of the Businesses

Rival Parents → Parenting Advantage ← Trends and Scenarios

Decisions about the Parent —— Fit —— Decisions about the Portfolio

These headings for examining the characteristics of the parent and its businesses can be added to our previous framework for corporate strategy (see Exhibit 2–5).

SUCCESSFUL CORPORATE STRATEGIES

Our research focused on multibusiness companies that have some claim to parenting advantage for at least a significant proportion of their portfolios. We wanted to understand what distinguished these companies from others that we knew well. What was the basis of their success? What patterns or themes linked them together?

At first sight, it was hard not to focus on the differences, since companies seemed to adopt fundamentally conflicting approaches. Canon's large corporate center and complex organizational structures seemed totally at variance with BTR's emphasis on low overheads and unambiguous personal accountability. Emerson's rigorous use of the strategic planning process, encompassing at least 5 years of historic data and 5 years of projected results, differed dramatically from Hanson's complete lack of involvement in any strategic planning process. As noted previously, however, the more we talked to managers both within the parents and within the businesses, the more we discerned the existence of some underlying features that are shared by successful parents. These features relate to different dimensions of fit between a parent and its businesses, regardless of the particular corporate strategy that is being pursued.

First, successful parents' attempts to create value do fit well with the parenting opportunities in their particular businesses. But there is much more to observe. Successful parents not only focus on relevant opportunities; they have unusual insights about how they can create value from them. These insights distinguish them from the pack, and come across in how they talk about their role. Successful parents:

- Either focus on parenting opportunities that are specially significant and hence unlock major value.
- And/or focus on opportunities that others have not perceived.
- And/or have a particularly deep and rich understanding of why specific improvement opportunities exist and how they can be exploited by a parent.

Successful parents do not rely on general assertions such as "Our main role is to allocate resources across the portfolio and provide the business managers with an informed second opinion." They are guided by more focused, more penetrating and more insightful statements such as "In mature, manufacturing businesses, we pay special attention to cost recovery because we find that managers are frequently not bold enough in asking customers for price increases."

We describe this first feature of successful parents as the possession of *value creation insights.*

Successful parents also excel on a second dimension of fit. Not only are they generally well equipped to address their chosen improvement opportunities, but they also have distinctive characteristics that are unusually helpful in exploiting those opportunities. Very often, their parenting characteristics are mutually supportive, providing a consistency and coherence that reinforces the power of each element. We describe this second feature of successful parents as the possession of *distinctive parenting characteristics.*

Finally, successful parents focus on businesses where their parenting is likely to lead to high net value creation. In particular, they avoid businesses where parenting misfit is likely to lead them to destroy value. They have an unusually strong sense of the criteria defining businesses where:

- Their insights are valuable.
- Their "feel" for the critical success factors will minimize the risk of serious damage.

Many companies have criteria for shaping their portfolios, such as a desire to spread geographical coverage or enter high-growth industries. Successful parents, however, employ criteria that expressly recognize their own parenting characteristics, and the potential of these to create or destroy value. They have a well developed, and often an articulated, sense of the businesses with which these characteristics fit, and they actively focus their portfolio around them. We describe this type of business, where the parent in question can create high levels of net value, as a *heartland* business. The third feature of successful parents is a clear recognition of the criteria that define their own heartland, and a determination to focus the portfolio on this heartland.

These three features of successful parents—value creation insights, distinctive parenting characteristics and heartland businesses—can be mapped onto our framework for corporate strategy. (See Exhibit 2–6.)

As our understanding of these common features of successful parents developed, we found it useful to identify them explicitly and succinctly in the research companies. In each case, we outlined the areas in which the parent had particular value creation insights, the distinctive parenting characteristics that helped to exploit these insights, and the criteria that defined the company's heartland. These elements make up a "parenting advantage statement." Subsequent chapters provide parenting advantage statements for 15 companies based in the U.S., Europe, and Japan. Here, we include as illustrations summary statements for three companies—Asea Brown Boveri (ABB), Canon, and Emerson Electric (Exhibits 2–7, 2–8, 2–9). We describe each of these companies in much greater detail later in the book. At this stage,

EXHIBIT 2–6 Corporate strategy framework

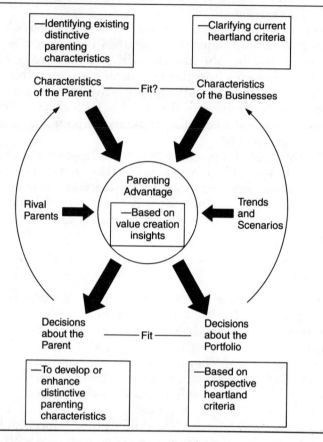

however, they serve to illustrate some basic points about parenting advantage statements.

The *value creation insights* of the three companies appear to overlap somewhat at a superficial level. Canon and ABB both focus on certain types of linkage. ABB and Emerson both focus on cost reduction through understanding product profitability. But in reality, the insights are far more specific to each company. For example, ABB's insights about linkage concern the value of being "global and local, big and small, decentralized with centralized reporting," as their chief executive puts it.[15] Insights about how to achieve this, and about when it is most valuable, distinguish ABB from other parents with somewhat similar strategies.[16] Furthermore, although the general heading of the insight can be summarized briefly, as in these statements, it is the depth of the parent's specific understanding that is critical. Emerson does not just perceive a parenting opportunity related to sharper strategic thinking and analysis, it has insights into how the parent can realize this opportunity. Canon does not just perceive the value of blending different

EXHIBIT 2–7   ABB parenting advantage statement

Value Creation Insights	Most companies make direct tradeoffs between centralization and decentralization, or scale and focus. There are opportunities for a parent that can combine the various benefits in new ways.
	Many European engineering businesses have been relatively fragmented in global terms. Consolidation can reduce costs while increasing coverage and global muscle.
	Many engineering businesses do not have a strong commercial focus and are prone to increase sales volume and product range at the expense of margin. A parent can help redress the balance.
Distinctive Parenting Characteristics	Ability to combine decentralized small business units into a global network through the ABB matrix structure.
	Systems and corporate initiatives that focus on profitability, customer needs, and simplification of operations.
	Ability to integrate acquisitions and improve their performance rapidly.
	Ruthless approach to cutting of overhead costs.
Heartland Businesses	Engineering-intensive, electrotechnical businesses, usually involving complex integration into systems. Customers are large industrial or governmental institutions.

technologies and experiences from different markets, it has insights into the parent's role in achieving such blends. Most parents are not even clear as to the parenting opportunities that they wish to address; even fewer have deep insights about how to address them.

But insights in themselves are not enough. It is the *distinctive parenting characteristics* that enable the successful company to realize unusually high value from its insights. Once again, at a superficial level, others seem to share these characteristics. Many parents have a strategic planning process, or a vision, or a matrix structure. What distinguishes successful parents is the way they operate these mechanisms. Emerson's strategic planning process, for example, is unusually rigorous and effective.[17] The time and effort devoted by senior managers, the availability of comparable data over long periods, the use of specific forms and ratios to highlight trends and relationships, the depth of corporate knowledge and understanding, the structure of the meetings, the challenging culture of the organization, and the personal characteristics of the chief executive combine to create a strategic planning process that is far more valuable than in the vast majority of other companies. Attempts to copy other companies' distinctive parenting characteristics often confuse the label with the underlying reality. By no means all

EXHIBIT 2–8   Canon parenting advantage statement

Value Creation Insights	Individual businesses have resourcing difficulties in pursuing a range of technologies in depth and can benefit from shared resource within the parent.
	Businesses find it difficult to create linkages and cross-fertilization between different areas of technology, between technologists and market needs, and between different markets; and there is a role for a parent in facilitating these linkages.
	An inspiring corporate vision can help businesses to stretch for growth beyond the confines of each business.
Distinctive Parenting Characteristics	Ability to manage cross-fertilization: • Across different technologies. • Between technical and market specialists. • Across different markets.
	A high level of corporate commitment to technology and learning.
	Company vision that energizes staff toward growth and stretch without prompting inappropriate risks.
Heartland Businesses	Businesses in which overall performance depends heavily on product performance and new product development, which in turn are driven by superior understanding and linking of three core technology areas: precision mechanics, fine optics, and microelectronics; where technology advantage is embodied in certain key components; where international presence and ability to manage multiple channels to market provide a major advantage; selling business machines, cameras, and specialist optical products.

strategic planning processes represent valuable and distinctive parenting characteristics.

Differences in value creation insights and parenting characteristics are reflected in different criteria for *heartland businesses.* Many companies might be interested in high-growth technology businesses, such as those addressed by Canon. But Canon's success in parenting such businesses is based on far more than the selection of attractive markets.[18] Underlying features, such as the importance of linking three core technologies in complex ways, or the embodiment of technological advantage in key components, link Canon's heartland businesses. Furthermore, Canon has actively built up its knowledge and feel for the critical success factors in certain businesses, such as office products, to limit the risk of value destruction through unexpected misfits with the parent. It is therefore familiar with the types of sales channels, product lead times, investment decisions, and other critical success factors that

EXHIBIT 2–9   Emerson parenting advantage statement

Value Creation Insights	Even in businesses which have basically sound management and adequate profitability, a parent with suitable skills can often improve performance substantially by helping to sharpen strategic thinking, analyze the components of cost and revenue in the business, and focus on manufacturing cost reduction.
Distinctive Parenting Characteristics	Intensive strategic planning process that identifies key issues and opportunities in the businesses, and creates a constructive and open dialogue about them.
	Focus on the performance and responsibility of each business's management team, including 15% return on sales expectation.
	Corporate Best Cost Producer (BCP) program.
	Skills in identifying and acquiring businesses that will respond well to Emerson's parenting.
	Personal experience and style of the CEO and top corporate managers.
Heartland Businesses	Businesses that manufacture electrical, electromechanical, or electronic products of medium technology and capital intensity for industrial customers. Ideally, businesses with a reasonable level of profitability, but scope for improvement; sound underlying market position, but scope to build on it; moderate market growth rates.

characterize its businesses. Although Canon and ABB are both successful parents of some "high technology" businesses, their heartlands are very different. Canon would not have a good feel for the issues involved in building nuclear power plants, or in bidding for and managing multi-million-dollar contracts for governmental customers, any more than ABB would feel comfortable with consumer marketing of camcorders.

These three successful companies illustrate the power of even a one-page parenting advantage statement. Focusing on their value creation insights, distinctive parenting characteristics, and heartland business criteria exposes the differences between the companies, while underscoring the underlying pattern of similarity: They all achieve exceptional fit between the characteristics of the parent and the characteristics of their businesses.

THE EVOLUTION OF PARENTING ADVANTAGE— THE HANSON STORY

Summary parenting advantage statements are succinct and powerful. However, they also risk being static snapshots. In reality, parenting advantage evolves over time as parents develop unique insights or parenting characteristics and then find these advantages gradually eroded by rivals.

One of our research companies, Hanson, can be used to illustrate in much greater depth what happens to parenting advantage over time—in this case, three decades. It is particularly interesting to look at a company like Hanson because many frameworks for corporate strategy have nothing to say about this type of conglomerate. Labeled as "opportunistic," "deal-driven," and sometimes just "lucky," companies such as Hanson are considered by many to have no corporate strategy at all. We disagree with this conclusion. The parenting advantage framework can be applied as usefully to understanding the corporate strategy of a 'conglomerate' such as Hanson as to understanding more integrated or networked companies such as Canon or ABB.

Lords Hanson and White have been prolific wealth creators since they teamed up in 1963. An investment of £100 in the company when it went public in 1964 would have been worth £38,357 by the end of 1993. They have not succeeded by riding on the back of some remarkable invention or investing in glamorous, intrinsically attractive sectors. They have focused on mature, often dull, and sometimes declining business areas such as bricks, aggregates, cigarettes, coal mining, batteries, and basic chemicals. How did they develop parenting advantage? And is their corporate strategy sustainable?

The Hanson family had a small transport business which was partly nationalized after World War II. James Hanson and his brother used their share of the compensation to set up a haulage company in Canada in the early 1950s, but James returned to England after his brother's death. He then took over what remained of the family transport business: "Under his father's influence, Hanson learned to rely on successful individuals running their own depots—a hands-off policy that endures today."[19] This experience shaped the mental maps that have guided Hanson's parenting.

During the 1950s, Gordon White owned a printing, publishing, and advertising company. He was, in Hanson's words, "wearing off shoe leather" tramping around pubs selling advertising space for garage calendars.[20] In 1963, the two combined their transport and printing businesses to form a small conglomerate and began buying other companies. From the beginning of the partnership, White was the deal maker and Hanson the manager. The nature and skills of these two individuals were undoubtedly the most important characteristics of the parent at this stage.

In 1964, Oswald Tillotson Motors, the original Hanson family firm, was acquired by Wiles Group; Hanson and White joined the board. They gained control of the group the next year, and Hanson became chairman. During the late 1960s, Wiles acquired a number of businesses. These included Scottish Land Developments in 1967; and

West of England Sack, British Agricultural Services, Nathaniel Lloyd, Dufaylite, and Butterley Engineering in 1968. In 1970, Wiles Group changed its name to Hanson Trust.

Based on their experience, Hanson and White determined that "good quality basic businesses providing essential goods and services"[21] were capable of producing high profitability, provided their managers were given the right responsibilities and objectives. In these sorts of businesses, they believed, the parent needed to decentralize responsibility, within a framework of tough financial targets and suitable performance incentives, to bring about the best results. At the time, these observations represented a value creation insight and provided the beginnings of a heartland definition.

Hanson also perceived that, in the Britain of the 1970s, many mature businesses in basic industries were performing poorly. The businesses were following overambitious growth objectives, were subject to loose profitability controls, and were bedeviled with excessive corporate costs. Particular problems arose with companies that, deciding that their historic core businesses were mature, had started to diversify in search of growth or more attractive businesses. Hanson and White found that they could acquire companies of this sort and create value through an approach to parenting that stressed tight financial controls. There was no shortage of improvement opportunities that matched with their basic insights. Since Hanson's approach to parenting mature businesses created and captured more value than the approaches of their previous owners, Hanson had parenting advantage when it came to getting the best out of many mature businesses.

Hanson was also willing to sell businesses to other parents that would pay more than the holdings were worth within the Hanson portfolio. For example, in 1970 Tillotson Motors was sold to Lex. "When Tillotson's got to a certain size," Hanson recalls, "Donald Stokes (later Lord Stokes) said we couldn't have any more British Leyland dealerships. Lex said they'd buy it all. I'd been in it all my life but we were better off selling it in 1971 for £4m. That was our launch pad."[22] The sale of Tillotson to Lex was an example of a portfolio decision based on unsentimental parenting advantage logic. If a rival has parenting advantage, it makes good economic sense to capture some of the increased value through a sale to the new parent.

But Hanson faced competition from other aggressive, financially driven parents such as Slater Walker and Jessel Securities. These parents had also recognized the opportunity in mature and basic businesses and were aiming to create value in a similar way. Why should Hanson have created more value and been more successful than its rivals?

The secret of Hanson's success during the 1970s and into the 1980s was not only identifying an opportunity to add value through tight financial control but also developing distinctive parenting characteristics that could realize this value. First, Hanson developed a small, highly competent team for acquisition identification, screening, and deal making. By the 1980s, Hanson had screened hundreds of possible acquisition candidates and had completed dozens of deals. The M&A (mergers and acquisitions) team, led by Martin Taylor, the vice chairman, was generally regarded as more experienced and skillful than the M&A departments in many leading investment and merchant banks, let alone in other industrial companies. Furthermore, Gordon White's instincts and daring were superior to those of most other deal makers.

Second, Hanson fine-tuned its skills in managing new acquisitions through the first 12 to 18 months of ownership. It developed an especially speedy and cost-effective way of making decisions about which businesses and managers to keep after the acquisition, and for managing the culture change that most acquisitions needed. Hanson learned to achieve these changes without losing momentum, demotivating managers, or losing the best people. Senior Hanson managers such as Tony Alexander and Ron Fulford worked together on assimilating acquisitions ranging from British EverReady through London Brick to the Imperial Group. They developed a phased approach to the postacquisition restructuring process that created maximum value.

Third, these acquisition management skills were reinforced by an increasingly sophisticated financial control process, administered by a strong central finance team. The tightness of Hanson's budget and capital expenditure control process became legendary, and its finance department became a training ground for a generation of financially driven industrialists. The finance directors in all the businesses had a strong dotted-line relationship to the corporate center, and were responsible for safeguarding the integrity of the group financial systems and processes.

These parenting skills, superior to those of most other financially driven conglomerates in the 1970s and early 1980s, provided the basis for Hanson's parenting advantage. Hanson was able to bring off successfully a series of bigger and bigger deals, such as SCM Inc., Imperial Group, and Kidde Inc., and by the mid-1980s was widely recognized as an outstanding restructurer.[23]

As the 1980s progressed, Hanson further refined these skills and added new ones—skills in managing megabids, in selling businesses on to other parents to release value, in tax management, and in managing an industrial empire split between the two sides of the Atlantic. As a result, Hanson has been able to draw on several mutually reinforcing and distinctive parenting characteristics. Furthermore, the development of parenting advantage has been the driving force in determining key corporate strategy decisions. Parenting advantage logic provided the criteria for picking suitable acquisitions. It determined which businesses would be kept within the portfolio or sold to other owners, and the sort of objectives that would be set for each business. Hanson's value creation insights also determined the type of management structures, processes, and culture that the company built up. Success has stemmed from identifying clear sources of parenting advantage, and from applying them consistently in corporate strategy decisions over the past 25 years. Exhibit 2–10 is a summary parenting advantage statement for Hanson.[24]

Yet perversely, Hanson's parenting characteristics may now be worth less than its smaller array of skills in 1980. There may now be fewer suitable opportunities in the form of underperforming acquisition targets, while more high-quality rival parents are playing a similar role. By the end of the 1980s, fewer large companies were being seduced into dubious diversifications that took their eyes off mature core businesses, and more companies, sensing the threat from Hanson-type predators, were moving to restructure themselves and to tighten their own management controls. American LBO (leveraged buyout) specialists such as Kohlberg Kravis Roberts & Co. (KKR) have stalked similar targets and pushed up the prices of acquisitions. In the United Kingdom, smaller

EXHIBIT 2–10 Hanson parenting advantage statement

Value Creation Insights	Companies that seek growth from mature businesses tend to destabilize competitive conditions, indulge in unnecessary investments, and take on excessive costs. This gives an opportunity for a parent that stresses tight profitability controls to create value.
	In acquisitions of diversified companies with mixed portfolios of businesses, value can be created by a parent that is willing to sell on different businesses to other owners to whom they are worth more.
Distinctive Parenting Characteristics	Acquisition screening and deal-making skills.
	Tried and tested process for integrating new acquisitions into Hanson's management process.
	Decentralized responsibilities for running businesses, coupled with strong personal profitability incentives.
	Emphasis on financial control processes and culture.
	Willingness to sell any business that is "worth more to others than we think it's worth to us."
Heartland Businesses	Mature businesses that are not facing rapid technological change and where there is a basic and continuing demand for the product. Ideally, they should neither require long payback investments, nor globally integrated strategies, and they should hold strong, preferably branded, positions in their markets. Manufacturing and natural resource businesses are preferred.

conglomerates such as Williams Holdings and Tomkins have been increasingly active. As a result, the extent and value of Hanson's advantage may be diminishing, and as we discuss in Chapter 9, Hanson may now be seeking a new corporate strategy.

RIVAL PARENTS—THE RANKS HOVIS MCDOUGALL STORY

Parenting advantage, like competitive advantage, is relative. It can be undermined by similar parents who focus on similar opportunities efficiently enough to close the gap. Advantage can also be challenged by parents who focus on quite different opportunities for enhancing business performance, supported by quite different parenting characteristics. A case in point concerns Hanson's 1992 bid for Ranks Hovis McDougall (RHM).

RHM's core business was bread baking, but it also owned flour mills and a number of food brands, such as Mr. Kipling cakes. On October 5, 1992, Hanson bid 220 pence per share for RHM, valuing the company at £780 million, a 26 percent premium over its previous closing price. This price had already risen by 25 percent in September on bid speculation. Hanson argued that the RHM management had underperformed for many years and had no clear strategy for its portfolio of businesses. The press speculated on a classic Hanson move, suggesting that the company would resell all RHM's valuable brands to specialist food parents such as Nestlé, Unilever, Philip Morris, or United Biscuits. That would leave the flour milling and bread-making business, to which Hanson's financial control approach would be applied.

Three weeks after the bid, however, Greg Hutchings, chief executive of Tomkins, topped Hanson's bid by 18 percent. Tomkins also has a track record of restructuring businesses, although in the past these had been engineering firms such as Pegler Hattersley, the valve company, and gun manufacturer Smith & Wesson. Interestingly enough, Hutchings is Hanson-trained. He spent 10 years helping to build the group for Lord Hanson before setting up his own rival parent. Challenged as to how an engineering company could improve the management of a food company, Hutchings replied that Tomkins was not an engineering company, but an organization with the management skills to revitalize struggling companies and enable them to flourish.[25] This was essentially a claim that RHM lay within the Tomkins "heartland."

Hanson chose not to counterbid, and Tomkins gained control of RHM. Most observers believe that its approach to parenting RHM will be very similar to Hanson's. Value probably can be added to RHM, but the rivalry between the two parents has deprived Hanson of the prize and led Tomkins to pay a high price. The example shows how emergence of strong rival parents has eroded the level of parenting advantage enjoyed by Hanson—or any other restructurer with a Financial Control style. Initially, Tomkins' shares dropped by 20 percent because the market thought the price too high. It took a strenuous communication campaign by Hutchings before the share price partly recovered.[26]

In assessing parenting advantage, it is necessary to recognize that different parent companies may seek to create value in different ways. Other parent companies with very different approaches to parenting might also have bid for RHM, and sought to exploit different improvement opportunities. While we do not know how actively such thoughts were entertained, it is easy to hypothesize about other companies that may have considered RHM an interesting target.

Grand Metropolitan, a large and acquisitive British food and drinks company, was a possible rival bidder. Under its chief executive Allen Sheppard, Grand Metropolitan transformed itself in the late 1980s and early 1990s from a sprawling conglomerate to a lean and aggressive acquirer. It concentrates on rejuvenating branded goods companies.[27] With a distinctive and challenging management style, Sheppard successfully turned round three companies in the Grand Metropolitan stable—Watneys in brewing, Express Dairies, and most recently Pillsbury in food. Grand Metropolitan's parenting advantage is based on combining sensitivity to brand management issues with tough operating controls. Sheppard might have thought that RHM was an ideal target, and that Grand Metropolitan could create even more value than Hanson or Tomkins—particularly since it already knew flour milling through Pillsbury.

Another possible bidder was Northern Foods. Like RHM, it is focused mainly on the British market, but specializes in working closely with large food retailers such as Sainsbury and Tesco, which have a high proportion of own-brand, or private label, sales. Northern Foods has been particularly successful in working with retailers to offer a mix of own brands and manufacturer brands. The parenting team of Northern Foods might have seen potential in improving the relationship between RHM businesses and the large retailers—for example, by extending its presence in retailer own-brand bread and flour to increase RHM volumes and profits. If Northern Foods had bid for RHM, it would have hoped to create value based on its expertise in retailer branding and in managing relationships with retailers.

Another possible bidder was Unilever,[28] whose vast portfolio of food businesses makes it one of the world's largest food companies. Unilever's parenting philosophy is particularly suited to the food industry because it aims to give primary responsibility to national company management, but to release selected international synergies. A high percentage of food products and food brands are national and require strong national companies for their marketing and distribution. Moreover, many of the synergies are in distribution and sales, both of which are best managed nationally. This demands a high degree of decentralization to country-based operating companies. However, Unilever also promotes opportunities to internationalize products and to centralize research and development. Furthermore, Unilever is renowned for brand management skills, an area where RHM appeared to be weak. Finally, Unilever's experience in branding commodity items such as margarine and frozen vegetables might have been helpful in parenting RHM's bread and flour brands. Unilever could have claimed a number of distinctive sources of parenting advantage.

The Kraft General Foods subsidiary of Philip Morris might also have been a potential bidder. Kraft General Foods has been an aggressive acquirer of food and confectionery businesses in Europe, such as Jacobs Suchard and the Terry's Group. RHM could have been seen as an excellent opportunity to strengthen distribution in the United Kingdom, an area where Kraft General Foods is relatively weak. Kraft General Foods would also have been able to internationalize RHM's strongest brands.

Many different approaches to creating value are therefore possible. Rival parents compete for the chance to exploit performance enhancement opportunities. The opportunity spotted by Hanson and Tomkins was not the only one that a new parent could have exploited. The question of which company could create the most value out of RHM's businesses depends on the relative abilities of each parent to identify particular opportunities and to realize them. Parenting advantage can be achieved either by superior realization of the same insight, or by the possession and realization of a superior insight. In either case, it is the degree of fit between the characteristics of the parent and the businesses that underlies the advantage.

SUMMARY

This chapter has outlined the concept of parenting advantage and compared its role in corporate-level strategy to the role of competitive advantage in business-level strategy. The concept of competitive advantage provides a goal, a measure, and a test for business-level strategy. Parenting advantage can play the same role for corporate-level strategy. It provides a goal that currently may or may not be met, but toward which the parent should constantly be striving. It provides a measure to gauge how the parent is performing overall, and to highlight where this performance is strongest and weakest. It provides a test for proposed corporate strategies, to determine how or why a given policy, direction, or action will enhance parenting advantage in the future.

The parenting advantage concept can and should inform all major corporate strategy decisions about a company's portfolio of businesses and the ways in which they will be parented. It emphasizes the need for high levels of fit between the characteristics of the parent and the characteristics of its businesses. This fit leads to value creation by matching opportunities in the businesses with a parent that can realize them. Fit is maintained by focusing on businesses for which the parent has an appropriate feel. By understanding the critical success factors in these businesses, the parent reduces the risk of causing inadvertent damage. We have shown how this logic underlies the success of very different companies such as ABB, Canon, Emerson Electric, and Hanson. We have shown that parenting advantage is built on three bases: (1) insights about particular opportunities for the parent to create value, (2) distinctive characteristics that allow the parent to realize this value in a unique or special way, and (3) the identification of a heartland on which to focus the portfolio.

We have also shown that parenting advantage is not everlasting. Even if a parent is improving its ability to create value, its relative advantage may be declining. Other parents are also honing their skills and insights, so that advantage is constantly under attack. This attack may be based on developing better skills to exploit the same basic insight. But it may also be based on different insights supported by different skills and characteristics.

Our framework for corporate strategy is founded on the pursuit of parenting advantage. It combines inputs about the characteristics of the parent, the characteristics of its businesses, the nature of rival parents, and trends and scenarios for the future. These form the basis for parenting decisions and portfolio decisions that will lead toward parenting advantage.

NOTES

1. For a discussion of business definition, and the difference between organizational and economic definition, see Appendix A.

2. For a discussion of the definition of the parent, and different structures in parent organizations, see Appendix B.

3. Many managers that we have spoken to have clear views as to whether their parents are creating or destroying value in their businesses. The potential significance of the parent's impact is also suggested by changes in corporate performance and market capitalization following significant changes in the parent's composition. Some academics believe, however, that the parent makes little real difference to the performance of its businesses. Although we do not accept this view, some claim that it is at least partly supported by statistical analysis of U.S. manufacturing businesses between 1974 and 1977, although the interpretation of the analysis has provoked much debate. See Richard P. Rumelt, "How Much Does Industry Matter?", *Strategic Management Journal*, vol. 12, 1991, pp. 167–185.

4. In Chapter 3, we will consider different definitions of value, but we will assume in this chapter that value is defined by the parent.

5. The issue of determining when and why a parent, or "hierarchy," is likely to outperform arm's length transactions, or "markets," is central to much so-called transaction cost literature. See, for example, O. E. Williamson, *Markets and Hierarchies,* New York: The Free Press, 1975.

6. Michael Porter, "From Competitive Advantage to Corporate Strategy," *Harvard Business Review,* May–June 1987.

7. Other authors have commented on the importance of fit in more specific aspects of multibusiness management. For example, Sumantra Ghoshal and Nitin Nohria document the relevance of a so-called contingency approach to the organization and structure of multinational corporations (Sumantra Ghoshal and Nitin Nohria "Horses for Courses: Organizational Forms for Multinational Corporations," *Sloan Management Review,* Winter 1993). They argue that appropriate fit is driven by requisite complexity—the complexity of a firm's structure must match the complexity of its environment. Similarly, Hill, Hitt, and Hoskisson examine the importance of fit between strategy, structure, and control systems in achieving different economic benefits associated with different diversification strategies (Charles W. Hill, Michael A. Hitt, and Robert E. Hoskisson, "Cooperative Versus Competitive Structures in Related and Unrelated Diversified Firms," *Organization Science,* vol. 3, no. 4, November 1992).

8. We will explore the nature of this fit more fully in Parts Two and Three. In particular, Part Two provides a detailed discussion of the extent and type of fit achieved by successful parents. Part Three, particularly Chapter 12, then provides tests of current fit, and tools and techniques for improving future fit.

9. Michael Goold and Andrew Campbell, *Strategies and Styles,* Oxford: Basil Blackwell, 1987.

10. In *Strategies and Styles,* we had not yet developed the concept of "parenting," and therefore simply referred to "management styles."

11. Appendix C provides a fuller account of the parenting styles. It describes the styles, shows how a company's style can be assessed, and reviews the implications of following each style. It draws on our earlier work, updated to reflect further research carried out subsequently.

12. For a fuller description of these characteristics and tools that help to elucidate them, see Chapter 12.

13. For a fuller description of these characteristics, and tools that help elucidate them, see Chapter 12.

14. For a discussion of economic business definition, see Appendix A. For a discussion of value creation through business redefinition, see Chapters 9 and 14.

15. "The Logic of Global Business: An Interview with ABB's Percy Barnevik," *Harvard Business Review,* March–April 1991.

16. For a fuller discussion of ABB and its network, see Chapter 7.

17. For a fuller description of Emerson's planning process and corporate strategy, see Chapter 6.

18. For a fuller description of Canon's corporate strategy, see Chapter 7.

19. Shirley Skeel, "The Enhancement of Hanson," *Management Today,* August 1991, pp. 34–39.

20. Charles Leadbeater and Roland Rudd, "What Drives the Lords of the Deal?", *Financial Times,* July 20/21, 1992.

21. "Management for Prosperity," Hanson company document, 1984.

22. Tom Lloyd, "A Muscular Hanson Bides Its Time," *Financial Weekly,* January 26, 1989, pp. 22–27.

23. See, for example, sidebar entitled "An uncanny British restructurer," in Michael E. Porter, "From Competitive Advantage to Corporate Strategy," *Harvard Business Review,* May–June 1984, p. 55.

24. See Chapter 9 for a further discussion of Hanson's corporate development skills and corporate strategy.

25. Rufus Olins and Alan Ruddock, "An Exceedingly Big Gamble," *Sunday Times,* November 1, 1992.

26. Since the takeover of RHM, Tomkins's share price has underperformed the Financial Times All Share Index. By the end of 1993, it had just about returned to the level at which it stood the day before the bid. Despite a recognition of benefits from rationalization and integration, analysts continued to question whether Tomkins had overpaid for RHM.

27. See Chapter 11 for more details of Grand Metropolitan's corporate strategy.

28. See Chapter 7 for more details on Unilever's corporate strategy.

3 QUESTIONS ABOUT PARENTING ADVANTAGE

In discussions of the parenting advantage concept with managers, we have encountered several recurrent questions. These include:

- What is meant by "value creation"?
- Why focus on the parent?
- When is parenting advantage a relevant concept?
- How accurately can parenting advantage be assessed?
- Is it necessary to be "the best" parent for each of your businesses?
- Why use the "parenting" metaphor?

In this chapter, we provide an immediate response to these questions, though we will cast further light on each of them elsewhere in the book.

WHAT IS MEANT BY VALUE CREATION?

So far in our discussion of parenting advantage we have talked loosely about "value creation" and "adding value" without defining precisely what we mean by value. The need to operationalize the term "value" is not a requirement peculiar to parenting advantage, since all approaches to strategy presuppose some definition of value. Nevertheless, we will address this issue first.

Enterprises affect the interests of a wide range of stakeholders (see Exhibit 3–1 illustrating the stakeholder model). If the interests of any of the stakeholder groups are consistently ignored, the enterprise will become unviable. For example, if customers are consistently given a

EXHIBIT 3–1   Stakeholder model

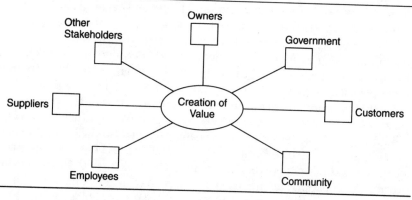

poor deal relative to the alternatives available to them, they will stop buying from the enterprise. If employees are consistently given a poor deal, they will stop working for the enterprise. Similarly, other stakeholders whose needs are consistently ignored will remove their support. There is a minimum requirement for each group to sustain its involvement with the enterprise. At the simplest level, value creation is the creation of a surplus over and above these minimum requirements.

If a surplus is created, how should it be distributed? In essence, this is a matter for each company to determine, given its own priorities and preferences. Many companies, however, argue it should be distributed in a way that will maxmize future surpluses. Rather like a net present value calculation, the current surplus should be used to maximize the present value of future flows. This may involve giving a better deal to customers, to increase market share and generate greater advantage in the future. It may involve giving a better deal to employees, to attract higher caliber staff or provide better working conditions that increase productivity. It may involve paying out higher dividends, to enhance shareholder loyalty and reduce the overall cost of capital. It may involve investing in new assets and R&D. As there is no agreed way to measure future surplus generating capacity, companies that claim this as their objective can, and do, differ significantly in how they distribute today's surplus. Decisions about the relative priority to give to different stakeholders therefore reflect each company's own distinctive purpose and judgments.

Many firms are strongly focused on the stock market and use shareholder value as a guide to their decisions. Some argue, simply, that the shareholder is the owner of the company, and deserves priority over rival stakeholders. Others view shareholder value as more of an indicator than a goal in itself. They argue that the stock price is the best available indicator of the value of future surpluses. If the company makes decisions that improve its ability to generate future surpluses, its stock price rises. If the company allocates resources in ways that reduce the likelihood or size of future surpluses, the stock price falls. The market is therefore judging the future impact of current surplus distribution. In practice, however, the response of the stock market to any given decision remains somewhat unpredictable, so that the overall objective of maximizing shareholder value cannot provide detailed guidance on how to distribute surpluses, and the judgment of management about the relative priority to give to different stakeholders remains important.

It is appropriate, then, to define value in terms of the prime purposes and priorities of the company. Value is created if these purposes, whatever they may be for each company, are furthered. Thus value creation cannot be assessed until the company has laid out what its main purposes and priorities are. Once this has been achieved, the parenting advantage concept can be used to help maximize value creation in these terms, whether or not it is equated with shareholder value. Furthermore, if shareholder value is not of central importance, even as an indication of the company's ability to generate future surpluses, the discipline of attempting to assess parenting advantage will help to clarify what purposes and priorities are assumed by management. This is a matter of significance to all stakeholders, and underlies one element of the corporate governance debate. If stakeholders disagree fundamentally with management's view on this topic, they may wish to withdraw their support.

WHY FOCUS ON THE PARENT?

We distinguish between the parent organization and the corporation as a whole. The corporation as a whole includes every person throughout the company, whereas the parent organization includes only those people who work at levels above or outside the business units, whether in the corporate center, or at divisonal, group, sector, or country levels. In a large, multibusiness company, more than 100,000 people may work for the corporation as a whole, but as few as 1,000 or even 100 may work in the parent organization. Our emphasis is on the role of the comparatively small group of people in the parent. Some managers argue that this is inappropriate. Corporate strategy is about the whole corporation, all 100,000 people, not just the 1,000 people in the parent. Surely we should be focusing on issues of corporatewide advantage, and on what the businesses and the parent achieve together, rather than on our narrower concept of parenting advantage, which deals exclusively with the role of the parent.

We disagree. Obviously, we are interested in the overall results achieved by the parent and the businesses working together. However, our concept of corporate strategy, as distinct from business strategy, stresses the difference made by the parent to the results that the businesses would otherwise achieve.[1] Indeed, it is the failure to focus on this difference that leads many corporate strategies to be little more than the sum of the business unit strategies. This almost always leads to parenting influence that fails to justify its cost. Worse still, confusion about the parent's role usually leads to active value destruction. The businesses each need to develop and implement their own business strategies; the 99,000 should be focused on their respective business strategies. The parent, however, is attempting to influence the businesses in ways that will change, and improve, their collective performance. This is the field of corporate strategy, and it is, by definition, the concern of the parent. Put simply, corporate strategy is about what parent organizations do, and business strategy is about what businesses do. Business strategy provides guidance for the 99,000. Corporate strategy provides guidance for the 1,000.

Many managers then add a further concern. They point out that corporate strategy influences business strategy: Separating the two is therefore artificial. We agree that the parent can significantly influence the strategies of the businesses. The question of whether this influence creates or destroys value, and whether the net result is better than would be achieved by rival parents, is vital in assessing parenting advantage. But to address such questions, we must be able to identify the parent and its influence. It is for this reason that we place the value-creating activities of the parent itself at the center of corporate strategy.

A related challenge which is sometimes raised is that the parent organization is not the main source of corporatewide value creation. Managers in businesses argue that they get more help and support from colleagues in other businesses than from managers in the parent. Again, we recognize that this is often the case, and we deal with value creation of this sort in Chapter 7. But we believe that the parent company has a special role to play in enhancing this "linkage" value. The culture that the parent fosters, the networking mechanisms and coordination systems that the parent promotes, are critical in encouraging or discouraging the flow of value from one business to another. If the linkage value could be created equally well between independent businesses not under common parenting, there would be no need for a parent—no need for common ownership. It is therefore important to identify the particular influence and impact of the parent organization rather than simply to look at cross-company activities.

Other managers claim that the flow of useful ideas and information is mainly upwards into the parent. Again, this may often be true. The question is whether or not it leads to value creation. If there is simply a flow of ideas going into the parent, but no action coming out, value is not created. It is only when the parent translates such ideas or information into action, either influencing its existing portfolio or changing the portfolio composition, that value can be created. Many of the good ideas that lead to parental influence and actions may indeed come from within the businesses, but the main focus must be on what the parent does with them.

When we make the distinction between the businesses and the parent organization, we are often challenged by managers who say that it is impossible in practice to distinguish between them. They explain that, in their company, managers and staff move freely between the businesses and the center; service departments operate at the center, but do important jobs for businesses; and some businesses have joint sales forces or buying teams that report to the center. We recognize these issues and overlaps and discuss the complexity of parent structures in Appendix B. But we have seldom found that it is impossible to identify the parent, even though a particular individual may be working partly for the parent and partly for the businesses. Moreover, we have always found that distinguishing between the businesses and the parent has helped to clarify the value creation role of different managers.

In summary, we see the parent as playing the central role in the creation and execution of corporate strategy. Corporate strategy is about what people in the parent organization do to create value.

WHEN IS PARENTING ADVANTAGE A RELEVANT CONCEPT?

Some managers have questioned the relevance of the parenting advantage concept to their own company. Is the concept only suitable for an Anglo-Saxon culture, or for conglomerates that trade businesses in and out of their portfolios? Is it equally relevant for companies that grow organically, shun acquisitions and divestments, and focus on company-wide performance rather than the achievements of individual businesses? Alternatively, is it a relevant concept for companies who attempt to do little more than pick good businesses to invest in? Our answer is clear: Parenting advantage is relevant to all multibusiness companies. It is as applicable to those that have developed organically from single business companies as to those that have developed through acquisitions and diversification. It provides a rationale for creating or maintaining multibusiness companies based on value maximization, whether for the company's owners or for any other stakeholders.

Most large companies are now multibusiness companies. There are, however, many different sorts. Some, such as Hanson or BTR, bring together a large number of clearly identified, individual units, often operating in quite distinct industry sectors. Others, such as Canon or Shell, are much more closely integrated, with less pronounced and clear-cut boundaries between their different businesses. The parenting advantage concept, however, can be usefully applied across the whole of this broad spectrum, as we shall see in Chapters 6 through 10.

But where does the spectrum end? At one end lies the single business company. Its structure and activities are so integrated that, whatever its size, it cannot be viewed as comprising multiple businesses. Its strategic decisions should be guided by the concept of competitive advantage. Corporate-level strategy and parenting advantage are relevant to such a company only if it is considering diversifying or restructuring itself into more than one business.

At the other end lie fund managers. Although they hold potentially significant stakes in many businesses, they have no direct management authority over them. Like parents, they are intermediaries between the providers of capital and individual businesses, but they are on the other side of the management-owner fence. Fund managers should engage with questions that parallel those we have posed for parents: If they are to justify their cost as intermediaries, they must create some value for the individual shareholder, and they should aim to excel in comparison with rival fund managers. But they cannot influence the businesses they partly own in the same way as a company's management. Close to this end of the spectrum lie those parents who adopt a minimalist management approach. They aim to create value for their shareholders primarily by picking the right businesses to buy and sell, while maintaining a completely hands-off style. But the mere fact that they have legal authority to become more closely involved if they so choose changes the nature of the influence that they exert, intentionally or not. This makes them parents rather than investment trusts. Close to this position are the leveraged buyout partnerships, such as KKR. These organizations exert significant influence in relation to a very small number of issues, such as financial structure and senior management compensation, but deliberately avoid involvement in many normal areas of parenting.[2]

The spectrum of multibusiness companies is therefore broad. Fully integrated single business companies, at one end, and fund managers, at the other, have ownership positions in their businesses, but neither are parent companies. Parents operate between these two extremes, and the corporate strategies they develop should be based on parenting advantage thinking.

HOW ACCURATELY CAN PARENTING ADVANTAGE BE ASSESSED?

Given the difficulties in defining value, and the existence of a variety of parent companies each with its own sources of parenting advantage, some managers have questioned whether the parenting advantage concept can be made precise and accurate enough to be useful.

We accept that parenting advantage is not a precisely measurable concept. Indeed, the difficulty of disentangling the contribution of the parent from that of the business means that it is even harder to quantify than competitive advantage. However, we believe that the concept remains useful as a guide to decisions. It may not be possible to use it with mathematical accuracy, but it can provide the overall direction for corporate strategy.

Furthermore, in Part Three of this book, we will provide some suggestions for analysis and quantification of parenting advantage. While we do not claim that these analyses are simple to carry out, they do provide a basis for assessing value creation by the parent. They also highlight areas of clear parenting advantage or disadvantage. Looking at the track record of acquisitions over a period of years, for example, can reveal broad patterns that do not depend on exact quantification of the parent's influence. Our experience has been that even fairly blunt tools can provide useful insights. However, as greater attention is focused on parenting advantage, methods of measurement will no doubt improve, as has happened in many other apparently soft areas.[3]

DOES A COMPANY NEED TO BE THE BEST PARENT FOR ALL ITS BUSINESSES?

We are frequently challenged by managers who say that to aim to be the best parent is too demanding a target. These managers can usually identify a business under their ownership that would clearly benefit from being owned by one of their rivals. In some cases, the rival is a specialist in the business area concerned and could bring international experience or particular technical knowledge to the business. In other cases, the rival owns a large competing business and would be able to create cost savings and synergies if the two were combined. But if it is a good business, earning more than its cost of capital, managers resist the implication that selling out to the rival would make sense. They may not have parenting advantage, but they refuse to contemplate a sale. Even if they are not the best parents, they argue, they can create value for their stakeholders by continuing to own the business. They sometimes draw an analogy with the business-level concept of competitive advantage. They point out that number two and number three players can exist profitably even though they are at a disadvantage to the number one player. They argue that the same is true for parent companies.

Our response is that it is indeed possible to be a number two or number three parent and still create value. In our experience, most successful companies are in this position for some, if not most, of the businesses they own. But, since the objective of corporate strategy is to maximize value creation, we encourage managers to look for, and focus on, situations where they can aspire to have parenting advantage. We therefore seek to use parenting advantage at the corporate level in exactly the same way as competitive advantage is used at the business level. It is the objective, the guiding thought. A company may not currently have it. In fact, it may never attain true advantage. But it is always trying to improve its relative position, in the knowledge that ultimately a company is not secure unless it can rightly claim to be the best at what it does.

But some managers are uncomfortable with the idea that corporate strategy should be judged against the standards set by rival parents. They point out that hostile takeover bids are rare occurrences and suggest that the market for corporate control is imperfect and only occasionally active. Furthermore, they claim, corporations do not see themselves as competing with other companies for the ownership of their existing businesses.

Our retort is that parent companies are indeed competing with each other. This competition is evident in different ways. For example, competition between parent companies exists whenever a business is put up for sale. It is not unusual, particularly during acquisition booms, for an investment bank to receive 30 or 40 inquiries for each business it is selling. Maybe only a few of these are serious bidders, but, whatever the number of inquiries, one parent company has to decide that it is prepared to pay more for the business than other parent companies. If all the decision makers are rational, the parent company that is prepared to pay the most should also be the parent company that can create the most value out of the acquisition. All the "interested" parent companies are competing with each other to see which one can create the most value out of the particular business that is for sale.[4] In competitive tenders or hostile takeover situations, the competition between parent companies is quite evident. But it also exists in other ways and in less obvious transactions.

Parent companies compete with each other for people and talent. When Allen Sheppard became chief executive of Grand Metropolitan, he brought with him a small cadre of managers he had been working with in one of the divisions. He then set about recruiting high-quality managers and poaching talent from the best companies. The attraction of Grand Metropolitan for these managers was not primarily the financial package offered. Sheppard was able to communicate to them an exciting corporate strategy and interesting job responsibilities within the parent company. His corporate strategy and management style seemed more attractive to them than what they were leaving behind. Grand Metropolitan's position in the mid-1980s was unusual, in that the company changed most of its parent managers. Normally, the competition for management talent is more muted, but nonetheless discernible. Rather than direct poaching, competition occurs indirectly, as managers in businesses look at the career prospects and interests for them at the parent company level, and decide whether to leave or stay.

In the financial markets, parent companies also compete with each other. They compete for ratings from the debt rating agencies; for the loyalty of their bankers; and for the attentions of shareholders through movements in their share prices. A parent company with a poor debt rating, a history of abrasive negotiations with its bankers, and a record of underperforming the Index is unlikely to be able to raise money on favorable terms. The financial community has better-performing companies to support.

Most fundamentally, parent companies compete with each other in causing their businesses to perform better. A company with parenting advantage will enable its businesses to outperform their competitors. This shows through in the increasing strength of the company's individual business units, and in the damage they inflict on less well-parented rivals. If each business in a company is competing with better-parented rivals, the performance of the whole company will suffer. Competition between parents is implicit in the competition between their businesses.

Parent companies therefore compete with each other in various ways. We acknowledge that the market for corporate control is not highly active in most countries, and even in the United States and United Kingdom, competition between parent companies through hostile bids is a difficult and expensive process. In practice, it is quite normal for poorly performing parent companies to go unchallenged for long periods. However, the underlying pressure from competing parent companies gradually emerges in different ways: Active shareholders will encourage management to sell off businesses that would be worth more to others; business managers will draw attention to better ways of parenting, or will seek to capture unrealized value through management buyouts; nonexecutive directors and employee representatives will question whether corporate management is doing its best for all stakeholders or is succumbing to temptations of self-aggrandizement and self-delusion; finally, businesses with second-best parents will gradually lose ground to those with better parents. Despite the infrequency of hostile bids, the competitive pressure on parent managers is increasing.

Some managers are concerned by the apparently radical conclusions of our concept. They argue that if you accept the notion of parenting advantage, you would have to believe that every industry will become dominated by one company—the best parent for that industry. If our concept is correct, they argue, such parents would ultimately gain ownership of all the businesses in their industry—with the only restriction being monopoly and antitrust legislation. We do not support this view. First, as we saw in the discussion of different parenting approaches to RHM, there are many sources of advantage, allowing radically different parent companies to compete on fairly equal terms even in the same industry. Second, the relevance and value of specific advantages changes over time. The best parent in an industry at one stage may be disadvantaged as the world evolves. The problems of IBM, long acknowledged as a world leader, reveal the importance and difficulty of maintaining fit between the parent's characteristics and the changing requirements of its businesses.

WHY USE THE PARENTING METAPHOR?

Managers have sometimes questioned the validity of the parenting metaphor. Where does it come from, and why do we use it? The term "parenting advantage" derives, in the first instance, from the familiar language of parent companies and their subsidiary businesses. The notion of parenting, however, also has connotations from the family setting. For this reason, some people have criticized the term as potentially misleading. While we recognize that the family analogy is not totally apt, we nevertheless believe that the parenting metaphor is richly suggestive.

The strength of the metaphor is in its implication that there are different roles within the family for the parent and the businesses (children) and that the parent has great influence over the businesses (children). The parent needs to balance advice and encouragement with control and discipline. It also needs to recognize that the businesses (children) change and mature over time, and that a relationship that may have worked well in their early years will probably need to change as they grow. Businesses (children) like to know where they stand with their parents, including what will be regarded as good and bad behavior. While businesses (children) can learn an enormous amount from each other, they also tend to compete with each other, as well as against the outside world; the parent has an important role in creating a family environment in which friendly relationships between the businesses (children) are fostered, and mutual antagonism is diffused. Parents that smother their businesses (children) with close attention may end up by being rejected as interfering bores, while parents that let their businesses (children) go entirely their own way are abdicating their responsibility to attempt to help them maximize their true potential.

Some managers, especially within parent organizations, argue that the parenting metaphor is needlessly hierarchical. They explain that they operate more as a facilitator, or even a support structure. While such attitudes may be helpful in challenging assumed superiority by the parent or undue deference from the businesses, they seldom reflect the reality of power within multibusiness companies. Just as in family life, the corporate parent may not know better than its businesses (children), but it has legal and managerial authority that creates an unequal relationship.

For all these reasons, corporate parents do well to bear in mind the family analogy, and can promote better relationships with their businesses by remembering and learning from the mistakes they have made with their children.

The metaphor works less well in other areas. Corporate parents are able to work with systematic new business criteria when planning the development of their portfolios, while parents have much more limited choice, at this stage, regarding the nature of new children that are born into the family. There are circumstances in which corporate parents can and should consider divesting businesses, whereas relationships between parents and their children are seldom broken except in extreme and painful circumstances.[5] All children eventually grow up[6] and need their parents less, while many businesses continue to benefit from good parenting indefinitely. The goals and values of the corporation differ from those of the family,[7] placing less emphasis on loyalty, belonging, and family relationships, and often giving pride of place to shareholders, for which there are no family equivalents.[8] Perhaps the most fundamental difference is that corporate parents, we argue, have no role other than as intermediaries between their businesses and the external world, a limitation that even the most dedicated father or mother would want to reject.

So the metaphor is far from perfect. But we use metaphors to help us gain new and helpful insights about the things that they describe, not because they are universally exact. Good metaphors are neither complete nor accurate, but they are suggestive.[9] We could have written this book about "corporate advantage," a safe and dreary term that would have led to little confusion but would have inspired few new perceptions. We have preferred the richer, but riskier, alternative of parenting advantage, relying on the reader to interpret it in ways that are appropriate for the context.

NOTES

1. See Chapters 1 and 2.

2. For an interesting view of KKR's approach to parenting, see George Anders, "The 'Barbarians' in the Boardroom," *Harvard Business Review*, vol. 70, no. 4, July–August 1992, pp. 79–87.

3. For example, consulting companies have recently moved beyond a focus on more readily quantified "positional" advantages, such as market share dominance and the ownership of tangible assets, to a consideration of less tangible "capability" advantages. The growing importance of the latter category has prompted new attempts to quantify the nature and value of competences and capabilities. See, for example, George Stalk, Philip Evans, and Lawrence E. Shulman, "Competing on Capabilities: The New Rules of Corporate Strategy," *Harvard Business Review*, March–April 1992.

4. See Chapter 2 for a discussion of how rival parents might have assessed RHM.

5. Children are also more likely to sever their connections with their parents than vice versa.

6. Exceptions are regarded as abnormal or retarded.

7. Bruno Bettelheim, the well-known child psychologist, wrote a book entitled *A Good Enough Parent,* London: Thames & Hudson, 1987. While arguably a suitable family goal, our parenting advantage concept suggests that this is not ambitious enough in the corporate setting.

8. The bank manager, however, may play a closely similar role in both contexts.

9. Other metaphors that have relevance for relationships between the center and the businesses in the multibusiness company include the sports team (coach and players), the clan (chieftain and members), and the orchestra (conductor and players). For many companies, especially in the United States, the sports analogy is attractive, pointing up the collective drive to win and the role of the coach in bringing out the best performance from his players, individually and as a team. The clan, which Bill Ouchi has used as a metaphor for corporate life, is more like an extended family, but is a less familiar social form to most of us (see W. G. Ouchi, "A Conceptual Framework for the Design of Organizational Control Mechanisms," *Management Science,* vol. 25, no. 9, September 1979; "Markets, Bureaucracies and Clans," *Administrative Science Quarterly,* vol. 25, March 1980). The orchestra analogy highlights the difference in role between the players and the conductor. The conductor has an indirect role, but is invested with authority and overall responsibility. The need for close coordination between the players in the orchestra, however, is by no means always appropriate in a multibusiness context. On balance, we have found the parenting language to have the most meaning for the managers we have worked with.

4 CORPORATE STRATEGY: THE BACKGROUND

The broad nature of thinking about corporate strategy decisions has shifted over the past four decades. Increasing enthusiasm for diversification and multibusiness companies during the 1960s and 1970s, built on concepts of decentralization, general management skills, synergy, and portfolio balance, has been replaced in the 1980s and early 1990s with scepticism about the results achieved by diversified companies, a return to core businesses, and a renewed search for the key to corporate strategy. In this chapter, we will trace the evolution of this thinking and show the background against which the parenting advantage concept has been developed. We will also illustrate how different strands of corporate strategy thinking can be illuminated by the notion of parenting advantage. Successive ideas have drawn on different aspects of parenting advantage logic, without previously pulling them together into a comprehensive framework. We will start by reviewing the ideas in their historical context, before turning to their relationship with the concept of parenting advantage.

DIVISIONALIZATION

Alfred Chandler, the eminent business historian, has shown how the divisionalized, multibusiness company first emerged in the years before and during World War II.[1] In Chandler's view, companies like General Motors, Du Pont, and Standard Oil were forced to adopt a divisional structure because they had grown too large and complex to be managed with their previously functional organizations. These companies had been drawn into a wider and wider range of products and markets to exploit the opportunities arising from their base businesses and competences, and found that the only way to avoid overload at the center was by decentralization. Divisional structures were therefore introduced that separated day-to-day management responsibilities for the businesses from corporate strategy and resource allocation. These divisional structures recognized, for the first time, a distinction between business-level decisions, which were now the primary responsibility of management within the division, and corporate-level strategy, which was the responsibility of the corporate center.

The success of companies such as GM led to increased popularity for divisional structures in the years after the war. Richard Rumelt's *Strategy, Structure and Economic Performance* estimates that the percentage of divisionalized companies in the Fortune 500 rose from 24 percent in 1949, to 51 percent in 1959, and to 80 percent in 1969.[2] In many cases, divisionalization was coupled with, or initiated a move toward diversification.

DIVERSIFICATION

During the 1960s, many newly divisionalized companies embarked on a quest for corporate growth. Even companies in relatively mature, slow-growth industries believed that they could achieve faster corporate growth by diversifications that built on their general management skills and on opportunities for synergy in businesses that were related to their original, base businesses.

From the 1950s onward writers such as Peter Drucker were beginning to put forward the proposition that good managers needed to master certain general principles of management that were applicable in any business setting.[3] Given a belief in general management skills, it was not a great leap to conclude that professional managers might be able to use their skills in a variety of different business areas. An example of this view can be found in a 1955 *Harvard Business Review* article, entitled "Skills of an Effective Administrator," by Robert Katz. It states: "We are all familiar with those 'professional managers' who are becoming the prototypes of our modern executive world. These men shift with great ease, and with no apparent loss in effectiveness, from one industry to another. Their human and conceptual skills seem to make up for their unfamiliarity with the new job's technical aspects."[4] Businesspeople were even encouraged to apply their general management skills to improve the effectiveness of charities, universities, and government.[5]

In Europe, too, there was interest in general management skills. The founding of business schools in the United Kingdom and in France during the 1960s and the growing interest in management training were in part motivated by the perceived need to provide European managers with the same kind of general management skills as their U.S. competitors. Indeed, there was concern in Europe that the management skills of U.S. companies were so powerful that Americans would take over large chunks of European industry.[6]

The new divisional structures, coupled with the rise of "general managers," provided fertile ground for diversification strategies during the 1960s and 1970s. At one extreme, conglomerates such as Litton, ITT, and Textron sought growth by entering a wide range of different businesses. The bosses of these conglomerates believed that they possessed distinctive new management skills and that, by applying them to a large number of different businesses, they could grow profitably. For example, David Judelson of Gulf & Western argued in 1969: "Without the high degree of sophistication, skill, and effectiveness that management has developed only in the past two decades, the conglomerate could not exist. These management techniques provide the necessary unity and compatibility among a diversity of operations and acquisitions."[7] And Harold Geneen, chief executive of ITT from 1959 to 1977, reflected on the company's numerous acquisitions as follows: "I think our acquisitions were based largely upon intuition, experience, and a sense of confidence that we at ITT could help manage that company better than it had been managed before. In most instances, we kept on the same management and introduced the company's managers to the ITT system of business plans, detailed budgets, strict financial controls, and face-to-face General Managers Meetings."[8] These new American conglomerates were admired abroad. In the United Kingdom, Bob Heller wrote glowingly of Litton Industries and its spectacular growth across high-tech industries, claiming that the company was ". . . a technological achievement of its own, an operation in the technology of management as much as the management of technology."[9]

Many other industrial companies, which did not regard themselves as conglomerates, also diversified during the 1960s and 1970s. Particularly where the companies' base businesses were maturing, corporate managers looked for growth opportunities in new areas. Diversification was attractive to such companies as a means of meeting corporate growth objectives and spreading risks across different sectors. Typically, the new businesses were not in "unrelated" areas, as with the true conglomerates but were built on some links into the base business, however tenuous.[10] Such diversifications could be justified by a belief in synergy, which writers such as Igor Ansoff were claiming as a primary basis for corporate strategy. Ansoff advised firms to analyze their capabilities in areas such as manufacturing, marketing, and general management and to identify new product-markets where these capabilities could be exploited to achieve synergies.[11] Rumelt's research on diversification suggests that, by 1969, 44 percent of the Fortune 500 companies had diversified into related businesses, while only 12 percent had diversified into unrelated areas.[12]

A typical example of this sort of diversification is provided by the British Oxygen Company (now the BOC Group). From a base in industrial gases, BOC's quest for growth took it into a series of loosely related businesses during the 1960s and 1970s. The company developed a major welding equipment and consumables division, since oxyacetylene welding was a user of its cylinder gases. It created a healthcare division, based initially on its anesthetic gases. It went into high vacuum engineering, which had a link with its cryogenic know-how. A computer services business was established, to take advantage of its central computing staff, and a distribution business was set up to utilize its logistics skills. There was even a business called King Harry Pizza, which manufactured frozen pizza; the rationale was that gases were used in the freezing process. By the late 1960s, BOC—in common with many other old established and professionally managed industrial companies—had become a highly diversified group.[13]

Managers recognized that diversification was not an easy corporate strategy. But during the 1960s, a belief in the value of general management skills coupled, in many cases, with the pursuit of synergy in related activities, provided a rationale for entry into new businesses. Kenneth Andrews, Harvard Business School's leading business policy expert, summarized the basic premise, arguing that "successful diversification—because it always means successful surmounting of formidable administrative problems—develops know-how which further diversification will capitalize and extend."[14]

PORTFOLIO PLANNING

By the early 1970s, however, many of the new diversified companies, both conglomerates and otherwise, were beginning to encounter performance problems. The benign economic environment of the 1960s had given way to slower growth, higher inflation, and more competition. In companies like BOC, and in conglomerates like Textron, by no means all of the businesses in the portfolio were performing equally well. Managers increasingly recognized the need for selectivity in resource allocation, objective setting, and acquisitions.

But, in diversified companies, selectivity in resource allocation is difficult. "General" management skills are severely tested, where the corporate center must take a view on the relative merits of investment proposals coming from a range of businesses in different sectors, with different time horizons, different competitive positions, and different risk profiles, not to mention management teams with differing credibilities. In the early 1970s, a company such as ITT had to attempt to allocate resources between businesses that included telecommunications, insurance, rental cars, bakeries, and construction, while BOC had to divide its investments between its businesses in gases, healthcare, welding, high vacuum engineering, transportation, computer services, and frozen pizza.

Companies faced with resource allocation problems of this kind turned readily to the new techniques of portfolio planning that were introduced by the Boston Consulting Group and others in the 1970s. Portfolio planning gained wide acceptance during the 1970s because it helped corporate executives tackle the problems of capital allocation in the context of an overall corporate strategy.[15]

Portfolio planning provided corporate managers with a common framework to compare many different businesses. The industry attractiveness-business position matrix developed at GE, the Boston Consulting Group's growth-share matrix, and variations developed at other consultancies, were used to classify businesses in terms of their strategic position and opportunities. On the BCG matrix, businesses fell into one of four generic categories, and the terms cash cow, star, question mark, and dog became part of the business vocabulary.[16] By classifying businesses according to their positions on a growth-share matrix, managers could more easily determine appropriate objectives and resource allocation strategies for the different businesses in the portfolio.

The helicopter view provided by portfolio planning techniques was widely perceived as useful. For example, one CEO explained: "Portfolio planning became relevant to me as soon as I became CEO. I was finding it very difficult to manage and understand so many different products and markets. I just grabbed at portfolio planning, because it provided me with a way to organize my thinking about our businesses, and the resource allocation issues facing the total company. I became and still am very enthusiastic. I guess you could say that I went for it hook, line, and sinker."[17] During the 1970s, more and more corporations adopted portfolio planning, with the largest diversified companies among the earliest adherents. By 1979, 45 percent of the Fortune 500 companies were using some form of portfolio planning.[18]

In many companies, portfolio planning techniques became more than analytical tools to help chief executives direct corporate resources toward the most profitable opportunities: They became the basis of corporate strategy itself. The key concept here was the idea of a "balanced" portfolio made up of businesses whose profitability, growth, and cash flow characteristics would complement each other, and add up to a satisfactory overall corporate performance. "Imbalance" could be caused, for example, either by excessive cash generation with too few growth opportunities or by insufficient cash generation to fund the growth requirements elsewhere in the portfolio.[19]

Frequently, the first step toward balancing the corporate portfolio was to identify businesses that were a drain on corporate resources. These were the "dogs," and because of their weak competitive position in low-growth industries, they had to be divested. Some companies dramatically improved their overall performance by selling off weaker businesses in which they had no competitive advantage. Divestitures made funds available to invest in the kinds of businesses required to provide the appropriate balance for the corporate portfolio. Corporations with businesses in growth industries needed cash-generating businesses to finance their growth, while companies with profitable cash-generating businesses in mature industries needed to invest in higher growth businesses for the future. Monsanto, for example, used portfolio planning to restructure its portfolio, divesting low-growth commodity chemicals businesses and acquiring businesses in higher growth industries such as biotechnology.[20]

Portfolio planning reinforced the virtuous circle of corporate growth and diversification that had originally been founded on general management skills. It helped corporate-level managers correct past diversification mistakes, leading to the divestiture of weak businesses, and it encouraged them to invest in a mix of businesses, with different strategic (and cash) characteristics to balance their corporate portfolios and ensure future growth.

But even as an increasing number of corporations turned to portfolio planning, problems emerged in managing "balanced" portfolios. Companies discovered that, while certain businesses appeared to meet all the economic requirements of the corporate portfolio, they did not fit easily into the corporate family. It turned out to be extremely difficult, for example, for corporate managers with long experience of managing cash cows in a particular industry sector to manage effectively their acquired growth businesses in new, dynamic, and unfamiliar sectors. Many companies discovered that common systems and approaches, when applied to different kinds of businesses, could detract value from those businesses.[21]

The recognition that different types of businesses had to be managed differently undermined the argument that general management skills, buttressed by the framework of portfolio planning, provided the rationale for diversified companies. Portfolio planning helped corporate executives sort out the contribution of each of their businesses to the corporate portfolio, but it did not answer the other critical question confronting a diversified company: What contribution, if any, can the corporation make to each of its businesses?

RESTRUCTURING

During the 1980s, widespread scepticism about the ability of companies to manage and add value to diverse portfolios gained ground. Raiders such as Carl Icahn and T. Boone Pickens demonstrated that they could acquire even the largest companies, break them up, and realize huge profits. The takeover activity of the 1980s prompted a rethinking of both the role of the corporate center in large companies, and of the appropriate kinds of strategies for diversified companies.

Moreover, consultants and academics were less and less favorable to diversification. For example, Michael Porter published a study showing the high rate of divestiture of acquisitions among American corporations, arguing that the diversification strategies of many companies had failed to create value. "I studied the diversification records of 33 large, prestigious U.S. companies over the 1950–1986 period and found that most of them had divested many more acquisitions than they had kept. The corporate strategies of most companies have dissipated instead of created shareholder value. . . . By taking over companies and breaking them up, corporate raiders thrive on failed corporate strategies."[22]

Faced with the threat from raiders and the criticism of academics, chief executives devoted themselves increasingly to the task of restructuring. Delayering, downsizing, and reducing corporate costs became popular, coupled with divestment of businesses that were seen as less attractive for the company. In many cases, this led to a reversal of the diversification trend of the previous two decades.

Restructuring was given added impetus by a fresh emphasis on the importance of creating shareholder value. Managers were encouraged to evaluate corporate performance in the same terms as the stock market (and raiders), using economic rather than accounting measures, and to take whatever actions were necessary to improve their company's stock price. "Value-based planning," using the financial tools of discounted cash flow, ROE spreads, and hurdle rates, provided corporate managers with a fresh perspective on the linkages between stock prices and competitive strategy.[23] Value-based planning techniques gained many adherents, especially among American corporations. In 1987, an article in *Fortune* described how "managements have caught the religion. At first reluctant, they pound at the door of consultants who can teach them the way to a higher stock price—a price so high it would thwart even the most determined raider."[24] Frequently, these consultants ended up by recommending strategies that involved getting out of the low-profit, low-value businesses in the portfolio, and concentrating on the high-profit, high-value ones.

Against this background, a concept of corporate success based on core businesses, or a "stick-to-the-knitting" philosophy, gained popularity. Peters and Waterman observed in *In Search of Excellence* that successful corporations did not diversify widely. They tended to specialize in particular industries and focused intently on improving their knowledge and skills in the areas they knew best.[25]

Stick-to-the-knitting advice was also a reaction against the analytical techniques and impersonal approach of much of corporate strategy and portfolio planning. Bob Hayes and Bill Abernathy voiced these concerns in their article "Managing Our Way to Economic Decline." In their view, too many American corporations were being run by

"pseudoprofessional" managers, skilled in finance and law, but lacking in technological expertise or in-depth experience in any particular industry. They warned that portfolios diversified across different industries and businesses were appropriate for stocks and bonds, but not for corporations.[26] The need for experience and deep knowledge of a business was also emphasized by Henry Mintzberg, who criticized the "thin and lifeless" strategies that result from treating businesses as mere positions on a portfolio matrix. He argued that instead of broad diversity, we need "focused organizations that understand their missions, "know" the people they serve, and excite the ones they employ; we should be encouraging "thick" management, deep knowledge, healthy competition and authentic social responsibility."[27] The widespread conviction that companies should stick to the knitting reinforced the practical pressures created by the corporate raiders and contributed to the wave of restructuring.

Restructuring (whether voluntary or not) has frequently led to the disposal of corporate assets and reduced diversification. In 1985, for example, General Mills announced its intention to focus on its core businesses of consumer foods and restaurants, and the company sold off its toy and fashion businesses.[28] More recently, General Signal embarked on a strategy of "back to the basics," retreating from its earlier major investments in high-tech businesses to focus on its traditional "boring" products such as industrial mixers.[29] In a study of diversification among the Fortune 500, Constantinos Markides found that the proportion of diversified companies fell from 63 percent in 1974 to 41 percent in 1987, reversing the trend of the previous two decades.[30] Furthermore, Markides concluded that the companies that restructured to reduce diversity were those characterized by poor performance relative to their industry counterparts.[31]

CORE BUSINESSES

Restructuring has been widely regarded as a salutary correction to the excesses of broad diversification. Michael Jensen has argued that corporate breakups, divisional sell-offs, and LBOs are critical developments that can prevent the wasteful use of capital by managers of large public corporations, and other recent academic studies support the view that restructuring does help improve the performance of corporations.[32] But restructuring implies a sense of which businesses a company should retain and which it should divest. How should the "core" businesses be selected?

One answer was that companies should restructure to focus their businesses on one, or a few, closely related industries. In this way, managers can stick to what they know well, and best exploit corporate expertise. This approach was consistent with stick-to-the-knitting advice, but it has not provided a complete answer. Successful companies such as GE, Hanson, and Cooper Industries continue to have businesses in many different industries. Furthermore, sticking to a single industry does not necessarily limit complexity or ensure that companies expand into areas they "know." During the 1980s, companies such as Prudential and Merrill Lynch sought to combine different types of financial services businesses. They discovered that businesses such as insurance, stockbroking, and banking, though all in the financial services industry, nonetheless required very different approaches, resources, and skills.[33]

Another reservation about a corporate strategy based on limiting diversification to closely related businesses is that, despite extensive research, empirical evidence on the performance of companies pursuing more and less related diversification strategies is ambiguous and contradictory. Many studies have compared the performance of single-product companies, companies that diversify into related products, markets, or technologies, and unrelated conglomerates; but no firm relationship between different diversification strategies and performance has been discovered.[34]

A more promising basis for focus concentrates on the idea of a company's "dominant general management logic." C. K. Prahalad and Richard Bettis argue that the more diverse a firm, the more complex the problems in managing it. Diversity, however, cannot be defined simply in terms of the number of product/markets in which a firm competes; the strategic variety of the firm's businesses is a more significant measure of its diversity. With firms in strategically similar businesses, the center can employ common methods and approaches, using a single managerial dominant logic: "A dominant general management logic is defined as the way in which managers conceptualize the business and make critical resource allocation decisions—be it in technologies, product development, distribution, advertising, or in human resource management."[35] The dominant general management logic of the corporate management team provides the basis for selecting the core businesses for the portfolio.

Prahalad and Bettis's views are compatible with our own work on parenting styles, described in *Strategies and Styles*.[36] The concept of parenting style is reviewed more fully in Appendix C of this book, but our basic contention in *Strategies and Styles* was that companies have different parenting styles, and that these styles are suitable for different sorts of businesses. Thus both dominant logic and parenting style argue for focusing the portfolio onto businesses that share common strategic characteristics. In this way, the corporate portfolio is composed of a group of businesses that are more readily manageable by the corporate team.[37]

Other experts, however, have claimed that the links between the businesses in the corporate portfolio need to be more substantial and that the only valid justification for a diversified company is sharing of resources and competences across the businesses. Michael Porter, for example, views the management of interrelationships between businesses as the essence of corporate-level strategy, arguing that without this, a diversified company is little more than a mutual fund.[38] He maintains: "Both the strategic logic and the experience of the companies I studied over the last decade suggest that a company will create shareholder value through diversification to a greater and greater extent as its strategy moves from portfolio management toward sharing activities. Because they do not rely on superior insight or other questionable assumptions about the company's capabilities, sharing activities and transferring skills offer the best avenues for value creation."[39] Thus Porter returns to the idea of synergy, originally put forward by Ansoff in the 1960s.[40]

Perhaps the best-known advocates of the view that corporate strategies need to rest on shared core competences are C. K. Prahalad and Gary Hamel. Hamel and Prahalad argue that the corporate portfolio should not be perceived simply as a group of businesses, but also as a collection of competences. In managing the corporate portfolio, managers must ensure that each part draws on and contributes to the core competences the corporation is seeking to build and exploit. Even a poorly performing business may be contributing to an important core competence, and if managers divest such businesses they may also be discarding some of their competences. If corporations are unable to transfer a core competence from one business to another, then they are wasting their resources. According to Prahalad and Hamel, many of the current management approaches of Western corporations, including SBUs, decentralization, and resource allocation practices, undermine the ability of corporations to build core competences, since autonomous businesses seldom have the resources or vision to build world-class competences.[41]

Several other writers have stressed the importance of a company's underlying competences, capabilities, skills, and resources.[42] This work has generated much interest. Walter Kiechel, in *Fortune* magazine, describes how some executives are perceiving their role, and that of the corporate center, as guardians and promoters of the company's core skills, and concludes: "To the extent that such skills can be exploited by each of the company's businesses, they represent a reason for having all those businesses under one corporate umbrella."[43]

But corporations that do base their strategy on core competences have found that it can be difficult to judge when an investment in a business is justified in terms of building a core competence, particularly if it means suspending normal profitability criteria and if the investment is in an unfamiliar business area. Another danger with the competence approach to corporate strategy is that businesses may require similar core competences but demand different overall strategies and managerial approaches.

In practice, therefore, many companies have found it difficult to gain benefits from a corporate strategy based on linkages, core competences, and synergy.[44] Acquisitions aimed at realizing synergies can be especially risky. A British study concluded: "Benefits of synergy are now truly legendary. Diversification and synergy have become virtually inseparable in texts and business language. Yet . . . those particular benefits show an almost unshakeable resolve not to appear when it becomes time for their release."[45] Quantitative evidence appears to support the observation that synergies are hard to achieve; a recent study on takeovers concluded that most gains arise from asset disposals and restructuring rather than from synergy.[46]

A LASTING BASIS FOR CORPORATE STRATEGY

Over the past four decades, therefore, there have been various waves of thinking concerning corporate strategy in diversified companies. Different concepts and approaches have proved fashionable at different times but have all ultimately appeared incomplete. Each wave of thinking has been helpful in addressing particular issues, as summarized in Exhibit 4–1. The topicality of each issue drew out helpful new concepts, but the corporate strategies embodying the new concepts seemed to fall prey to fresh problems, leading to a need for further rethinking. The resulting overlays and contradictions have led to some confusion.

There is now renewed interest in finding a sound and lasting basis for corporate strategy. We believe that the concept of parenting advantage can fill this need, and provide the practical and comprehensive framework that has been lacking. A focus on parenting advantage and parenting value is distinct from any of the previous waves of thinking. However, it can be seen as an underlying theme that runs through many of the concepts described, and provides a link that reconciles apparently divergent approaches. Reviewing these approaches from a parenting perspective therefore sheds new light on their interrelationships and validity.

A PARENTING PERSPECTIVE ON PREVIOUS APPROACHES TO CORPORATE STRATEGY

In this section, we will adopt a parenting perspective to review the main approaches to corporate strategy described earlier. In each case, we will identify an underlying thought about value creation that gave power and attraction to the particular approach. Successful parents have focused on this underlying thought and had insights about it that distinguished them from less successful "followers of the fad." We will also show that past approaches each spawned some misconceptions.

EXHIBIT 4–1   The development of corporate-level strategies

	Issues	Concepts	Corporate Strategies
1950	Overload at the center	Decentralization	Divisionalization
1960	Quest for growth	General management skills Synergy	Diversification —conglomerate —"related"
1970	Resource allocation problems	Portfolio planning	"Balanced" portfolios
1980s	Value gaps and raiders Poor performance of diversifications	Value based planning "Stick to the knitting"	Restructuring
1990s	Defining the core businesses	"Dominant logic" and "management styles" Core competences and shared resources	Manageable portfolios Linked portfolios
	Lasting basis for corporate strategy	Parenting advantage	Managing portfolio to maximize value creation

These misconceptions continue to cause some parents to make bad corporate strategy decisions today. We therefore highlight where and how they come into conflict with the parenting advantage approach we are proposing. By focusing on the value creation of the parent, we can explain the underlying power of previous concepts, while clarifying where they may be misleading or incomplete.

Divisionalization

Divisionalization created the parent. By distinguishing between the center and the divisions, a role was established for managers outside the businesses. The underlying source of value creation was the opportunity to improve business definitions. Rather than defining all the activities of the company as a single business, top corporate managers saw that narrower business definitions could reduce managerial complexity and improve the tradeoffs between size and focus. Parenting advantage was achieved by companies that had particular insights about appropriate business definition.[47] They captured the most valuable combinations of size and focus by creating a separation between the divisions and the parent organization, and in the particular ways that they divisionalized.

But, although divisionalization enabled some parents to create value, it was not a formula for success in its own right. Parents who followed the trend but had no insights about business definition divided up their activities in ways that were inappropriate and value destroying. In the quest for parenting advantage, there is still a role for improved business definition,[48] and many of the parents we examine in this book have had powerful insights in this area.[49] Divisionalisation is therefore helpful when it leads to better business definitions but harmful when it leads to worse business definitions.

Diversification

Diversification in the 1960s was based on three underlying thoughts about value creation. First, that it was possible for a parent to leverage professional general management skills across a broad range of businesses. Second, that there were opportunities to coordinate or share across businesses that had some form of overlap. Third, that rapid corporate growth could be achieved through acquisitions and moves into new business areas.

Successful parents were able to create value and gain advantage by applying professional management skills when they were in short supply. But as general management skills spread, the ability of a parent to create value from generalist guidance concerning things such as organization structure, planning, and budgeting was severely reduced. Even though individual businesses presented parenting opportunities, other parents were equally able to realize them. This pushed up the price of acquisitions and reduced differentiation between parents. As the value of generalist professionalism played out, the importance of the heartland concept was revealed. The need for parents to have a good "feel" for their businesses increased,[50] as the opportunity for basic improvements declined. Without a feel for their businesses, generalist professional managers could not create as much value as professional, but more focused, rivals. A misconception about the continued value of leveraging general management skills led many parents not only to lose advantage, but to destroy value. Generalists found themselves spread across portfolios with widely differing parenting needs. It was problems from this overextension that led to the development of portfolio planning techniques.

The second thought underlying diversification concerned synergy. Successful parents gained advantage by creating valuable links across businesses. As well as "managerial synergy" already described, they exploited synergies in resources, market knowledge, and other forms of know-how. But, once again, misconceptions about the nature and role of synergy led many parents to destroy value. One problem was the failure to distinguish between mere relatedness and the existence of a value creation opportunity that parents could exploit. Simply having two businesses that use the same technology or share the same markets is no guarantee that a parent can create value through joint ownership. Many parents had no value creation insights, and simply hoped that their presence in related areas would lead to benefits. Worse still, as we saw with BOC's entry to frozen pizza, misconceptions about the value of relatedness tempted parents into areas completely outside their heartland. Companies were not only ill-equipped to parent such businesses, but their recognition of the dangers of misfit was clouded. The comforting thought that they were not conglomerates, but owned a series of related businesses, lulled many parents into a false sense of security and paved the way to value destruction.

Another misconception concerning diversification relates to the value of risk spreading. Parents were encouraged in their diversifications by the thought that they would benefit from a greater spread of risk across different businesses. In such cases, it is important to note that the risk they reduced, if any, was senior management risk rather than shareholder risk. Shareholders can reduce their own risk more effectively by diversifying their equity holdings. But diversifications intended to spread risks across different businesses often increased the risk of value destruction. The very fact that parents sought diversifications that balanced existing exposures led them into unfamiliar businesses. As a result, they often entered businesses that fitted poorly with their parenting characteristics and lay outside their heartland.

The third thought about value creation concerned corporate growth. Successful parents recognized that they could expand their portfolios more rapidly by making acquisitions and entering new business areas. Inasmuch as they brought parenting advantage to these new areas, this led to "healthy" growth. Furthermore, it attracted high caliber managers and stock market support, based on the career opportunities and dynamism of the companies. Ability to attract the best professional managers and to fund further acquisitions based on a high stock rating reinforced parenting advantage. The desire to grow rapidly to make use of and reinforce parenting advantage was entirely appropriate. But a focus on growth can become an end in itself and lead to dangerous temptations. It can encourage a cavalier attitude toward value creation, for example by making acquisitions that do not fit the parent's characteristics in a scramble to reach aggressive growth targets. It can undermine the status or morale of low-growth businesses, which fit well with the company's parenting but are felt to be dull or inadequate. It can encourage mature businesses to seek growth that is unprofitable or destabilizing. It can prevent the sale of high-growth businesses, even if they are being poorly parented.

A desire for growth as an end in itself often shapes an attitude to corporate strategy built on "gap-filling." Corporate managers establish some aspiration regarding total company growth. They then add up the constituent parts of the existing portfolio and identify the size of the gap. This gap becomes the target of corporate strategy: How can we fill it, with new acquisitions or new developments or increased pressure on the businesses? Such an attitude encourages ill-founded decisions that destroy value. The order of priorities shifts from "We must create value in our portfolio and aim for parenting advantage; it would be nice to expand the portfolio in which we do this by 20 percent a year," to the all-too-frequent "We must expand the portfolio by 20 percent a year; it would be nice if we could create some value in doing so." This confusion of priorities prompted many companies to diversify inappropriately and overrapidly, sowing the seeds for later restructuring.

، As with divisionalization, diversification has therefore provided opportunities for some parents to create value. Many others, however, have followed the fashionable trend without a clear sense of how they would create value, and, as a result, have destroyed value instead.

Portfolio Planning

When successfully applied, portfolio planning created value by helping parents improve their processes for resource allocation and objective setting. Businesses in rapidly growing markets, for example, should be subject to different cash, profitability, and market share goals from businesses in mature settings. Some companies improved their parenting through a clearer focus on the different competitive and market contexts of their businesses.

But portfolio planning techniques also spawned misconceptions. These concerned the role of the parent in picking "attractive" businesses, and in "balancing" the portfolio. Having categorized their businesses, many parents concluded that they should focus on attractive ones that were profitable and offered high growth potential and should exit from less attractive ones. But, while it was obviously sensible not to invest in businesses insufficiently profitable to generate their own cost of capital, a focus on inherent business attraction obscured the role of the parent. Unless the parent could spot growth opportunities that were unnoticed by rivals or contribute to profitability in ways that others did not, it had no basis for creating value. Acquisition prices or new business entry costs reflect the attractions of the businesses. If the parent cannot add some additional benefit, it pays fully for the opportunity it is buying into. Some corporate managers perceive their main task as finding good businesses to invest in, but they are normally less well positioned to do this than fund managers.

The other misconception concerned balance. Many parents sought to balance their "cash cows," which were generating large cash flows, with "stars" or "question marks" that needed significant investment. While access to capital markets was restricted, this provided a potential source of parenting advantage. Balanced parents could fund investments that others could not. But the development of capital markets has reduced this parenting opportunity, since there is now generally no shortage of funds for good investments.[51] Furthermore, parents with balanced portfolios, containing mature and profitable businesses together with others that were growing and cash hungry, typically had businesses with very different parenting needs. It was correspondingly difficult to have value creation insights or distinctive parenting characteristics that were relevant to the whole portfolio. Characteristics that created value with one business or division were likely to be damaging to another. While parenting advantage requires focus on heartland businesses with similar parenting needs and opportunities, the search for balance often pushes in the opposite direction. Just as with risk spreading, an emphasis on balancing cash flows or growth patterns across the portfolio frequently prompts a dilution of parenting advantage.

Restructuring

Based on the previously described misconceptions, many parents were destroying value by the 1980s. Businesses were often worth less under the control of their parents than they would have been as stand-alone entities or in some other grouping. This was the value creation opportunity that underlay restructuring. So-called predators found that they could pay a premium of 50 percent on the stock price of their targets and still release enough value to make good returns. In some cases, simply reducing the size and complexity of the parent organization created value. It not only saved central costs, but reduced unhelpful interference and delays. In other cases, parents with no value creation insights and no heartland were broken up. Their businesses were floated off or sold to other parents with whom there was better fit.[52]

Under the threat of hostile takeover, many parents decided to restructure and refocus themselves. But the basis for refocusing was inconsistent. In particular, two misconceptions developed which once again cut across the underlying thought about value creation. One was the inclination to restructure around the businesses that were inherently most attractive, rather than those to which the parent had most to add. This was subject to the problems we have already noted. The other misconception was to assume that delayering and cutting central costs was necessarily the right answer. A concern with the parent's value creation will always challenge the size of head office. In many cases, it will help to isolate staff functions or parenting layers that add little value to the businesses, or indeed that destroy value through their influence. The challenge however, does not always imply downsizing. In building parenting advantage, it is also quite possible that the center should be expanded and that its role should be extended into new areas of involvement. In several companies, a clash between parenting advantage thinking and the pressure to downsize has emerged. The aim of reducing the size of head office has made managers reluctant to hire the staff needed to make the parent more effective. Cutting corporate costs as an end in itself is therefore not compatible with parenting advantage logic. Although delayering is often appropriate, in some circumstances it will undermine the achievement of parenting advantage. This is the concern at the heart of much "core competence" thinking, which criticizes Western management for focusing too heavily on cost reduction rather than on value creation.[53]

Core Businesses

The benefits available from focus meant that value was often created when companies shed their non-core businesses. Parents could become successful by focusing on certain businesses and withdrawing from or deemphasizing others. But, from the perspective of parenting advantage, the thinking behind a move to core businesses was often confused or incomplete.

Focusing on a particular industry may increase a parent's chances of having a good understanding of the markets and technologies facing its businesses. This can reduce the risk of value destruction. However, in itself, it does not guarantee any value creation. Furthermore, within an industry, different businesses may present very different parenting opportunities. For example, the parenting opportunities available in a group of community branch banks are completely different from those in international investment banking. In contrast, the same parenting opportunity may apply to businesses spanning different industries, as we saw in the example of Hanson. As a result, core business definitions based purely on specified industries seldom map well onto a parent's real heartland.

The notions of dominant logic and parenting style provided clearer guides for avoiding value destruction. If businesses did not fit the dominant logic or the parenting style of the parent, the misfit would cause problems. Such businesses would risk being harmed by inappropriate parental interventions. Building a portfolio around the parent's style or dominant logic therefore improved the parenting of many companies. But, again, neither concept fully addressed the basis of value creation rather than the avoidance of value destruction. Absence of misfit was not sufficient to create value, let alone parenting advantage. Many parents that adopt a Strategic Control style,[54] for example, have no style misfit with the businesses in their portfolio. But, if they lack value creation insights, distinctive parenting characteristics, and a clear sense of their heartland, such parents do not prove successful.

The notion of core competences suffers from almost the opposite problem. It focuses on a value creation opportunity to the exclusion of avoiding value destruction. The need for similar competences in a number of businesses in the portfolio provides one potential opportunity for a parent to exploit. By building the competences and facilitating the transfer of know-how and skills across business boundaries, a parent may indeed create value and even advantage. Canon's value creation insights largely fit this pattern. But too heavy an emphasis on core competences can understate the dangers of value destruction from other areas of misfit between a parent and its businesses.

Texas Instruments, for example, attempted to exploit the core competence it had developed in its semiconductors business in areas such as calculators, watches, and home computers. It failed in these new areas not because it lacked the core semiconductor competence, but because its top management had no experience in managing such consumer-oriented businesses.[55] Similarly, Procter & Gamble applied its skills in product innovation and consumer promotion to a soft drinks business, Crush, but eventually divested the business because it ran into unfamiliar problems managing the local bottlers who largely control the distribution of soft drinks.[56] Core competences may add value in specific areas in a variety of different businesses, but this is no guarantee that, overall, a company will be able to manage those different businesses successfully. Businesses that can be linked together by core competences frequently have other parenting needs that differ widely. As a result, the parent may destroy more value through a failure to appreciate these differences fully than it creates through the sharing of core competences.

If the sharing of core competences is not a sufficient condition to ensure parenting value, neither is it a necessary condition. Companies such as Berkshire Hathaway and BTR are collections of independent businesses, whose successful strategies are not based on exploiting core competences, at least as defined by Prahalad and Hamel,[57] across the portfolio. For some companies, the advantages of concentrating on raising the performance of stand-alone businesses outweigh the long-term investment required to create and share core competences among those businesses; and, in many corporate portfolios, the potential for sharing may simply not exist. Corporate strategists need to be able to determine when shared competences represent an important and viable rationale for a multibusiness company, and when their appeal is likely to prove illusory.

A Lasting Basis for Corporate Strategy

Throughout the ebb and flow of corporate strategy thinking, the parenting advantage concept can be seen to provide a means of distinguishing between successful, enlightened application of new ideas and the unenlightened following of fashionable bandwagons. No doubt, there will be other bandwagons in the future. We believe that the distinction between successful companies and those who blindly follow these bandwagons will continue to depend on the underlying logic of parenting value and parenting advantage. Whatever the trends of the time, multibusiness companies seeking a lasting basis for corporate strategy will be best served by a clear focus on the concept of parenting advantage.

NOTES

1. Alfred D. Chandler, Jr., *Strategy and Structure,* Cambridge, MA: MIT Press, 1962; reissued 1982.

2. Richard P. Rumelt, *Strategy, Structure and Economic Performance,* Boston: Harvard Business School Press, 1974, reissued 1986.

3. Peter Drucker, *The Practice of Management,* London: Heinemann, 1955, reissued Pan Books, 1968; Harold Koontz, "The Management Theory Jungle," *Academy of Management Journal,* vol. 4, no. 3, December 1961, pp. 174–188; Harold Koontz, "A Model for Analyzing the Universality and Transferability of Management," *Academy of Management Journal,* vol. 12, no. 4, December 1969, pp. 415–430.

4. Robert L. Katz, "Skills of an Effective Administrator," *Harvard Business Review,* January–February 1955, pp. 33–42.

5. Arthur B. Langlie, "Top Management's Responsibility for Good Government," and Thomas Roy Jones, "Top Management's Responsibility to the Community," both in H. B. Maynard, ed., *Top Management Handbook,* New York: McGraw-Hill, 1960; Kenneth R. Andrews, "Toward Professionalism in·Business Management," *Harvard Business Review,* March–April 1969, pp. 49–60; Y. K. Shetty, and Newman S. Perry, Jr., "Are Top Executives Transferable across Companies?" *Business Horizons,* June 1976, pp. 23–28.

6. Richard Whitley, Alan Thomas, and Jane Marceau, *Masters of Business? Business Schools and Business Graduates in Britain and France,* London: Tavistock Publications, 1981; J.-J. Servan-Schreiber, *The American Challenge,* translated by Roland Steel, London: Hamish Hamilton, 1968.

7. David N. Judelson, "The Conglomerate—Corporate Form of the Future," *Michigan Business Review,* July 1969, pp. 8–12; reprinted in John W. Bonge, and Bruce P. Coleman, eds., *Concepts for Corporate Strategy,* New York: Macmillan, 1972.

8. Harold Geneen, with Alvin Moscow. *Managing,* New York: Doubleday, 1984.

9. R. Heller, "The Legend of Litton," *Management Today,* October 1967; reprinted in Igor Ansoff, ed., *Business Strategy,* London: Penguin Books, 1969, pp. 360–378.

10. Rumelt, *Strategy, Structure and Economic Performance.*

11. Igor Ansoff, *Corporate Strategy,* New York: McGraw-Hill, 1965; London: Penguin Books, 1968.

12. Rumelt, *Strategy, Structure and Economic Performance.*

13. During the 1980s, BOC, which had acquired Airco of the United States in 1978, divested over 30 companies under its then chief executive Richard Giordano, and concentrated its portfolio around the two main sectors of gases and healthcare.

14. Kenneth R. Andrews, "Product Diversification and the Public Interest," *Harvard Business Review,* July 1951, p. 98.

15. Joseph L. Bower, *Managing the Resource Allocation Process,* Harvard Business School Classics Edition, Boston, MA: Harvard Business School Press, 1986; Richard G. Hamermesh, *Making Strategy Work,* New York: John Wiley & Sons, 1986, pp. 17–21.

16. Barry Hedley, "Strategy and the 'Business Portfolio,'" *Long Range Planning,* February 1977, pp. 9–15.

17. Richard G. Hamermesh, *Making Strategy Work,* p. 7.

18. Philippe Haspeslagh, "Portfolio Planning: Uses and Limits," *Harvard Business Review,* January–February 1982, pp. 58–73.

19. Barry Hedley, "Strategy and the 'Business Portfolio,'" pp. 9–15; Charles W. Hofer, and Dan Schendel, *Strategy Formulation: Analytical Concepts,* New York: West Publishing, 1978.

20. Hamermesh, *Making Strategy Work,* p. 71.

21. Richard G. Hamermesh, and Rokerick E. White, "Manage beyond Portfolio Analysis," *Harvard Business Review,* January–February 1984, pp. 103–109; Philippe Haspeslagh, "Portfolio Planning: Uses and Limits," *Harvard Business Review,* January–February 1982, pp. 58–73.

22. Michael E. Porter, "From Competitive Advantage to Corporate Strategy," *Harvard Business Review,* May–June 1987, pp. 43–59.

23. William W. Alberts, and James M. McTaggart, "Value Based Strategic Investment Planning," *Interfaces,* January–February 1984, pp. 138–51; see also Enrique R. Arzac, "Do Your Business Units Create Shareholder Value?", *Harvard Business Review,* January–February 1986, pp. 121–126; Alfred Rappaport, *Creating Shareholder Value: The New Standard for Business Performance,* New York: Free Press, 1986; Bernard C. Reimann, *Managing for Value,* Oxford: Basil Blackwell, 1987; Tom Copeland, et al., *Valuation,* New York: John Wiley & Sons, 1990.

24. John J. Curran, "Are Stocks Too High?", *Fortune,* September 28, 1987, p. 24.

25. Thomas J. Peters, and Robert H. Waterman, *In Search of Excellence,* New York: Free Press, 1982.

26. Bob Hayes, and Bill Abernathy, "Managing Our Way to Economic Decline," *Harvard Business Review,* July–August 1980, pp. 67–77.

27. Henry Mintzberg, *Mintzberg on Management,* New York: Free Press, 1989.

28. Michael E. Porter, "General Mills, Inc.: Corporate Strategy," HBS Case Study 9-388-123, 1988.

29. Seth Lubove, "Dog with Bone," *Forbes,* April 13, 1992, p. 106.

30. Constantinos Markides, "Corporate Refocusing," *Business Strategy Review,* vol. 4, no. 1, Spring 1993, pp. 1–15. Markides gives the following figures:

	1974	1981	1987
Single business	14.4%	23.8%	30.4%
Dominant business	22.6	31.9	28.1
Related business	42.3	21.9	22.4
Unrelated business	20.7	22.4	19.0

31. The restructuring phenomenon became so popular that it formed the subject of a special issue of the *Strategic Management Journal,* edited by Edward H. Bowman, and Harbir Singh, in 1993 (volume 14). See also Milton L. Rock, and Robert H. Rock, eds., *Corporate Restructuring,* New York: McGraw-Hill, 1990.

32. Michael Jensen, "The Eclipse of the Public Corporation," *Harvard Business Review,* September–October 1989, pp. 61–74, and "Corporate Control and the Politics of Finance," *Journal of Applied Corporate Finance,* vol. 4, no. 2, Summer 1991; S. Chatterjee, "Sources of Value in Takeovers: Synergy or Restructuring—Implications for Target and Bidder Firms," *Strategic Management Journal,* vol. 13, no. 4, May 1992, pp. 267–286; S. Bhagat, A. Shleifer, and R. Vishny, "Hostile Takeovers in the 1980s: The Return to Corporate Specialization," *Brookings Papers on Economic Activity: Microeconomics,* 1990.

33. Robert M. Grant, "On 'Dominant Logic,' Relatedness and the Link between Diversity and Performance," *Strategic Management Journal,* vol. 9, no. 6, November–December 1988, pp. 639–642; Robert M. Grant, "Diversification in the Financial Services Industry: Why Are the Benefits of Synergy So Elusive?" in A. Campbell, and K. Luchs, eds., *Strategic Synergy,* Oxford: Butterworth Heinemann, 1992, pp. 201–242.

34. There is an extensive literature on this topic. See Rumelt, *Strategy, Structure and Economic Performance;* Richard P. Rumelt, "Diversification Strategy and Profitability," *Strategic Management Journal,* vol. 3, 1982, pp. 359–369; Richard A. Bettis, "Performance Differences in Related and Unrelated Diversified Firms," *Strategic Management Journal,* vol. 2, 1981, pp. 379–393; Kurt H. Christensen, and Cynthia A. Montgomery, "Corporate Economic Performance: Diversification Strategy versus Market Structure," *Strategic Management Journal,* vol. 2, 1981, pp. 327–343; Gerry Johnson, and Howard Thomas, "The Industry Context of Strategy, Structure and Performance: The U.K. Brewing Industry," *Strategic Management Journal,* vol. 8, 1987, pp. 343–361; Anju Seth, "Value Creation in Acquisitions: A Re-Examination of Performance Issues," *Strategic Management Journal,* vol. 11, 1990, pp. 99–115; V.

Ramanujam, and P. Varadarajan, "Research on Corporate Diversification: A Synthesis," *Strategic Management Journal*, vol. 10, 1989, p. 523–551.

35. C. K. Prahalad, and R. A. Bettis, "The Dominant Logic: A New Linkage between Diversity and Performance," *Strategic Management Journal*, vol. 7, 1986, p. 490.

36. Michael Goold, and Andrew Campbell, *Strategies and Styles*, Oxford: Basil Blackwell, 1987. In *Strategies and Styles*, we used the term "management style" rather than "parenting style."

37. See also Charles W. L. Hill, "The Functions of the Headquarters Unit in Multibusiness Firms," in R. Rumelt, D. Teece, and D. Schendel, eds., *Fundamental Issues in Strategy Research*, Cambridge, MA: Harvard University Press, 1994.

38. Michael E. Porter, *Competitive Advantage*, New York: Free Press, 1985.

39. Michael E. Porter, "From Competitive Advantage to Corporate Strategy," *Harvard Business Review*, May–June 1987.

40. The importance of synergy, or sharing across business units, has been emphasized by other authors in the recent management literature. Rosabeth Moss Kanter also argues that the achievement of synergy is the only justification for a multibusiness company. She describes new kinds of organizations emerging in the United States—"postentrepreneurial corporations"—that "make the search for synergies a central part of their strategies . . . . They make sure each area contributes something to the others" (see Rosabeth Moss Kanter, *When Giants Learn to Dance*, New York: Simon & Schuster, 1989). Christopher Bartlett and Sumantra Ghoshal focus on the complex problems facing multinationals and the emergence of a new organizational form—the transnational. This is an integrated network where resources, products, people, and information flow between interdependent units. See C. Bartlett, and S. Ghoshal, *Managing across Borders*, Boston, MA: Harvard Business School Press, 1989. A recent review of the academic literature on mergers found that managers almost always justified diversification moves in terms of the synergies available and that most of the advice in the management literature on diversification was based on the concept of realizing synergies. See Friedrich Trautwein, "Merger Motives and Merger Prescriptions," *Strategic Management Journal*, vol. 11, 1990, pp. 283–295.

41. C. K. Prahalad, and Gary Hamel, "The Core Competence of the Corporation," *Harvard Business Review*, May–June 1990, pp. 79–91; Gary Hamel, and C. K. Prahalad, "Strategic Intent," *Harvard Business Review*, May–June 1989, pp. 63–76.

42. Hiroyuki Itami, a Japanese academic, focuses on building the corporation's "invisible assets," such as expertise in a particular technology, brand names, reputation, or customer information. Such assets, he argues, can be employed throughout the firm without being used up, and they are the only sustainable source of competitive advantage (H. Itami, *Mobilizing*

Invisible Assets, Cambridge, MA: Harvard University Press, 1987). Philippe Haspeslagh and David Jemison, authors of a recent study on acquisitions, support a capabilities-based view of corporate value creation, defining core capabilities as managerial and technological skills gained mainly through experience. Such capabilities can be applied across the corporation's businesses and make an important contribution to customer benefits. It can be difficult to define a corporation's capabilities objectively, but understanding what they are can provide important insights into its sources of competitive advantage and the strategic options of the firm (P. Haspeslagh, and David Jemison, *Managing Acquisitions,* New York: Free Press, 1991).

The core competences or capabilities view of corporate strategy is part of a broader stream of academic research, which is often referred to as the Resource-Based Theory of the Firm. This theory focuses on the firm's internal resources and capabilities and on how a firm's unique resources create competitive advantage. David Collis uses this model to analyze global competition (David Collis, "A Resource-Based Analysis of Global Competition: The Case of the Bearings Industry," *Strategic Management Journal,* vol. 12, 1991, pp. 49–68). Robert Grant explores the impact of the resource-based theory on strategy formulation (Robert M. Grant, "The Resource-Based Theory of Competitive Advantage," *California Management Review,* vol. 33, no. 3, Spring 1991, pp. 114–135). See also David J. Teece, et al., "Firm Capabilities, Resources and the Concept of Strategy," Consortium on Competitiveness and Cooperation, CCC Working Paper No. 90-8, December 1990; Jay B. Barney, "Organizational Culture: Can It Be a Source of Sustained Competitive Advantage?" *Academy of Management Review,* vol. 11, no. 3, 1986, pp. 656–665; and "Firm Resources and Sustained Competitive Advantage," *Journal of Management,* 1991, vol. 17, no. 1, pp. 99–120; George Stalk, et al., "Competing on Capabilities: The New Rules of Corporate Strategy," *Harvard Business Review,* March–April 1992, pp. 57–69.

43. Walter Kiechel, "Corporate Strategy for the 1990s," *Fortune,* February 29, 1988, p. 20.

44. Vasudevan Ramanujam, and P. Varadarajan, "Research on Corporate Diversification: A Synthesis," *Strategic Management Journal,* vol. 10, 1989; Andrew Campbell and Kathleen Luchs, *Strategic Synergy,* Oxford: Butterworth Heinemann, 1992.

45. Richard Reed, and George A. Luffman, "Diversification: the Growing Confusion," *Strategic Management Journal,* vol. 7, 1986, pp. 29–35.

46. S. Chatterjee, "Sources of Value in Takeovers: Synergy or Restructuring," *Strategic Management Journal,* vol. 13, no. 4, May 1992, pp. 267–286. Those who view synergy as the essence of corporate-level strategy acknowledge that the failure rate is high, and much of the current literature on synergy therefore focuses on implementation issues. See Michael Porter, *Competitive Advantage,* New York: Free Press, 1985; Kanter, *When Giants Learn to Dance;* Bartlett and Ghoshal, *Managing across Borders.*

47. For a discussion of economic business definitions, and the problems of a mismatch between these and organizational definitions, see Appendix A.

48. See Chapter 9.

49. See, for example, the discussion of different approaches to business definition and linkage in Chapter 7.

50. See Chapter 6 for a fuller discussion of the importance of an adequate feel for a parents' businesses in order to avoid value destruction.

51. Despite the evidence of academic studies on this topic, and the supportive assertions of finance providers, many managers remain skeptical that sufficient funds are available for good opportunities. One explanation for this divergence is that the assessment of certain investments requires very specialist expertise not possessed by the market at large. This topic is explored in Chapter 6 in relation to RTZ.

52. For further details, see Chapter 9.

53. E.g., Prahalad and Hamel, "The Core Competence of the Corporation": "During the 1980s, top executives were judged on their ability to restructure, declutter and delayer their corporations. In the 1990s, they'll be judged on their ability to identify, cultivate and exploit the core competencies that make growth possible."

54. See Appendix C for discussion of the Strategic Control style.

55. C. K. Prahalad and R. A. Bettis, "The Dominant Logic: A New Linkage between Diversity and Performance," *Strategic Management Journal*, vol. 7, 1986, p. 495.

56. Patricia Winters, "Crush Fails to Fit on P&G Shelf," *Advertising Age*, July 10, 1989.

57. In "The Core Competence of the Corporation," Prahalad and Hamel define core competences as "the collective learning in the organization, especially how to coordinate diverse production skills and integrate multiple streams of technologies." They also provide three tests to identify core competences in a company: "First, a core competence provides potential access to a wide variety of markets. . . . Second, a core competence should make a significant contribution to the perceived customer benefit of the end product. . . . Finally, a core competence should be difficult for competitors to imitate. And it *will* be difficult if it is a complex harmonization of individual technologies and production skills." In their sense, therefore, core competences are contained within the company as a whole, rather than within the parent. Others, however, including some consulting firms, use the term core competences or corporate center competences to refer to ways in which the parent adds value to its business units. This usage equates far more closely with our notion of distinctive parenting characteristics.

PART TWO

SUCCESSFUL CORPORATE STRATEGIES

5 HOW PARENTS CREATE VALUE

Our primary concern in this book is with the value created by corporate parents. Sound corporate strategies lead to high value creation, whereas poor corporate strategies frequently result in value destruction. It is, therefore, vital to understand how, and under what conditions, corporate parents succeed in creating value.

This chapter will argue that four main sorts of value creation are open to the parent. In each case, however, the parent faces difficulties that make most of them more likely to destroy than to create value. We express these difficulties as four paradoxes that all parents must strive to overcome. We then examine the conditions under which parents are able to overcome the paradoxes they face and create value. This leads us to a fuller understanding of the ingredients of successful corporate strategies to achieve parenting advantage, and of the underlying circumstances that make such strategies possible.

The chapter describes the framework that will guide our detailed analysis of successful corporate strategies throughout Part Two. Chapters 6 through 9 provide detailed discussions of the four sorts of parental value creation and give illustrations of corporate strategies that realize value from each of them. These chapters deepen our understanding of the conditions under which value is created. Chapter 10 shows how successful corporate strategies evolve and change over time. Chapter 11 summarizes our conclusions concerning successful corporate strategies.

FOUR SORTS OF VALUE CREATION

We have found it useful to analyze corporate strategies in terms of four main sorts of value creation by the parent:

1. Stand-alone influence, through which the parent enhances the stand-alone performance of the business units.
2. Linkage influence, through which the parent enhances the value of linkages between the business units.
3. Functional and services influence, through which the parent provides functional leadership and cost effective services for the business units.
4. Corporate development activities, which create value by altering the composition of the portfolio of business units.

Although there is some overlap between the four sorts of value creation, we have found it useful to distinguish between them since they bring out different issues concerning parental value creation.[1] (See Exhibit 5–1.)

Stand-Alone Influence

Stand-alone influence is about the parent's influence on the strategies and performance of each business in the parent's ownership, viewed as a stand-alone profit center in its own right. All parents exert considerable stand-alone influence on their businesses. Even a parent such as Hanson, with a decentralization contract that pushes maximum responsibility onto the business units, will be involved in agreeing and monitoring basic performance targets, in approving major capital expenditures, and in selecting and replacing the business unit managing directors. These activities, in themselves, are powerful influences on the businesses. Many parents, however, go further, exercising influence on a wider range of issues, such as product-market strategies, pricing decisions, and human resource development. The range of issues in which the parent is involved reflects the nature of its decentralization contracts.

Stand-alone influence is of vital importance in the vast majority of companies. Our research, however, indicates that, although the parent's stand-alone influence is frequently critical to performance, it is often overlooked or underestimated. A focus on the stand-alone influence of the parent is essential for understanding corporate strategy.

While the parent can create substantial value through stand-alone influence, it can also destroy value. By pressing for inappropriate targets, by starving businesses of resources for worthwhile projects, by encouraging wasteful investment, and by appointing the wrong managers, the parent can have a serious adverse effect on its businesses. The potential for value creation must always be balanced against the risk of value destruction.

Indeed, the likelihood is that most parents will destroy value through their stand-alone influence. In a multibusiness organization, managers in the parent can devote only a small percentage of their attention to the affairs of each business, while the managers in the businesses are fully engaged in their own units. Why should the parent managers, in 10 percent of their time, be able to improve on the decisions being made

EXHIBIT 5–1   Four types of parental value creation

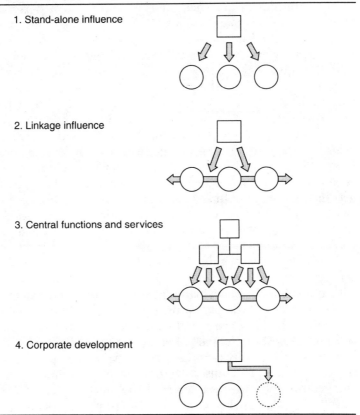

1. Stand-alone influence

2. Linkage influence

3. Central functions and services

4. Corporate development

by competent managers who are giving 100 percent of their efforts to the business? The very idea that part-time managers at one remove (or more) will be able to enhance the performance of the business's own dedicated management is, in some sense, paradoxical. We refer to this as the "10 percent versus 100 percent" paradox.

Successful corporate parents find ways of overcoming the 10 percent versus 100 percent paradox and are able to create value through stand-alone influence. However, we need to understand the circumstances under which this can be achieved, since the large majority of corporate parents inadvertently end up destroying value through their stand-alone influence. In Chapter 6, we shall focus on Dover, BTR, Emerson, and RTZ, as examples of companies that succeed in creating value through stand-alone influence.

Linkage Influence

Many parents seek to create value by enhancing the linkages that exist between their different business units. Through corporate decision-making processes and structures, through policies and guidelines, through transfer pricing mechanisms, and through personal pressure, they encourage, or mandate, relationships between their business units that would not occur if the businesses were independent companies. In this way, they aim to create value by making the "whole" worth more than the "sum of the parts." Whether all units benefit, or some benefit more than others lose, the purpose is to release net value for the company by affecting the ways in which the units link with each other. This objective is captured in the familiar notion of synergy.

But the quest for synergy has led to many disappointments. The efforts of the parent to encourage linkages may be cumbersome, inappropriate, or ineffective. Equally, they may lead to linkages that are not economically justifiable. Indeed, the limited payoff from, and the dangers inherent in, most linkage initiatives have led us to conclude that the value of linkage influence is often overestimated and that the desire to exploit synergies has played too prominent a role in many companies' corporate strategies.

The difficulty of value creation from linkage influence stems from another paradox. The managers of each business unit are free to link with other units without parental involvement, and indeed frequently do so. Why should the parent managers be able to perceive linkage opportunities, if they have not already been perceived as a result of mutual self-interest on the part of energetic and enlightened business unit managers? It is hardly surprising that corporately inspired synergy initiatives so often prove unsatisfactory, since, by definition, they have not engaged the spontaneous interest of the business managers directly involved. We call this the "enlightened self-interest" paradox.

Some corporate parents, however, do succeed in creating value through linkage influence despite the enlightened self-interest paradox. But we shall have to examine the conditions under which they do so with care, since the track record of most synergy seekers is not good. In Chapter 7, we shall discuss Banc One, Unilever, ABB, and Canon as examples of companies that succeed in creating value through linkage influence.

Functional and Services Influence

The main responsibility for exercising parental influence typically lies with the chief executive and other senior line managers in the parent. However, the parent also contains a range of corporate staff functions and services. These functions and services can create value by providing functional leadership and cost-effective services for the businesses, as well as by assisting the line management in exercising stand-alone or linkage influence. The importance of such functions and services in some companies, and the variations that exist between companies in the size, cost, and influence of corporate staffs, have led us to devote separate attention to them as potential sources of value creation.

Corporate functions create value to the extent that they bring about, or contribute to, beneficial influence. Obviously, the benefit to the businesses must more than offset both the costs of maintaining the functions and, importantly, the knock-on costs that the functions cause to be incurred in the businesses. Corporate staffs that provide services can also create value if the services are more cost-effective than the businesses could provide for themselves or purchase from outside suppliers. Some companies believe that corporate functions and services play an essential role in creating value.

But there is widespread scepticism about the value of large corporate staffs, and the fashion for downsizing corporate functions and services is not groundless. In many companies, the corporate staffs create overheads and bureaucracies that far exceed their value; and it is not uncommon for business units to regard them as out-of-touch, ineffective, and interfering.

The trend to downsize corporate functions and outsource services brings out another paradox that lies behind the difficulties that corporate staffs face. A specialist, external supplier stands or falls by its ability to provide the most responsive and cost-effective expertise in its chosen field, whether it be market research, manufacturing advice, or strategic planning. Why should an in-house staff department be able to create value, if specialist competitors are available to undertake similar tasks and services on a third-party basis? It is this "beating the specialists" paradox that has led many companies to disband large parts of their corporate functions and services.

Nevertheless, some companies continue to believe strongly in the value of their corporate staffs. To understand their corporate strategies, we need to assess whether and how corporate functions and services can beat the specialists and create value. In Chapter 8, we shall discuss Cooper Industries, 3M, and Shell, whose central functions and services do succeed in creating value.

Corporate Development Activities

As well as influencing the units that are already in the portfolio, the parent determines the composition of the portfolio itself. The parent can buy or sell businesses; it can create new businesses through corporate venturing; it can redefine businesses by amalgamating units or by separating them out. In such activities, the parent is doing more than influencing its existing businesses. It is changing the businesses in its portfolio. Its initiatives in these corporate development activities can create, or destroy, value in their own right. This value is, in principle, distinct from the value that may subsequently be created through ongoing parenting influence on the businesses that are brought into the portfolio.

Many corporate parents believe that they create substantial value in their corporate development activities, for example by spotting opportunities to buy businesses cheaply, by creating new ventures that provide profitable future growth opportunities, or by redefining businesses in ways that lead them to be more competitive in their marketplaces. We have found, however, that such initiatives can also frequently misfire. Parents can overpay for acquisitions, support losing ventures, and redefine businesses in the wrong way. The weight of research evidence indicates that the majority of corporately sponsored acquisitions, new ventures, and business redefinitions fail to create value. The odds against bringing off a value-creating deal or launching a successful new business are long. It can even be argued that proactive corporate development enthusiasts face their own value creation paradox: Why should their activities beat the odds that appear to be stacked so heavily against them?

Yet successful corporate strategies often do include an active corporate development role. Our final question will therefore concern the underlying conditions that allow corporate development activities to work well and overcome the "beating the odds" paradox. In Chapter 9, we shall discuss several companies, including the British TI Group and Hanson, whose corporate strategies include value-creating corporate development activities.

CONDITIONS FOR VALUE CREATION

Our research with many companies has led us to conclude that the majority of corporate parents fail to create value in their businesses, and the paradoxes we have identified express basic reasons why we should expect that it will always be difficult for parents to create value. Nevertheless, some companies have successful corporate strategies that do lead to value creation. Under what conditions do corporate strategies succeed in creating value?

Three conditions must be satisfied for a parent's corporate strategy to create value:

1. There must be opportunities for a parent to improve performance in the businesses in its portfolio, and the parent must perceive these opportunities and the role that it can play to realize them. In other words, the corporate strategy must be based on and fit with parenting opportunities in the businesses.
2. The company must have some parenting characteristics that allow it to realize these opportunities. It must have specific characteristics, whether they be mental maps; structures, systems, or

processes; functions, services, or resources; people or skills; that match the opportunities, and therefore lead to value creation.

3. The company must not have other parenting characteristics that fit so poorly with the businesses that they lead to value destruction which more than offsets any value that has been created. In particular, the company's decentralization contracts must not encourage it to interfere in areas where it is likely to destroy value, and its overall parenting style must not be inappropriate for its businesses.

In the remainder of this chapter, we shall discuss these conditions in general terms, bringing out the underlying circumstances under which they can be met and their implications for successful corporate strategies. In Chapters 6 through 9, we shall explore the conditions more fully in the course of analyzing and illustrating each of the four sorts of value creation.

Parenting Opportunities

For a parent to create value, it is necessary that there should be real opportunities for performance improvement in the portfolio. Furthermore, there must be some essential role for the parent in their realization; otherwise the paradoxes imply that business managers will usually be in a better position to make the necessary decisions than the parent.

For stand-alone value creation, there must, for example, be opportunities to change strategy that will lead to enhanced results; and there must be reasons why these opportunities would not be taken by business unit management without the influence of the parent. For linkage value creation, there must be benefits available from closer links between businesses; and there must be blockages preventing the links from occurring, which the parent can help to remove. For central functions and services to create value, there must be opportunities to improve performance through the use of their expertise; and there must be reasons why the businesses would not use, or could not find, superior specialist external advice. For corporate development decisions, the parent needs to unearth specific opportunities to improve performance through changes in the composition of its portfolio.

It is far from easy to find opportunities of this sort. Normally, competent managers in the businesses can be relied on to optimize the performance of their own units, to establish any links with other business units that will have genuine mutual benefits, and to build up, or hire in, the specialist staffs they need to discharge their responsibilities. Opportunities for parents to create value occur, in a fundamental sense, only in circumstances in which the usual effectiveness of business unit managers, under the spur of competitive markets, breaks down.[2] Furthermore, there is usually no reason to suppose that decisions to buy or sell business units, or to create new units will, in themselves, create value, since competition between parent companies in the market for corporate control means that the scope for value creation is limited.[3] In many cases, there is little that a parent can contribute to enhance the performance of a well-run independent business.

Opportunities for a parent to create value, nevertheless, can and do arise. Managers in individual businesses may be less than competent, and the forces of competition alone may be insufficient to weed them out rapidly. The external capital markets may encounter difficulty in understanding some businesses and may fail to provide appropriate financial support. Conflicts between the personal interests of managers and those of other stakeholders, in particular the shareholders, can occur and lead to suboptimal decisions. Blockages to links between independent business units, such as lack of information, mutual suspicions, and poor communications, can prevent sensible relationships from developing. In all these circumstances, business units may not optimize their performance, and there can be a basis for a parent to intervene and create value.

Furthermore, parents may build up, or have access to, unusual skills or resources that individual businesses could not expect to match.[4] For example, a staff group may have developed unique skills in a given functional specialism, such as property development, the corporate brand may have acquired a special power and authority, or the chief executive may have unusually wide experience of certain types of business situations, such as turnarounds. Even a well-run business could not expect to have comparable skills or resources of its own. In addition, some parents have built up special corporate development skills. Unusual skills and resources can therefore provide a basis for parents to enhance performance.

In circumstances of this sort, opportunities can exist for parents to overcome the paradoxes and create value. For any given corporate parent, however, the key point is that it will only create value if its corporate strategy is focused on specific opportunities in its businesses. BTR's corporate strategy concentrates on its role in unearthing previously unrecognized opportunities to push up profit margins in its businesses. Banc One's corporate strategy emphasizes its role in improving performance by sharing information and best practice between previously separate affiliate banks. The corporate strategy of 3M majors on the contribution that its central technical function can make to businesses' new product development programs. The parent needs a corporate strategy that is targeted on real opportunities in its portfolio of businesses and that identifies the role it can play in realizing them.

Due to the paradoxes, a parent that lacks a clear focus on value creation opportunities in its businesses is more likely to destroy value than to create it. Such a parent may believe that it can usefully provide an informed but objective second opinion for its businesses, supporting them when their proposals and performance are sound and intervening only if problems arise. But, in such cases, the chances are that the parent's valuable interventions will seldom justify its cost and offset its more misguided initiatives. It is only parents that base their corporate strategies on substantial parenting opportunities that are likely to create value.

Parenting Characteristics That Fit Parenting Opportunities

The existence of a parenting opportunity is a necessary, but not a sufficient, condition for a parent to create value. In addition, the parent must possess skills, resources, and other characteristics that allow it to realize value from the opportunity.

The nature of the opportunity determines the type of parenting needed. For example, businesses that could improve their stand-alone performance through a better understanding of cost and margin structures need a parent with the sort of rigorous profit planning processes found in BTR. Businesses with opportunities to increase the sharing of best practices between units need a parent, such as Banc One, with an appreciation of what can be achieved by the businesses and with the mechanisms to make it happen. Businesses that could benefit from specialist technical skills need a parent, such as 3M, with the relevant staff expertise. And opportunities that exist to profit from brokering the breakup of overdiversified companies will be taken only by a parent, such as Hanson, with the willingness and skills to embark on deals of this sort. Once the nature of the opportunity is clear, it is possible to see what type of parent will be best suited to it. To create value, a parent must have characteristics that match the parenting opportunity.

The extent to which an improvement opportunity is realized, and hence the amount of value that is created, depends on the suitability of the company's parenting characteristics. Without suitable parenting characteristics, even a corporate strategy that is targeted on large parenting opportunities will fail. In recent years, many companies have recognized the opportunities that exist to benefit from sharing of best practice between their businesses: Far fewer have been able to establish processes that successfully bring about as much sharing as they would like. In other words, the highest value will be created by the parent with the most suitable parenting characteristics for realizing a given opportunity.

Avoidance of Value Destruction

However much value a parent creates, there is always a danger that some aspects of its parenting may destroy value. A parent may add value by promoting more stretching budget targets but destroy value by denying justified investment proposals or by promoting worthless linkages. A parent may see, and realize, synergy opportunities between two businesses, but destroy value through inappropriate stand-alone influence in one or both businesses. A parent may have a specialist corporate function that is vital to the success of some of its businesses, but may destroy value by pushing the businesses to follow the wrong overall strategy or by forcing other businesses to use the function although it is not suitable for them. A parent may create value through acquiring a business cheaply, but may destroy the value through ill-judged subsequent influence. Net value will be created only if value-destroying interventions can be reduced to a level that does not outweigh any value that has been created.

Value is destroyed when one or more of the parent's characteristics fit poorly with the business in question. Mental maps that are based on a false understanding of the critical success factors in the business; planning and budgetary processes that are either too burdensome or too skimpy for the issues faced by the business; central staffs that do not have skills that are relevant for the business: These are all sources of value destruction that we have encountered frequently.[5] Furthermore, parenting characteristics that create value in one business may destroy value in others. A mental map that is supportive of risky, long-term technology investments may create value in one business, such as oil exploration, but destroy value in others, such as bricks. A thorough, systematic capital expenditure review process may be the key to value creation in RTZ's businesses, but would be much less appropriate for Dover's. A complex matrix structure may be the best way to create valuable linkage between ABB's businesses, but would probably destroy value if imposed on BTR's. The need to match the characteristics of the business and the parent has implications for portfolio composition as well as for the parenting of the businesses in the portfolio.

One way to reduce the risk of value destruction is to decentralize extensively to the businesses, and to limit the parent's involvement as far as possible to issues related to specific parenting opportunities. However, there is a minimum set of parenting tasks that cannot be delegated: These include appointing the general manager of the business, approving major decisions and investments proposed by the business, agreeing on basic performance targets and monitoring and following up on results that are achieved, and reacting to disputes between businesses. Moreover, many parents feel unable or unwilling to step back from involvement across a considerably wider range of issues. In practice, therefore, decentralization is not, and cannot be, the complete answer to avoiding value destruction.

To avoid value-destroying interventions, parents need to have a "feel" for their businesses. A feel for a business means that the parent's instincts and intuitions about it are generally sound, that the parent understands the critical success factors in the business, that it can judge whether the business is on track and performing well or in need of some change of direction or management. As a result, the parent has a sense for when and how to exercise its influence. By not interfering when things are, in fact, going well, it can avoid destroying value. Furthermore, if it does need to intervene, its influence is likely to be positive. A parent with a feel for a business will also know what sorts of management systems and processes, and what functions and services, are likely to be suitable for it. It can therefore avoid imposing a parenting approach and style that are basically unsuitable for the business.

A feel for a business is normally grounded in a depth of personal experience of managing or parenting businesses of a particular sort. Typically, senior managers build up experience with certain types of businesses during their careers and are able to avoid value-destroying interventions in them. They are much more prone to destroy value in other types of businesses, with which they are less familiar and for which they have a less good feel.

To create net value, the parent must avoid parenting characteristics that represent misfits with its businesses and will eliminate the beneficial impact of its parenting in other areas. Underlying this requirement is the need for a sufficient feel for all the businesses in the portfolio.[6]

CONDITIONS FOR PARENTING ADVANTAGE

The conditions for value creation that we have identified are necessary, but not sufficient, for parenting advantage. To create more value than rival parents, a company needs:

1. A corporate strategy targeted on parenting opportunities which have not been seen by other rivals, or which are more substantial than rivals', or in which the parent's depth of understanding of its role distinguishes it from rivals. In Chapter 2, we introduced the term *value creation insights* to refer to the perceptions of value creation opportunities on which successful parents base their corporate strategies.

2. Parenting characteristics that are more suitable for realizing the opportunities it is pursuing than the characteristics of rivals that are targeting similar opportunities. We call these *distinctive parenting characteristics*. In Chapter 2, we claimed that corporate parents that aspire to parenting advantage need to develop parenting characteristics that have some distinctiveness, some superiority.

3. A clearer understanding than rival parents of the sorts of business in which its value-creation insights and distinctive parenting characteristics are most potent, and in which misfits with parenting characteristics that would lead to value destruction can be avoided. In Chapter 2, we referred to the sorts of businesses in which the

parent can create high value and avoid value destruction as *heartland businesses*. Companies that achieve parenting advantage have a clearer understanding of their heartland business criteria, and a higher degree of focus on these sorts of businesses, than rival parents. In other words, the corporate strategy maintains a better match between the company's parenting characteristics and its businesses than rivals achieve.

Using these three concepts, we have developed a succinct framework within which to summarize and describe successful corporate strategies, which we call a *parenting advantage statement*. In Chapter 2, we gave some illustrations of summary parenting advantage statements. In Chapters 6 through 10, we will lay out and discuss more fully the parenting advantage statements for 15 different companies.

For each of these companies, we have attempted to identify value creation insights, distinctive parenting characteristics, and heartland businesses. Unequivocal evidence that the parent does create value is, however, hard to come by. It is always difficult to disentangle the contribution of the parent from the contribution of the business, and there are no simple measures of parental performance to monitor. It is possible, however, to put together a picture from a variety of sources. How well have businesses of this type in the company's portfolio performed in comparison to their competitors? While this evidence is clouded by the competence, strategy, and positioning of each of the businesses, it gives some idea of the overall results of the company's parenting. What sort of influence did the parent have on specific major decisions in the businesses? This allows a more focused assessment of whether the parent has actually added value. What sort of relationship exists between the business-level managers and the parent, and do the business managers endorse the parent's claims about its value creation? The cross-check provided by asking the views of the business managers is, we believe, one of the best ways to validate parental value creation. By examining the performance of the businesses over a period of time, talking through the major decisions that have been made, and distilling out the role of the parent, we have been able to form a view of whether the parent has created value.

Comparing the parent's value creation with other rival parents is an even harder task. Our purpose, however, has been to identify companies that had unusually insightful corporate strategies in terms of the value-creation opportunities they were targeting; that had unusually suitable parenting characteristics for realizing the opportunities; and that had an unusually clear focus on businesses in which they could create net value. It is our judgment that, given the standards of parenting that prevail in the 1990s, the companies in our research have all attained parenting advantage for a significant proportion of the businesses in their portfolios. We shall therefore use these companies as the main evidence for the conclusions we draw in Chapter 11 concerning the value-creation insights, distinctive parenting characteristics, and heartland businesses that lie behind successful corporate strategies.

NOTES

1. David Collis puts forward a similar classification in *Managing the Multibusiness Corporation,* (Harvard Business School Teaching Note 9-391-286, 1992). Consulting companies, such as McKinsey & Co and Bain & Co also use classifications that are similar; see, for example, "Corporate Center Design," *McKinsey Quarterly,* 1991, and "The Role of the Center," internal Corporate Strategy Practice document, Bain & Company.

2. Indeed, classical economic theory suggests that competitive forces will ensure that only businesses run by competent, efficient managers will survive in the longer term. Opportunities for a parent therefore depend on "market failures" that depart from the classical economic model. See Chapters 6, 7, and 8 for further discussion.

3. Due to the competitive nature of the "market for corporate control," buying and selling units per se, as opposed to subsequent performance improvement through better parenting, seldom creates value. Similarly, competition between parent companies means that there are seldom opportunities to earn more than the cost of capital in new ventures. See Chapter 9 for further discussion.

4. Recent academic work on the so-called Resource Based Theory of the Firm provides insights into the circumstances in which this occurs. See Chapters 6, 7, and particularly 8 for fuller discussion.

5. Appendix C shows how mismatches between a company's overall parenting style and its businesses can also lead to value destruction.

6. The depth of feel required depends on the nature of the decentralization contracts with the businesses. See Chapter 6 for a fuller discussion of the need for a feel for the businesses in the portfolio.

6 STAND-ALONE INFLUENCE

The corporate parent has a variety of powerful ways of influencing its businesses as stand-alone entities. It can appoint the general manager of each business and influence management development and succession planning within the businesses. It can approve or reject budgets, strategic plans, and capital expenditure proposals, and can influence the shape and implementation of these plans and proposals. It can provide advice and policy guidance to the businesses. The parent also influences the businesses by the hints and pressures passed on through both formal and informal line management meetings and contacts, and, more indirectly, through the corporate culture.

The influence that the parent exercises on the stand-alone performance of its businesses reflects the full range of parenting characteristics identified in Chapter 2. The parent's mental maps, its structures, systems and processes, its functions, central services and resources, its people and skills, and its decentralization contracts collectively determine the sorts of issues on which the parent intervenes, and the direction of the influence that it exercises. Due to differences in these characteristics, parents differ greatly in the nature and extent of stand-alone influence that they exercise. However, stand-alone parenting is of profound importance in all multibusiness companies. Our research indicates that, in most companies, stand-alone influence has more impact on performance than any other area of parenting and is a vital component of corporate strategy.

Despite its importance, stand-alone influence is sometimes overlooked. Corporate strategists, and, even more, writers about corporate strategy, are beguiled into concentrating on "synergy" or "corporate renewal" to the exclusion of stand-alone influence. It may be that the very pervasiveness of stand-alone parenting allows it to be taken for granted, and therefore neglected.

The basic premise behind stand-alone influence is that the corporate parent's influence can result in better individual business strategies and performance than would otherwise have occurred. The parent, as representative of the shareholders and other investors, checks that the businesses have sound managements, strategies, and plans; allocate resources in support of these strategies; and monitors performance to ensure that implementation of plans remains on track. The parent can draw on more knowledge and information about its businesses than is available to external capital markets and should therefore be able to do a better job of monitoring and controlling businesses' plans and performance. Furthermore, the parent may be able to provide valuable expertise to its businesses, act as a useful sounding board for ideas, open up thinking about strategic issues, prevent undue preoccupation with day-to-day concerns, and press for awkward or unpleasant issues to be dealt with in a timely fashion.

But the impact of stand-alone parenting can be either positive or negative. Stand-alone parenting can be a major source of added value and performance improvement for the businesses. However it can also seriously damage performance through inappropriate influence and excessive overhead costs. Our research has persuaded us that, while the best corporate parents undoubtedly succeed in creating value through stand-alone influence, the majority of parents end up by inadvertently causing more harm than good.

In this chapter, we shall therefore begin by exploring the causes of value destruction through stand-alone parenting. Against this background, and recognizing the difficulties that must be overcome, we will go on to describe a number of companies that succeed in creating value through stand-alone influence. Our objective will be to achieve a fuller understanding of the conditions under which parents can create value and achieve parenting advantage through their influence on businesses as stand-alone entities.

VALUE DESTRUCTION

Too often, criticism of corporate parents focuses exclusively on the level of corporate overhead costs. Certainly, these costs must be paid for out of the profits of the operating businesses and are, in many companies, excessive. But the real sources of value destruction typically lie much more in mistakes that the parent causes through its influence on the businesses than in the corporate overhead as such. Poor appointments, invalid objectives, inappropriate strategies, and unsuitable, slow and costly review processes damage performance much more than the corporate overhead charge.

Examples of Value Destruction

Some examples from our research will illustrate how value can be destroyed by ineffective stand-alone parenting.

- A major business in a large diversified group picked up signals that the corporate team was looking for at least 10 percent per annum profit growth from all the businesses in the group. The business in question was a mature and profitable cash cow, whose first priority should have been to maintain its profitability and cash generation, not to search for growth options. The corporate growth objectives distracted the business's management from this priority task and led only to a waste of time and resources on investigating and pursuing ultimately fruitless growth initiatives.

- An oil company decided that it would help its newly acquired minerals business to perform better by suggesting some new approaches to exploration. Unfortunately, these approaches, which were based on oil industry practices, were quite inappropriate for the minerals business. However, the minerals management team felt compelled to try some of the suggestions from its corporate parent—and took several years to recover from the losses that resulted.

- Group management in an industrial services company devised an extensive and sophisticated strategic planning process, through which the businesses in the company were expected to review their strategies with the center. Most of the businesses, however, were facing their main competition from low overhead, local entrepreneurs, and needed to focus their attention on driving down costs and improving customer relationships. By insisting on the strategic planning process, which led simply to sterile and inconclusive debates about issues that the business managers felt were not of immediate importance, the parent not only imposed extra costs and delayed decisions, but also encouraged the wrong sorts of decisions and priorities.

The damage caused by stand-alone influence is often seen most clearly in the experience of management buyouts. A buyout removes the influence of the parent, for good or ill, and forces the business to stand on its own feet and make its own decisions. Again and again, buyout teams seem able to improve their performance[1] and can identify the ways in which their previous parents inhibited their development. A case in point is Premier Brands, a buyout from Cadbury Schweppes.

Cadbury Schweppes has built its portfolio around two core businesses: chocolate confectionery and soft drinks. In both these businesses it has strong brands and leading market share positions, particularly in the United Kingdom, but also in other markets. Cadbury Schweppes has enjoyed considerable success as a parent of these businesses, despite strong competition from companies such as Mars, Philip Morris, Nestlé, Coca-Cola, and Pepsico.[2]

Although the strategy of concentrating on these core businesses was decided in 1977, for several years thereafter Cadbury Schweppes continued to operate in a number of other business areas. Several of these businesses were grouped together into a Foods Division, whose products included canned foods, jams, tea, coffee, chocolate beverages, biscuits, instant mashed potato, and dried milk. Throughout the 1980s, the Foods Division consistently underperformed, with trading margins declining to a low point of 2.1 percent in 1985. Finally, in May 1986 Cadbury Schweppes decided to sell the division, and a group of managers raised £97 million for a management buyout. The new company was established under the name of Premier Brands, with the right to use the Cadbury name on some of its products.

After the buyout, there was a rapid improvement. Profits rose strongly from £6.6 million in 1985 to £31 million in 1988, with trading margins climbing to over 8 percent. Market share was also gained. How was this turnaround achieved? Why did Premier perform so much better as an independent company than as part of Cadbury Schweppes?

Paul Judge, a career manager with Cadbury Schweppes who became chairman of Premier, believes that the first essential point concerns awareness of the need for change. As part of Cadbury's, there had been a feeling that, despite moderate results, the division was protected by the resources and reputation of the parent company. Once Premier became independent, with a substantial debt burden as part of the buyout, the whole management and workforce realized that performance had to improve. Opportunities were found to reduce indirect workers by 500 (25 percent of the workforce) and to cut working capital in half, releasing a cash inflow of £20 million. Suddenly, there was a new sense of urgency and an ability to grasp issues that previously had been ignored. As one member of the buyout team put it: "All we lost was the comfortable feel of an old pair of slippers."

A second important factor concerned investment priorities. The Foods division businesses were not part of Cadbury Schweppes's "core." Accordingly, there was, in principle, much less enthusiasm for investment in the Foods division than elsewhere. This meant that there had been little expenditure on product development or acquisitions since the mid-1970s. As Paul Judge put it: "It was easy for corporate to shoot holes in the sort of proposals that came up because there are always uncertainties in trying to develop new brands and making company acquisitions." As a result, investment was spread too thinly and failed to pay off, thereby reinforcing the center's unwillingness to invest more heavily. The noncore status meant that the division did not receive the resources and attention it needed to break out of the vicious circle of low profitability and low investment.

Lastly, the Cadbury Schweppes corporate center did not have a good understanding of strategy in the Foods businesses. In its core businesses, Cadbury's enjoyed high market shares in strongly branded product areas. In Foods, there was less brand recognition, more fragmentation of market shares, and a higher private label presence. The sources of competitive advantage and the nature of successful strategies were therefore fundamentally different. While this was intellectually accepted, the gut reaction to the sorts of strategies being put forward by the Foods businesses was to judge them by criteria that would have been appropriate in the core businesses, but were wrong for Foods. Today, Sir Adrian Cadbury, chairman of Cadbury Schweppes at the time, accepts that the pressures and inhibitions created by these wrong criteria were probably among the most profound causes of the Foods division's underperformance.

How far did the removal of negative parenting influence in and of itself bring about the turnaround? It is, of course, difficult to be precise about how much improvement could have been achieved without the buyout solution. But it is noteworthy that, with only one or two exceptions, the managers that presided over the buyout renaissance were the same as the team that was running the business previously. The goals were clearer and sharper, but the people were largely unchanged. This suggests that inappropriate parenting was the root cause of the division's underperformance.[3]

In our research, we have come across numerous examples of detrimental stand-alone parenting, many far more blatant than the Premier example. And, within large multibusiness companies, "I'm from head office, I'm here to help," is a standard joke. We have little doubt that, in the majority of multibusiness companies, stand-alone parenting is a cause of value destruction, not value creation. Why is it that value destruction seems to be so widespread?

Underlying Reasons for Value Destruction

There is a basic and unavoidable reason for the difficulty that corporate parents find in creating value through stand-alone influence. The chief executive and the parenting team have a variety of objectives, interests, and concerns. Each business can receive only a fraction of their attention, and must be reviewed along with all the other businesses in the portfolio. But, to improve performance, stand-alone influence must result in different and better decisions than the team dedicated to running the business would have reached. Why should the chief executive in 10 percent of his time be able to perceive better strategies for a business than energetic managers devoting 100 percent of their time to the business? Why should top-down corporate objectives draw more performance out of a business than objectives built on a detailed understanding of what the business is capable of? Why should common corporate review processes imposed across all the businesses bring out issues that would not be surfaced by the management process built for each business by its own team? Intrinsically, the parent must almost always be less well informed and less close to each business's needs than the business's own management. Unless one assumes omniscience on the part of the parent, or incompetence on the part of the business team, the difficulty of the task facing the parent is evident. We refer to this basic problem for corporate parents as the "10 percent versus 100 percent" paradox.

Reinforcing the 10 percent versus 100 percent paradox, it can be argued that the nature of stand-alone parenting in many multibusiness companies systematically perverts business decisions. If each business feels that it must compete with every other business in the portfolio for corporate attention and resources, an incentive exists to bias information and proposals to win the competition with the other businesses. This does not lead to open and productive discussion of plans and strategies for the business. We met recently with a business that faced significant uncertainties but had produced a "whitewash" strategy for presentation to the corporate team. After the presentation of the strategy, we asked the business's general manager how it went. "Excellent," was his response. "They didn't ask us a thing." This is a standard of excellence that has nothing to do with improving strategy and enhancing performance, and everything to do with "selling" the business's desired way forward.

In these circumstances, the parent is liable to regard the business managers as biased and untrustworthy. Lord Weinstock, chief executive of the British GEC, expressed this view in extreme form to us: "All managers," he said, "are liars. It's just a question of how big the lies are." The impact of this sort of review process was brought out by a senior partner in one of the major strategy consulting firms, who told us that, in his experience, his firm could invariably guarantee to save any multibusiness company at least $1 million simply by improving the flow of objective, unbiased information between the different levels in the company. "The competition for resources between the units," he claimed, "is so intense that most of the information that moves upwards from the businesses is intended to conceal the true situation, not reveal it."

What is more, businesses that are part of a well-resourced parent organization may not feel the same urgency to perform as independent companies. For Premier, the quest for better results only became serious once the support of Cadbury Schweppes was removed by the buyout. The businesses in many large corporations feel able to propose plans, budgets, and investments that imply performance that would simply not be acceptable for stand-alone companies. The parent's influence on these businesses is to allow them to get away with performance that would not otherwise be tolerated. It is a sorry reflection on this state of affairs that many corporate managers seem to believe that the question "Would you do this if it was your own money?" provides useful insights in reviewing businesses' investment proposals. Without a parent organization, the question would have much less point.

Conversely, businesses with parents that face financial pressures, or that place a heavy stress on continuous increases in quarterly earnings, frequently complain about short-termism. The parent puts them under more severe constraints than they would face from external sources of capital, and cuts off investments or initiatives that the businesses would have been quite capable of funding as independent entities.[4]

It is, therefore, only too easy for corporate parents to destroy value through stand-alone influence. They must always overcome the problems caused by being less close to their businesses than the managers that run them on a day-to-day basis; in many companies, they must grapple with biased information from the businesses; and they must avoid cushioning businesses from the need to manage themselves keenly and efficiently, or else creating short-term pressures that will inhibit desirable investments and initiatives. Any discussion of stand-alone influence must start with a recognition of these difficulties, which mean that the first essential objective must be to avoid destroying value. If corporate parents could stop pushing their businesses into the wrong strategies and demotivating their managers with unproductive second guessing and interference, a great leap forward would be taken.

VALUE CREATION

Despite the difficulties that parent companies face, value can be created through stand-alone influence. Indeed, in many businesses there are opportunities for performance improvement that are only likely to be realized with the help of a suitable parent.

When a business is being run by a management team that has gone off the boil, or that lacks skills or motivation, a parent can move more speedily and effectively to rectify the position than can outside owners. In situations where the business management team is committed to pursuing its own agenda, irrespective of shareholder or other interests, a parent can redress the balance. In businesses that are difficult for outside investors to understand, a parent can play a constructive intermediary role. And, last but by no means least, some parents can bring to bear special skills or knowledge that would not normally be found within an individual business. In all these circumstances, as we shall see in the examples we discuss in this chapter, a parent has the potential to create real value.

However, to succeed in creating value, the parent's characteristics must be suitable for realizing the opportunities in its businesses. It needs to have sufficient understanding and feel for the businesses to make suitable interventions and to avoid destroying value through inappropriate pressures. It needs management processes that provide effective vehicles for exercising its influence, and functions and services that support and contribute to the main sources of value creation. It needs people with the requisite skills to work constructively with the businesses. And it needs decentralization contracts that focus on issues where it has the most to contribute, and away from issues where it is liable to destroy value.

In this chapter, we shall concentrate on four main areas of stand-alone influence: the appointment of business unit general managers, budgetary control, strategy reviews, and capital investment decisions. In each area, we shall discuss the ways in which value can be created and destroyed, and we will describe in some detail a company with a successful corporate strategy that emphasizes value creation in the area in question. The companies that we will cover are Dover, which emphasizes appointments; BTR, which emphasizes budgetary control; Emerson, which emphasizes strategy reviews; and RTZ, which emphasizes capital investments.[5]

Business Unit Senior Appointments

One of the most powerful ways for a corporate parent to influence its businesses is through the appointments it makes to the senior management positions in the businesses. Almost all corporate parents recognize that these appointments are critical and that well-chosen appointments can greatly improve a business's performance, while mistakes cause serious harm. As a result, the selection of business unit heads is high on the agenda of the large majority of parent companies.

To add value in senior business unit appointments, the parent must make better and more timely selections for the top jobs than would emerge for an independent business, and for parenting advantage, the appointments must be better than would be made by rival parents. By no means all corporate parents can claim to meet this requirement. Career planning is often driven by corporate politics more than by merit, so that inadequate managers are supported and allowed to remain in post for too long, or are replaced by new appointees who lack the qualities necessary to succeed in the business. Particularly in newer, less familiar businesses, appointments can be made that astound those most directly involved with the business. Individuals who have succeeded in the company's core business (or, even worse, are being moved aside because they have failed) are assigned to run a new, quite different business in the naive belief that a track record in, say, defense contracting is relevant in choosing a general manager for a consumer durables business. Or else, a candidate known personally and trusted by the corporate CEO is preferred to others with far more suitable experience and qualifications. There is no doubt about the power wielded by corporate parents in the appointment process; there is much more question about whether the power adds value.

We need, therefore, to understand what it takes for the corporate parent to achieve an above-average hit rate with its appointments. To ground the discussion, we shall concentrate on Dover Corporation, a company that has been unusually effective at appointing the right people for its businesses, and that believes this is a crucial part of its parenting. We will discuss the appointments process in Dover, and we will show how it fits into the company's overall corporate strategy.

DOVER: APPOINTMENTS.   Dover Corporation is a $2.5 billion company, with about 50 different businesses in a variety of industry sectors including elevators, pumps, valves, controls, heat exchangers, and food-processing equipment. These businesses are grouped into five "subsidiaries." Gary Roubos, the chairman and chief executive, believes that the ability to pick the right people as general managers of the businesses is his most essential parenting skill. "One of the key responsibilities that I and the subsidiary heads have is picking the people who run the businesses in Dover."

In Dover, this responsibility is not exercised through any formal personnel evaluation or succession planning system. Instead, Roubos and the subsidiary heads rely on the judgments they form from a constant round of personal visits to their businesses. These visits provide what one senior Dover officer termed "intimacy" of personal contact between the parent and the businesses. A typical Roubos visit was described as follows: "He (Roubos) was a noticeable drag on the procession, taking care to pause at every office and at every station on the factory floor, listening patiently and talking amiably with nearly everyone he encountered, from the company president to the clerical staff, from the plant manager to the shipping supervisor."[6] There are no standard control reports and no structured agendas to guide these visits, since Dover allows each company to determine its own management information requirements. But the visits provide an opportunity, in Roubos's words, "to surround the man with questions," from which a view can be formed about his stewardship of the business. Dover does not believe in a "hire and fire" culture, and managers whose businesses are not performing well will, in the first instance, receive support and advice from Roubos and his colleagues. But it is one of the main planks of Dover's parenting to remain closely enough in touch with these situations to be able to determine whether and when a new manager needs to be appointed.

Roubos stresses that his ability to form people judgments depends on his extensive experience in Dover's sorts of businesses. "Almost all our businesses are of modest technology. They are also niche businesses, focusing on small market segments and making manufactured products for sale to industrial customers. I am the third chief executive of Dover, and we have all had operating backgrounds in businesses like that, as do our subsidiary heads. We have a good feel for the sorts of issues that come up in these businesses and for the sorts of people who succeed in managing them."

It is because Gary Roubos has made dozens of appointments of general managers in Dover's type of businesses that his judgment about who will succeed or fail tends to be sound. He would not claim a 100 percent hit rate ("We've had to fire a few company presidents—not many, but a few"), but he gets it right more often than most other parents would. Furthermore, the large number of similar businesses in Dover's portfolio gives Roubos an extensive pool of candidates—each known personally to him and his subsidiary heads—to choose from. This pool of candidates reinforces Dover's ability to add value in the appointment process.

Roubos, however, concedes that Dover has had more difficulty picking the right people to run less familiar businesses. "We have struggled in higher technology and in defense businesses." In one such business, Dover was falling behind technically and spending its R&D money on the wrong areas. Roubos now blames himself, not for failing to see that the business's decisions were wrong, but because "we failed to understand that the company president wasn't doing it right." Eventually, changes at the top of the business were made, but even then, "they were bad changes." Further changes have now been made, and over time, Roubos believes that Dover is getting to grips with parenting businesses in higher technology, higher R&D fields. But he acknowledges that his people selection skills have been less well developed in these businesses.

Good appointments to senior positions in the businesses depend on the judgment of the managers in the parent. Some companies believe that a sophisticated human resource and succession planning system is helpful in forming these judgments. Dover relies on a more informal approach to arrive at its decisions. But, in all companies, the ability to add value through good appointments comes down to the quality of parental judgments, based on knowledge of the businesses and the people who work within them.

DOVER: CORPORATE STRATEGY.   Exhibit 6–1 is a parenting advantage statement for Dover, which shows that an emphasis on good and timely general manager appointments is one of the *value creation insights* around which Dover's corporate strategy is built.

Dover's value creation insights, however, are concerned with corporate development as well as stand-alone influence. Dover believes that a parent with a supportive, informal management style is attractive to entrepreneurial managers. Such a parent can be a preferred buyer for owners of small businesses who wish to sell a stake in their companies, and Dover has been able to acquire some excellent companies, such as Blackmer (pumps), De-Sta-Co (valves), and Dietrich Standard (flow

---

EXHIBIT 6-1   Dover Corporation parenting advantage statement

Value Creation Insights	In many businesses, the greatest contribution that a parent can make is through well-judged and timely general management appointments. A parent with a depth of relevant experience in making such appointments can create substantial value.
	A parent with a supportive, informal management style is attractive to entrepreneurial managers and to many owners of small businesses who wish to sell their companies, which leads to opportunities to make acquisitions at favorable prices.
Distinctive Parenting Characteristics	Informal, MBWA process for corporate management to get to know businesses and people running them.
	Judgment about when a general manager should receive continuing support or be replaced.
	Pool of candidates for general manager positions.
	Lack of formal corporate management processes, systems, and overheads.
	"Honor roll" targets.
	Reputation for having an attractive culture to entrepreneurial sellers.
Heartland Businesses	Small, niche, low- to medium-technology manufacturing businesses, selling to industrial customers in primarily national markets and with leading market share positions.

---

sensors) at keen prices. Dover's parenting also helps in recruiting and retaining the sorts of entrepreneurial managers who are most likely to make a success of its type of businesses. It provides an unconstrained and low overhead environment, in which the business managers can develop their own businesses, but with a vigilant and well-informed parent to ensure that they do so.

Several *distinctive parenting characteristics* support Dover's value creation insights. For example, the informal MBWA (Management by Wandering Around) process is important in guiding judgments about when a general manager should receive continuing support or be replaced. It is interesting that, when Dover's number of businesses grew to exceed 20, this approach to parenting was threatened by the sheer number of businesses in the portfolio, and the difficulty of retaining close contact with all of them. Dover's response has been to create five subsidiary organizations, each a mini-Dover, with a senior executive, supported by three or four staff, playing the traditional Dover parenting role in each. This has allowed the informal parenting approach to continue, despite Dover's overall size. Gary Roubos and the corporate team remain responsible for the overall corporate culture, for appointing the five subsidiary heads, and for investor relations.[7]

The lack of formal management systems is a long-standing Dover tradition. There are no corporate budgeting, planning, or human resource processes imposed on the businesses, and corporate staff are kept to a minimum: In 1992, Dover had 22 people at the corporate center, primarily in the finance function. To promote ambitious targets, however, Dover distributes monthly, quarterly, and annual "honor rolls" of businesses that achieve any of the company's key targets, such as 25 percent after-tax return on total capital, 20 percent pretax profit margin, and 15 percent pretax income growth. Peer pressure is the main motivating force to achieve these targets, but they also feature in compensation bonus calculations.

Dover now has a reputation as the sort of company that a family-owned business should consider selling to, as and when the family is ready to realize its capital. Dover will make no hostile bid before that time, will be pleased to allow the family to continue to run its business with a minimum of interference after the change in ownership (always provided results remain satisfactory), and understands the sort of culture in which such businesses thrive. "We don't just let a company president run his own business," says Roubos. "We insist he do so—on his own. We want to make being president of a Dover company the next best thing to owning your own." As a result, it sees an unusual flow of opportunities to make friendly acquisitions at favorable prices.

Dover's parenting skills and approach are most suitable in small, niche, low- to medium-technology manufacturing businesses, selling to industrial customers in primarily national markets and with leading market share positions. These *heartland business* criteria have guided Dover's portfolio development. As Roubos states: "We have a pretty disciplined view of what is a Dover-type business. You won't see us owning a hotel chain or insurance company or airline."

Based on this corporate strategy, Dover's sales have grown from just over $1 billion in 1983 to $2.5 billion in 1993, with return on equity moving in a range between 15 and 20 percent during this period. It has enjoyed a strong positive cash flow, sufficient to support its acquisition and stock repurchase program as well as the organic growth of its businesses. These results suggest that Dover's parenting, based around selecting and motivating the right managers to run each of its businesses, has created value. Profitability has been lower in some of Dover's higher technology businesses, which conform less well to its heartland criteria. It can also be argued that Dover's parenting philosophy of minimal interference adds relatively little value to ongoing businesses within the portfolio; unless a business is facing a crisis and the need for fresh management, Dover will seldom exercise strong influence to alter the decisions of the individual company presidents. But these reservations must be set against the cost of Dover's parenting, which is extremely low. Our impression is that, as a result, the net value creation remains clearly positive, and that Dover is a better parent for its businesses than most other, more interventionist parents would be.

Budgetary Control

Budgetary control provides the basis for corporate parents to review and test their businesses' operating plans and targets for each year, and to monitor results against plan as the year progresses. Some companies regard budgets as vital and believe it is through budgetary control that they add the most value. Other companies give less prominence to budgeting, but most still regard it as an important part of parenting.

The budget process creates value if it leads to better operating effectiveness and results than would otherwise be achieved. Good budgetary control can also enhance motivation and provide the basis for corporate financial planning and investor relations. But, in many companies, the budget process is unproductive. If businesses find it easy to bamboozle the parent into accepting budgets with large amounts of slack, or if the process involves extensive data gathering, analysis, and debate but no significant impact on business decisions or performance, budgets add cost but no value. Equally, if businesses are pressed into agreeing to unrealistic, top-down objectives, or if the control process is so severe that it leads to demotivation and fear, budgeting will damage performance. Budgeting may be part of the management process in nearly all companies, but it by no means always creates any value.

One company whose budget process is a vital value-creating component of its corporate strategy is BTR.

BTR: PROFIT PLANNING. BTR is a diverse British company, with sales of £9 billion, which has achieved rapid growth and high levels of profitability during the past two decades. Its origins were in the tyre and rubber industry (BTR stood for British Tyre and Rubber), but it has now branched out into a variety of different sectors, including power transmission, electric motors, materials handling, diesel engines, aerospace, construction, control systems, electrical products, packaging, paper technology equipment, sports goods, and healthcare. This portfolio of businesses has been put together through a series of major acquisitions, such as Thomas Tilling (1983), Nylex (1984), Dunlop (1985), ACI (1988), Hawker Siddeley (1991), and Rexnord (1993).

BTR has a distinctive management philosophy, developed under its former chairman Sir Owen Green, who was managing director from 1967 through 1987, and carried on by the current management under the leadership of Alan Jackson, the chief executive. This philosophy stresses the importance of detailed budgeting and close monitoring of performance, through the BTR profit planning process. BTR uses this process as a key source of corporate added value. Indeed managers throughout the company are careful to point out that BTR calls the process "profit planning," not "budgeting," because, as one senior corporate officer put it: "It's about making money, not spending money."[8]

The profit planning process begins in July, when corporate guidelines are issued to each of BTR's 1,300 profit centers, all of which have a high degree of freedom to set and follow their own strategies and a correspondingly high level of responsibility for the results they achieve. The guidelines state BTR's corporate assumptions for the coming year in terms of growth rates, inflation rates, and exchange rates in the main world economies. They also give suggestions for what BTR will be expecting from the profit centers in terms of key ratio and profitability trends. For example, they will suggest the sorts of improvements that should be targeted in margins (e.g., to improve by 1%), working-capital-to-sales ratios (e.g., to reduce debtor days by 2 days), and value-added per employee (e.g., to increase by 5%). The guidelines are not tailored for each profit center, and do not give specific profit center targets. However, they do convey BTR's expectation of constant improvement in trends and ratios, and provide a framework within which the profit centers draw up their plans. Given the product and geographic scope of a business, its cost structure, and its past performance, profit center managing directors can readily see the implications for the sort of profit plan that is expected from them.

During the summer, the profit centers put together their plans. The guidelines usually mean that developing a credible plan that is likely to be acceptable to the center is a stretching task. The preparation of the profit plans, therefore, forces a rigorous and wide-ranging discussion within the managements of each profit center about plans for the coming year.

Profit plans must be prepared in accordance with BTR's standard forms and definitions. The complete profit planning package runs to some 15 schedules, which break down the income statement and the balance sheet for the business into considerable detail, and which highlight certain ratios that BTR regard as key control variables. For example, sales per employee versus cost per employee; analysis of revenue changes into volume, price, and mix effects; and a variety of asset turnover ratios are all required items. The cross-references within the schedules ensure that the implications of proposed changes in one area of the business are thought through in terms of their impact elsewhere, and the key ratios bring out any inconsistencies or anomalies in the proposed plan.

Each profit center reports to one of 25 group chief executives (GCEs), and in September the profit center's managing director and financial controller[9] meet with their GCE and the GCE's financial controller to review the proposed plan. Part of the meeting is devoted to checking the technical correctness of the way the schedules have been filled in—not a trivial task given the detail and complexity of the forms. A profit center controller commented: "In order to be able to prepare these schedules for historic data, the current year's forecast and the next year's plan, you have to have first class management information on product profitability that is capable of being reconciled directly back to financial results. There is never any compromise on the standard and quality of financial information expected. If the plan reveals shortcomings in information, then the center takes it as an indication that the management team in the profit center has inadequate systems to run its own business." If these shortcomings cannot be speedily rectified, new people will be brought in to run the business.

But the bulk of the meeting is used to test the thinking behind the plan. Are the objectives sufficiently ambitious? Do the key ratios conform to the corporate guidelines, and, if not, why not? Are the plans realistic and achievable? Does the plan fit together and are the key ratios internally consistent and compatible? For obvious reasons, these meetings are called "challenge" meetings within BTR. "The profit plan meeting," we were told by a profit center MD, "is normally a grueling session, which is anticipated with apprehension. Poor plans, badly thought out or illogically compiled, show their weakness very quickly." Based on the detailed analysis in the schedules and on familiarity with the businesses, the GCE can frequently make constructive suggestions about how a plan can be improved or made more robust. "Decisions have to be justifiable to an audience that has vast experience of past plans and their results. It is a free-and-easy discussion, with no holds barred and no quarter given."

The challenge meetings end with an agreement on any changes that need to be incorporated into the plans. Subsequently, the GCEs review the plans for all of their profit centers at a "second challenge meeting" with one or more members of the main board.[10] The board members look both at the aggregate results for each group and at the results of the individual profit centers behind them. But they are primarily concerned with overall performance and trends, and with comparisons between profit centers, rather than with the details behind the figures, which should have been covered in the first challenge meeting. The overall corporate profit plan is formally agreed by the full board in November.

Monitoring of actual results during the year is intensive and frequent. Each profit center reports weekly on its sales and order intake. Sir Owen Green, who retired as chairman in 1993 but was the original architect of the profit planning process, was always particularly concerned with order intake, and saw it as a key indicator, providing early warning of future prospects. Deviations from the planned level of order intake lead to pressure from the center for corrective action well before problems manifest themselves in actual results.

Monthly results provide the main basis of detailed monitoring. By the end of the third working day after the month end, all profit centers must provide a "flash" report on orders, sales, profits before interest and tax, interest, and manpower. These flash reports allow GCEs and the corporate center to react quickly to any problems that are arising. The full monthly report is submitted seven working days after the end of the month. It provides confirmation of the flash data, and additional detail on costs, balance sheet, and cash flow items. The monthly reports are the subject of face-to-face meetings between each profit center and its GCE. While BTR recognizes that circumstances can arise that prevent plans from being realized, these meetings are powerful motivators to profit center managers to do everything within their power to deliver their planned results. Failure to make plan is not necessarily terminal for profit center managing directors, provided they can show convincingly why problems have arisen and what they are doing about them. But consistent underperformance is not acceptable, and BTR's close monitoring is designed to weed out quickly those who do not deliver. Even GCEs are at risk if their profit centers, collectively, appear to be below par. Moreover, the competitive spirit in BTR means that profit center managers strive to be at the top of the league in terms of the performance they achieve.

BTR's profit planning process creates value in several ways. Firstly, the rigor and detail of the profit planning forms ensure that there is high quality, reliable and consistent financial information and analysis available in every profit center. BTR's profit planning package has been developed and fine-tuned over 20 years or more. Although it is time consuming to fill in, experience has shown that the information generated is relevant and useful for BTR's businesses. There are also few, if any, ways of "fudging the numbers" to distort the process.[11] The forms and ratios are most suitable for businesses with the sorts of cost and profit structures found in industrial manufacturing companies, which make up the bulk of BTR's portfolio, but they are used throughout the company. The discipline of using the BTR forms raises the standard of financial literacy throughout BTR, and gives a better basis for discussing future plans and past performance than exists in most companies.[12]

A second source of value arises from the way that the GCEs and the corporate center draw out plans with more ambitious goals from the profit centers. The corporate guidelines and the plan review meetings make clear what standards of performance are expected, and challenge the profit centers to devise plans that will come up to these standards. A lackluster plan, or a failure to show sufficient energy in seeking out improvements, will be quickly identified and rejected. Ultimately, the plans must be proposed and owned by the profit centers, but the process is designed to raise their ambitions as high as possible. A key skill for BTR's corporate managers is, therefore, to judge what targets are appropriate for each profit center. "We want plans that are stretching but achievable, not over the top," says Bob Faircloth, the chief operating officer. BTR corporate managers' ability to sense what level of ambition is right rests on their exposure to, and experience of, a very wide range of basically similar manufacturing profit centers.

A heavy emphasis is placed on margin improvement in the profit planning process. "We don't go for volume," explained Alan Jackson. "We go for the quality of the sale. It's all about margins. We target businesses to increase their margins by 1 percent per year, and it's amazing how long they can go on achieving this!" To reinforce this drive, the corporate center carries out "price audits" during the year to check that the profit centers are moving their prices ahead as planned, and to put pressure on any laggards. As a result, businesses seek out and develop the most profitable niches in their markets, rather than concerning themselves with market share or volume growth.

The third benefit of the process is the motivation it creates. Profit center managers are in no doubt about what their targets are and have full authority within their businesses to do what is necessary to achieve these targets. They therefore know that their success or failure depends entirely on their own decisions and efforts. The constant monitoring and personal feedback on performance reinforces their commitment to deliver their planned targets. Profit center managers in BTR seem that much hungrier and more motivated than in the large majority of other companies.

The secret of the motivation provided by the BTR profit planning process lies in a collective pride in the culture of constant effort and improvement that pervades the company. The challenges provided by the profit planning process act as a stimulus to the best BTR managers, and the constant feedback is a source of recurrent satisfaction—provided that results are being achieved. There is strong competition between profit center heads to be able to report the best results, and it is the consequent sense of achievement rather than high salaries or bonuses that primarily motivates BTR managers. Indeed one told us that he would be willing to forego £10,000 of salary in exchange for the satisfaction of being ahead of plan at each of his monthly review meetings. The culture is summed up by one senior manager who stated: "The key thing about BTR is that everyone is driven by this restless passion to improve performance."

A fourth benefit is that the tight control process is well designed to help profit center managers to identify problems early and to take action fast. In the 1990–1992 recession, BTR's profit margin only fell from 16 percent to 14.4 percent, but, in achieving this, the company shed over 30,000 employees. In many companies, the redundancies would have come as a response to a severe fall in profitability rather than as a means of preventing it. The ability to push for timely changes in direction—or indeed in senior management—depends on the quality of the center's judgment about what should be possible in each BTR business. If a change in profit center management is needed, BTR can draw on a large pool of potential candidates for the job from the many other similar profit centers in the company.

Lastly, the frequent contacts between the profit centers, the GCEs, and the corporate center allow for a continuous exchange of views about how best to develop the business. Whether the center is pressing for a reconsideration of pricing policy, a more aggressive attack on the cost base, or a new campaign to reduce working capital, the profit center can count on advice that is well-informed and based on experience across many similar business situations. Almost all the GCEs and members of the corporate team have personal backgrounds in running the sorts of businesses that make up BTR's industrial manu-facturing heartland, and they have a vast accumulation of data and ex-perience through profit planning on all of BTR's profit centers. Their influence builds on this unique experience base.

In many companies, budgetary control is regarded as no more than an administrative necessity: an exercise in form filling that provides the basis for the routine of corporate financial reporting but is of little value to managers in running their businesses better. There are, however, companies such as BTR where the budget process is a vital value cre-ation component of stand-alone parenting influence. To achieve this end, the parent must have a good sense for targets that are appropriate for each business, must create a context for budgeting that leads to agree-ment on suitably stretching targets, and must design a budget process that provides a vehicle for motivating business unit managers to find ways of delivering on these targets.

BTR: CORPORATE STRATEGY. Exhibit 6–2 is a parenting ad-vantage statement for BTR. Its key *value creation insights* focus on the opportunities that exist in many businesses to raise profitability through closer control of product profitability and a focus on productivity and margin improvement. BTR has long believed that many—perhaps most—businesses do not achieve the efficiency levels and profit margins of which they are capable. They are run by management teams that are not ambitious enough, or that lack key skills or sufficient motivation. "They don't know what can be achieved until you push them," stated a senior corporate manager; and a business manager who had come into BTR via an acquisition boasted to us that his business was now obtain-ing margins on sales in excess of 15 percent, in an industry where he and his competitors had traditionally been happy with 5 percent. An im-portant part of BTR's insight is a realization that in many businesses a focus on return on sales produces a better financial result than a focus on volume or market share. Managers are therefore encouraged to push prices up to achieve full "cost recovery," even if this results in some lost sales, and, if necessary, to cut costs back to match sales volumes. Many of BTR's businesses are mature, so that an emphasis on profitability and margins rather than sales growth can prevent wasteful initiatives.

EXHIBIT 6-2   BTR parenting advantage statement

Value Creation Insights	Many manufacturing businesses in mature markets do not have a close enough control of product profitability and have opportunities to push prices up and improve productivity. Such businesses can greatly benefit from a parent that insists on tight profit planning disciplines and stretching targets, and emphasizes margin improvement rather than volume growth.
Distinctive Parenting Characteristics	Intensive profit planning process that • Improves the financial management of the businesses. • Creates high personal motivation to deliver. • Leads to stretching targets. • Identifies key issues and opportunities in the businesses early. • Allows for continuous exchange of views between parent and businesses. Decentralized, stand-alone business structure, coupled with strong personal responsibility for results. Low corporate overheads and constant improvement culture. Skills in identifying and integrating acquisitions.
Heartland Businesses	Industrial manufactured product businesses of moderate technology and capital intensity. Ideally, these businesses operate primarily in noncyclical, niche markets.

BTR's profit planning process is probably its most essential *distinctive parenting characteristic.* There are, however, several other important and mutually reinforcing aspects of its parenting. Under BTR's decentralized structure, the profit centers are treated as stand-alone businesses and most deal with other BTR profit centers only on a third-party basis, if at all. BTR is committed in principle to the overriding responsibility of each profit center for its own affairs, and strongly resists establishing staff or functions at levels above the profit center. "It is very important to remember that each business remains separate," says Jackson. "We certainly do not have any nonsenses like central marketing or group marketing directors. We do not blunt the edges of the clear business unit focus. That would be criminal."

BTR's distinctive culture also supports the drive for constant profit improvement. Its head office still occupies the modest building in Vincent Square that it moved into in 1978, and the furnishings and fittings show little sign of renovation or replacement since that time either. Its corporate staff number around 60 in the United Kingdom with similarly small corporate offices in the United States and Australia. The chief executive takes pride in the fact that he drives a second-hand car that he took over from a manager who had taken early retirement. It is evident that this is a head office where costs are kept to a minimum and where extravagance is frowned on. Moreover, the top team lead by example. Hard work, constant improvement, and bottom-line results are the watchwords in BTR. The culture of the company is epitomized by the inscription on the boardroom clock. It reads: "Think of Rest and Work On." This culture provides the ideal background for BTR's approach to parenting.

BTR has also recognized that many corporate parents view BTR's type of businesses as "unglamorous" and have focused their attention elsewhere; and that independent companies in such businesses are often run by less sophisticated management teams. As a result, there are plenty of opportunities to acquire underperforming businesses at attractive prices, and to use BTR's profit planning processes to restructure the businesses and boost margins. Thus, it is no surprise that BTR has been an active acquirer. From this experience, it has developed skills in the identification and assessment of candidates, and in the integration of them into BTR.

BTR's acquisition, in November 1992, of Hawker Siddeley, a £2 billion British diversified engineering group, is a case in point. Alan Jackson, Bob Faircloth and Kathleen O'Donovan (the finance director) undertook the bulk of the initial screening and analysis themselves. "We don't use consultants. We don't have staffs. We like to do the analysis ourselves." "If you looked at the 10-year record, you could see no growth in earnings, no growth in sales and a big growth in employees. Their sales per employee numbers didn't stack up with anything we remotely recognized." After a hotly contested bid, BTR finally won control. Drawing on experience from previous acquisitions, an integration team of BTR managers under Bob Faircloth worked through the whole of Hawker Siddeley during the first two months after the acquisition. "We needed to move fast," says Faircloth, "to create a sense of urgency and the real true profit motivation, which had evidently been lacking previously." Within a year, Hawker Siddeley's profits have been pushed up from a budgeted £130 million to over double this amount. Despite the success of the integration, Bob Faircloth convened a meeting on the first anniversary of the acquisition to review what BTR could learn from the process, and what should be done differently in future acquisition integrations. By building on experience, BTR has honed its skills in acquisition identification and integration.

BTR adds most value in businesses that involve manufactured products of moderate technology and capital intensity for industrial customers. It is around these *heartland businesses* that BTR's profit planning process has been designed, and it is in these businesses that most of the senior corporate executives have personal experience and feel. Alan Jackson states: "Our game is really in industrial manufacturing. We know how to set up a plant. We know how to get productivity improvements. We know how to downsize and squeeze when volumes fall." Most of BTR's recent acquisitions consist primarily of industrial manufacturing businesses.

Although BTR has businesses in other areas, such as consumer products and distribution, it has more difficulty making judgments about people, plans, and targets the further away from the industrial manufacturing heartland that a business lies. "We have been less successful away from industrial manufacturing. Distribution businesses, for example, need a different sort of philosophy," says Jackson. Thus, in distribution businesses, which tend to have many small locations each with its own fixed costs, it is harder to cut back costs quickly and incrementally in response to a volume decline. A cost-reduction program soon encounters the need to close branches, which may then damage the business's market coverage. This means that BTR is less able to maintain margins through tight control and timely reaction to events, and BTR's distribution businesses have been less profitable than other parts of the portfolio. BTR has accordingly divested businesses such as National Tyre Service (a UK tyre distributor and retailer), Pretty Polly (a consumer business making hosiery), Heinemann and Octopus (publishing businesses), Cornhill (an insurance business), and Newey & Eyre and Graham Builders Merchants (construction materials distributors).

Ideally, BTR prefers businesses in which profit improvements are possible through close control of costs and prices, and through a multiplicity of small, incremental, optimizing decisions. Niche products, which face limited competition and are less price sensitive, respond particularly well to BTR's profit planning disciplines. Conversely, cyclical businesses, which are exposed to large swings in demand, are less suited to BTR's approach.

BTR's parenting has undoubtedly brought about great improvements in performance in many of the businesses it has acquired and succeeds in maintaining the profitability of most businesses in the portfolio at unusually high levels. It is an outstanding example of the Financial Control style, with a record and reputation that is superior to the great majority of rival parents that pursue this style.

Some of BTR's businesses, such as sealing systems, are becoming more international in their market and competitive scopes, and, in these businesses, the company is beginning to place somewhat more emphasis on the role of the GCE in enhancing linkages between national profit centers. The GCE may, for example, play a role in encouraging some profit centers to use a development laboratory in another profit center, or in allocating responsibilities for new product developments between profit centers. While such moves may be desirable, given the nature of competition in these businesses, they entail some conflict with BTR's long-standing tradition of separate profit center responsibilities. It will be necessary for BTR to preserve the strength of its established parenting approach, while introducing these modifications to it. The company will also need to maintain a portfolio focus on businesses where its distinctive parenting characteristics are most valuable.

Strategy Reviews

Many parent organizations believe they can create value by helping their businesses to think more strategically. They feel that their business heads may overlook longer term trends in their businesses, fail to think through their key competitive success factors, or adopt too narrow horizons in their planning. A corporate strategic planning process is seen as a way to rectify these errors.

Our research over many years has convinced us that such beliefs are frequently both arrogant and wrong. Weak management teams may indeed make the sort of errors implied, but competent, professional business unit managers are, in general, no more likely to fall into these traps than their corporate parents.[13] Indeed, the considerably greater detailed knowledge of their businesses of such managers usually gives them a rather better appreciation than their bosses for the strategic developments that are taking place, and for the longer term objectives that are desirable and realistic. This is why so many business managers find the corporate strategic planning process a distraction rather than a source of added value.

There are, however, companies that derive real benefit from the strategic planning dialogue between the businesses and the parent. In Emerson Electric, for example, the annual strategic planning process for each business (called "divisions" in Emerson) is regarded as a vital event.

EMERSON ELECTRIC: STRATEGIC PLANNING.   Emerson Electric is a company that focuses on businesses that are somewhat similar to those of BTR. Emerson's origins are in the electrical industry, while BTR's are in rubber-based products such as belting. Emerson now has sales of $8 billion, spread across about 40 different business divisions, ranging from industrial electric motors to process control. Both BTR and Emerson have remarkable records of squeezing extra performance from their businesses. But, whereas BTR focuses on the budget process as its main vehicle for creating value, Emerson focuses on the strategy process.

Each Emerson division has an annual strategy review. The reviews are conducted personally by Chuck Knight, Emerson's CEO, at full-day sessions known as divisional "planning conferences." For some divisions, the planning conference lasts two days. The divisional management team spend a great deal of time during the preceding two months in preparing for the planning conference. It is up to the divisions to decide what to cover in their presentations, but they will be influenced by the nature of the discussions at the previous year's conferences, and in other reviews with corporate management throughout the year.

Emerson has an extensive package of charts and tables that divisions must fill out, as background for their presentation. These forms identify cost, growth, and profit trends in the division in considerable detail, and allow the comparison of past results (going back five years), current performance and future plans (going forward five years). The full documentation for a typical division, consisting of slides, charts, and forms can run to some 400 pages; of these there are about 75 required charts that must be completed by all divisions.[14] The corporate center in Emerson, however, believes that the required charts ask only for information that any competent manager needs to run a division.

Before the planning conference, there is a premeeting between the division management and Al Suter, the Chief Operating Officer, to review the required charts that focus on cost and profit trends. The purpose of this meeting is to deal with some of the more detailed aspects of the plan, and to check that the plan is internally consistent and robust. The main planning conference then focuses more attention on growth plans and prospects.

The conference begins with a one- to two-hour presentation by the division president. Subsequent presentations may be made by other members of the team, down to relatively junior product manager level. The presentations are intended to focus on the key issues in the division and do not go through the great majority of the required charts in the background pack. While Knight discourages long and involved presentations, he is willing to go into whatever detail is necessary to get to grips with the real issues.

A major purpose of the day is for the center to challenge the division's plans, to test their validity, and to see whether the division has the potential for better growth or profit performance. "The objectives and standards of the corporation should be clearly established with the dialogue," claims Charlie Peters, vice president of Corporate Development and Technology. The debate takes off from the prepared slides and charts but is not constrained by them. Typically it ranges much more broadly, with the standard data acting as background information only. Knight describes the conferences as follows: "Though we're not trying to put anyone on the spot, we do want to challenge assumptions and conventional thinking and give ample time to every significant issue. We want proof that a division is stretching to reach its goals, and we want to see the details of the actions division management believes will yield improved results. Our expectations are high, and the discussions are intense. A division president who comes to a planning conference poorly prepared has made a serious mistake."[15]

Through the planning process, a division may come under pressure to do more to contain its labor costs or its working capital, with Knight using comparisons with other divisions' achievements to ratchet up targets; or it may be challenged to think again about its underlying competitive position and the dynamics of its marketplace. Both the 1992 acquisition of Fisher to complement Rosemount's position in process control and the joint venture in power tools between Skil and Robert Bosch were ideas that were developed during planning conferences.

By design, the atmosphere is combative and confrontational. "Emerson is a contact sport," as one manager put it. But though the arguments are often heated, they are not intended to be personal. Furthermore managers at all levels are encouraged to speak out and to defend their own views strongly, and there is no deference to rank and position. The belief is that this sort of dialogue results in superior plans, more commitment, and a more constructive relationship between the center and the divisions. The day ends with dinner when any residual personal animosities can be smoothed out.

At the end of the meeting, Knight writes a brief (e.g., 3-page) memo, summarizing what he believes emerged from the conference. This forms the basis for a meeting called the post planning conference. The post planning conference is a half-day session to confirm and agree on objectives, action items, and forecasts. A clear set of action programs will be identified and documented, and will then be reviewed monthly at division board meetings. In this way, the implementation follow-up to the plan is strengthened.

Despite the amount of time involved in preparing for and attending the planning conferences, managers throughout Emerson perceive the process as valuable. In particular, the division presidents recognize that the planning process is helpful to them, rather than some bureaucratic imposition. "The value of the planning discipline makes itself felt in the period of preparation. The process forces us not only to do our homework, but also to think through the issues." And the planning conferences themselves are regarded as constructive, and the source of valuable new ideas and perspectives. Not all of the time involved or all of the required charts are seen as equally worthwhile ("about half are extremely important; the rest are not so productive"), but the overall balance is clearly positive. The consistently high level of profitability achieved by almost all the Emerson businesses suggests that there is also a payoff in terms of results.

The success of Emerson's strategic planning process depends on the top team's understanding of their businesses. Among the comments we received were: "You'll not find a chief executive who knows his company better than Chuck Knight. He is very informed and very objective about the businesses." "It is amazing to me how much Knight is on top of the issues in my division." As a result, the quality of the planning dialogue is high and leads to added-value decisions.

Three main factors contribute to central understanding of the businesses. First, the center spends a great deal of time gathering and processing information about the businesses. Knight, for example, claims to spend well over half of his time on planning, and believes that other senior managers spend even more of their time on this activity. Second, there is a vast accumulation of data and experience on the Emerson businesses, gathered through the systematic annual processes of planning and control, pursued year in, year out for decades. The forms and analysis packages ensure that fundamental data on all the businesses are available, in a format that is readily accessible to the center, comparable across businesses, and structured in a way that brings out key issues. And the intensive, continuing dialogue with businesses means that, over time, the center has seen the results of different sorts of strategies in each of the businesses, and therefore has a basis for judging new proposals. Third, the businesses within Emerson are comparatively homogeneous in terms of basic technologies and key success factors. An emphasis on manufactured electrical products of medium technology for industrial customers means that the vast majority of Emerson's businesses have similar cost structures, and that the standard Emerson planning charts and ratios are therefore useful and applicable. More importantly, the businesses play to the strengths and experience of the corporate management team. These are businesses which confront similar strategic issues, so that the center's feel for how to react to plans, proposals, and results is usually sound, and ideas and approaches that have been shown to work well in one business are likely to be valid in others.

It is also important that the planning process is managed in a way that surfaces new ideas and strategies. A key skill in Emerson is the ability to create an atmosphere in the company where managers can express different points of view forcibly, but without degenerating into unconstructive conflict. There are many factors here: a respect for each individual's opinions; rewards for fresh thinking, not conformism; a search for data-based conclusions; behavior that demonstrates that specific disagreements do not imply a generally low regard for those who differ. "Knight invites people to punch back. He takes positions to provoke a response and expects one." Openness of communication and debate is vital to make the Emerson process work well.

The process is also managed to create a sense of personal commitment to planned targets. These may be the result of a strenuous and intense wrestling match with the center, but at the end of the day, the division managers feel personally committed to targets that they feel to be their own and not imposed as top-down objectives. Again, this concerns atmosphere and personal relationships as much as formal process design.

Emerson's use of the strategic planning process resembles BTR's use of budgeting in so far as it concentrates on testing the businesses' plans and targets, and on motivating them to deliver. But Emerson places more emphasis on growth plans and strategic issues, and covers a longer time horizon. Both companies, however, expect careful preparation for planning meetings by their business managers, use detailed data and analysis about the businesses as a means of informing the discussion, concentrate on making the financial implications of plans as precise as possible, and encourage open—even confrontational—debate.

The dialogue between the parent and the businesses about strategy is not, of course, limited to the formal strategic planning process. Very often, the most important strategy debates take place ad hoc, around specific decisions or issues as they arise, or informally in the course of Dover-type visits or other encounters, or as a by-product of other management processes such as the budget or the capital expenditure process. Indeed, in some companies, such as BTR, very little (or even no) emphasis is placed on a formal strategic planning process as such. But the conditions under which strategy dialogues create value remain the same as in the more formal processes we have described for Emerson.

EMERSON ELECTRIC: CORPORATE STRATEGY.   Exhibit 6–3 is a parenting advantage statement for Emerson. Emerson's *value creation insights* place emphasis on the opportunities that are available in many

EXHIBIT 6–3   Emerson parenting advantage statement

Value Creation Insights	Even in businesses which have basically sound management and adequate profitability, a parent with suitable skills can often improve performance substantially by helping to sharpen strategic thinking, analyze the components of cost and revenue in the business, and focus on manufacturing cost reduction.
Distinctive Parenting Characteristics	Intensive strategic planning process that identifies key issues and opportunities in the businesses, and creates a constructive and open dialogue about them.
	Focus on the performance and responsibility of each business's management team, including 15% return on sales expectation.
	Corporate Best Cost Producer (BCP) program.
	Skills in identifying and acquiring businesses that will respond well to Emerson's parenting.
	Personal experience and style of the CEO and top corporate managers.
Heartland Businesses	Businesses that manufacture electrical, electromechanical, or electronic products of medium technology and capital intensity for industrial customers. Ideally, businesses with a reasonable level of profitability, but scope for improvement; sound underlying market position, but scope to build on it; moderate market growth rates.

businesses to improve performance by sharpening strategic thinking. They also stress the opportunities that exist for performance improvement through careful analysis of cost and revenue trends, and through manufacturing cost reductions.

Emerson's planning conferences have pride of place among its *distinctive parenting characteristics* for putting into practice the value creation insight, for reasons that we have explained. The planning conferences are also linked to Emerson's high performance standards. A 15 percent return on sales is regarded as the norm for Emerson's sorts of businesses, and the whole planning and control process is geared to finding ways of achieving it. The focus is also firmly on the responsibility for performance of each division as a stand-alone entity, rather than on linkages between divisions.

Emerson backs up the planning conferences by running corporate programs on issues that are currently regarded as important; for example, quality management or inventory control. The most important, and the most wide ranging, of these programs is the Best Cost Producer (BCP) program,[16] designed to make all of Emerson's businesses the lowest cost quality producers in the world in their product areas. This target, which has been driven through the organization by corporate management with a restructuring cost of $250 million in the 1980s, has now, Emerson claims, largely been achieved. BCP, however, remains as a sort of "doctrine of continuous improvement," and involves a wide cross section of employees throughout the company. Emerson believes it is a vital program to offset what is otherwise an inevitable tendency for costs to creep upward.

Acquisitions have been important in Emerson's impressive growth record and are integral to the corporate strategy. An essential part of the strategic planning process is to identify opportunities for acquisitions that will enhance the growth and profit opportunities of Emerson's businesses. Over time, the company has learned from its acquisition experiences, and it has refined both the process and the criteria for assessing candidates. In Emerson, acquisitions now receive a very thorough examination to determine whether the candidate will be compatible with Emerson's management approach and philosophy. ("It's like a marriage; you really need to get to know your potential partner before you decide to go ahead.") As with other areas of Emerson's parenting, the existence of a detailed acquisition screening process is not unique. The difference is the thoroughness and skill with which the screening is carried out, and the experience and track record on which it builds.

The parenting skills and style of Emerson's top team have evolved gradually with experience over a long period of time. Knight's regime as chief executive has already lasted nearly 20 years, and is itself, in many respects, a continuation of the management approach of his predecessor, Buck Persons, who took office in 1954. There has, however, been constant refinement of detailed aspects of the management process, a honing of the parenting skills in the company, and a pushing back and testing of the business boundaries within which the Emerson approach works best. As Knight observes: "Building a smooth-running operation entails years of effort and piece-by-piece construction."

Emerson is most at home in businesses that manufacture electrical, electromechanical, or electronic products of medium technology and capital intensity for industrial customers.[17] These are the *heartland businesses*. Conversely, Emerson generally avoids businesses that are not based on manufacturing, that do not have some connection to electrical technologies, that involve high capital or research intensity, or that serve consumer markets. "Our ability to strategize in consumer products is less good. We like a slower rhythm. We don't do well with advertising, short product cycles and the like." "We don't like highly capital intensive businesses like major chemical process plants. What we are good at is managing an hourly work force and buying things like steel."

The Emerson parenting approach emphases sharpening strategies and improving operating margins in businesses that are basically sound and well run. It adds less value for a business that is already highly profitable and tightly managed. Equally, it is less suited to basically weak businesses and poor management teams, since it is more about fine-tuning and building than about radical turnarounds. Thus Emerson concentrates on acquisitions that have scope for margin improvement, but a reasonable basic level of profitability; sufficient size and scale to compete with the industry leaders (underlying position sound, but possible to build on it); moderate market growth rates (not facing market stagnation or decline, but also not growing so fast that the tight Emerson control system might be inhibiting). "We build on good fundamentals which are already in place. Our approach is really to fix up sound businesses rather than to turn round unsound ones." With businesses of this sort, Emerson can usually make a major impact on performance within two to three years, pushing margins up from the 5 to 10 percent range to in excess of 15 percent, and supporting strategic initiatives to strengthen long-term prospects.

Although the heartland criteria have not been explicitly laid out, they appear to be embedded in Emerson's management thinking, and their influence can be seen in the moves that Emerson has made to develop its portfolio. Successful acquisitions such as Morse Industrial (a former division of Borg Warner that manufactures power transmission equipment), Branson (a former division of Smith-Kline Beckman that operates in the ultrasonic welding, cleaning, and testing fields), Copeland (a leading compressor manufacturer), and ASCO (solenoid valves and industrial automation controls) all conformed to the prototype of suitable members of the Emerson family. Emerson has also exited from businesses that did not fit the heartland criteria. Beaird-Poulan, for example, a manufacturer of chain saws and garden equipment, which Emerson sold to Electrolux in the early 1980s, was in a relatively weak competitive position, in a market that had peaked and was now declining, in an unfamiliar technology (gas engines rather than electrical), and, largely, in a consumer rather than an industrial market. Reflecting on the underlying rationale for divestments, a senior corporate manager stated: "We have well established management systems that have been around for a long time. Once you get into businesses that lie outside the boundaries where these systems are effective, you cease to add value."

The success of Emerson's parenting is evident from the company's record. Sales have increased eightfold since Knight became chief executive in 1973, while earnings and dividends per share have grown consistently in every year. Return on equity has moved in a range from 17.7 percent to 20.2 percent in the period 1983–1993. This remarkable record is based on clear sources of parenting advantage, systematically developed and exploited, and depends heavily on the strategic reviews it conducts of its businesses.

Critics of Emerson have charged that its structured approach to planning and tight control process do not encourage organic growth in its businesses. They claim that Emerson is highly effective at generating extra profits from a given level of sales, but less good at promoting sales growth. Given the pressures placed on consistent, predictable, planned increases in profits, it may be true that Emerson is less comfortable in rapidly growing, high-risk businesses. But it has nevertheless succeeded in achieving solid growth from its ongoing businesses, and new businesses that have been brought into the portfolio have yielded performance improvements and contributed to growth in corporate earnings per share. This form of growth should continue into the future under Emerson's corporate strategy.

Emerson's success has hinged on preserving and fine-tuning the fit between its parenting characteristics, the businesses in its portfolio, and the sort of value creation that it targets. Through a management process that has been refined with experience over the past 20 years, it has achieved a balance between profit pressure and strategic development that has eluded most other followers of the Strategic Control style.[18] As a result, it has achieved parenting advantage across the bulk of its portfolio.

Capital Investment Decisions

Traditionally, the allocation of capital investment resources has been seen as one of the key functions, and potential sources of stand-alone value, of the corporate parent. The businesses could perform better, it was alleged, because they raised their capital from an informed, sympathetic, and well-financed corporate parent rather than directly from banks or the capital market.

All major companies do indeed devote corporate effort to capital expenditure authorization processes. In some companies, especially those with low capital intensity or where the sources of competitive advantage are not seen as depending on major capital investment, the capital expenditure process may be relatively low key. In almost all companies, however, the parent needs to know what capital spending is planned by the businesses, and to be in a position to authorize or reject such plans, in order to balance cash requirements with the company's sources of funds.

Unfortunately, the parent's influence is often detrimental rather than positive. The capital expenditure process can involve a sequence of presentations and approvals, each representing a hurdle to be crossed. At each successive hurdle, knowledge about the basis of the investment becomes thinner and decisions to support or reject it are taken on less and less adequate grounds. Businesses, knowing that the focus will inevitably be on quantitative criteria, such as the payback period, the return on investment (ROI), or the net present value (NPV), become adept at providing projections that meet the corporate criteria, while suppressing the real uncertainties behind the figures. Where capital rationing exists, with each business knowing that it must compete for funds with all the others in the portfolio, it sows the seeds from which biased information and overoptimism flow. What is more, given the quantity of investable funds in the capital market, a corporate role that involves turning down a good investment simply because there are other even better ones available is destroying rather than creating value. In these circumstances, the corporation is unlikely to make better decisions about capital investments than would result from independent businesses having to justify their own capital requirements directly to the capital markets. Frequently, the businesses within such corporations view the corporate capital expenditure process as slow, arbitrary, and ill-informed, and envy independent companies that can deal directly with their bankers.

But we have also found examples of companies where capital expenditure processes do create value and, indeed, play a vital role in the corporate strategy. RTZ is a case in point.

RTZ: CAPITAL INVESTMENTS. RTZ's early history in the 1950s was as a mining finance house, taking equity interests in projects operated by other companies. Over the years, it has extended its role into operations, and has grown rapidly and profitably. It is now one of the largest and most profitable diversified mining and minerals groups in the world. Its interests cover exploration, mining, and downstream processing of copper, silver, gold, bauxite, molybdenum, talc, borates, and many other minerals, with operating companies in many different countries.

In RTZ, the businesses move forward through infrequent, major capital projects. A new mine may involve an investment of several hundred million dollars, and the investment will largely predetermine the success of the business for decades thereafter. Not surprisingly, the capital investment review process is therefore seen as crucial in RTZ.

Within the operating companies, capital project submissions provide a focus for detailed planning activity. These submissions are often worked up in collaboration with central staff departments, and are, in any case, carefully scrutinized by these departments once they have been completed. RTZ have corporate departments that specialize in technical aspects of mine planning, in commercial and strategic evaluation, in financial project analysis and planning, and in environmental issues. There is also a central economics department that provides specialist advice on the outlook for supply, demand, and prices in the metals or minerals concerned. Each of these departments is staffed by experts in their respective fields, and aims to be at the forefront in its area. For example, RTZ has particular expertise in computer-based modeling and conceptual mine planning.[19] It has also been in the forefront of analytical techniques for capital expenditure evaluation, from the development of DCF analysis in the 1960s, up until the introduction of risk-weighted hurdle rates today. And the company's finance staff has particular skill in putting together creative financing packages for projects. It is worth noting that the company does not believe in the sort of capital rationing system that encourages competition between businesses for funds. As Tony Lighterness, the corporate treasurer, put it to us: "Our job is to raise finance for all good projects."

Ultimately, capital investment proposals are presented to an investment committee comprising all of RTZ's executive directors. Almost all the directors have long experience in the minerals business and are therefore able to make informed judgments concerning the proposals that come up to them. The top team is used to taking a view on the economic attractiveness of the ore body in a mine, and, in particular, understands the tradeoffs involved in conceptual mine planning. "None of us could run the optimization software ourselves, but we all understand the nature of the output produced," says Bob Adams, the planning director. It is also understood that prices of minerals are set as commodities on a world market. Therefore, cyclical swings in profitability as prices rise and fall are inevitable, which means that it is essential to concentrate on long-term, underlying cost position. Typically, decisions on proposals are reached at the meeting of the committee when they are presented, or within a few days thereafter.

The RTZ capital expenditure process is, therefore, a vehicle for delivering added value in several ways. It motivates the local management to plan investments more carefully; it allows special knowledge and expertise at the center to shape the proposal and influence the ultimate decision; it ensures that rigorous analysis supports proposals; and it provides a speedy decision once the review has been presented. But, most importantly, the corporate team are experienced in the judgment calls that typically arise with these huge investments. The mid-1980s investment in the Escondida copper mine, which began operations in 1990, is a good example.

Escondida involved spending a total of $820 million, of which RTZ had a $280 million financial exposure. The characteristics of the investment were that RTZ was to be a 30 percent minority shareholder and would therefore lack management control. The project was in Chile, a country in which international bankers felt, at the time, that it was too risky to lend any further money. The mine was to produce copper, which was then at the bottom of its price cycle, implying the need for a major price rise to justify the investment with a financial payback. For all these reasons, the vast majority of companies would have regarded Escondida as an unacceptably risky investment.

RTZ, however, went ahead with the investment. The willingness to do so stemmed from RTZ's long experience in the mining business. First, RTZ's directors were familiar with minority partnership situations, knew that they were essential to participating in many good minerals investments, and were comfortable with handling the management problems that are likely to arise. Second, they were also familiar with investing in geopolitically risky areas. The best investments in the mining business are often located in politically difficult, less developed parts of world, such as South America and Africa. RTZ's senior managers have therefore developed an ability both to assess and manage the political risks involved in operating in these areas. In this instance, they were in fact able to put together a financing package that laid off much of the political risk onto equipment suppliers and ultimate customers in Japan and elsewhere. Third, and perhaps most importantly, they focused their attention on the extremely low cost position of the high-grade ore to be extracted from the mine and were confident, rightly, that the copper price would in due course rise sufficiently to make such a mine profitable. Senior people in the company have always appreciated that the key to success is the underlying cost position of a mine, rather than the current price level of the metal or mineral that it produces. "We have got a very simple success formula. All you need to do is to have the lowest costs in the business."

As the Escondida story shows, RTZ's capital expenditure review processes make it more likely to support the right investments in their minerals businesses than the external capital markets. This is a substantial source of added value, and has allowed the company to grow from a modest size in the 1950s to its preeminent position today.

RTZ lays particular emphasis on the capital expenditure process due to the importance of major, long-term investments in its businesses. Moreover, it has sufficient expertise and understanding in the parent company to make insightful decisions about capital projects, and it sees its role as raising sufficient finance to fund all good investments, rather than as allocating a fixed pool of money between investments. In this way, RTZ creates value through its capital expenditure process.

RTZ: CORPORATE STRATEGY.   Exhibit 6–4 is a parenting advantage statement for RTZ. RTZ's *value creation insights* depend on a recognition that operating companies in minerals businesses often need a well resourced, sympathetic, and knowledgeable parent to fund and support major investment opportunities. External investors may be uncomfortable with the risks and the timescales of these investments, whereas a parent with an understanding of the business is in a much better position to decide what investments to support and can provide specialist expertise to help to make the investments succeed.

RTZ has various *distinctive parenting characteristics* that support these value creation insights. An effective capital expenditure review process, supported by a senior management team with a good feel for the difficult judgments that arise in minerals investments and by a treasury team with sophisticated skills in international project finance, are essential for RTZ's type of value creation. Project management and supervision are also important areas of corporate expertise. For example, RTZ has always maintained one or two experts at the center, who are available to handle negotiations with engineering contractors on major projects, and to ensure that the job is carried out in a timely and cost-effective manner. On one recent investment, this led to cutting a 32-month construction program to 28 months, and to reducing the cost from over $1,100 million to just over $800 million.

EXHIBIT 6–4   RTZ parenting advantage statement

Value Creation Insights	In minerals businesses, a well-informed parent can identify, fund, and help to carry through major, risky, but profitable investment opportunities that other investors would not support. It can also add value through specialist expertise that is provided to its operating companies.
Distinctive Parenting Characteristics	Effective capital expenditure review process.
	Senior management feel for the difficult judgments in minerals investments.
	Skill in international project finance, management, and supervision.
	Decentralized management philosophy.
	Comfort with joint ventures and minority holdings.
	Reputation for successful investment and for completing projects on time and within budget.
	Skill in the technical aspects of minerals extraction and processing.
Heartland Businesses	Capital intensive, cyclical, major project based businesses in the metals, minerals, and mining industries.

RTZ believes strongly in the importance of decentralizing as many decisions as possible to local operating management. This belief goes back to the company's origins in mining finance, when its role was limited to providing finance for investment opportunities and projects that it found in different local companies around the world. Although RTZ is now much more than a mining finance company, it retains the belief that decentralization attracts more energetic and entrepreneurial local managements, and leads to faster and more cost-effective decision making than in other more centralized minerals companies. Our discussions with local RTZ managers confirmed the importance of the philosophy to them. For example, the managing director of one of the major subsidiaries stated: "The RTZ style means that I feel personally responsible for my business. The way they manage is not a matter of standing and saluting to the boss."

RTZ's decentralized style of parenting has been compatible with joint venture and minority investments in which RTZ lacks a controlling interest. Such situations are common in natural resource investments, where small local exploration companies or local governments are often looking for larger, more technically sophisticated international partners to develop opportunities, or where the sheer scale of investments makes it attractive to share the risks among several partners. RTZ's belief in decentralization allows it to contribute its expertise in these situations, without feeling the need to dominate decision making, and its experience of joint ventures over the years has led to skills in managing the sensitivities and relationships that arise.

One of RTZ's greatest assets as a minerals parent is now its reputation in the industry. It is seen as a good partner and a reliable investor, able to identify sound opportunities and to contribute in a major way to their successful completion. For this reason, it receives an unusually high flow of opportunities to participate in new investments from local companies, governments, and banks, which in turn allows it to be more selective and discriminating in the investments it makes. As a senior manager in another minerals company put it to us, rather ruefully: "RTZ has got into virtually every one of the real "cherries" that have come up in the last 20 years."

During the 1990s, RTZ has begun to focus more on opportunities to give targeted technical support to local management teams. Although it has always stressed the importance of local operating company autonomy and has avoided interfering in local operations, the size and spread of RTZ's minerals operations now give it a unique ability to develop and share skills in specialist technical areas that are of relevance to most of its minerals businesses. For example, we were told about a $70 million investment in one operating company that had had an 18-month payback, and which had depended on some new technology that RTZ's technical staff had been able to offer to the company for extracting low-grade ores. Specialist technical staff at the center are available to local management, but RTZ is careful to avoid imposing them in a way that would curtail the independence of local companies. "They give you an objective, but they don't tell you how to achieve it. You can always get advice from head office if you need it, but basically it is up to you to find the right way forward," was a comment from the president of RTZ Brazil.

RTZ's portfolio now concentrates on its *heartland businesses* in mining, metals, and minerals. During the late 1970s and early 1980s, however, the company went through an era of diversification away from minerals, based on the belief that the competitive environment in minerals was becoming unfavorable. RTZ was concerned about excess capacity and slower growth in many of their product areas, and was worried that local governments were increasingly hostile to foreign natural resource investors. The company therefore sought opportunities in new businesses that were not dependent on the metals price cycle and had a different risk profile. During the early 1980s, it acquired substantial businesses in cement, chemicals, and oil and gas.

As the 1980s progressed, however, RTZ became less and less comfortable with these new businesses. In cement, it came to realize that it faced entrenched competition in the United Kingdom from companies such as Rugby and Blue Circle, and to feel that its relatively low market share was a source of weakness. These problems might have been discerned before entering the business, given a better understanding of the cement business. After initial successes in oil and gas, the investment requirements for further participation and development in the North Sea began to escalate, and as Ian Strachan, then finance director and now deputy chief executive, put it: "We were horror-struck at spending these amounts in areas where we had no expertise and no basis for control." Chemicals, which were furthest from the minerals heartland, presented even greater problems. These businesses did not involve major capital expenditures, required high levels of product development and technical work for specific customer applications, and were less price sensitive than the more commodity-oriented minerals businesses. What is more, they took RTZ into completely new products and technologies. Bob Wilson, RTZ's chief executive, described the problem vividly: "We couldn't even pronounce the names of the products, leave alone understand the markets or the technologies." By the end of the 1980s, RTZ had therefore sold its businesses in all of these new areas. In 1993, it also announced the sale of most of its Pillar subsidiary. Pillar was a diversified light engineering and construction division, originally created during the 1960s to integrate forward into downstream businesses. However its parenting needs and opportunities were very different from those of the heartland minerals businesses, and RTZ concluded that it did not fit within its portfolio.

The cash released by the disposal of the nonheartland businesses has allowed RTZ to make substantial fresh investments that reemphasize its commitment to the minerals businesses. In 1989, it acquired the bulk of BP's Minerals businesses for £2.25 billion; in 1993 it spent over $1 billion on U.S. coal acquisitions; and it has made a number of major investments in its existing businesses, including $880 million on a new copper smelter for Kennecott.

RTZ is an outstanding parent of minerals businesses, as its success within the industry demonstrates. It seems to have been able to participate in more good projects and to attract more entrepreneurial local managers than other rivals, and it has shown exceptional investment judgment. These characteristics, coupled with its constantly developing technical skills, suggest that it has achieved parenting advantage in its heartland businesses. The minerals industry, of course, remains cyclical, and RTZ is not invulnerable to the downturns. However, its spread of minerals interests gives some protection against excessive exposure to any individual mineral or metal. What is more, as a well-resourced parent, RTZ has opportunities at the bottom of the cycle to make keenly priced acquisitions and investments, as the 1993 acquisitions of Nerco and Cordero Mining, which establish RTZ as a major U.S. coal producer, demonstrate. RTZ is right to have concluded that it is better to concentrate on the cyclical minerals industry, in which it holds parenting advantage, than to diversify into other businesses, in which it lacks parenting advantage.

In our view, the development of RTZ's corporate strategy over the past two decades shows the importance and value of parenting advantage as a guiding principle. In businesses where the company has held parenting advantage, it has grown and prospered. In other businesses, it has encountered difficulties. And over time, the focus of the corporate strategy has moved increasingly onto those businesses where it holds parenting advantage, and onto those aspects of parenting that are most important in creating advantage.

CONDITIONS FOR VALUE CREATION AND PARENTING ADVANTAGE

The four companies described in this chapter all have successful corporate strategies that include an important component of stand-alone value creation. In this section, we will lay out more fully the conditions that must be satisfied for corporate strategies to create value through stand-alone influence, and we will illustrate these conditions from the companies we have researched. We will then identify the additional requirements that must be met to achieve parenting advantage.

Opportunities for Stand-Alone Value Creation

For a parent to create stand-alone value, there must be unfulfilled potential in its businesses. Furthermore, there must be a particular role for the parent in bringing about improved performance. We shall discuss the circumstances in which such parenting opportunities can arise, and we will argue that, to create stand-alone value, a company's corporate strategy must be based on specific performance improvement opportunities in its businesses.

Weak Management.   If businesses have weak or incompetent management teams, there are obvious opportunities for a parent to add value. Companies such as Dover, BTR, and Emerson frequently create value by ratcheting up the performance of businesses, which were previously run by managers who were insufficiently able or motivated to achieve their full potential.

The ability to find businesses run by weak managers has been the basis of many successful corporate strategies. Yet the opportunity this has presented may diminish in the future.[20] The pressures of competition at the business level, coupled with a capital market capable of allocating funds to profitable uses and replacing nonperforming managements, should reduce the number of weak managers. But, in reality, capital markets are slow to discipline poor performance. The mechanisms of corporate governance make it difficult for external investors to influence a weak management unless their performance has resulted in a crisis. Even companies that are, by common consent, performing well below par often continue with the same senior management for several years. Without significant changes in corporate governance, and in the relationship between large investors and the companies they invest in, many businesses will continue to be run by less competent managements,[21] and will provide opportunities for acquisitive corporate parents to create value.

But stand-alone parenting does not have to rely exclusively on business management incompetence to create value. There are other parenting opportunities, which would exist even if management teams were to become universally competent.

Difficult Businesses for External Capital Markets.   Some businesses are particularly difficult for external investors to understand. If the technology is complicated and difficult to grasp for nonexperts, as in pharmaceuticals or biotechnology; if investments only pay off after very long periods, as in many natural resource businesses; if the business faces unusual risks, for example from political upheavals in distant countries or from rapid changes in consumer fashions; in all these circumstances normal capital providers such as banks and equity markets will struggle to arrive at good decisions about a business. A competent management team that is performing well may not find it possible to obtain support for worthwhile investments, while other companies may be able to raise funding for projects that a better informed and more expert investor would reject.

In these businesses, a knowledgeable parent can play a particularly valuable role. The capital market interfaces with the parent, relying on the parent's overall reputation and performance to guide its decisions; and the parent deals with the businesses, allocating resources, approving plans, and monitoring performance with a sensitivity and judgment that it would be unreasonable to expect of external investors. We have described RTZ's support for the Escondida copper mine as an example.

It can again be argued that the increasing efficiency and specialization of capital providers will erode this opportunity over time. Venture capital or other specialized funds may be able to provide the expertise that has previously only resided in parent companies. However, we do not expect such funds to eliminate the opportunity for a parent. Parents will continue to have access to much more information from inside their businesses and to be able to question their managers in much more depth than even the most specialized external investors. Therefore we see a continuing opportunity for parent companies to create value by supporting good investments that might not get funding from the capital markets.[22]

Conflict between Managers' and Other Stakeholders' Interests. Managers running businesses have a variety of interests and objectives. These may include personal goals such as preservation of a power base, expansion of an empire, improvement in life-style through more luxurious office space, better corporate entertainment facilities, or shorter working hours. Such goals can evidently conflict with the interests of other stakeholders such as customers, employees and, in particular, shareholders and investors. This is a matter of management motivation rather than management competence. However, as with management competence, there are particular opportunities for a parent to prevent behavior that would be detrimental to other stakeholders.

We do not suggest that business managers are typically Machiavellian schemers, plotting ways to feather their own nests at the expense of everyone else, nor that corporate parents are free from any self-interested motivations of their own. However, we do believe that there are circumstances where business managers face particular temptations. For example, managers in cash cow businesses are liable to want to reinvest more in their own businesses than may be justified by the opportunities they face. Such investments are attractive to business managers because they represent new, expansionist challenges in an otherwise more mature situation, and can open up wider fields of interest, opportunity, and power. Sometimes, such investments pay handsome commercial rewards; more often, they destabilize what should be highly profitable businesses. Parents such as BTR and Hanson have specialized in correcting temptations of this kind.

Temptations also arise in businesses that face the need for radical change. Managers—and their loyal subordinates—may have their careers invested in a given business structure or in the preeminence of certain functional skills. It may, for example, be difficult for the heads of businesses that have previously been defined as national entities to accept that a new strategy is needed in which they will be subordinate to a worldwide business entity. A parent such as Emerson can add value by overcoming resistance of this kind.

We therefore believe that parents may face opportunities to redress these temptations.[23] But, by the same token, it is important for the parent itself to avoid falling into such natural temptations as the desire to diversify into new businesses rather than to pay free cash flow out to investors, to preserve the corporate entity at all costs even if it adds no value to the businesses, or even to relocate the corporate offices into more sumptuous premises. To recognize that there can be a role for the parent in preventing the businesses from succumbing to temptations is not by any means to believe that the parent itself is beyond temptation.

Specialist Expertise.   It is evident that many businesses can benefit from skills or resources possessed by their parent companies. Often, however, this is a matter of rectifying management weaknesses in the businesses, which we have already discussed, or the result of specialist corporate staff expertise, which we shall discuss more fully in Chapter 8.[24]

There are, however, circumstances in which the senior line management in the parent can provide valuable specialist expertise or guidance to a competent management team. This is particularly evident when businesses encounter the need for major change and must face upheavals in their strategies. It may be a matter of rapid growth (or decline) in their markets; it may involve a radical change in technology; or it may require a fundamental shift in priorities, for example from a strategy to gain market share to a strategy of consolidation. Such changes may call for new skills that the existing management of the business did not previously need. A competent team will, over time, acquire these new skills, but a parent can often accelerate the learning process.[25]

Furthermore, parents that have experience of similar transitions in other businesses may have built up specialist expertise in assisting with them. For example, BTR has wide experience and expertise in parenting businesses that face the need for cost reduction and turnaround strategies, and Canon[26] has skills and experience in parenting businesses facing rapidly changing technological possibilities. The transition management skills of the parent are particularly relevant because businesses can become overcommitted to a prevailing strategy;[27] attachment to the status quo creates blinkers and barriers to change.

An Informed but Objective Second View.   Many corporate parents believe that there is unfulfilled potential in most businesses and

that the informed but objective second view provided by a parent can almost always help to optimize performance.

We accept that a parent can often play this sort of role. It may introduce a somewhat different perspective from the views held by the managers in the businesses. It may be more dispassionate in reviewing the results from following a favored strategy. It may simply provide a useful sounding board for testing new ideas.[28] But, without more tangible improvement opportunities, these activities are unlikely to add much value for a competent business management and certainly do not provide the basis for parenting advantage. Either the influence exercised by the parent is modest and therefore creates little value; or if more substantial, it runs considerable risks of distracting a competent management team and destroying value.

Corporate parents that can identify no specific parenting opportunities in their businesses, relying only on the generally beneficial effects of an informed but objective second view, need to think again about whether they can really justify their ownership of the businesses in question. Successful corporate strategies that create value need to be based on, and fit with, specific opportunities for performance improvement in the businesses.

Parenting Characteristics That Fit the Opportunities

To realize the unfulfilled stand-alone potential in their businesses, parents need suitable skills, resources, and other characteristics. Their parenting characteristics must match with the opportunities they are targeting.

The parent's mental maps must fit the opportunities and be conducive to good decisions and value-creating interventions. RTZ's success formula for the minerals business ("All you need to do is to have the lowest costs in the business") is a case in point, as is BTR's belief that, in mature, manufacturing businesses, a focus on margin rather than volume is preferable.

The parent's structures, systems, and processes can be vital for bringing about value creation. BTR's profit planning process is a highly effective and integral part of its corporate strategy. Similarly, Dover's subsidiary structure and informal approach to parenting its businesses are essential to its value creation. These companies have very different management processes, but in both cases, the processes are designed to fit well with the focus of their value creation.

The parent's staff functions and services can play an important role, as we shall discuss in more depth in Chapter 8. But we have already seen, for example, that Emerson's strategic planning staff are closely involved in the success of its planning conferences, and that RTZ's capital expenditure reviews benefit from the advice of several expert staff functions. The parent's functions and services must match the stand-alone parenting opportunities.

It is hardly necessary to stress the part played by the senior people in the parent, and the key role of the skills they bring to the task. Strong chief executives, together with the teams they have assembled around them, personally drive through the value creation in their companies. For example, Emerson's confrontational approach to strategic planning works well and adds value; but, in many companies, a confrontational strategic planning process leads to resentments, secrecy, and bruised feelings. The difference lies in Chuck Knight's skill at handling the process in a way that is constructive and motivational for business managers. This is much more about the way that the management process is operated, and the skills of the people who operate it, than about its formal design.

Lastly, decentralization contracts need to focus the parent on those issues where it believes it can create value, and away from issues of less importance or potential. Dover emphasizes people appointments, and tends not to interfere in most other aspects of its businesses. RTZ also embraces decentralization, but does see a role for the parent on a wider range of issues, especially those related to major investments, such as commodity price forecasting, project management and supervision, and technical aspects of mine planning.

To succeed in stand-alone value creation, the parent needs characteristics that give it the ability to realize the stand-alone parenting opportunities in its businesses. All the successful parents we have researched have built parenting characteristics that are tailored to the sort of stand-alone value that they aspire to create in their businesses.

Avoidance of Value Destruction

Good parenting is as much about avoiding value destruction as it is about value creation. All parents, even those that have identified significant value creation opportunities for which they have suitable parenting characteristics, run the risk of destroying value through negative influence in areas in which their parenting characteristics are less appropriate. We have seen, for example, that each of the companies we have described has been less successful in certain sorts of businesses.

In discussing how to avoid value destruction, corporate managers talked again and again about the importance of a "feel" for the businesses in their portfolios. This feel is a sense of how to compete effectively in the business. It covers issues such as what sorts of managers succeed best in running the business, what strategies and targets are appropriate, what sort of management processes are most suitable for it. An understanding of how to compete effectively in a business is a precondition for creating value through any form of parenting influence. Without a good feel for its businesses, the parent will almost certainly destroy value, since it is always liable to be exerting the wrong sorts of pressure, for the wrong sorts of reasons, through the wrong sorts of processes. Referring to BP's parenting of its ill-fated minerals diversification, one manager stated graphically: "The problem was that the BP managing directors couldn't really get to grips with the minerals business or feel that they understood it. There was always that vestige of suspicion about the business, that in turn led to a temptation to say "no" to proposals from the business, or, alternatively, if they said yes, to say yes for the wrong reasons."

Given a feel for a business, the mental maps that the parent employs to guide its parenting of the business are likely to be suitable. These mental maps include biases, instincts, success formulas and decision criteria. They are often expressed as rules of thumb such as "If the gross margin falls below 35 percent, you know you're in trouble," or "If new products can't command a price premium of 10 percent, they shouldn't be launched," or "No one should be promoted to managing director without at least two years' experience in the sales function." The parent's mental maps also guide judgments about the sorts of management processes, staff functions, resources, and overall parenting style that will be effective for influencing the businesses. Mental maps help the parent to interpret events in the business and provide a way of focusing attention and arriving at decisions.[29] Without some well-developed mental maps to guide them, there is no way that Alan Jackson could handle profit plan reviews for BTR's 1,300 profit centers or that Chuck Knight could add value in the strategic planning conferences for Emerson's 40 divisions. It is by having a good feel, a good mental map for their businesses, that successful corporate parents overcome the 10 percent versus 100 percent paradox.

Mental maps that work well in one sort of business are often inappropriate in others. Indeed, many parents find it easier to specify the characteristics of the businesses for which they believe they have appropriate mental maps than to articulate the maps themselves. Often the response patterns, biases, and rules of thumb are embedded in the parent's behavior rather than explicitly stated. Some key aspects may be clearly laid out and "top of mind." Many other aspects, however, can only be inferred from examining the parent's behavior patterns. The parent will normally acknowledge that these patterns exist and recognize them when they are made explicit, but will not find it easy to give anything like a full list of them. We have found, however, that successful parents can usually lay out the characteristics of the businesses for which they believe they have a good feel. Dover concentrates on modest technology, niche, manufacturing businesses; RTZ on mining and minerals businesses; and so on.

The depth of feel that a parent company needs depends on the nature of the decentralization contract it establishes with its businesses. A "hands-on" parent, such as Shell or Canon,[30] is liable to be drawn into disputes about technical tradeoffs and priorities, new product positioning issues, and decisions about capacity expansion and sourcing. It therefore needs mental maps that will guide it on a whole variety of detailed, business-specific matters, as well as on broader issues of strategy and performance. A "hands-off" parent, such as Dover or Hanson, concentrates on only a few issues that it regards as vital, delegating responsibility for other matters to the business's management team. It consequently has less need for an in-depth feel for its businesses since it exercises its influence on fewer issues. However, even a parent that believes in a high degree of decentralization must be involved, as the representative of the shareholders, in certain minimum areas of stand-alone influence, such as key appointments and resource allocation decisions, agreeing the businesses' overall plans, strategies, and targets, monitoring their performance, and intervening in the event of crises. At the least, it needs mental maps that will guide it in these areas, and a sufficient feel for its businesses to be able to avoid destroying value through its influence on them.[31] In general, parents need a sufficient depth of feel for their businesses to discharge the responsibilities that the decentralization contract allocates to them.

A feel for a business is typically not arrived at through a process of careful analysis and data gathering. Rather, it follows from long experience of managing, and of parenting, businesses of a particular sort, from which an intuitive grasp of the things that matter most in the business is developed. A more analytical, intellectual understanding of the business is usually no substitute for this intuitive feel, since the parent normally has too little time to devote to the business to undertake detailed analyses of the issues it faces.[32] Furthermore—and even more importantly—many of the major parental interventions, for example in responding to crises or choosing between two similarly qualified candidates for a top position, depend ultimately on judgment calls. It is here that a sufficient feel for the business is indispensable.

Personal experience in one business can carry over and remain valid for other businesses, provided they are similar. BTR, for example, has hundreds of different profit centers, and the members of the parenting team have certainly not had close personal experience with all of them. Nevertheless the bulk of the profit centers are industrial manufactured product businesses, of moderate technology and capital intensity, often in noncyclical, niche markets. As such, the key competitive success factors, the cost structures, the critical ratios and targets, the appropriate reactions to a market downturn, the major risk categories, and the profiles of successful general managers tend to be common. Thus, Alan Jackson and his team are comfortable with the sort of parenting issues that arise. The parent's feel normally extends to other businesses whose key success factors are similar to the businesses in which they have personal experience.

Different members of the parenting team may have a feel for somewhat different sorts of businesses. The chief executive may have a background in the core businesses of the company, while other members of the team may have experience in different areas. Equally, the divisional parenting team may have a different or deeper feel for their businesses, when compared with the corporate team. Ideally, the different members of the parenting organization will complement each other and enlarge the area within which the parent has an adequate feel. However, the danger is that the different members of the parenting organization take responsibility for different parts of the company, rather than acting collectively as a team, in which case there is little reason to keep the parts of the company together. Furthermore the chief executive will always be tempted—and occasionally required—to intervene on issues in businesses for which he or she lacks a feel, rather than deferring to others' better judgment. Ideally, all members of the parenting team need a sufficient feel for each business in the portfolio to avoid these dangers.

Corporate parents that lack a sufficient feel for a business—often the case with diversifications into new and unfamiliar fields—or whose feel for a business is faulty are likely to destroy value. With no feel for the business, the parent is likely to dither indecisively when faced with decisions and to have difficulty in engaging in constructive debate about issues. While the problem can be reduced by delegating more responsibility to the businesses, the requirement to be involved on certain key minimum parenting issues means that parents that have insufficient feel for their businesses are always liable to damage their performance. With a faulty feel for the business, the parent will wade in, imposing inappropriate objectives and targets, offering unhelpful advice and focusing away from the issues that matter most. A "wrong" feel is even more dangerous than a lack of feel, and inevitably leads to large amounts of value destruction. If BTR's sense of appropriate profit margins in its businesses was wrong, it would destroy substantial value through its profit planning process. A further condition for net value creation is therefore that the parent should include within its portfolio only businesses for which it has a sufficient feel to avoid value-destroying influences that overcome the beneficial influences it provides.

Stand-Alone Value Creation and Parenting Advantage

For parenting advantage, the corporate parent must not only meet the conditions for stand-alone value creation that we have laid out. It must create more value than other rivals would.

For stand-alone influence to provide the basis of parenting advantage, either the corporate strategy must be targeted on stand-alone opportunities that are unusual or the parent must have characteristics that are specially suitable for realizing the opportunities it is targeting, or both. In our descriptions of Dover, BTR, Emerson, and RTZ, we have described their stand-alone value creation insights and their distinctive parenting characteristics, and we have indicated why we believe that these companies' corporate strategies create more value than the bulk of their rivals.

Successful corporate parents that achieve parenting advantage through stand-alone influence also have a clearer sense than their rivals of the criteria that define their heartland businesses, and they act more decisively than their rivals to focus their portfolios on heartland businesses. The moves that companies such as Dover, BTR, Emerson, and RTZ have made to focus their portfolios on certain sorts of businesses, and to avoid or exit from others, demonstrate the importance of understanding the heartland business criteria and using them to guide portfolio moves.

In Chapter 11, we will explore more fully the ingredients of parenting advantage, summarizing the nature of the value creation insights, the distinctive parenting characteristics, and the heartland businesses in the companies we have researched. However, in all the companies, stand-alone influence plays an important role in the corporate strategy. Unless a company's stand-alone influence on its businesses is positive, it is most unlikely to achieve parenting advantage.

SUMMARY

In this chapter, we have described how different parents create value through stand-alone influence. We have also stated the conditions that are necessary to overcome the intrinsic problems, which, due to the 10 percent versus 100 percent paradox, so often occur in the stand-alone parenting relationship.

Questions that any corporate parent needs to address concerning its stand-alone parenting are:

- Have we identified specific stand-alone performance improvement opportunities in our businesses? Why do they exist, and are we, as a parent, focusing our efforts on these opportunities? Are the opportunities we have seen of more potential value than those of rival parents?
- Do we have characteristics as a parent that mean we are well placed to realize these parenting opportunities and what are we doing to build them up further? Are our characteristics more suitable than those of rival parents for realizing the opportunities?
- Do we have a sufficient feel for all of the businesses in our portfolio? If not, are we sure that we are not destroying value

through our influence in those businesses where we lack a sufficient feel?

- What criteria define the heartland businesses, in which we can both add value and avoid destroying value? How much of our portfolio consists of heartland businesses, and what moves are we making to increase the proportion of heartland businesses in our portfolio?

Parents that can answer all these questions positively will be well on the way to achieving parenting advantage.

NOTES

1. See, for example, Sebastian Green and Dean F. Berry, *Cultural, Structural and Strategic Change in Management Buyouts,* London: Macmillan, 1991; Michael Jensen, "Corporate Control and the Politics of Finance," *Journal of Applied Corporate Finance,* vol. 4, no. 2, Summer 1991, pp. 13–33; Steven Kaplan, "The Effects of Management Buyouts on Operating Performance and Value," *Journal of Financial Economics,* vol. 23, 1989, pp. 217–254; John Kitching, "Early Returns on LBOs," *Harvard Business Review,* November–December 1989, pp. 74–81; William F. Long and David J. Ravenscraft, "LBOs, Debt and R&D Intensity," *Strategic Management Journal,* vol. 14, 1993, pp. 119–135; Anju Seth and John Easterwood, "Strategic Redirection in Large Management Buyouts: The Evidence from Post-Buyout Restructuring Activity," *Strategic Management Journal,* vol. 14, 1993, pp. 251–273. These authors show that performance tends to improve in the immediate aftermath of a buyout. It is less easy to research the longer-term effect of buyouts, in part because the impact of the buyout as such becomes harder and harder to disentangle from other factors. Some commentators suggest that the long-term effects are less favorable, but there is, as yet, little systematic evidence to support this view.

2. See Michael Goold, Andrew Campbell, and Kathleen Luchs, "Strategies and Styles Revisited: Strategic Planning and Financial Control," *Long Range Planning,* October 1993.

3. Premier Brands has subsequently been acquired, at a price that made the buyout team and their investors a great deal of money, by Hillsdown Holdings, an acquisitive company that operates mainly in food businesses (poultry and eggs, fresh meat and bacon, processing and distribution). Hillsdown follows a highly decentralized management approach, and is more accustomed than Cadbury Schweppes to competing in unbranded and less strongly branded product categories. It appears that Premier's results have continued to be satisfactory under Hillsdown's ownership, although margins fell during the recession in the United Kingdom in the early 1990s.

4. This is part of the short-termism debate. See, for example, Michael Porter, "Capital Disadvantage: America's Failing Capital Investment System,"

Harvard Business Review, September–October 1992, and Paul Marsh, *"Short-Termism on Trial,"* Institutional Fund Managers Association, London, 1990.

5. The sorts of stand-alone influence that companies emphasize reflect their parenting styles. For example, Financial Control style companies emphasize their role in budgetary control, whereas Strategic Planning companies emphasize their contribution to long-term strategies. Indeed, the emphasis on short-term profitability control of Financial Control companies is incompatible with the encouragement of a long-term strategic perspective that is found in Strategic Planning companies. See Appendix C for further discussion.

6. See George D. Smith and Robert Sobel, *"Dover Corporation: A History 1955–1989,"* Cambridge, MA: Winthrop Group, 1991, p. 138.

7. See Appendix B for a fuller discussion.

8. See Michael Goold and Andrew Campbell, *Strategies and Styles,* Oxford: Basil Blackwell, 1987, for further description of BTR's management processes in the mid-1980s. Though there have been changes in detail since that time, the philosophy remains the same.

9. Other members of the profit center's management team may be invited to attend, depending on the agenda, and the corporate main board director ultimately responsible for the profit center may also choose to attend.

10. The GCEs report either to Alan Jackson, the chief executive, or to Bob Faircloth, the chief operating officer, or to one of two other main board members.

11. One form is dedicated to examining all provisions that have been made, an area that managers often use to smooth performance figures.

12. "The ratios and forms are very illuminating. They showed me things I should have bloody well known: for example relationships between different elements of costs in the business, and how their movements compare to movements in price," was the comment of one manager. See Goold and Campbell, *Strategies and Styles,* p. 303.

13. The idea that the parent should, at least, be able to provide an informed second view is discussed later in this chapter.

14. In 1993, a computerized analysis package was introduced, which generated the required charts from specified data that the division had to input.

15. Charles F. Knight, "Emerson Electric: Consistent Profits, Consistently," *Harvard Business Review,* January–February 1992, p. 62.

16. See Charles F. Knight, "Emerson Electric: Consistent Profits, Consistently," *Harvard Business Review,* January–Feburary 1992.

17. Joe Adorjan, for many years head of corporate development and now Emerson's president, describes Emerson's diversification and growth as "concentric." "The original core of Emerson was in motors, fans and defense. Most of the other businesses bear some relationship to these original businesses, either in terms of common technology or markets, or at least in terms of common strategic issues. All the businesses are manufactured products, in

electrical, electromechanical or electronic technologies, and they all face similar sorts of key success factors and issues."

18. See Appendix C.

19. In mining operations, difficult decisions must be made about how much ore to extract and by what means. Based on limited exploration data, a plan must be drawn up that makes tradeoffs between the likely cost of extraction versus the likely revenues. This is referred to as "conceptual mine planning," and makes use of sophisticated software for modeling alternative options as well as experience in different mines around the world.

20. See Michael E. Porter, "From Competitive Advantage to Corporate Strategy," *Harvard Business Review*, vol. 65, 1987.

21. The view that weak managers can be no more than a transitory phenomenon goes back to classical economics, where the forces of competition supposedly ensure that all surviving businesses are efficient. But economic theory now recognizes that the models of classical economics are not a good representation of the real corporate world. Investors have information that is far from perfect on the businesses they invest in and can only bring about changes in strategy or management with considerable difficulty. "Transaction costs" exist, particularly where there is a separation between owners and managers of a business. These costs provide a theoretical underpinning for the "stickiness" that we find in practice in replacing weak management teams. See Oliver E. Williamson, *Markets and Hierarchies*, New York: Free Press, 1975, and *The Economic Institutions of Capitalism*, New York: Free Press, 1985. See also David J. Teece, "Transaction Cost Economics and the Multinational Enterprise: An Assessment," *Journal of Economic Behaviour and Organization*, 1985, no. 7.

22. A theoretical basis for this belief is again provided by transaction cost economics. Given the sorts of information necessary to make good decisions in these businesses, there is a particularly strong case for "internalizing" investment and resource allocation decisions within the firm.

23. The whole question of the conflict between the personal interests of managers and the interest of owners, where management and ownership are separated, has been extensively examined from a theoretical perspective in a branch of behavioral economics called "agency theory." Agency theory reviews the relationship between owners and their "agents" (the managers), and examines the distortions and costs introduced into economically efficient outcomes by these "agency" relationships, in which the interests of owners and their agents can diverge. The parent may be seen as a device for the owners to monitor the performance of their agents in the businesses, and to ensure that their interests are protected, in a relatively cost-effective fashion. Others have argued that the real agency problem for owners is to prevent parent companies from ignoring the owners' interests in the decisions that they make, and that parents should be replaced by a direct relationship between more accountable business managers and more active investors. See M. C. Jensen and W. H. Meckling, "Theory of the Firm: Management Behaviour, Agency Costs and Ownership Structure," *Journal of Financial Economics,*

vol. 3, 1976 pp. 305–360; S. Baiman, "Agency Research in Managerial Accountancy: A Survey," *Journal of Accounting Literature,* vol 1, 1982, pp. 154–213; Michael C. Jensen, "The Eclipse of the Public Corporation," *Harvard Business Review,* September–October 1989.

24. Specialist expertise is best understood in terms of the resource-based theory of the firm. See Chapters 4 and 8.

25. There is increasing attention in the academic world to the idea of the learning organization. One of the best established principles concerns the difficulty that organizations have "unfreezing" sufficiently from past practices to see the need for new approaches. In order to learn, the first step is to open up awareness of the need to learn. A parent can help to create an awareness of this need, as well as provide coaching for the new skills. See Chapter 10 for further discussion of learning within organizations.

26. See Chapter 7 for a full discussion of Canon's corporate strategy.

27. See, for example, B. Staw, "The Escalation of Commitment to a Course of Action," *Academy of Management Review,* vol. 6, 1981, pp. 577–587.

28. Ideally, parent managers should be selected for their abilities in these areas. However, by no means all parents have the sensitivity and perception to provide a second view that is helpful to their businesses.

29. Many writers have stressed the extent to which we all interpret our experiences in terms of our prior convictions: Bertrand Russell, for example, stated: "Every man, wherever he goes, is encompassed by a cloud of convictions, which move with him like flies on a summer day." This phenomenon has also been widely observed in the field of management, and many experts have claimed that managers invariably interpret events by using mental maps or recipes or formulas. See, for example, Ari Ginsberg, "Connecting Diversification to Performance: A Sociocognitive Approach," *Academy of Management Review,* vol. 15, no. 3, 1990, and "Constructing the Business Portfolio: A Cognitive Model of Diversification," *Journal of Management Studies,* vol. 26, July 1989; Richard R. Nelson and Sidney G. Winter, *An Evolutionary Theory of Economic Change,* Cambridge, MA: Harvard University Press, 1982; J. C. Spender, *Industry Recipes: The Nature and Sources of Managerial Judgement,* Oxford: Basil Blackwell, 1989; Karl E. Weick, *The Social Psychology of Organizing,* New York: Random House, 1969; P. M. Senge, *The Fifth Discipline—The Art and Practice of the Learning Organization,* New York: Doubleday/Currency, 1992.

30. See Chapters 7 and 8 for fuller discussion of these companies' corporate strategies.

31. The depth of feel needed to discharge these minimum stand-alone parenting activities is by no means trivial. Recognizing the right sort of managers and targets for a business, for example, is not easy; it requires a level of feel that not all parents possess.

32. It is partly because feel depends more on experience and intuition than intellect and analysis, more on "hearts" than "minds," that we have chosen the term "heartland" businesses.

7 LINKAGE INFLUENCE

In addition to influencing the stand-alone performance of its businesses, the corporate parent is able to encourage or require its businesses to work more closely with each other. We refer to this as linkage influence.[1] Linkage influence creates value when it leads the businesses to achieve increased benefits from internal trading, sharing of skills and resources, coordination of product ranges, or other forms of mutual relationships. Exhibit 7–1 is a list of the types of benefit that can be achieved.

If a business has no parent, it will still form linkages with other businesses. It will, for example, buy from some, sell to others, join trade associations, exchange information, sometimes even share distribution facilities or a manufacturing plant. The parent's influence is beneficial only if it creates more value through linkages than the businesses would if they were independent. A crucial assumption behind linkage influence must, therefore, be that the parent can help to realize opportunities for valuable linkages that the businesses themselves would overlook or avoid, or can improve relationships between businesses.

Linkages can be influenced through many different vehicles. These include sourcing policies, transfer pricing mechanisms, cross-unit task forces, reward and recognition systems, staff rotation, central policies or guidelines, arbitration processes, central experts, forums to encourage sharing, and straightforward information exchanges. General management processes such as budgeting, strategic planning, and capital expenditure authorization, which were discussed in Chapter 6, and functional influence, which will be examined in Chapter 8, are also relevant.

Linkage influence can be an important source of added value and performance improvement. But, as with stand-alone influence, the parent can also damage performance through inappropriate pressures and

139

EXHIBIT 7–1   Linkage benefits that can be achieved

---

1. Improved internal trading.

2. Benefits from coordinating strategies:
   —Avoid unhelpful competition.
   —Avoid unintentional damage.
   —Help outmaneuver competitors.

3. Pooling power relative to outside groups:
   —Suppliers.
   —Employees/unions.
   —Customers.
   —Shareholders/bankers.
   —Governments.
   —Pressure groups.

4. Better utilization and development of tangible assets:
   —Physical plant, machinery, buildings.
   —Logistics and distribution facilities.
   —Salesforces, functions, departments.
   —Databases, brochures, experts.

5. Better utilization and development of intangible assets:
   —Ideas.
   —Knowledge.
   —Skills and competences.
   —Contacts and relationships.
   —Reputation and brands.

---

excessive overhead costs. Although the search for linkage benefits, often referred to as "synergy," has been a powerful prompt to parental involvement, our research suggests that such involvement is frequently ill-advised, badly thought through, and poorly executed. As a result, linkage influence is often a major destroyer of value rather than a source of value creation.

Our discussion of linkage influence in this chapter will therefore parallel our treatment of stand-alone influence in the preceding chapter. We shall explore the causes of both value destruction and value creation through linkage influence, with the intention of identifying the conditions under which corporate strategies create value through linkage influence. We shall also discuss the role of linkage influence in building parenting advantage.

VALUE DESTRUCTION

Linkage influence can destroy value in two different ways. One is the overhead cost associated with the parent's attempts to influence or manage linkages. This cost can be considerable, since significant numbers of central staff may be involved in determining, codifying, communicating and policing linkage policies. The other is the less visible cost of wasted business management time, lengthened decision processes, inappropriate compromises, loss of control or accountability, and sapped enthusiasm. As with stand-alone influence, these less easily quantifiable costs are often far more damaging than the direct overhead costs involved.

Examples of Value Destruction

In our research, we encountered many examples of value destruction due to inappropriate linkage influence. Typical examples include businesses that were forced to share purchasing, leading to "lowest common denominator" decisions with which few were happy; businesses that were required to devote time to joint conferences and exploratory meetings to identify synergies, despite the fact that little or no value had ever emerged from these events; and businesses that were pushed into using common marketing policies when a more focused approach was needed. As a result, many managers have an allergic reaction to the very mention of the word "synergy."

A diversified worldwide consulting firm provides a classic example of the dangers of synergistic visions by the parent. As part of a "one firm" policy, it strongly encouraged its different business units in each country to seek synergies by sharing computer systems and office space. It also insisted on a "coordinated" approach to clients and established client managers to manage the client relationship for the whole firm and to cross-sell its various services. Unfortunately, these initiatives backfired. The shared billing system, which cost several million dollars to develop, was considered by most units to be more expensive and less useful than their previous systems; indeed, several units used their old systems in parallel to ensure reliability. Sharing office space proved useful for a number of small units, especially new operations in Continental Europe. But, as each business grew, the importance of the small cost savings dwindled. The coordinated approach to client management was a disaster, since many clients resented the imposition of a gatekeeper between themselves and the providers of the specialist services they were buying, and most of the relationship managers were not familiar enough with the services of the different consulting operations to be effective. After the near collapse of some of the businesses, management was eventually refocused on distinct "lines of business." Although both profitability and market share increased subsequently, the scars of failed synergy remained. Many units now deliberately avoid contact with "sister operations" if opportunities for joint work arise.

Underlying Reasons for Value Destruction

As with stand-alone influence, there are underlying reasons for the difficulty that corporate parents find in adding value through linkage influence. These follow from the fact that business unit managers are perfectly able to collaborate with other businesses without parental involvement, if they perceive that it is beneficial to do so. Intelligent managers are quite capable of getting together and reaching a mutually beneficial agreement themselves. If the linkage opportunity benefits one business more than the other, or even destroys value in one while creating value in another, the managers can agree on a deal under which the benefits and costs are fairly shared out. What starts out as potentially a win-lose situation can be turned into a win-win by redistributing the value that is created. The existence of value-creating linkages is, therefore, no direct evidence that a parent is playing a useful role.

Where there is a genuine opportunity to create value, even competitors in different companies can form effective linkages. In the music industry, for example, the six major players (BMG, Sony, EMI, MCA/Geffen, Polygram, and WEA) compete aggressively for artist signings, chart positioning and market share. However, they also coordinate efforts around the world to reduce "piracy" (unauthorized commercial copying of music), share information on market trends, supply each other's production needs in markets that can support only one or two CD or vinyl plants, engage in joint distribution systems, and produce compilation albums that bring together tracks from their different artists. Similarly, within the same company, business units can agree to share information or coordinate buying activities without parental involvement. Such linkages are based on enlightened self-interest.

To add value through linkage influence, the parent must bring about linkages that would not have arisen through enlightened self-interest. In so doing, it must second-guess and improve on decisions from which it is necessarily distant. As a result, it can easily misperceive the potential size of linkage benefits, and impose costly or inappropriate linkage vehicles. In other words, it is liable to fall into all the traps of a centrally planned system that attempts to beat a market system. Linkage influence therefore raises a parallel concern to the 10 percent versus 100 percent paradox discussed in Chapter 6: How can a parent expect to judge linkage opportunities better, and manage their realization more effectively, than the business managers who are closest to them and who should themselves be pursuing any worthwhile opportunities? We shall refer to this concern as the "enlightened self-interest" paradox.

Indeed, the existence of a parent company can hamper the workings of enlightened self-interest: Merely bringing the businesses under joint ownership creates distortions that reduce the effectiveness of arm's-length dealings. In some cases, these distortions encourage linkage activity that would be better ignored. Thus many managers feel that, as a matter of principle, they should work more closely with members of the corporate family than with outsiders. Though this can foster helpful teamwork, it can also lead to low-value linkages and an excessively internal focus. For example, many companies that emphasize the need to spread best practice have focused on internal benchmarking, while ignoring external world standards. The company's own expert on a particular issue, or the company's most productive plant, is too readily seen as a suitable exemplar. As one manager summed up the danger: "In the land of the blind, the one-eyed man is king."

At the other extreme, opportunities for valuable internal linkages are often denied. Some managers admit that they deliberately conceal potential opportunities and avoid internal partners or suppliers, for fear of losing control of negotiations to some centralized procedure or third party. As one manager put it: "I would always prefer to deal with an outsider, because you don't have to watch your back on the political issues." There is also widespread concern that sensible one-off agreements can become precedents for other less appropriate agreements. As a result, opportunities are concealed to avoid initiating a process that could get out of control. Fear of pressure to overcoordinate can cause managers to hide opportunities or deny the existence of valid benefits.

Other distorting factors include poor monitoring of linkage costs, lack of clarity in internal communication and contracting, and political influences. Costs involved in internal linkages, particularly those in the parent company, are usually not monitored as closely as in external linkages. This can lead to the pursuit of marginal benefits, the use of inefficient mechanisms, and the inaccurate assessment of net gains. Internal communication and internal contracting are often sloppier than with outside parties. Internal customers, for example, may agree to use an in-house supplier but fail to clarify required service levels in the way that they would with an outsider. Typically, this leads to smoldering dissatisfaction as differences between the expectations of the two parties gradually emerge. Because the linkage is with a sister unit, there is less initial concern about clarifying details, supported by a belief that "we can work it out as we go along." In practice, this often leads to unpleasant surprises and misunderstandings. Lastly, the political implications of internal linkages also distort the market. A value-creating linkage that gives extra powers to a political rival may be blocked; a value-destroying linkage that cements a political alliance may be pursued.

Enlightened self-interest suggests that the most valuable linkages between business units should be identified and pursued by the interested parties without the need for parental influence, and that parental interference is seldom justified. Furthermore, simply bringing businesses into the ownership of a parent tends to distort the workings of enlightened self-interest and reduce the linkage benefits that would otherwise be achieved. As a result, parents often destroy value through their linkage influence.

VALUE CREATION

Despite the danger of value destruction, our research has convinced us that opportunities do arise for a parent to improve performance through linkage influence. The basis for these parenting opportunities is that blockages get in the way of enlightened self-interest. Managers are not always enlightened; self-interest does not always result in the best outcome. These blockages can inhibit valuable linkages from occurring, and provide opportunities for parents to create value.

Some opportunities to overcome blockages arise for reasons that directly parallel the circumstances in which stand-alone parenting opportunities occur: the presence of a weak management team; the temptation for managers to value personal interests and outcomes over those of other stakeholders; the need for specialist expertise to identify and eliminate certain blockages. Other circumstances in which opportunities to overcome blockages arise include lack of information about other units; competition between units; inertia and problems associated with establishing complex contracts between units. In all these circumstances, there can be opportunities for a parent to create value.

However, just as with stand-alone influence, to succeed in creating value, the parent's characteristics must be suitable for realizing the opportunities. For example, the parent needs to have sufficient knowledge and understanding of the businesses to pick suitable areas for intervention and to avoid destroying value through inappropriate pressures. Furthermore, it needs processes, skills and resources which will unlock potential value that the businesses would not achieve on their own.

When we examined stand-alone influence in Chapter 6, we focused on four main types of stand-alone value creation: through appointments, budgetary control, strategy reviews, and capital investment decisions. In analyzing linkage influence, we have found it more helpful to focus on different overall approaches to linkages, rather than on particular types on linkage. Although some parents place more emphasis on sharing best practice, while others concentrate more on resource sharing or internal sourcing, most parents target a combination of linkage benefits. More insight can be gained by understanding the fundamentally different approaches to linkage influence that companies take than by focusing on specific types of linkages.

Exhibit 7–2 illustrates the different approaches to linkage influence. At the top of the exhibit is a fully integrated, single business company. Moving clockwise, we start with Approach 1, in which two or more businesses are brought together under common ownership, but in which the parent attempts, as far as possible, to allow enlightened

EXHIBIT 7–2   Different linkage approaches

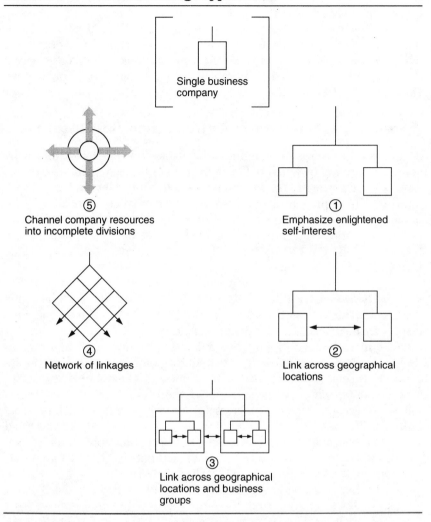

Single business company

⑤
Channel company resources into incomplete divisions

① Emphasize enlightened self-interest

④ Network of linkages

② Link across geographical locations

③ Link across geographical locations and business groups

self-interest to guide linkages. Under Approach 2, companies aim to influence linkages between essentially similar businesses operating in different geographic locations, but not across different business groups. With Approach 3, companies influence linkages both across geographic locations and across business groups. Under Approach 4, companies network their business units in a matrix that covers multiple dimensions. Finally, in Approach 5, we come to companies that maintain significant central resources, which their businesses draw off and feed into, and which also encourage linkages in other ways, such as through shared sales forces, functional matrices, and ad hoc task-forces. Further integration leads back to the single business company. There are no hard and fast boundaries between the approaches. They do, however, represent different roles and ambitions for the parent's linkage influence.[2]

To illustrate the different approaches, we will discuss five companies: BTR, Banc One, Unilever, ABB, and Canon. As in Chapter 6, we will follow our discussion of each company's approach to linkages with a discussion of their overall corporate strategy, bringing out how linkage value creation fits into the fuller picture.

Approach 1: Emphasize Enlightened Self-Interest

As previously discussed, enlightened self-interest can be distorted by common parental ownership. One approach to linkage influence, therefore, is to endeavor simply to emphasize and reinforce enlightened self-interest. This approach recognizes the danger of value destruction from inappropriate parental pressure. It also recognizes that the parent starts at a disadvantage and must work actively to restore the operation of a free market. It does not attempt, however, to create additional value through linkage influence.

BTR: SEPARATE PROFIT CENTERS.   Traditionally, BTR has been keen to emphasize that linkages between its businesses should only take place on the basis of enlightened self-interest. The center does not attempt to encourage or promote linkages, and does not attach great weight to benefits supposedly created for some undefined corporate good. If linkage benefits are to be achieved, they should accrue to specific units, whose managers should therefore pursue them themselves. As a result, internal linkages are treated very much like external linkages. Business managers do not anticipate central interference and so have no reason to conceal promising but uncertain opportunities. Negotiations with other units can take place without the fear that an unsatisfactory solution will be imposed by the head office.

BTR may not create extra value through linkage influence,[3] but it avoids value destruction. First, the parent does not incur overhead costs from coordinating departments and corporatewide initiatives. Second, and more importantly, it reduces the risk that internal linkages will be pursued or ignored for noneconomic reasons. Finally, it enhances the sense of ownership and responsibility at the business unit level. If the business is not performing, it cannot blame other parts of the company, or central pressure for inappropriate linkages. These benefits tie in well with the type of stand-alone influence that BTR exerts, and with its overall corporate strategy, which does not depend on encouraging linkages between its businesses.[4] Other companies that adopt this approach to linkage influence include Hanson and Dover.

The essence of the approach is that it avoids the potential problems with linkage influence rather than seeking the potential benefits. It is most effective in situations where business definitions are clear and stable, where linkages are either limited or relatively easy to identify and assess, and where local management focus and commitment can significantly improve performance. In contrast, it is not so effective where business definitions are unclear or changing, where linkages can have a significant impact on performance, where linkage opportunities are complex or contracting arrangements are difficult, and where valuable linkages do not align with the personal interests of business unit managers. Parents that adopt this approach therefore need businesses in their portfolios that are suitable, as well as the self-discipline to act in ways that support enlightened self-interest—even when the decisions made by the businesses seem suboptimal to the parent.

Approach 2: Link across Geographic Locations

Under Approach 2, the parent wishes to maintain an emphasis on clearly defined local business units, with separate profit accountability. But it also seeks to enhance linkages between these local units. The parent identifies potential linkage blockages and acts to "unblock" them.

While there are greater potential benefits from this approach, there are also greater risks. Even a parent that stresses voluntary cooperation between similar units may bring about unjustifiable and costly linkages. For example, a forum set up to share information on common customers may lead to a fruitless search for joint selling, even if no such opportunities exist. As one manager told us: "Merely bringing people together gives them the feeling that they really should be coming up with some joint activities, even if the meeting was only intended to explore possibilities." The more active role played by the parent under Approach 2 has a downside. However, we have found several companies, such as Banc One, in which this approach to linkages leads to major value creation.

BANC ONE: "UNCOMMON PARTNERSHIPS." Banc One is a uniquely successful bank holding company, based in Columbus, Ohio, that concentrates on retail banking for local communities. Banc One has made more than 100 bank acquisitions over the past 25 years, and has created one of the largest and most successful banks in the United States.

Rather than merging its acquisitions into a single operation, Banc One has maintained a number of distinct and separate entities (81 in 1993). "I feel much more comfortable having a decentralized organization rather than a strong, centralized one," says the CEO, John B. McCoy. "Our management structure is very decentralized with a president heading up the various affiliates. Each affiliate also has its own board of directors, its own business plan, and its own strategy for marketing and product pricing in its local territory. Consequently, each bank president is directly responsible for its performance."[5] All the affiliates are relatively free to design their own marketing strategies and pricing for their local markets.

But despite the decentralization philosophy, linkages mandated from the center play a significant role in guiding local decisions. All the local affiliates operate under the Banc One brand and follow certain common policies. For example, they are all required to concentrate on serving their local communities and to focus on three main measures of service quality: customer retention rates, response time for customer requests, and the proportion of "highly satisfied" customers. Their back office systems are converted to standard Banc One processes, and all data-processing operations are transferred to a central office in Springfield, Ohio, which, by 1992, had become the second biggest automated clearing house transaction processor in the United States. All affiliates also adopt the "Uniform Product Line," a standard Banc One range of products and services. More specialist services, such as corporate banking, credit card management, and trust activities are centralized or transferred to an affiliate bank with particular skills in that area. The focus for each bank is placed firmly on marketing to and servicing of local customers, and banks are encouraged to offer locally tailored services or products in addition to the Uniform Product Line.

Within this framework, there is strong pressure to spread best practice between the affiliate banks. A key role in spreading best practice is played by Banc One's uniquely detailed monthly reporting system, known as the Management Information Computer System (MICS). This enables all affiliates to gauge their performance against a range of other similarly focused retail banking operations, and identify both areas for improvement and potential leaders in "good practice." The information includes detailed performance measures covering at least 40 different product and market variables. This encourages "spirited competition among peers." McCoy believes that the opportunity to share good practice in a timely and efficient way is a major source of value: "Most people don't have anything to compare themselves to. We allow our guys to see who is doing things the best, and how they are doing it."[6] Implementation of the Uniform Product Line enhances the value of information sharing. As one vice president put it: "Unless all banks are operating the Uniform Product Line with the same systems, we are unable to have identical measures and performance statistics that can be compared across the banks."

The MICS performance statistics are reviewed with each affiliate each month. Every affiliate's performance is displayed and made available to every other affiliate. Poor performers are at the top of the list, good performers at the bottom, and the order is different for each performance variable. The focus is on differences from budget and comparative performance. The conversation is tuned to a discussion of what will be done to correct problem areas. The transparency of the data, the peer pressure it generates, and the relentless review of variances foster a performance orientation that is reinforced by a clear bonus formula. Bonuses are paid against an absolute performance indicator—return on assets. If the affiliate's return is below 1.1 percent of assets, there is no bonus. Above that level, there is a sliding scale. The focus on performance measures and variances is unique among major banks, but similar to that of the best retailers.

But Banc One's management approach is more than a tight financial management system generating a performance culture. It is designed to foster a focus on best practice, continuous improvement, and know-how sharing. The MICS performance data is made available to all affiliates in order that they can learn from each other. As George Meiling, Banc One's Treasurer, explained, "They don't necessarily go to the affiliate with the best performance. That might be too threatening. But they will identify one with a similar profile that is a little better than them in some key areas and set up an exchange of ideas and experiences."

Other mechanisms to enhance valuable linkages include conferences, Banc One College, best practice manuals, and Quality Councils. Conferences address broad issues, such as commercial lending, but also specific products, such as Classic One for senior citizens. The largest is the retail conference, held once a year for 2½ days and involving about 750 people. This is run like an academic conference, with parallel tracks or sessions, and many speakers on the focus topics. Banc One College provides a high-level induction for senior executives in affiliates. It also exposes managers to the latest thinking on banking issues, and provides a forum for personal networking. Manuals are produced by central functions, such as marketing, to capture groupwide learning on specific topics such as home equity loans. The Quality Councils complete more than 500 projects per year, looking at issues that are relevant for all affiliates.

Banc One's approach to linkage influence is relatively straightforward. It focuses on obvious areas of overlap between fundamentally similar units. The value is not in developing complex or novel bridges between different types of business, but in maintaining focus while enhancing best practice sharing. If Banc One moved into significantly different activities in financial services, the value of what it calls its "uncommon partnerships" might well erode or require change. As John B. McCoy puts it: "I think our key achievement is that we are focused. We like to think of ourselves as the McDonald's of retail banking, selling the same thing everywhere: small and middle-market business loans, home mortgages, auto loans, trust services, credit cards, and the like."[7]

With an approach of this sort, the parent can remove blockages to linkages in several ways:

1. *Opportunity Recognition.* Units focused on a relatively small geographic area may not be aware of the opportunities for best practice sharing. Managers in the parent can see what might be obscured from a purely local perspective.
2. *Competition.* If Banc One's constituent businesses were not jointly owned, a system for sharing of detailed and accurate performance data would be unlikely to get off the ground, since lack of trust or fear of competitive disadvantage would block progress. Antitrust legislation would also block various forms of agreed cooperation, in a deliberate attempt to maintain competition.
3. *Inertia.* Without the peer pressure provided by MICS and affiliate rankings, opportunities to improve performance by examining other units could easily remain untapped. The difficulties in establishing clear benchmark comparisons would allow many managers to devote themselves to other priorities.
4. *Special Expertise.* Banc One's approach creates skills at the center in areas such as marketing, which can foster the spread of good ideas between affiliate banks.

Many multibusiness companies adopt a Banc One type of approach to linkages at the divisional level. The divisions are made up of similar businesses in different locations or countries, and the divisional parent aims to encourage linkages between these businesses. Companies such as Cooper in the United States and TI in the United Kingdom, for example, achieve linkage benefits of this kind.[8] Because the businesses are similar, the opportunities for sharing resources or best practices are often substantial.

BANC ONE: CORPORATE STRATEGY.   Exhibit 7–3 is a parenting advantage statement for Banc One. It shows how important Banc One's *distinctive parenting characteristics* for spreading best practice are in implementing its *value creation insights* and its corporate strategy. Mc-Coy believes that integration into the Banc One network can generally improve a bank's earnings by roughly 40 percent after an acquisition.[9] This improvement is due to a number of factors, including the benefits of enhanced stand-alone performance. However, a significant proportion of the gain comes from comparison and linkage across the units.

In addition, Banc One uses its size to pioneer new approaches to banking. This is particularly evident in its commitment to technology. In recent years, the company has invested heavily in a joint venture with Electronic Data Systems to develop a new bank management system based on distributed architecture. The objective has been to put user-friendly data on the desktops of customer-facing staff, so they have the latest customer details available to them and have prompts to remind them to offer services selected for that customer's profile. The project has cost over $100 million, and results from early tests show

EXHIBIT 7–3 Banc One parenting advantage statement

Value Creation Insights	In many regional and state banks in the USA, a parent can enhance performance dramatically by encouraging the spread of best practice in terms of product range, service, and operating systems.
	In addition, many such banks have been for sale cheaply due to historic mismanagement of their loan portfolios.
Distinctive Parenting Characteristics	Decentralized approach to the management of community-based affiliate banks.
	Shared systems and policies: • Use of Banc One name and brand. • Emphasis on customer service measures. • Back office processes. • Uniform Product Line. • MICS system.
	Pressure to spread best practice: • Use of MICS data and reviews. • Other mechanisms.
	Commitment to technology investment.
	Skill at assessing and acquiring banks.
Heartland Businesses	Banks involved in community retail banking and offering financial services to individuals and small- to medium-size companies. Banks need to be in the United States, be capable of being among the top three banks in the communities they serve, and to have sound managers.

that it will reduce system operating costs by 20 percent. A similar joint venture with Andersen Consulting has resulted in the development of "Triumph," a new credit-processing system. Behind this investment in technology is a 25-year commitment to spend 3 percent of profits on technology. Banc One as a portfolio of affiliates can afford to spend much more on technology than could be justified by any individual affiliate.

By the mid-1980s, Banc One's philosophy was well established. The U.S. banking industry then entered a period of unprecedented loan losses, defaults, and bankruptcies. As a community bank with tight credit limits and few loans to commercial property developers, Banc One was largely unaffected and soon became one of the few banks in the United States with a strong enough balance sheet and track record to make acquisitions. Moreover, literally hundreds of banks were calling on the FDIC (Federal Deposit Insurance Corporation) for help, or offering themselves for sale. Banc One was in a buyer's market. This created a further value creation opportunity for Banc One, which has been able to cherry-pick many of the best acquisition opportunities.

This area of value creation, however, depended on a further distinctive element of Banc One's parenting: its skill at assessing and acquiring banks. "In total, we have probably looked at a thousand banks and been involved in 137 acquisitions," commented George Meiling. This has enabled Banc One's top team to develop a well groomed acquisition and assessment process. Probably, the most important influence on whether Banc One is likely to make a bid or not is the strength of the management team. If the judgment is that more than four or five managers need to be replaced, Banc One is unlikely to be interested, because it does not have a pool of bankers available to move to the new company. "In the holding company, we have very few bankers. Nobody in the holding company is making loans, so we don't need bankers. We have people from companies like GE, Wendy's, or Arthur Andersen. The job at the holding company level is not a banking job." Banc One's experience with acquisitions has also made it skillful at laying off the loan portfolio risk onto the FDIC.

Banc One's distinctive parenting characteristics have gained it the reputation of being the best bank in the United States, with the fastest growing stock price, earnings record, and asset base. But Banc One has not succeeded in everything it has tried. It has been less successful in its nonbank affiliates. "The good news is that we have been cautious with our nonbank affiliates. The bad news is that we needed to be." This experience demonstrates that Banc One's parenting capability appears to be limited to its *heartland businesses* in retail community banking and services that support these banks. It is in these businesses that Banc One creates the most value through its parenting.

Approach 3: Link across Geographic Locations and Business Groups

Some parents are more ambitious in their linkage influence. Rather than focusing only on links across geographic locations in similar businesses, they also encourage linkages across different business groups. In this way, they aim to create additional value. But, since the business unit managers involved will have less in common than in Approach 2, more problems tend to arise. Parents must be particularly careful that they do not stimulate overzealous pursuit of ill-conceived ideas. As one manager summed up the danger: "If you put bright, motivated people in charge of finding synergies, they are bound to come up with something, even if it makes no commercial sense. We do not want to encourage coordination for the hell of it or in order to meet managers' personal objectives [for the bonus plan] regardless of economic value."

Parents adopt Approach 3 for different reasons. The new chief executive of a broadly diversified group may see it as a previously untapped source of value creation. A company that has exploited a key resource by venturing into new businesses may see it as a way of avoiding fragmentation. A parent eager to expand may see it as a logic for acquisitions and diversification. Regrettably, our research suggests that many companies with this approach have failed to create net benefits, since the linkage benefits between separate business groups are often minor, the costs of achieving them can be high, and there is always a danger that the linkage influence may have a negative impact on stand-alone performance. Nevertheless, there are some companies, such as Unilever, that successfully parent linkages across different business groups as well as across geographic locations within business groups.

UNILEVER: LATERAL LINKS.   Unilever is a company with a long history of managing cooperation and coordination between operating companies in different businesses and different countries. It was formed in 1930 by the merger of Margarine Unie, a Netherlands margarine company, and Lever Brothers, a U.K. detergents company. Its ownership structure, and corporate head office, have continued to be shared between The Netherlands and the United Kingdom ever since. The company is structured into four global groups of businesses—food, detergents, personal products, and speciality chemicals.

Like Banc One, Unilever promotes linkages between similar businesses in different geographic locations. For example, Unilever has personal products businesses selling items such as shampoo and hand cream in more than 30 countries. Linkages between these country-based businesses involve sharing product and marketing information, internal trading, exchanging best practice ideas, transfer of people (particularly product managers), and coordinating research. Because the environments and consumer tastes in each country are different, Unilever is unable to impose as much standardization on its businesses as Banc One. But the objective of raising standards and promoting information sharing is the same. As one manager in Unilever explained, "We do not standardize for the sake of standardizing, we are seeking to standardize on best practice." Instead of a Banc One type MICS database as a pivot for sharing, Unilever has many systems and processes. For example, each business produces a strategic plan in a standard format; each month a video is distributed to all countries of the new advertising campaigns around the world; where possible, there is only one advertising agency worldwide for each international product; and so on.

Unilever differs from Banc One in the diversity of its product line. Alongside the personal products businesses, Unilever has food businesses, selling margarine, tea, ice cream, and other food stuffs; detergent businesses, selling soap powder and cleaning materials; and chemical businesses, selling chemical ingredients both on the open market and to many of its other businesses. Although each of these business groups is distinct, Unilever attempts to create valuable linkages between them. It is this fact that makes Unilever a good example of Approach 3.

Unilever influences linkages across business groups in four areas: (1) in functional areas such as research and marketing; (2) in supply relationships between chemicals and the other businesses; (3) in the operations of different businesses in less developed countries; and (4) in the development and sharing of management talent. This is achieved within the context of a highly decentralized management philosophy, where the chairman of a country-based business has extensive power to accept or reject the advice of managers in the parent company. The parent influences these cross-product group linkages by creating a culture of coordination, by building elaborate networks and lateral relationships between managers in different businesses,[10] by retaining tight control over career management and promotion decisions, by influencing strategy development, and by structural means where these are necessary. We will concentrate on two important influence processes: career management and the management of linkages between businesses in less developed countries.

Unilever's management of human resources is vital in establishing lateral links between product groups, and in fostering a culture in which such links thrive. Unilever's Personnel Division lays down corporate policies, such as the requirement that managers must gain experience in more than one country or product line and that all managers must be formally appraised. It runs a large management training activity through which 400 managers a year from all over the world are brought together. It manages the policies that make Unilever's large expatriate system work. It is involved in helping to keep salaries and remuneration packages in a reasonable state of comparability. It also orchestrates the career-planning process and is influential in all cross-business appointments.

The parent becomes involved at the earliest stage in the recruitment of university graduates. Floris Maljers, a joint chairman of Unilever, underlined the importance of managing recruitment and early training. "The greatest challenge of recruiting is to find the best and brightest who will fit into the company. We certainly do not want *homo unileverens,* but for international careers in our current operating companies, we look for people who can work in teams and understand the value of cooperation and consensus. Preparation includes both on-the-job experience and training courses. In fact, many have joked that Unilever is really a management education institute financed by soap and margarine." Unilever recruits about 1,000 graduate management trainees a year, who enter the company in over 50 countries.

Once in management ranks, the Unilever parent monitors four grades. The lowest grade includes about 15,000 managers worldwide; the second 4,000; the third 1,400; and the top level includes all directors of operating companies with sales over £500 million and chairpersons of smaller companies. Personnel Division maintains lists of managers in each grade and notes those with the potential to move to the next grade. It has a template of what type of cross-geographic and cross-functional experience is necessary for each position and helps to orchestrate the development of those coming forward to the next grade.[11] For example, Personnel Division acts as secretary to the annual personnel review that is held in each company and chaired by the main board director responsible for the procedure. Due to Unilever's marketing culture, appointments of brand managers or marketing directors receive particular attention. Thus, a new marketing appointment in Portugal would be discussed at the annual review meeting. If there was no natural internal successor, a list of candidates from other countries and product groups would be developed. The local managers would be the main influence on this list. But Personnel Division would also have the right to put names on the list, especially of managers who could benefit from exposure to the country or product group. Moreover, senior personnel officers meet every 3 weeks to discuss all vacancies and could ask for a name to be added to the list. Finally, every 6 weeks, the main board directors concerned with Europe would review the vacancies list and might add names.

Unilever's system for managing its human resources creates a direct linkage benefit by providing the businesses with a larger pool of suitable managerial talent to draw on. It is also a mechanism that promotes other linkages. By fostering a common culture, promoting networks, and exposing managers to a broad range of experiences, the Unilever system speeds up the circulation of product knowledge and best practice. Like the Banc One approach, it helps to overcome many of the typical blockages that hinder linkage development. It reduces blockages from weak or parochial management. It encourages a unity of interest between managers and the company's international commercial objectives. It lowers the barriers to communication.

Unilever's human resource management process is sophisticated and complex. It has been developed gradually over a number of years. In contrast, its method of managing linkages between businesses in less developed countries (LDCs) is simple and structural, and has been in place almost since the company began. In LDCs, the different businesses (with the exception of chemicals) report to a single country manager, and in smaller countries are often integrated into one business. The country managers in turn report to regional managers. The structure for LDCs is different from that for developed countries, where the business groups represent the main line of reporting, because the opportunities for linkages between businesses in less developed parts of the world are greater. A detergent business in Kenya has more to share with a food business in Kenya than it has with a detergent business in Germany; it can share scarce management talent, combine sales and distribution activities, leverage off good government relations, and build country-based brand recognition.

Unilever's success in influencing linkages across product groups depends on the existence of important commonalities between its businesses. Its businesses share common marketing skills, common general management skills, and have overlapping technical interests. Finding mechanisms to harness these opportunities, given the company's history and culture, has been an ongoing challenge for at least 30 years. Success has been possible because parent managers have a deep understanding of the main product groups, as a result of career experience in all or most of the groups. Those product areas not part of the mainstream, such as tea plantations and animal feed, have been divested.

Successful use of Approach 3 may require a significant period of evolution. Some companies, such as American Express, have achieved partial benefits from less deeply embedded processes than those described in Unilever, but difficulties often reemerge. American Express's "One Enterprise Program," involving a range of linkage mechanisms, from joint taskforces to incentives for cooperation to shared management development activities, was hailed in the mid-1980s as a major producer of synergy. But links between the base traveler's check and credit card business and newer additions to the portfolio, such as the Shearson brokerage, were sometimes superficial. Following disappointing performance, and the departure of its chief executive James Robinson III, American Express sold off some of its businesses in 1993[12] and focused on linkages between less diverse areas of financial service.

For Approach 3 to work well, there need to be important untapped linkage opportunities across product groups. Marginal opportunities will seldom justify the cost involved in these sorts of linkages unless the linkage mechanisms adopted are designed to be as light, voluntary, and low cost as possible. Managers in the parent must also understand the different product groups well enough to appreciate the opportunities and develop linkage mechanisms which remove the communication barriers, competitive rivalries, and other blockages that prevent the linkages from occurring through enlightened self-interest.

UNILEVER: CORPORATE STRATEGY. Exhibit 7–4 is a parenting advantage statement for Unilever. It shows the importance of linkage management in Unilever's corporate strategy. But the parent's *value creation insights* also involve recognizing that many fast-moving consumer goods (FMCG) companies have a tendency to underinvest in research and product development. The parent's belief in research and product development, and its understanding of what sort of research expenditure is appropriate, enable it to prevent businesses from underinvesting. Unilever applied these value creation insights after its acquisition of Cheeseborough Ponds, the U.S. personal care business, and improved its flow of new products and its market share.

EXHIBIT 7–4 Unilever parenting advantage statement

Value Creation Insights	By creating a network of operating companies in FMCG businesses in different countries, a parent can generate value through the exchange of product, marketing, and technological information, ideas, and skills.
	By promoting investment in new products and research, a parent can improve performance, since most independent FMCG businesses tend to underinvest in these areas.
Distinctive Parenting Characteristics	Decentralized structure: • Developed countries. • LDCs.
	Mechanisms to encourage networking across businesses and countries: • Expatriate cadre and HR development. • Business "Coordinations" and information flows. • Corporate culture.
	Balance of centralized and decentralized research. • Fat technology skills. • Close relationship between research and marketing.
	Marketing Division
Heartland Businesses	Fast-moving consumer packaged goods for the mass market, where opportunities exist to gain advantage by centralized research and product development and international linkages between country-focused business units.

Supporting its value creation insights, Unilever has some highly *distinctive parenting characteristics.* Its decentralized structure gives substantial autonomy to local country managers, particularly in LDCs. But the local businesses are tied together by a number of mechanisms to encourage networking and coordination. These include the human resource management process, the expatriate management cadre, the corporate culture, and, probably most importantly, the product group "Coordinations."

Unilever aims to achieve networking and coordination without building a bureaucracy or making central management top-heavy. "I am proud to say that usually there are only four management layers between myself and a brand manager," explained Sir Michael Angus, the recently retired chairman. A vital role is played by the Coordination (a product division in normal managerial language). For example, the Personal Products Coordination is staffed by about 15 people. More than 10 of these are senior executives, called "members" of the Coordination, who have previously been marketing directors or chief executives of operating companies, and who can expect to return to the field after a few years in the Coordination. These members have no direct staff and an intentionally wide-ranging responsibility. For example, a marketing member may have responsibility for dental products worldwide and overall liaison responsibility for the personal products businesses in Latin America and India. To execute this responsibility, he or she may need to have a direct relationship with 50 or 60 chief executives, marketing directors, and product managers around the world. With this work load, it is impossible for the member to be excessively interfering. The role is to provide a vehicle for linkages between countries, guidance on worldwide product strategy, and a mechanism for best practice transfer—a light linkage influence. The Coordination also has a role in providing information to all business units on the performance and practices of other units. Due to the culture, the light linkage influence works well. "In Unilever, there is an unwritten rule that before you embark on a particular decision you allow others to shape that decision," stated Angus. The term "Coordination" is therefore appropriate and represents an important use of language.

In addition, Unilever's management of two vital functional areas is particularly effective. In research and development, Unilever has an unusual balance between centrally controlled research laboratories and decentralized control of budgets. The central laboratories have to persuade the businesses to continue to fund them. The company also has a process for involving research, marketing, and market research in product development decisions that is unusually effective. Combined with its technical prowess in fat-related technologies, and senior managers' feel for the appropriate level of spend on research, this has led to Unilever's excellent product development track record.

Unilever also gains important technical benefits from the range of technologies it is involved in. Although the laboratories are organized to support the business groups and each business group has a process for coordinating the research demands of its operating companies, many important innovations have come from cross-fertilization of technologies. A new toothpaste was developed as a result of an idea for plaque reduction that came from detergent research activity. A new lipstick was developed as a result of work on fat technology. The fact that Unilever's laboratories are not clearly divided by product type helps this cross-fertilization.

The company has also developed world beating skills in concept marketing to mass-market consumers. Through its central Marketing Division, which specializes in raising skills in market research, trade marketing, promotions, and advertising; through careful development of its product managers; and through the fostering of a marketing culture, Unilever has built a companywide marketing skill that is recognized as among the best in the world. But, like other central activities,

Marketing Division is not a classic, authoritarian central function. The division is a service organization, working for the operating companies and gaining support for new initiatives only when the operating companies acknowledge the need. There is a quarterly meeting between the marketing members from the Coordinations and Marketing Division and a similar meeting with the advertising members. These meetings are used to sort out priorities and activities. Throughout its history, Unilever has sought to be at the forefront of marketing techniques, setting up one of the first international market research agencies and an internal advertising agency to help advance the state of the art and service its own needs. As both of these industries have matured and Unilever has been able to buy equally good service from external agencies, the two internal agencies have been sold off and become successful external competitors.

Unilever's *heartland* has become increasingly clear over the past 10 years. It adds most value in businesses involved in fast-moving packaged goods for mass-market consumers, where there are opportunities to gain advantage through research and product development, superior concept marketing, and international and cross-product group linkages. Unilever has been focusing its portfolio on these sorts of businesses and has exited from businesses such as animal feeds, packaging, and transportation during the past decade. Unilever's heartland criteria certainly include personal products, detergents, and food products, but do not obviously include Unilever's chemical activities. The links between chemicals and the other businesses are important, particularly in research and product development, but the stand-alone parenting needs of the chemicals businesses are different. Unilever therefore faces a difficult decision concerning whether to retain the chemicals activity within the portfolio.

Unilever is among the most effective parents in the world for its heartland businesses. Procter & Gamble has been equally successful, with a somewhat more centralized approach, and Kraft General Foods and Nestlé have also been powerful international rivals. But Unilever's ability to balance global and cross-product group coordination with local responsibility has given it a strong claim to parenting advantage in many of its businesses.

Approach 4: Network of Linkages

Under Approach 4, linkages are essential to the whole viability of the organization. At the heart of the network are individual units, few of which would be viable as external stand-alone businesses. These are networked together in a matrix, so that they can create and benefit from linkages of different sorts for different purposes. Thus, to create a more interlinked whole, the parent builds the organization on individual units that are not fully self-sufficient. In contrast to Approach 3, such networks imply greater balance, or tension, between different lines of coordination. Rather than emphasizing a primary dimension of linkage with other overlays, the network simultaneously exploits different dimensions of linkage, whose relative power may be constantly shifting.

In the recent past, academics and managers have been particularly interested in this approach,[13] due to its ability to combine attributes previously considered mutually exclusive. The individual units can match the customer responsiveness, speed of decision making, and entrepreneurial enthusiasm of a highly focused, small business. But they can also access the power, scale, and government contacts of a large multibusiness organization. As a result, the concept of a network organization, deemphasizing divisions and reemphasizing multiple lines of linkage, has been gaining in popularity. Furthermore, improvements in information technology are making previously unworkable organization structures more viable.[14] At another level, changes in political structures and attitudes to multinationals are calling for creative new types of organization.[15] Management demands for "empowerment" and the need for more rapid local responsiveness are also leading thinking in this direction.[16]

But, like the other approaches, Approach 4 can lead to value destruction. If the networking mechanisms become cumbersome, costly, and bureaucratic, the end result may be to combine the worst of all worlds rather than the best.[17] Similarly, if certain dimensions of linkage are economically far more significant than others, seeking to network on multiple dimensions may prove less beneficial than a clear focus on one. Many companies regard the complexity of matrix organizations and networks as anathema.

One company that has made much of its commitment to a network of linkages in a matrix structure is Asea Brown Boveri (ABB).

ABB: MATRIX LINKAGES.   ABB is one of the largest electrotechnical companies in the world, with 1993 revenues of about $28 billion. It was formed in January 1988 through the merger of Asea, a Swedish company created in 1883, and Brown Boveri, a Swiss company founded in 1891. Although a young company, its heritage therefore stretches back over a century. The company employs around 206,000 people, in about 5,000 profit centers of roughly 40 employees each. These profit centers are grouped into approximately 1,500 local companies, few of which would be entirely viable as stand-alone units. Within ABB, however, they are linked together in various ways.

On one dimension, each profit center is part of a "Business Area," that focuses on a particular group of products or services throughout the world. For example, there are Business Areas focused on drives, process engineering, hydro power plants, air pollution control, mass transit vehicles, and signaling. In 1993, there were about 50 Business Areas or "BAs," each operating, to some extent, as a global business.

However, on another dimension, each profit center is also part of a regional company, such as Asea Brown Boveri Aktiengesellschaft in Germany or ABB Inc. in the United States. These national or regional companies represent another linkage dimension, often echoing the historically national roots and focus of the companies that have been brought together to form ABB (such as Asea in Sweden; Brown Boveri, with dual bases in Germany and Switzerland; Strömberg in Finland; or Combustion Engineering in the United States).

In this way, ABB acknowledges three rival business definitions simultaneously, each with a different blend of focus and scale.[18] The first definition is embodied in the "atomic" units at the heart of the organizational matrix. They have significant freedom and responsibility in making tradeoffs to meet budgets and plans, and their individual identity encourages a clear sense of employee belonging and ownership. In the words of Percy Barnevik, the chief executive: "We are fervent believers in decentralization. When we structure local operations, we always push to create separate legal entities. Separate companies allow you to create real balance sheets with real responsibility for cash flow and dividends. Separate companies also create more effective tools to recruit and motivate managers. People can aspire to meaningful career ladders in companies small enough to understand and be committed to."[19] These units, then, are actual "businesses" in some very real ways.

However, a second business definition focuses on the global integration inside each Business Area. In some BAs, such as those producing power plants, the same competitors fight for nearly every contract and, Barnevik maintains, "national borders are virtually meaningless."[20] In this context, the BA must function as a global business, with tight integration across its operations.

The third business definition stresses regional or national identity, based on the value of integrated local presence: first, with national labor pools (e.g., through attracting talent by offering career development across units in the same country); second, with customers (e.g., through maintaining higher level contacts); third, with governments and communities (e.g., through being a significant local operation, which can expect to receive government support and preference, especially in areas of national sensitivity or pride).

Although this multiple approach may seem unnecessarily ambiguous and complex, in some ways it reduces complexity for many of ABB's staff. Individuals within a local company have a reasonably clear sense of what their particular unit is supposed to be doing, and they can see the local company president as a focal point of decision making who is visible and close at hand. Company presidents do not have to be "global managers" in themselves, though they do need to accept and manage a dual reporting responsibility. Country or Region managers have a potentially bewildering array of businesses under their local control; but their function is primarily to keep these units in line with their agreed budgets. They are not required to understand all the global cost trade-offs or specific technology changes in each of the businesses, but rather to ensure that short-term financial performance is meeting agreed expectations and that local relationships are managed to the company's advantage. If financial performance is not in line, they will immediately meet with the relevant BA and business unit heads to work out an improvement plan.

Business Area leaders do have a more global, and potentially awkward, role. They must work across national boundaries and encourage resource shifts, product specialization, and export allocation, which may be sensitive or threatening to the individual units. Furthermore, they have little direct power or resources. Typically, the BA head will chair a BA management board consisting of the presidents of the largest companies in the business area from around the world. His staff is usually a handful of experienced managers, often six or less, who travel around the world focusing on specific opportunities for knowledge sharing, optimization or spreading of best practice. His ability to make things happen depends more on an influence base than a power base, and the role of BA manager is one of the most difficult within the structure. It is made even more difficult because, historically, in most of the companies that now form ABB, there was a strong national power base in the home country. This creates some vested interests that do not take easily, for example, to major shifts of production capacity from one country to another.

The danger that the BA will perpetuate, rather than challenge, historical resource dispositions has been a management concern in designing the matrix. As a senior vice president in Baden, Switzerland, described it: "At first we tried to locate the BAs in the country operations that were strongest in that particular product or service area. However, this led to some prejudice in favor of the home region. Therefore, we took the BAs out of the countries, to make them more independent. But this leads to a different problem, as the BAs can end up in a sort of vacuum with no direct control of money or staff. If the worldwide BA manager says "right," and Germany says "left," there's not much the BA manager can do about it. The legal structure of the companies, being regionally based, lends significant weight and power to this dimension of the matrix." As a result, many senior managers are now wearing "two hats," with responsibilities and resources that span both sides of the matrix, though the desirability of this practice was a topic of review in 1993.[21]

Despite the potential ambiguity and complexity of the matrix, many managers feel that better overall decisions are reached. As the president of a local ABB company in Germany described it: "The advantages of the matrix are significant. The quality of the decisions that emerge is much higher than in a traditional system, as every issue is looked at from two sides. Second, there is much less change once a decision has been taken, so there is more of a sense of consistency." A vice president in the North American operation summed it up as follows: "For the matrix to work well, you need debate between the regional and BA management. This depends on three elements: conflict, teamwork, and trust. At the moment we probably have too much conflict, both healthy and unhealthy, but that is because we are still a very young company. We are only now developing the shared values, common language, and shared culture that need to underlie the matrix."

Although many commentators on ABB have focused on the matrix and the role of the parent in linking together separate units, perhaps the more significant achievement at ABB has been the breaking down of historical empires and hierarchies into more manageable pieces. In this context, the matrix has provided a framework to stop "atomization" becoming destructive and totally chaotic. It is not so much a system to create linkages between units that were already separate as a mechanism allowing the orderly separation and reformation of what was previously grouped together. ABB was put together from a series of powerful, country operations run in a hierarchical way. If these organizations had merely been acquired or had merged ownership interests, a number of blockages would have stopped them from achieving valuable linkages.

First, detailed performance measurement was not available, making it difficult to assess or even notice opportunities for linkage. The clarity of the group financial reporting system (called "Abacus"), which provides data on all of ABB's 5,000 decentralized profit centers, has vastly improved the visibility of individual units. Moreover, internal sales are made at market rates rather than at artificial transfer prices, and have focused attention on learning from operations that are particularly successful. A second blockage was the hierarchical decision-making process, which would have limited local exploitation of linkages between the previously separate companies. Paradoxically, large acquisitions have been integrated through a process of breaking things down, rather than by attempting to build them up into even bigger integrated structures. As a manager who had worked at Brown Boveri before the merger with ASEA commented: "Within Brown Boveri itself, we never even achieved the melding of our two main operations in Baden and Mannheim. But decentralization has enabled the units of ABB to come together as a single company." Third, the existence of BAs that cut across country operations removes blockages from contracting difficulties and deadlocks. For example, in determining the focus of different units within broader product ranges, or in allocating export markets, the BA manager can help units to gain specialization advantages rapidly without the complicated multipartite negotiations that would be required between fully independent companies or fully separated divisions. The BA can also provide a simple coordination focus for purchasing scale advantages, which is both efficient and credible to suppliers, and functional experts can be given responsibility for rooting out needless duplication or divergence.

The value of adopting a network approach depends on a number of factors. The characteristics of the businesses must be such that linkages on multiple dimensions are both valuable and subject to some shifting patterns. If this is not the case, clearer but less flexible structures will be adequate and easier to manage. It also seems to work better in some contexts than others. As an orderly means of breaking down complex, hierarchical structures, it may appear liberating. As a system for linking together previously independent units, it is more likely to appear over-complicated. Success in this approach also depends on the characteristics of the parent. If the parent is bureaucratic and heavy-handed, the individual units will be swamped by regulation and cost. Ideally, the parent requires facilitation skills and an ability to influence effectively, without the full weight of a hierarchy.

ABB: CORPORATE STRATEGY.   Exhibit 7–5 is a parenting advantage statement for ABB. Although the three *value creation insights*

EXHIBIT 7–5   ABB parenting advantage statement

Value Creation Insights	Most companies make direct tradeoffs between centralization and decentralization, or scale and focus. There are opportunities for a parent that can combine the various benefits in new ways.
	Many European engineering businesses have been relatively fragmented in global terms. Consolidation can reduce costs while increasing coverage and global muscle.
	Many engineering businesses do not have a strong commercial focus and are prone to increase sales volume and product range at the expense of margin. A parent can help redress the balance.
Distinctive Parenting Characteristics	Ability to combine decentralized small business units into a global network through the ABB matrix structure.
	Systems and corporate initiatives that focus on profitability, customer needs, and simplification of operations.
	Ability to integrate acquisitions and improve their performance rapidly.
	Ruthless approach to cutting of overhead costs.
Heartland Businesses	Engineering-intensive, electrotechnical businesses, usually involving complex integration into systems. Customers are large industrial or governmental institutions.

are distinct, ABB's matrix structure and linkage approach can be seen to play a major role in all three. Most directly, it supports the first insight by enabling the company to benefit from multiple dimensions of linkage at the same time. It also enables ABB to acquire and integrate complex national engineering companies and consolidate them rapidly into a shared framework. Less obviously, it sharpens commercial focus by pushing profit awareness and accountability down to small units that are close to local markets.

The value creation insights are also supported by other *distinctive parenting characteristics*. The parent's wholehearted support for customer focus programs has created further pressure to commercialize an engineering culture. In addition, by raising the visibility of time as a crucial competitive variable, ABB has encouraged all its units to reassess processes and simplify them wherever possible. The benefits include a 50 percent reduction in the time ABB takes to compile complex bids for power plants, which allows the company to incorporate more up-to-date information on customer requirements into its original designs. This improves the design concept and reduces the cost of reworking plans each time more information becomes available. Similarly, groupwide initiatives on issues such as tighter cash management have been led by Percy Barnevik himself and have benefited from the visibility that Abacus provides.

The focus on profit has also reshaped thinking about the size and scope of units. In power transformers, for example, ABB has gone against industry norms by reducing the size and complexity of individual operations, and focusing on flexibility and short throughput times rather than scale advantages. For example, in one transformer plant in Germany, staff and sales were reduced by nearly 60 percent and work-in-process inventory by 80 percent, but profits were substantially increased.

ABB has extensive experience in integrating acquisitions. Between 1988 and 1991, it acquired 126 companies, bringing well over 100,000 new staff on board; these included 15 acquisitions, employing more than 18,000 staff, in the former Communist bloc. The integration process concentrates on culture and management processes as much as technology. As a director of one of ABB's Polish businesses put it: "From the beginning our approach was to transfer the software first, the hardware second. We began with a lot of training, for instance in marketing and sales. Then we started the technological transfer. You don't give a kid an expensive toy before he knows how to play with it."[22]

ABB has often reached down several levels in the complex hierarchies of its acquisitions to find suitable general managers. In Eastern Europe, it has been particularly adroit in picking staff to take on in the joint venture or merged entity. This creates an environment responsive to change from day one, and reduces local bad press from subsequent firings. The process of delayering and breaking down unit size has also helped to bring in the ABB culture. Zamech in Poland had a 15-layer management hierarchy prior to ABB acquiring a 76 percent stake. A manager at the huge plant at Elblag described the old situation: "We were extremely centralized here. We had one manufacturing plant for everything, with our manufacturing director in charge. Every product was designed in one central design office: turbines, ship's propellers, gearboxes. We had central purchasing. We had huge overheads. It was a stupid way of doing things." Rationalization of product lines and allocation of defined export markets have also consistently improved the profitability of ABB acquisitions. Having focused its production range, ABB Strömberg has become a world leader in drives, supplying 35 percent of all ABB's group needs, and achieving a return on capital employed of 30 percent. As Barnevik says of ABB Strömberg "It is better to be the king of AC drives than to be a peasant in generators and transformers."[23]

A fourth distinctive parenting characteristic is a ruthless attitude to costs, especially corporate overhead costs. A normal objection to matrix management is the escalation in overheads that it incurs. In the case of ABB, however, corporate staff numbers have been kept to a minimum. The Head Office in Zurich is constrained to little over 100 staff, and Business Area heads seldom have more than a handful of assistants, many of whom carry out these global coordination roles part-time.[24]

ABB's *heartland* reflects the historical roots of its two main constituents, Asea and Brown Boveri. It includes businesses with a strong engineering content in electrotechnical fields and related service businesses. Although the engineering content may be embodied in specific products, such as boilers or drives, it is most evident in the complex integration of different products into complete systems. The delivery of these systems, such as power plants or power transmission systems (including cables, transformers, metering, and switchgear) involves sophisticated project management. Typically, the systems are sold to a small number of very large organizations, frequently with direct or indirect government involvement. The nature of sales and marketing is therefore completely different from consumer businesses. Individual projects may take several years to sell, design, and complete. Project values are often in tens or hundreds of millions of dollars, and bidding costs are high. Power distribution systems and environmental management and control systems are typical heartland businesses, as is the development of complete rail transportation systems, involving mainline rolling stock, signaling, and fixed railway installations. These sorts of businesses are fertile ground for ABB's value creation insights. They also share characteristics and critical success factors with which most of ABB's senior managers have long personal experience.

ABB has achieved an extraordinary amount in its brief history. However, the rate of acquisition activity has taken its toll in some areas and left other questions as yet unanswered. Some acquisitions have brought with them businesses that lie outside the heartland. A senior manager within ABB commented: "We have not taken a hard enough look at the acquisitions and pruned the portfolio. The main value added from Zurich should be to say: "I don't care if this business generates a ton of money—get rid of it: it won't always make money and we don't really understand it. It has been four years since some of the major acquisitions, but we haven't focused quickly enough on the core." Equally, while ABB has been held up as an exemplar of network or matrix management, the management demands of such a system are daunting. As one senior executive described it: "To manage this sort of organization you need very secure, mature people who are able to delegate as opposed to command. These are not easy to find among Western managers. ABB itself has a strong culture of hard-nosed, dictatorial people—they have been successful, and it is not easy to change." Significant progress has been made, but this is only the first phase of the new parent's development. As one competitor observed: "They are very impressive. They have certainly shown they can take out costs. But there is quite a lot of strain in the system. The real test will be in the years to come. Can they continue to deliver in a steadier state?"

Approach 5: Channel Company Resources into Incomplete Divisions

Approach 5, while sharing some of the ambiguity of business definition displayed in Approach 4, is less built around "decentralization with a safety net," and more around the rapid deployment of corporate resources and capabilities against shifting market opportunities. At its heart lies a strong sense of the unity of the company as a whole. But resources and capabilities are nevertheless concentrated behind focused thrusts into chosen product markets. It is an approach especially associated with Japanese corporations, and with the pursuit and management of "core competences," as described by C. K. Prahalad and Gary Hamel.[25] It involves a high level of linkage between units but falls short of a fully integrated, functionally structured approach. There is a strong emphasis on using learning that occurs in the context of one business or market opportunity, both to strengthen performance in other areas of the company, and to provide bridgeheads into new activities that may only just be emerging as businesses at all. Due to this focus on leveraging both tangible and intangible assets in new combinations, it is particularly appropriate in fluid business environments—areas where rapid evolution of technology and customer preferences creates opportunities for significant new business streams.

As with the other approaches, it brings certain risks. The existence of significant corporate resource held outside the business units can lead to costly and bureaucratic processes, divorced from market disciplines. The emphasis on the company as a single entity may also lead to lack of focus, overcoordination and introspection. The high level of linkage influence must imply major parenting opportunities to "beat enlightened self-interest," since otherwise it is hard to see the justification for such extensive parental involvement.

Difficulties with this approach have led to its abandonment by many North American and British companies over the past two decades. In the battle between synergy and focus, Anglo-Saxon managers have tended to opt for focus. More recently, however, the success of Japanese corporations and the appeal of the core competence notion has rekindled interest in this approach. Some argue that it only works within a cultural context where individuality is not paramount. Others believe that many Japanese corporations have succeeded in spite of it, rather than because of it. However, while acknowledging its risks, we believe that some companies, such as Canon, have adopted this approach to linkage influence with great success.

CANON: SHARED RESOURCES AND CORE COMPETENCES.   Canon was originally founded in 1933 as "Precision Optical Research Laboratory," developing camera products for the domestic Japanese market. By the early 1990s, it had become a significant world player in a wide array of products from photocopiers and laser copiers, facsimile transceivers and bubblejet printers, to cameras and videos, X-ray equipment, calculators, and even computers.

Canon's matrix structure is not so much the network of crossing lines observed in ABB, as a series of product division "spokes" emerging from a central corporate "hub," and bound together by strong global functions in R&D, production, and marketing. The product division spokes (such as "Peripherals" or "Camera Operations") provide the major thrust into the markets, but the functions and shared resources at the center enable full and frequent communication between all parties interested in a decision. This allows for global coordination of product group strategies, but also for local coordination of sales and channel strategies within national marketing organizations. Yasutaka Obayashi, Head of Corporate Strategy, believes that the weighting within the matrix is both clear and appropriate: "Although, as with any matrix structure, there are some confusions and ambiguities, it works well. The key to this is a clear sense of priorities. The product group is the primary axis in the matrix and the functional and geographical axes are secondary." For a decision to be reached, many individuals may need to be convinced, but, according to executives such as the general manager of the Copying Machines Product Group, this does not cause intolerable delay: "The process is not a step-by-step, level-by-level review, as might be typical of a Western company. Rather, the people concerned meet together and decide simultaneously. This speeds up the decision process and makes it less cumbersome."

The difference between the network of Approach 4 and the hub-and-spoke image of Canon depends on several factors. First, there are around 1,000 administrative staff and over 1,000 R&D staff at Canon's headquarters, in contrast to ABB's approximately 100 people at headquarters in Zurich. These staff are not so much an overlay on the Canon matrix, as a central resource from which, and into which, much learning flows. For example, most of the product groups share overlapping technologies that come together in the research rather than development phase, and central technologists are able to stimulate new combinations and generate new ideas. In this way, Approach 5 maintains considerable corporate resource outside the business units, whereas Approach 4 links together resources that are resident within individual units. Second, the hub-and-spoke image suggests more clearly the notion that all product groups radiate out of the company's resources; these product groups are conduits for corporate resources to generate value in specific markets. In the *Canon Fact Book* of 1991–1992, an interesting display shows how basic product groups (at the center of the circle) fan out into product families and in turn into specific end products (see Exhibit 7–6). A note under the diagram reads: "The composition of Canon's complete product lineup as shown here is the result of constant efforts to maximize the potential of the company's resources." This has a very different, and more centralist, flavor to it than ABB's networking of many hundreds of autonomous units. With Approach 5, the resources are essentially owned by the company as a whole, but are on loan to the individual units; with Approach 4, they are owned by the units, but are available to each other.

Despite the emphasis on corporate resource and shared corporate identity, Canon is by no means a unitary, functionally organized company. Its product groups have significant autonomy, and it is to them that the various functions in marketing or R&D are accountable. How, then, does the company maintain access to the skills and capabilities that are distributed across its units?

One crucial mechanism is the formation of short-term taskforces. These taskforces, which bring together employees from across the organization, have the authority, through their membership and the blessing of the most senior management, to act rather than merely recommend. They are not exempted from management review or veto, but they do have the same status in decision taking and action as more structurally fixed organizational forms. A classic example of Canon's approach was the large cross-company taskforce brought together to develop the AE-1 camera. This group combined skills and know-how from around the company to create the world's first electronically controlled totally automatic single lens reflex (SLR) camera with a built-in microprocessor unit. Following its introduction in 1976, the AE-1 achieved enormous success as a world trend-leader. Furthermore, the speed and success of the development process encouraged other breakthrough projects within Canon. One of these was focused on a new type of personal photocopier.[26] As in the case of the AE-1, the organizational unit for the development of the personal copier was the taskforce.[27]

EXHIBIT 7–6 Canon product circle

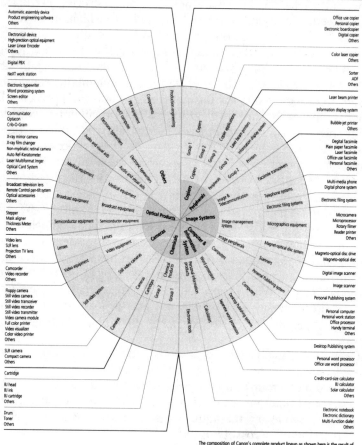

The composition of Canon's complete product lineup as shown here is the result of constant efforts to maximize the potential of the company's resources.

Source: Canon Fact Book, 1991/1992.

The composition of Canon's complete product lineup as shown here is the result of constant efforts to maximize the potential of the company's resources.

This group, known as "Taskforce X," was given high visibility. It was formally inaugurated on September 1, 1980, by Ryuzaburo Kaku, President of Canon. As with other Canon taskforces, its members were appointed by the company president, giving further organizational weight to this temporary entity. Taskforce X was very different from the lightweight teams that many companies establish to create linkages across units. It had around 200 members, divided between two prime development groups and six staff groups. Members were selected from many departments, including the reprographic products development center; the production engineering research center; the corporate technical planning and operation center; the corporate patents and legal center; the reprographic products planning and administration center; and the copier sales planning department. This membership reveals something of the importance and role of centralized groups in companies adopting Approach 5. For example, much of the specialist know-how and expertise of the production engineering research center had been gained from work on the mass production of cameras. This enabled K. Naito, Director of the Center, to redesign the copier production line using principles developed in camera manufacture. Furthermore, production engineering staff were involved from the earliest stages of the project, helping to shape product design with mass production in mind.

Canon's central staff provide another important mechanism for facilitating linkages. First, their briefings to senior executives help to enhance the understanding of cross-business or cross-functional issues, and to improve the flow of information. Second, the mere existence of so many staff positions provides an opportunity for many managers to spend some time in these roles. This can be an important part of "socialization" into Canon as a whole and provides a perspective from outside any given product group. Third, in a way that parallels the large negotiating staffs on international treaties, their existence enables a great deal of groundwork to be put in place. This smooths the way to multipartite decisions and lessens the danger of significant gaps developing between different parts of the company.

The center also plays an important role in gathering and disseminating information that can aid linkages. Data on the performance and cost structures of all the overseas manufacturing and sales subsidiaries are prepared in Tokyo and circulated to all locations. This "can stimulate questions which result in improvements," as one manager commented. Senior executives from the different dimensions of the matrix meet regularly face to face. At the top of the company, under the chairman and president, is an 8-man corporate team of senior managing directors. These are joined by the heads of the product divisions, the heads of the sales organizations for Japan, Europe, and the United States, and the heads of the main staff and functional departments to form a 22-man corporate executive committee that meets weekly and has final decision-making authority. This regular contact greatly reduces the risk of fragmentation or the development of unnoticed gulfs.

The culture of Canon, as of many Japanese organizations, is also well suited to a matrix structure with significant central resources.[28] On the one hand, the matrix reduces inappropriate deference to hierarchical authority by deemphasizing a single chain of command. This can help to flush out problems or disagreements that might otherwise be submerged. On the other hand, given a strong disposition toward consensus decision making, the matrix is unlikely to break down due to insoluble conflicts. Having flushed out the difficulties, there is a will to find solutions that are acceptable to all.

Another important mechanism to enhance linkages is the centrally driven career management process. This process not only moves individual managers through different functions and product groups, but recognizes and rewards the ability and inclination of individuals to network effectively. There is a strong central personnel department, with 25 staff who keep records on all employees, and are influential in promotion and training decisions for all senior staff. The systematic appraisal process includes written exams. The most senior personnel managers are themselves likely to have enjoyed a broad range of positions, perhaps starting in sales in one product group, then moving into a financial role in another group, then taking up an international position, before moving into the personnel function. The ability to create such career paths for many managers depends both on the parent's attitude to staff development and on the loyalty and long service of employees.

Finally, Canon's unifying culture creates an important backdrop in the search for linkages and their effective realization. Although there is lively competition between different product groups, there is a strong sense that all employees are primarily members of Canon as a whole. This sense of shared identity is based on a wide range of factors. The decision to grow organically rather than through major acquisitions has limited the risk of importing rival cultures. The movement of staff across units, the large number of centrally held resources, the formation of cross-company taskforces, and the clear corporate vision statement all support the sense of one enterprise.

The success of Japanese corporations such as Canon, which have substantial shared corporate resources available to their businesses, together with the tantalizing and mysterious accounts of building and leveraging tacit know-how and core competences, have led several Western companies to feel that they should explore this way of managing.[29] In many cases, however, companies have come to the conclusion either that they have no "core competences" or that the shared resources approach is of marginal relevance to their particular portfolio. In what business contexts, then, is the approach liable to be appropriate? Although it is important to distinguish between expertise in a particular technology and "core competences,"[30] it is easy to see that in technologically rich and fast-moving areas, Approach 5 is more likely to be relevant than in mature, low technology areas. Similarly, if opportunities exist for new combinations of skills and resources previously held in separate business domains, the approach is more likely to tease out these new combinations than one that is organized around tightly defined business units and business-specific ways of working. The role of the center is to encourage flexibility in product and business definition, and to avoid self-standing, complete divisions getting locked into ways of working that only optimize performance for a brief time span.

This fits with the notion that core competences can be applied to a number of different markets and that they remain the concern of the company as a whole. By maintaining a large center through which information and individual business managers regularly pass, the organization can benefit from local experiments and consolidate experience. It can also develop patterns of behavior that cross the organizational boundaries of the time. This fosters core competences that can be deployed in new settings and newly defined businesses.

CANON: CORPORATE STRATEGY. A parenting advantage statement for Canon is provided as Exhibit 7–7. Its *value creation insights* are all intimately related to its use of Approach 5. First, shared resources in core technologies allow all Canon's businesses to benefit from relevant expertise that they could not afford individually. Second, complex linkages are achieved through the use of large central staffs, the matrix structure, career development paths, and taskforces. Third,

EXHIBIT 7–7   Canon parenting advantage statement

Value Creation Insights	Individual businesses have resourcing difficulties in pursuing a range of technologies in depth and can benefit from shared resource within the parent.
	Businesses find it difficult to create linkages and cross-fertilization between different areas of technology, between technologists and market needs, and between different markets; and there is a role for a parent in facilitating these linkages.
	An inspiring corporate vision can help businesses to stretch for growth beyond the confines of each business.
Distinctive Parenting Characteristics	Ability to manage cross-fertilization: • Across different technologies. • Between technical and market specialists. • Across different markets.
	A high level of corporate commitment to technology and learning.
	Company vision that energizes staff toward growth and stretch without prompting inappropriate risks.
Heartland Businesses	Businesses in which overall performance depends heavily on product performance and new product development, which in turn are driven by superior understanding and linking of three core technology areas: precision mechanics, fine optics, and microelectronics; where technology advantage is embodied in certain key components; where international presence and ability to manage multiple channels to market provide a major advantage; selling business machines, cameras, and specialist optical products.

employees form an identification with Canon that goes beyond their current business unit and is based on shared access to the company's resources. But Canon's insights are not only supported by parenting characteristics concerned with sharing and linkages. Other *distinctive parenting characteristics* are also important.

Canon's commitment to technology development is spelled out in one of the company's corporate objectives, which states: "We will create the best and most unique products based on leading edge technologies. We have a responsibility to create the best products possible. To achieve this goal, we will concentrate our efforts in the areas of R&D, product planning and marketing, adopting an enterprising attitude." This involves both funding R&D and placing it in a central position within the company. Canon's total R&D expenditure averaged nearly 11 percent of sales in the second half of the 1980s and totaled $2.8 billion over the 5-year period from 1986 to 1990. Canon was granted a total of 3,363 patents in the United States between 1987 and 1990, which placed it in the top three achievers for each year, with Hitachi and Toshiba as its consistent fellows, well ahead of some much larger technology firms.

Commitment to R&D is not just demonstrated in the level of funding, but also in the parent's willingness to invest for long-term payoffs. As the 1992 annual report puts it: "In R&D, Canon will concentrate on developing products that will sell in the long term rather than making instant bestsellers." R&D has also had a distinctive status and role within Canon. As a Japanese business school professor, who had worked for many years at Canon, summed it up: "R&D drives Canon's strategic thinking and is central to Canon's behavior and management style. As an example, the medium-range management plan of each product division is drawn up by the development center of the product group. This 3-year product and development plan is then presented for discussion to the international meeting for product strategy held every autumn. Canon's R&D staff therefore believe that their work is essential to the growth of Canon."[31] This level of R&D commitment is clearly important in realizing benefit from the first value creation insight.

The third insight concerns the danger of psychological constraints imposed by rigid business definitions. These constraints are partly reduced by the linkage mechanisms and somewhat fluid organizational structure of Approach 5. But Canon has also been unusually successful in creating companywide visions that challenge employees to stretch well beyond their current businesses.

Canon has been guided by three company visions that have opened up new thinking and aspirations by concentrating on some form of strategic intent for the enterprise as a whole. Growth and stretch have been heavily emphasized in these visions. In 1976, Canon launched the first "Premier Company" plan. At that point, Canon was suffering badly from its overhasty entry into pocket calculators, and the devastating effects of the 1973 oil crisis. As Chairman Kaku later described it,

"Canon was like a ship that constantly changes course and goes nowhere." Against this difficult backdrop, Kaku, then a junior director, was the driving force in launching a plan to make Canon "The world's leading company." The plan covered a 6-year period aiming to make Canon a premier company within Japan during the first 3 years, and a premier company internationally during the second 3 years. The plan included high-level goals such as: "to time perfectly the release of new products which offer performance and quality unequaled anywhere in the world"; "to manufacture goods with the highest quality, at the lowest prices, and in the shortest time"; "to strengthen sales companies to achieve utterly efficient sales." The plan was not specific about how these objectives were to be attained but stressed issues such as the importance of innovation in technology, the need to develop human resources to the maximum, and Canon's social responsibilities. However, immediate practical steps were also taken, such as reorganizing the company into product groups, increasing automation in factories and offices, and supporting the corporate image. Furthermore, the grandiose high-level objectives were applied to specific projects, stimulating a level of aspiration that challenged basic assumptions. Middle-level managers were pressured into creative and unconventional ideas as the only possible way of meeting such aspirations. The development of the AE-1 camera or the personal copier were based on almost preposterous price targets. These acted as a ceiling under which the desired product functionality had to be delivered.

The extraordinary level of stretch in the 1976 vision was repeated in the second "Premier Company Plan" in 1982, and in the "Vision that Starts a New Canon" in 1988, which exhorts the "building of an ideal firm." These plans are strongly influenced by top management, but can involve a broad spectrum of Canon's employees. Their value lies not in the goals themselves, such as the apparently unreachable "trillion yen" sales goal proposed in 1976, but in the efforts that the vision and goals inspire. This inspiration is not simply generated by a document of intent. Senior management in general, and chairman Kaku in particular, regard the development and constant reemphasizing of the vision as their crucial role in the company. The company plan is not, therefore, seen as merely the output of senior management brainstorming, but as the driving force and energizer of the company as a whole.

Canon's *heartland* criteria emphasize the role of three core technologies. These technologies have been linked together to create innovative products for many different markets. Indeed, the ability to cross-fertilize ideas and know-how between these areas has been cited as a prime example of "core competences."[32] The competences are relevant to cameras, special optical products, and a variety of business machines, not just because all these areas use the three technologies, but also because they depend heavily on product performance and new product development. If this was not so, the relative value of the technological competences would be diminished. Within its heartland businesses, Canon also aims to produce the key components that embody technological advantage. By controlling these components, Canon is not reliant on the speed and capabilities of outside suppliers. It can also sell the key components to others, controlling the flow of technology, reducing reliance on single end product applications, and locking out would-be competitors through its own global dominance.[33]

But for a business to be included in the heartland, it is not enough simply to share benefits from a given core competence. To avoid the risk of value destruction, a parent must also understand the critical success factors of its businesses. Canon has proved itself particularly adept at achieving this requirement by acquiring a feel for new businesses. Its large center has helped it address the learning needs of the parent.[34] Its emphasis on organic growth rather than acquisition has also given it time to practice parenting new areas in comparatively low-risk contexts. Finally, it has so far focused on businesses that have elements of commonality beyond the importance of the three core technologies. For example, the value of international presence and the use of multiple sales channels are common to most Canon businesses. The parent is familiar and comfortable with the sorts of decisions that are important in such contexts. In contrast, a business that involved large-scale projects sold to government entities would be unfamiliar territory for Canon, even if it involved use of the three core technologies.

The nature and rate of Canon's growth is an impressive testimony to the quality of its parenting. It has grown organically rather than by acquisition and has successfully entered markets where it faced entrenched and dominant competitors. Its challenge to Xerox in photocopying was as audacious as its earlier challenge to Leika in cameras. But, to the extent that its parenting advantage has depended on technological competences and new product development, it may face new challenges as technologies mature in its major businesses. In the past, it has shown an unusual ability to bring new businesses successfully into its heartland. If it is able to continue this process in the future, for example with its current investments in computer businesses,[35] its parenting advantage will not play out for many years.

CONDITIONS FOR VALUE CREATION AND PARENTING ADVANTAGE

We have discussed five companies with successful corporate strategies, each of which adopts a different approach to linkages.[36] There are, however, many examples of companies that have been far less successful with each of these linkage approaches. What conditions must obtain for a parent's corporate strategy to create value through linkage influence and to overcome the enlightened self-interest paradox?

Opportunities for Linkage Value Creation

For a parent to create value through linkage influence, there must not only be benefits available from links between business units, but also blockages to enlightened self-interest that hinder the realization of these benefits. The businesses must be underperforming in some way due to a lack of linkages, and the parent must be able to help to remove the blockages that are stopping the linkages from occurring. If there are no such blockages, Approach 1, as practiced by BTR, which simply reinforces enlightened self-interest, is the best. But blockages often can and do arise. We shall examine six sorts of circumstances in which opportunities to remove blockages emerge.[37]

Weak Management. If the managements of the business units are weak, they may well fail to see, or to implement, opportunities to benefit from linkages. A parent can help such managements by providing prompts to valuable linkages, or tools for implementation. The linkage mechanisms in Banc One, Unilever, ABB, and Canon are intended, at a minimum, to prevent weak managements from overlooking beneficial linkage opportunities.

Conflict between Managers' and Other Stakeholders' Interests. Conflicts between the interests of managers and other stakeholders are particularly relevant in the context of linkages, since many linkages involve changes in the power, authority, or status of individual managers. Sharing a facility, coordinating prices or product ranges, or buying jointly from a shared vendor may all reduce a manager's degrees of freedom. This freedom may be valued more highly by the manager than by the shareholders or other stakeholders. Different interests lead to different assessments of the attraction of a given linkage.

To overcome this problem, parents adopt various approaches. In Canon, for example, the culture strongly identifies individual success with corporate success. By emphasizing corporate-level identity and moving managers across different businesses and roles, the parent aims to reduce the frequency of conflicts of interest. It is, however, important to identify whether failure to set up linkages follows from conflicts of interest or from sound business reasons. A manager may resist sharing a plant or giving up a key subordinate not merely because of personal inconvenience, but because it will not lead to the best outcome. There is a danger that resistance to linkages is dismissed as partisan or emanating from "not-invented-here syndrome" when it may, in fact, be well founded. Breaking down resistance to linkages will only create value if there are real benefits to be derived.

Specialist Expertise. Recognition of a valuable linkage opportunity may require specialist knowledge or creative, lateral thinking. In such cases, an expert or visionary in the parent organization may see potential that is initially invisible to others. One of the roles of Unilever's specialist marketing coordinators is to identify ideas or techniques that can be usefully shared across different businesses. Special expertise may exist because of the rare skills of individuals or teams. More normally, however, it exists on account of the parent's broad knowledge of its portfolio of businesses. Managers at the center have seen linkages operating successfully between certain businesses in the portfolio, and hence they can help other businesses to set up similarly valuable linkages.

Central expertise, however, has its dangers. Visions can be hallucinations; experience drawn from one part of the portfolio may be inappropriate to another part. The center's distance from the businesses creates a problem that can only be overcome by deep knowledge of the local requirements and conditions.

Lack of Communication. The range of concerns and other priorities confronting business managers are often such that they are less than fully informed about the possibilities to link with other units.[38] An important contribution that the parent can then make is simply to improve the flow of information. Within Banc One, for example, the MICS information system is designed to improve awareness of best practice in other affiliate banks. Without this information, affiliates might well not know which other banks to contact with a view to best practice sharing. In such cases, the parent is not enforcing or even sponsoring a particular linkage. It is aiding communication.

Inertia and Contracting Problems. Even if managers are aware of the possibilities for linkages, various forms of inertia may lead to the underexploitation of them. For example, each party to a potential linkage has an implicit veto: Until all parties concerned see the attractiveness of the linkage and are prepared to act on it, nothing will happen. The parent, by contrast, has a relationship of authority over its businesses, and can reduce inertia in various ways. Linkage policies can be established without unanimous agreement. Compliance can be policed. Confidence can be established among individual units that "cheating" will be punished. Within ABB, corporate enforcement of range specialization and market allocation reduces suspicion of unfair play, and Banc One's insistence on the Uniform Product Range provides the basis for useful best practice sharing. The parent can use its authority to overcome inertia and promote valuable linkages.

A parent can also sometimes help units in reaching complex linkage agreements, based on its negotiating and contracting skills, or its knowledge of what would be valuable to different parties.[39] With complex linkage agreements, the parent's contracting and negotiating skills can overcome blockages that would otherwise prevent businesses from working together.

Competition. As we saw at the beginning of this chapter, linkages can be formed between competitors. However, competition does create certain linkage blockages. These blockages may be legal, psychological, or commercial, but ultimately involve problems to do with "collaborating with the enemy." For example, although two stand-alone competing businesses may see the economic sense of sharing or coordinating activities, they may be legally constrained from doing so, for the very reason that it would limit competition. Alternatively, they may be psychologically constrained because they do not like to deal so closely with rivals. Finally, they may be commercially constrained because they fear that signals given or information passed on in exploring the linkage may be used by their competitors against them. In such cases, the move to joint ownership may remove the blockage, or at least lower the risks and psychological barriers involved.

Parenting Characteristics That Fit the Opportunities

To realize the linkage opportunities they have identified, parents need characteristics that match the opportunities and lead to value creation from them. The parent's mental maps must fit both the opportunities for value creation through linkage, and the blockages that will stop them from happening without a parent. ABB's understanding of opportunities to unblock linkages across nationally based engineering companies, or Canon's understanding of the opportunities to share technologies across different product groups, fall into this category. In businesses with less pressure to globalize and less value from a strong national presence, ABB's mental maps would be inappropriate. In businesses where technology transfer was simpler or less valuable to commercial success, Canon's mental maps would not fit.

The parent's structures, systems, and processes can also play a crucial role in removing blockages and realizing identified opportunities. Banc One's MICS system provides access to the quality of information that underpins its transfer of best practice. ABB's matrix structure enables business units to align on different axes of linkage. Unilever's personnel systems help to create the management networks that cut across countries, functions, and product groups.

The importance of the parent's functions, services, and other resources depends on the particular approach to linkage that is adopted. In Canon, and other companies maintaining "incomplete" divisions, they represent crucial mechanisms for capturing and disseminating experience. They also help the parent to learn rapidly about newer businesses. In Unilever, they act more as catalysts or facilitators, enabling the functions in different product groups to gain benefit from shared research or other joint activities that the operating companies see as desirable.

The importance of key individuals in the parent is as clear in linkages as in stand-alone influence. The personal association of Ryuzaburo Kaku with Canon's unifying company visions, or Percy Barnevik's ceaseless traveling and preaching of the need to network in ABB, underline the commitment of the parent to its particular linkage approach, and also provide distinctive mechanisms for furthering it.

Decentralization contracts are particularly important in linkage influence. A common danger of parental involvement in this area is a loss of local accountability. Concerns about fuzzy boundaries in the decentralization contract encourage some companies, such as BTR, to be extremely cautious in sponsoring linkages from the center. Even in companies where linkage influence is seen as more important, the terms of parental involvement must be clear, and due process observed. Banc One's "Uncommon Partnership" concept, with its stress on retaining independent affiliates rather than homogeneous branches, helps to retain local accountability and identification while encouraging cross-company links. Similarly, Unilever's use of personal networks and information exchange allows the product groups and operating companies to enjoy a high degree of independence, while benefiting from each other's know-how and experience. Even in Canon, product group managers are clear on the limits of their responsibilities and the bounds within which they are free to take initiatives.

Simply spotting opportunities for valuable linkage is not enough. Successful parents realize the value by developing relevant characteristics in support of the opportunities they are targeting. For value to be created, there must be a good fit between the parent's characteristics and the linkage opportunities in the businesses.

Avoidance of Value Destruction

Even if parents have identified opportunities to create linkage value and have suitable parenting characteristics to realize these opportunities, they must nevertheless beware of destroying value through other aspects of their parenting. In Chapter 6, we discussed extensively the importance of parents having a sufficient feel for their businesses to avoid value-destroying interventions in them, and the need for parents to avoid owning the sorts of businesses for which their parenting characteristics are unsuitable. These basic requirements remain important as conditions for creating net value through linkage influence.

One common source of value destruction is to parent businesses with a linkage approach that is fundamentally unsuitable. For example, BTR's approach, while suitable for most of the businesses in BTR's portfolio, would be unlikely to fare well in rapidly developing, high-technology areas, where new products can quickly emerge from combinations of previously discrete skills and processes. BTR's approach, therefore, would not fit the sort of businesses in Canon's portfolio.

Similarly, the Unilever approach would be wasteful and distracting if applied across businesses with little opportunity for sharing, and ABB's approach would be unnecessarily cumbersome if there were no tensions between rival business definitions of the units concerned. Such problems occur most frequently when companies apply an approach that has worked well in certain businesses to other businesses that are, in fact, rather different. The lure of applying a historically successful approach is real, since most managers have a strong predilection for one approach or another, which they regard as the "proper" way to do things. This is demonstrated in general statements such as "You simply can't make a matrix work; it's just too complicated," or "SBU thinking has been the biggest blind alley in the West. If you don't leverage companywide resources, you might as well trade shares," or "Synergy sounds fine, but synergy is the enemy of focus. If you start second-guessing the market, you end up running a central command economy." Such views express strongly held values and beliefs, which are liable to be applied regardless of the business context. This is a grave danger when companies move into new businesses that require an approach that differs from other businesses in their portfolio. It is also a danger when the business context changes significantly, as it appears to have done in computers over the past few years. If the basic linkage approach is not suited to the business, value will be destroyed.

Parents that concentrate on linkage value creation must also guard against destroying value through their stand-alone influence. A new business may be brought into the portfolio on the grounds that the parent can create value by linking it to other businesses that are owned. But, if the parent lacks a sufficient feel for the new business, the danger is that whatever value may be created from linkages is more than offset by damaging stand-alone influence. American Express, for example, may well have created substantial value through the linkages it parented between its different financial services divisions in the 1980s, but these successes were undermined by the difficulty of applying appropriate stand-alone parenting to businesses as different as Shearson brokerage, Lehman Brothers investment bank, the Boston company, and Amex Insurance.[40] We have encountered many similar examples of value destruction in our research. They arise because the prospect of linkage value creation can easily tempt parents to move into businesses for which they do not possess a sufficient feel.

Linkage Value Creation and Parenting Advantage

Linkage value creation can play an important role in corporate strategies that achieve parenting advantage, as we have seen in our analyses of Banc One, Unilever, ABB, and Canon. All these companies have value creation insights that stress linkage opportunities and distinctive parenting characteristics that are particularly well matched to implementing them.

However, positive linkage influence must be coupled with stand-alone influence that, at least, avoids value destruction; and very few companies achieve parenting advantage purely on the basis of linkage value creation. The companies we have discussed in this chapter all complement their linkage influence with strong contributions to the stand-alone performance of their businesses. Typically, parenting advantage comes from a combination of stand-alone and linkage influence, rather than from linkage influence alone.

The corporate parents in our research that major on linkage influence and achieve parenting advantage all have a clear view of their heartland business criteria, and they have applied these criteria to their portfolio decisions. Banc One has stuck largely to regional banking in the United States, Unilever has progressively concentrated on fast-moving consumer packaged goods in multiple national markets, ABB has targeted its acquisitions on complex and nationally focused engineering businesses, and Canon, while extending its heartland over time, has based its portfolio around its core technical competences and has been cautious about how it moves into new markets. This dedication to heartland businesses has been necessary both to yield unusual linkage value creation opportunities and to avoid value destruction pitfalls.

SUMMARY

In this chapter, we have analyzed how parents create value through influencing the linkages between their businesses. We have seen that linkage influence frequently ends up by destroying value, as parents pay insufficient attention to the nature of the parenting opportunities and the need to overcome the enlightened self-interest paradox. We therefore recommend that parents aiming to create linkage value should address these questions:

- What would the business units do if they were independent entities?
- Would this outcome be suboptimal? If so, what blockages are causing enlightened self-interest to fail? Can we remove the blockages at an acceptable cost, and by what means?
- Are we focusing our attention on specific linkage opportunities that have real value potential, and do we have suitable characteristics for realizing these opportunities?
- Is our linkage approach suitable for all the businesses in our portfolio, or do we run the risk of damaging some of our businesses by imposing the wrong approach on them?
- Are we sure that we can avoid damaging stand-alone influence on the businesses across which we are trying to create valuable

linkages? If not, should we refocus our portfolio to eliminate businesses where we lack a sufficient feel to avoid stand-alone value destruction?

Provided that parents address all these questions, linkage influence can be a powerful source of value creation within overall corporate strategies to achieve parenting advantage.

NOTES

1. Sometimes, linkage influence overlaps with stand-alone influence. For example, a parent may influence one of its businesses to adopt a particular computer system based on the past experience of another business unit. This might be viewed as encouraging the sharing of best practice, a typical form of linkage influence. However, it might also be viewed as a focused attempt to improve the stand-alone performance of the business, based on parental knowledge and understanding. Although such areas of overlap do exist, we have found that the concept of linkage influence is one that managers readily accept and use. The precise labeling of grey areas is of less importance than the identification of the mainstream intention, which is that the company should derive special benefit from the promotion of internal linkages between its units.

2. The approaches provide an overview of different ways of parenting linkages. They can be related to the different overall parenting styles, in the terminology introduced in Chapter 2:

	Financial Control Style	Strategic Control Style	Strategic Planning Style
Approach 1	✓	✓	X
Approach 2	X	✓	✓
Approach 3	X	✓	✓
Approach 4	X	✓	✓
Approach 5	X	X	✓

✓ = This approach is compatible with this style.
X = This approach is not compatible with this style.

3. In some of BTR's businesses, such as sealing systems, there are more linkage opportunities between similar profit centers in different countries. In these businesses, BTR's group chief executives have recently begun to play a more active linkage role, encouraging profit centers to share technical resources and rationalize product ranges, thus moving closer to Approach 2.

4. See Chapter 6.

5. "Banc One's Tactics for Excellence," an interview with John B. McCoy, *The Bankers Magazine*, September–October 1991, pp. 6–13.

6. *Financial Times,* Management Page, July 13, 1992.

7. "Banc One's Tactics for Excellence," op. cit.

8. See Chapters 8 and 9.

9. *The Business Magazine,* September–October 1991, p. 11.

10. We were told by a Unilever manager that an academic research project recorded the density of lateral relationships between business units in Unilever to be significantly greater than in any other company studied.

11. A computer program contains information on each individual, including details of experience, training, and qualifications. This system has been in place since the 1980s and is now a well-oiled machine. Unlike the systems in many companies, it is actively supported and used by line managers. "One of the beauties of the system is that people seem to try and make it work, rather than try and work against it," explained David Jones, head of management training.

12. The story of Shearson is particularly interesting. Sandy Weill sold Shearson to American Express for $900 million in 1981. He became president of American Express in 1983 and left the company in 1985. He created Primerica, a financial services group that includes broker Smith Barney. In March 1993, after integrating other acquisitions in this area and making internal investments, American Express sold the retail brokerage and asset management businesses of Shearson to Sandy Weill's Primerica for $1 billion.

13. See, for example, Christopher A. Bartlett and Sumantra Ghoshal, *Managing across Borders: The Transnational Solution,* Cambridge, MA: Harvard University Press, 1989; Sumantra Ghoshal and Christopher A. Bartlett, "The Multinational Corporation as an Interorganizational Network," *Academy of Management Review,* vol. 15, no. 4, 1990, pp. 603–625; Tom Peters, "Rethinking Scale," *California Management Review,* Fall 1992, pp. 7–29.

14. See Michael Scott Morton (ed.), *The Corporation of the 1990s,* New York: Oxford University Press, 1991.

15. However, the existence of joint ownership in the business context creates some important differences from political parallels. Through its ownership of subsidiary units, the parent can orchestrate a "federation" in a way that political entities find hard. See Charles Handy, "Balancing Corporate Power: A New Federalist Paper," *Harvard Business Review,* November–December 1992, pp. 59–72; James O'Toole and Warren Bennis, "Our Federalist Future: The Leadership Imperative," *California Management Review,* Summer 1992, pp. 73–90.

16. See Peter Drucker, "The Information-Based Organization," in *The Frontiers of Management,* Heinemann, 1987, Chapter 24; Peter F. Drucker, "The New Society of Organizations," *Harvard Business Review,* September–October 1992, pp. 95–104; Rosabeth Moss Kanter, *When Giants Learn to Dance,* New York: Simon & Schuster, 1989 (On the postentrepreneurial corporation, and the challenges and opportunities facing traditional corporations).

17. For a discussion of the strengths and weaknesses of a matrix structure, see Henry Mintzberg, *The Structuring of Organizations,* Englewood Cliffs, NJ: Prentice-Hall, 1979, pp. 168–175.

18. For a discussion of focus and scale in economic business definitions, see Appendix A.

19. William Taylor, "The Logic of Global Business: An Interview with ABB's Percy Barnevik," *Harvard Business Review*, March–April 1991, pp. 90–105.

20. Taylor, "The Logic of Global Business."

21. In August 1993, ABB announced a restructuring at board level, which distinguished between the tasks of 3 regional directors, covering the Americas, Asia, and Europe, and 4 divisional directors, each in charge of a group of BAs.

22. Tony Jackson, "Pioneer Looks East for Profit," *Financial Times*, April 4, 1993.

23. See Carol Kennedy, "ABB: Model Merger for the New Europe," *Long Range Planning*, vol. 25, no. 5, pp. 10–17, 1992.

24. For a description of ABB's approach to cutting of overhead costs, see Chapter 8.

25. C. K. Prahalad and Gary Hamel, "The Core Competence of the Corporation," *Harvard Business Review*, May–June 1990. See also the discussion of core competences in Chapter 4.

26. See Teruo Yamanouchi, "Breakthrough: The Development of the Canon Personal Copier," *Long Range Planning*, vol. 22, no. 5, pp. 11–21, 1989.

27. Yamanouchi, "Breakthrough."

28. Nigel Campbell, Michael Goold, and Kimio Kase, *The Role of the Centre in Managing Large Diversified Companies in Japan*, Ashridge Strategic Management Centre Working Paper, September 1990.

29. See, for example, Walter Kiechel, "Corporate Strategy for the 1990s," *Fortune*, February 29, 1988, p. 20. See also Hiroyuki Itami, *Mobilizing Invisible Assets*, Cambridge, MA: Harvard University Press, 1987.

30. Core competences involve an ability to combine technologies in ways that are not easy for others to replicate. It is the ability to transfer and cross-fertilize particular technologies in developing products that best exemplifies technological core competence.

31. Yamanouchi, "Breakthrough."

32. See Prahalad and Hamel, "The Core Competence of the Corporation."

33. Applying this logic, Canon had reputedly achieved an 84% share of the world market for desktop laser printer "engines" by 1990, although these were incorporated in many products and brands other than its own.

34. See Chapter 10 for a fuller discussion of Canon's approach to learning.

35. For a discussion of Canon's past heartland extensions and current moves, see Chapter 10.

36. We have considered linkage approaches across the company as a whole. However, within Approaches 2 and 3, it is possible to create linkages inside the specific business groups or divisions in rather different ways, although they will usually tend to be somewhat influenced by the corporate parent's headquarters approach.

37. The discussions of weak management, conflict between managers' and other stakeholders' interests, and specialist expertise parallel the similar points made in Chapter 6. Several of the points made in Chapter 6 are also relevant in this chapter.

38. In most large organizations that we have studied, managers of individual business units have only a partial sense of what is going on in areas of the organization distant from them. In such cases, they may not come across "natural" prompts to a particular linkage unless the path is smoothed. This is almost the reverse of the "10 percent versus 100 percent" problem noted in Chapter 6. Because the parent organization is necessarily spending time with each of its units, it is more likely than any one individual unit to see possibilities for mutually advantageous collaboration. For a discussion of the limits of knowledge and rationality within organizations, see Herbert A. Simon, *Administrative Behavior*, 2nd ed., New York: Macmillan, 1961, pp. 39–41. Oliver Williamson discusses the issue of bounded rationality in *Markets and Hierarchies*, New York: Free Press, 1975. See also Herbert A. Simon, "Theories of Bounded Rationality," in C. McGuire and R. Radner (eds.), *Decision and Organization*, Amsterdam, North-Holland Publishing, 1972, pp. 161–176.

39. The role of an intermediary in negotiations is discussed in academic literature on negotiation theory. By obtaining information that the negotiating parties will not share directly, an intermediary may be able to steer them toward areas of greater mutual benefit. See, for example, Howard Raiffa, *The Art and Science of Negotiation*, Cambridge, MA: Harvard University Press, 1982; Roger Fisher and William Ury, *Getting to Yes*, 2nd ed., Business Books, 1991.

40. For a fuller discussion of American Express and its search for valuable linkages, see *American Express's Corporate Strategy*, unpublished working paper, Ashridge Strategic Management Centre, 1994. For commentary on the many positive achievements at American Express, see "Synergy Works at American Express," *Fortune*, February 16, 1987, pp. 51–52; Michael Porter, *Competitive Advantage*, New York: Free Press, 1985, pp. 410–412; Rosabeth Moss Kanter, *When Giants Learn to Dance*, New York: Simon & Schuster, 1989, Chapters 3–4. For a more negative view, see John Friedman and John Meehan, *House of Cards: Inside the Troubled Empire of American Express*, New York: Putnam, 1992. For a discussion of the difficulties of managing diverse financial services businesses, including those once owned by American Express, see Robert Grant, "Diversification in the Financial Services Industry," in A. Campbell and K. Luchs, *Strategic Synergy*, Oxford: Butterworth Heinemann, 1992, pp. 203–242.

8 FUNCTIONAL AND SERVICES INFLUENCE

This chapter deals with the role in corporate strategy of central staff functions and services. Companies differ widely in the size, departmental composition, and cost of their central staffs.[1] However, in most companies central staff groups represent a significant part of the cost of the parent, and it is therefore important that they should be contributing to parental value creation. In reviewing the influence of central staffs, it is useful to distinguish between central functions and central services.

Central functions in areas such as finance, personnel, marketing, engineering, or technical services provide specialist functional leadership and guidance for the businesses, as well as assisting the senior line managers in the parent in exercising stand-alone or linkage influence. In addition to advising senior managers in the parent, functional staff may also set policies for the businesses to follow, act as centers of excellence to provide advice to the businesses, be involved in functional appointments and appraisal processes, and help to spread best practice between the businesses. Functional staffs aim to create value by raising professional standards in the businesses and by contributing to better decisions on functional matters.

In principle, central services, such as pensions administration, catering, or security, differ from central functions. The aim of a central service is simply to provide a cost-effective service, whereas functional staff are aiming to influence the decisions and policies of the businesses. The catering department, for example, is trying to give an economical and efficient catering service for each business, but is not trying to have an impact on the policies of the businesses.[2] In practice, however, many staff groups combine both roles. Cooper's manufacturing services department, as we shall see, not only exercises functional influence on Cooper's businesses but also provides a service to them. The justification

187

for the department is both that it raises the quality of manufacturing in the businesses and that it provides cost-effective services as a consultant on manufacturing issues. Central service departments in areas that go beyond routine administration or support usually combine functional influence with straight service provision.

The basic rationales for the parent to establish central staff departments concern specialist expertise and economies of scale. A central department can reach critical mass in terms of expertise or size in a way that may not be possible for some, or all, of the individual businesses. There may be benefits from specialization, making it possible, for example, to recruit better quality expertise or to develop scarce skills; or the benefits may concern economies of scale, allowing services to be provided more cost-effectively or functional skills to be better utilized. Eliminating duplication can also be a benefit; the interpretation of safety legislation only needs to be done once by a central unit, saving work in all the businesses. Claims about the added value available from specialization and the economies of scale in central staffs represent a classic and long-standing justification for the role of the corporate parent.

But the impact of corporate staffs is often negative rather than positive. In the 1980s and early 1990s, the trend in many companies has been to reduce central staffs. These companies not only aimed to reduce overhead costs but also expected the businesses to perform better, energized by the freedom to do things without functional interference and without relying on central services. The implication is that central staffs frequently do more damage than good.

As in the previous two chapters, we shall therefore begin by examining the causes of value destruction by central staffs. We will go on to describe three companies—Cooper Industries, 3M, and Shell—in which central staffs play an important value-creating role in the corporate strategy. We will conclude by focusing on the conditions for value creation that are relevant for central staff departments. Since central functions and services contribute to the stand-alone and linkage influence of the parent, many of the observations in Chapters 6 and 7 are relevant in considering whether and how they create value. However, the importance of staff groups in some companies, the variations between companies in their use of central staffs, and the particular issues faced by staff groups in attempting to create value through functional and services influence have led us to devote a separate chapter to them.

VALUE DESTRUCTION

Despite the theoretical benefits from economies of scale and specialization, our research has shown that central staffs are often less expert, less cost-effective, and less responsive than outside suppliers or than businesses' own departments.

Central staff departments often have difficulty recruiting top-quality talent, who see more challenge, greater rewards, and better career prospects in independent specialist organizations; this is particularly true of professional services such as tax, real estate, or legal advice. Equally, the best managers within a company tend to gravitate toward line positions in the parent or in the businesses, rather than toward central staff departments. Central staffs are frequently under less pressure to contain their costs than external suppliers or departments within businesses, since they may be protected by transfer pricing mechanisms or by parental preference. And they may be less responsive to the needs of individual businesses because they do not have to win the chance to serve the businesses in open competition with outside suppliers, and can often claim that "company policy" requires them to act in ways that are unsuitable or irritating for the businesses. In one company, we suggested to the chairman that he should consider allowing his businesses to buy property services from outside suppliers, in order to introduce more commercial edge into his in-house department. His response was that this would be quite impossible since, "How would our property people be able to plan their workflow with any certainty?" It appeared to have escaped the chairman's attention that the other side of certain workflow is sloppy cost control and inattentive customer service.

Even where central staffs add value for some businesses, they all too frequently negate this value by inappropriate involvement in others. It is insensitivity to the specific needs of each business in the portfolio that has brought many central activities into disrepute. In one company we researched, the retail division had a central department providing security to the businesses. Good security can add 5 or 10 percentage points to profit and, because it is a specialist area, the division chief executive was confident of the value of centralizing it. In addition, he believed that centralization helped to reduce costs. Over time, a policy had developed that all businesses should use the central department. The division then bought another retail chain from an entrepreneur. The plan was to professionalize the new business and help it grow faster than would have been possible under private ownership. One of the early decisions was to cancel the existing security arrangements and service the business's security needs out of the central department. Not only would the decision help to install parent company professionalism, but it would also result in an estimated saving in cost of $100,000. The management of the new business complained about the imposition of this central department, but the division chief executive assumed that the complaints were a sign of the "medicine working" and expected them to fall away over time. Some 3 years later, however, the complaints were still being voiced. A review of the security arrangements undertaken to appease the business management team finally pointed out the problem. The main security issue in the new business was very different from the other businesses. In the other businesses, security problems were created by customers taking products they had not paid for. In the new business, they were created by staff, not customers. A $200,000 investment in customer surveillance equipment, to bring the new business up to the standards of the existing businesses, had been largely ineffective and unnecessary. At the same time, shrinkage caused by staff had more than doubled through lack of security initiatives, costing the business more than $1.5 million over 3 years. A $100,000 cost saving through centralizing the activity had ended up costing the company nearly $2 million.

This story may seem trite and improbable. But in its essence, it is a story we have heard all too often: central activities destroying value because they did not understand the local issues and were not sensitive enough to the complaints from the businesses to distinguish between genuine problems and not-invented-here thinking.

The existence of a central department is therefore no guarantee that it will add value. If such departments are cozy homes for superannuated executives who have reached the end of their line management careers, if they are imposed on businesses with little attention to their professionalism and efficiency, or if they are insensitive to the specific needs of each business, they can do considerable damage to businesses' performance and to the relationship between the parent and the businesses. Even well-intentioned central departments, with hard-working and experienced staffs that strive to respond to businesses' needs, will often struggle to be as expert, as responsive, and as lean and hungry as competent external specialist suppliers, or as closely attuned to the needs of each business as a dedicated staff department within the business.[3] Indeed there is another value creation paradox here. If professional external specialists exist, and are willing to provide whatever functional expertise or services are required, why should an in-house staff department be able to outperform them? Why should a corporate function or service be superior to a dedicated firm that must survive and prosper purely on the basis of its expertise in the specialism in question? The rise of specialist providers in many areas has meant that it is harder and harder for central staffs to "beat the specialists" and create value. The beating-the-specialists paradox is of obvious relevance for central services that must compete with third-party providers. But it is also a useful challenge for staff that provide functional leadership, since many companies have found that they could outsource the role of "centers of excellence" in areas ranging from information technology (IT) to strategic planning to treasury advice, and benefit from the expertise of specialists.

Where there are doubts about the expertise of central staffs in comparison with specialists, the attention shifts rapidly to their costs; and as companies have become more aware of the costs of central staff, there has been a trend to downsize them. Companies such as ABB and

BP have outsourced many staff functions and services to external suppliers; have set up others as independent businesses that are free to trade with both internal and external customers, and will stand or fall by their success in doing so; and have decentralized others to be provided, if they are needed at all, within the businesses. By these means, ABB claims that it can normally reduce the size of acquired companies' head offices by 90 percent: 30 percent of head count are redundant, 30 percent are set up as independent businesses and forced to compete with outside suppliers as separate profit centers, and 30 percent are decentralized to businesses.[4] Following a similar philosophy, BP reduced the size of its head office in the early 1990s by well over 1,000 people by extensive outsourcing and decentralization.

Indeed, the tide is now running so strongly in favor of the outsourcers, the downsizers, and the decentralizers that it takes a brave chief executive to propose establishing, or enlarging, a central department to add more value to his or her businesses. Such a proposal risks being greeted with criticism and even derision, both from within and from outside the company. Empowerment and debureaucratization, not to mention good old-fashioned overhead reduction, all argue for sharpening the axe and taking it to central staffs.

VALUE CREATION

Yet, some companies continue to operate successful central departments and derive benefit from them. We shall discuss three such companies: Cooper, 3M, and Shell. Our purpose will be to see how and why their central departments create value, and how they fit into their corporate strategies.

Cooper Industries

Cooper Industries is a $6 billion company, headquartered in Houston, Texas. Until the 1960s, it was primarily a manufacturer of engines and compressors for natural gas pipelines. Since then, the company has diversified substantially, and now has businesses in hand tools, power tools, electrical products, electrical power equipment, and automotive parts, as well as in a variety of petroleum and industrial equipment sectors. A common factor in all these businesses is that manufacturing is an important part of the overall cost structure, and a key to competitive success.

COOPER INDUSTRIES: MANUFACTURING FUNCTION. Bob Cizik, the chairman and chief executive officer of Cooper, is personally committed to the importance of manufacturing for Cooper. He, and the other members of the parenting team, all have long experience of manufacturing businesses, and they believe that a focus on improving manufacturing is a key source of Cooper added value. Cizik has written about this in a company publication entitled "Manufacturing: Give Me an M," which deals with Cooper's so-called Big M manufacturing philosophy. The essence of the philosophy is that all functions in Cooper need to work together to recognize the importance of manufacturing. Manufacturing issues are high on the agenda in discussions between representatives of the parent company and the businesses, and feature prominently in planning and budgeting reviews.

The parent's influence on manufacturing is reinforced by the role of the corporate Manufacturing Services department. The department has a staff of 15 people, most of whom are divisional manufacturing people on 3- to 4-year tours of duty. "It is better," says Cizik, "to have people with a bit of grease under their fingernails." For many years, it was led by Joseph Coppola, a senior vice president with 14 years' service at Cooper, and a lifetime of experience in manufacturing positions.[5] The department is organized around different subfunctional specialisms, such as automation engineering, materials management, and environmental technology.

The department is involved in screening all Cooper acquisitions and is always brought in to advise on postacquisition improvement opportunities. It has a major role in vetting capital investment proposals from the ongoing businesses and will help them to develop their proposals if requested to do so. It is also available to advise any Cooper business on manufacturing issues. In addition, the department organizes a number of Cooper-wide "councils," which meet two or three times a year and bring together functional staff from different businesses around specific topics such as logistics management. The department also organizes a 2-year graduate training scheme in manufacturing management. The department therefore combines a functional influence role with a central service role.

Cooper's Manufacturing Services department can add value because the different Cooper businesses nearly all face similar manufacturing issues. "You would be amazed at the similarities in the processes in our divisions," explained Coppola. "Machining, fabrication, assembly, work measurement, materials management, quality assurance, and so on are all similar." This means that Cizik and the parenting team can develop a good sense of the issues and tradeoffs that the businesses face in their manufacturing operations, and that the Manufacturing Services department can become experts in these processes. Experience gained in one business carries over and is relevant to other businesses, and the department can draw on benchmarks and best practice established in one business in advising others. This raises standards and develops skills throughout the company. Cooper typically finds that new acquisitions fall far short of the company's expectations for manufacturing productivity, and major savings can be made by working with the Manufacturing Services department. Productivity at Champion Spark Plug, for example, increased by 30 percent during the 3 years after its acquisition by Cooper.

The Manufacturing Services department recognizes, however, that its skills do not cover all types and forms of manufacturing. "We can contribute less on the sort of sophisticated forging they do in the Cameron business," stated Coppola. "And if we went into something like a speciality chemical, I doubt whether we could contribute much at all."

The way in which the Manufacturing Services department exercises its influence is also noteworthy. Except with new acquisitions, the department only works with Cooper businesses if it is invited to do so. Businesses are free to establish their own specialist departments or to use the services of an external consultant, if they so choose. However, in the words of one division head: "It would be very difficult to have all that expertise within the division, and outside suppliers would be very expensive and probably not as close to the state of the art as the Manufacturing Services people." It is seen as crucially important for the department to regard the businesses as "clients," who must be persuaded of the views of the department. "We give out no edicts," was Coppola's claim. Furthermore members of the department are trained to treat the personal relationships in client businesses with care, and to aim to win the respect and support of the businesses for the department. To achieve this end, the department always tries to involve divisional staff closely with projects on which it works, and to structure the projects to show early successes. A quick identification of a measurable cost reduction opportunity gains credibility for the department, and improves the chances of major, longer-term proposals being accepted. Although the department draws on its experience with other divisions in making best practice suggestions, it is careful to avoid "gossip" about problems or personalities elsewhere. Establishing a confidential relationship with each business, in which openness about issues is possible, is the goal. To encourage divisions to seek the help of the department, Cooper makes no charge for its services, a policy that applies to all of Cooper's central departments.

Cizik believes that an internal department working in this way can create much more value than outside consultants and advisers. "It helps us to demonstrate our commitment to manufacturing. Our people know Cooper plants, products, and people better than outsiders, and can spread the Cooper way of doing things. And, with our own staff, we can control the interpersonal interfaces better and make sure that we are developing the skills in our people throughout the company."

The attention and priority given to manufacturing in Cooper reflects the key success factors in its businesses. The Big M concept and Cooper's understanding and support for manufacturing investments distinguish the company from many other parents that have neither the commitment to, nor the feel for, what is necessary to succeed in manufacturing businesses. Furthermore, the Manufacturing Services department creates value because it has a unique depth of expertise, based on its extensive experience with Cooper's particular types of businesses, and ways of working that develop positive relationships with the businesses. The fact that businesses do not have to pay for the services of the department obviously means that they are seen as good value. But the primary purpose of the "no charges" policy is to overcome any initial resistance to calling on the department for advice; our clear impression is that Cooper businesses that have experience of working with the department would continue to use it, even if it made "commercial" charges for its work.

COOPER INDUSTRIES: CORPORATE STRATEGY.   Exhibit 8–1 is a parenting advantage statement for Cooper Industries. Cooper's basic *value creation insight* has been to perceive that many U.S. businesses in the manufacturing sector have failed to make the most of their opportunities. Often, their parent companies have become disenchanted with manufacturing, seeing it as an unattractive or unglamorous activity in which to engage. As a result, these businesses have not been aggressively managed. They have suffered from underinvestment, have given up the initiative to strong labor unions, have allowed unnecessary costs to be taken on, and have lost focus on those products and markets where their profit opportunities were best. A typical example was Champion Spark Plug, acquired by Cooper in 1989.

Champion was the leading U.S. manufacturer of spark plugs and wipers, with a strong domestic market share in these products, and a brand name that was recognized throughout the world. However, the company had been reinvesting only 2 percent of sales revenues in its businesses since the mid-1970s, and the main thrust of Champion's strategy during the 1980s was to deemphasize its core products, and to diversify into new products that could carry the Champion brand name. These included oil additives, hand cleaners, automotive tools, and even a chain of car washes in Mexico. Most of these new businesses proved unprofitable, and in 1988 Champion incurred an operating loss of $6.4 million in its U.S. operations. Cooper believes that a corporate parent that is committed to manufacturing can help businesses such as Champion to realize their true potential, by focusing them back on their core businesses and helping them to identify ways of improving their productivity and profitability in those businesses. Thus Champion is now concentrating on spark plugs, wipers, and aircraft ignitions. With the help of the Manufacturing Services department, it has also consolidated five North American production facilities down to two, and has introduced major process changes and investments and eliminated restrictive practices at the remaining plants. The business is now much more profitable.

Cooper's second value creation insight concerns the synergies available from bringing together different businesses that serve similar

EXHIBIT 8–1   Cooper Industries parenting advantage statement

Value Creation Insights	Companies that see manufacturing as unattractive lose focus on their profit opportunities, give up the initiative to strong unions, and fail to control their costs. This gives opportunities for a parent committed to manufacturing, particularly if it has specialist expertise in manufacturing technology and other relevant areas.
	Many independent businesses serving similar markets can derive synergy benefits in manufacturing and distribution, if brought under common parental ownership.
Distinctive Parenting Characteristics	Commitment to manufacturing: • Strong, specialist corporate staffs in manufacturing and other related areas.
	"Cooperization" process: • Structuring into semiautonomous divisions that report directly to the corporate center, with no intermediate layers. • Reviewing top management appointments in the businesses, and bringing in managers from elsewhere in Cooper as needed. • "80/20" focus on most profitable opportunities. • Imposing Cooper policies and practices, and clarifying what issues will be handled by the center and by the business. • "Clustering" businesses with linkage potential into the same division.
Heartland Businesses	Manufacturing businesses, drawing on selected, fairly mature technologies, with leading positions and brand recognition in their markets; focusing mainly on the U.S. market; where consumer marketing is not key to success; and preferably where individual customers do not have high bargaining power and capital intensity is not high.

markets into divisional "clusters." The clusters allow Cooper to overcome the competition and mutual distrust that prevent independent businesses from achieving the sort of benefits that are possible. Cooper now has clusters in hand tools, oil field equipment, and lighting products, as well as automotive parts.

Cooper's value creation insights are supported by *distinctive parenting characteristics* that stress the importance of manufacturing, and the role of the Manufacturing Services department and other corporate staff departments, such as industrial relations, management development, finance, and planning. Other distinctive parenting characteristics are drawn together in the concept of "Cooperization," an approach to parenting that is applied to all Cooper businesses, but especially to new acquisitions. The ingredients of Cooperization include:

- Fitting the business into the Cooper organization structure and, in particular, cutting out unnecessary layers of overhead and reporting. The Cooper structure stresses "semiautonomous" divisions (for example, the Lighting division, the Hand Tool division, the Oil Tool division) that report direct to the corporate center. There are some 20 divisions, which each report to one of three executive vice presidents. The EVPs have very small, one- or two-person staffs and do not act as a consolidation or review level in the corporate structure. Rather they act as representatives of Bob Cizik and the corporate center for the divisions in their areas. The structure therefore has a minimum of layers and often allows substantial cost reductions for new acquisitions. Champion's corporate, international, and regional head offices, for example, were all closed by Cooper. The divisions are largely free to propose their own strategies, subject to corporate functional policies, as described later in this section. If necessary, Cooper also tightens up on redundant working capital, SG&A costs and other areas of overhead.

- Appointing new managers from elsewhere in Cooper to senior positions in the business, as needed. Typically, the general manager and financial controller in newly acquired businesses come from other Cooper businesses and, in some cases, a much larger number of new appointments are made: In Champion, for example, 19 out of the top 20 positions were filled by new Cooper people after the acquisition. Cooper's human resource planning tracks the top 800 people in the company, with the expectation that cross-divisional moves will be common and beneficial. In 1991, no fewer than 45 senior managers moved into new divisions.

- Insisting that all businesses focus on their most profitable products, markets, and customers. Cooper believes strongly in the 80:20 rule, especially for companies that have strayed into peripheral diversifications. A firm steer from the parent is sometimes needed to move business managers away from peripheral products to which they have become unduly committed.

- Imposing Cooper's policies and approaches on industrial relations, management development and succession planning, environmental issues, benefit plans, accounting, planning and budgeting, and real estate. In areas such as real estate and industrial relations, corporate functions take over responsibility from the divisions, and believe that they can achieve economies of scale and specialization not open to individual divisions. With accounting, planning, budgeting, and benefit plans, it is more a matter of following the Cooper way of doing things. "When we make an acquisition," says Alan Reidel, vice chairman of the board, "we tend to impose the

Cooper culture and processes. To begin with, we were less confident in doing this, but during the last few years we have gained increasing confidence that this is right for the sort of businesses we acquire." Support for this view comes from most of the division heads. One, from a recent acquisition, observed that during the first year of Cooper's ownership he felt that he was being "mothered" and became restive. But now that the disciplines have been established, he accepts that they work well. "It is more supportive than restrictive."

- Bringing in the Manufacturing Services department to identify manufacturing improvements and investments that should be made. Often, this involves factory relocation and the introduction of new working practices.

- Lastly, designing the divisional structure to facilitate resource sharing between businesses clustered into the same division. For example, with the acquisition of Moog Automotive in 1992, a new automotive parts cluster has been created, with a view to sharing and rationalizing distribution and sales between Cooper's "under-car" chassis part businesses. The structure is intended to locate businesses with significant potential for sharing within the same division, and to avoid the need for strong linkages between divisions.

Cooperization is possible due to the similarities between Cooper's businesses, and the opportunities this gives for common approaches between them. Indeed, sharing best practice between businesses is a pervasive philosophy in Cooper. As one division head claimed: "To me, the strength that comes out of corporate is that if they see something that works in one division, then they get it into the others too." Thus, although Cooper's portfolio has evolved over the past 25 years to include a variety of different businesses, they all conform to the *heartland criteria*. Most essentially, all of Cooper's businesses have manufacturing as an important part of their cost structure, and a significant basis for competitive advantage. "The business of Cooper Industries is value-added manufacturing. We come from a long line of people who forge, cast, draw, drill, bore, grind, heat treat, and fabricate things out of metal. Now we use other materials and processes as well. But it all comes down to manufacturing. We know a lot about that."[6] Continuous process manufacturing or simple assembly businesses do not build on Cooper's particular competences, but businesses where cell-based manufacturing is the key to success are particularly suitable.

In addition to the manufacturing theme, Cooper concentrates on businesses in relatively mature technology areas, where high levels of R&D spending and rapid product obsolescence are not found. Cooper is less comfortable judging the risks in more rapidly changing, technically unstable businesses. Ideally, businesses should, however, have some distinctive products or technologies to give them a competitive edge. Cooper prefers businesses that have leading market share positions and enjoy brand recognition in their markets. It is also familiar with the types of issues that arise where products are handled through extensive channels of distribution, involving wholesalers, dealers and, for consumer goods, retailers. Most of Cooper's businesses are primarily focused on U.S. production for U.S. markets. Cooper avoids businesses that require high consumer marketing expenditures or that are dominated by a few large customers. It also avoids high capital intensity businesses and businesses that face intractable labor relations problems or large environmental or product liability risks. Businesses should also be large enough to support the Cooper overhead.

Nearly all of Cooper's many acquisitions during the past 25 years conform, to a greater or lesser extent, to these specifications. Companies such as Crescent, Lufkin, Nicholson, and Triangle in the Hand Tool division, Crouse Hinds, McGraw Eddison, and RTE in Electrical Products, Cameron and Gardner-Denver in oil field equipment, and Champion and Moog in automotive parts, all fall within the heartland. Equally, Cooper Airmotive, an aircraft engine overhaul and service business, the Industrial Machinery division of Gardner-Denver, the specialty forged products business of Cameron, and other smaller businesses have been divested because they did not fit the heartland criteria.

Bob Cizik, Cooper's CEO, expresses the importance of the heartland criteria as follows: "Because our businesses are all reasonably closely related in terms of depending on basic manufacturing processes and using similar sorts of distribution channels, we can get a pretty good understanding of the issues they each face quite quickly." "You don't have to know the details of how a turbine is made as against a file, but the language is the same. There are tremendous similarities in the sorts of strategic issues that come up in the different businesses in our group." "Flags pop in your mind when certain ratios are getting out of line. I know what sort of ratios we need to make money, given the cost structures in our sort of businesses. These sort of understandings get developed over time due to constant experience with our businesses." It is in the heartland businesses that Cooper's manufacturing-based corporate strategy adds the most value.

Cooper's record through the 1980s is one of significant success in the majority of its businesses. Its Cooperization approach has yielded real performance improvements in many businesses and has allowed profits before tax to rise from $240 million in 1982 to $625 million in 1993, on sales up from $2,390 million to $6,274 million. Earnings per share have risen during the same period from $1.38 to $2.75.

These impressive results would have been even better without the negative impact of the oil and gas sector, which has remained depressed for the bulk of the past decade, and which is likely to cause 1994 earnings to fall. Cooper's long-term commitment to this sector has prevented the quality of its corporate strategy from being fully reflected in its bottom-line results since the early 1980s. Oil and gas equipment is one of Cooper's original businesses and provided excellent profits, particularly during the late 1970s oil boom. But Cooper's willingness to continue to support and invest in it during bad times and good has proved expensive. During the late 1980s and early 1990s, Electrical Power Equipment has also faced a depressed market.

Cooper also paid full prices for its major late 1980s acquisitions, such as Champion, Cameron, and RTE, with the result that, by 1992 it was carrying $2.8 billion of intangible assets, primarily goodwill, in its balance sheet. This has depressed return on assets and means that Cooperization needs to yield high levels of performance improvement in these businesses to justify the acquisitions. Progress has already been made, but Cooper will be looking for substantial advances when the markets in which these businesses compete improve.

Cooper's success has come, therefore, not from corporate development activities that have positioned it in profitable sectors or allowed it to make cheap acquisitions, but from performance improvement in the businesses in its portfolio. Its parenting influence, based on its manufacturing commitment and skills and its Cooperization process, creates unusual value. Some commentators point to Cooper's diversity as the source of its strength. We believe, in contrast, that it is its focus on the kinds of businesses and the sorts of parenting opportunities that it knows best that accounts for its success.

3M

For many years, 3M has been one of the most admired companies in the United States. It has an enviable record for innovation and new business creation, and it has a portfolio diversity that most rivals have found difficult to manage. The company's $14 billion of sales are derived from some 40 product divisions. The product divisions range from businesses selling abrasives to the automotive industry to businesses selling dental products to the pharmaceutical industry. One division makes roofing tile granules, another makes Post-it notes for use in office work. But there is a common factor within this diversity. Nearly every product made by 3M has been developed by its technical staff in its divisional laboratories. On average, 3M's laboratories produce many more successful new products than its rivals. Much of this success is due to the parenting influence of 3M's central technical function.

3M: TECHNICAL FUNCTION.   Each division in 3M has its own laboratory for developing new products, and the duty of the divisional technical director is to develop products that secure the business's future. It is the technical function, not the marketing function, that is the main source of new product ideas. The management of laboratories, the prime task of the divisional technical director, is therefore a vital activity in 3M. In total, there are some 150 laboratories working on some 1,500 new product development programs. Divisional technical directors report to divisional chief executives. But they also have dotted-line relationships with sector technical directors and the central technical function. The sector technical director has overall responsibility for the technical development of the sector and works closely with the central technical function. Good relationships between technical people at the center, the sector level, and the divisions are essential to the smooth working of the 3M system.

In this description of 3M's technical function, we will focus on two areas of influence—improving the quality of laboratory management and ensuring that technology is shared throughout 3M. The quality of laboratory management is maintained and improved in a number of ways. First, the central technical function helps to develop and select technical directors. The final selection decision is made by the division chief executive, but the candidates will all be internal technical people, identified by the technical function and imbued with 3M's approach to laboratory management. One unusual aspect of 3M's approach is the close working relationship between marketing and technical staff. Technical staff frequently visit customers and go on calls with marketing staff. As a result, 3M technical people are usually skilled in marketing and new product development as well as technical research. It is the central technical function's responsibility to make sure that these qualities are being developed in the technical staff and that there are sufficient potential candidates for new technical posts.

The second way that the quality of laboratory management is developed is through an audit process. The central technical function manages a peer audit process, in which technical directors from other laboratories visit a laboratory and write a report on their findings. The main focus is on operational procedures such as how patents are handled or how the new product introduction system is working. The importance attached to these audits helps to reinforce the natural desire of technical directors to get a clean bill of health from their peers. Both the audits themselves, and the work that goes into deciding what the audit standards should be, help to accelerate the continuous learning process at 3M. In addition, learning flows both ways, from those doing the audit to those being studied and vice versa.

The third way of raising the quality of laboratory management is through the policies, procedures, and cultural norms that have grown up and become institutionalized in 3M. The managers in the central technical function are the keepers of these "3M ways of doing things," and they have the task of deciding whether to enforce a particular policy or norm. They recognize the need for continuous improvement and experimentation, and hence, they keep a healthy balance between rigid policies and management chaos. One policy or norm is the 15 percent rule. This 40-year-old norm permits technical people to spend 15 percent of their time pursuing their own ideas. It is a management policy that 3M has cherished as part of its technical culture. Not all technical people choose to use the opportunity to follow their own projects. But some do, and the fact that the opportunity is available encourages individuals to take more responsibility for innovation. Another part of the "3M way" is the new product introduction system. This consists of a centrally written four-page guideline, stating that all laboratories should have an organized system for product introduction. The guideline was developed in 1967 and has been revised a number of times since then. As a divisional technical director explained: "I don't feel constrained by the guideline. It is not an instruction. I am free to develop my own system if I believe it will be more effective. But it is a standard against which to measure yourself and it is used in the audit process."

The fourth way of raising the quality of laboratory management is through the Technical Forum. All technical staff in 3M are members of the Forum, and the Forum has its own central staff. It is like a professional association within 3M. There are regular meetings to discuss the "hottest technical areas" and the "hottest management issues." Attendance is voluntary, ensuring that managers only attend if they consider the sessions useful.

Another important role of the central technical staff is to ensure that technology is shared between 3M's 150 laboratories. This commitment to share is backed by a strong 3M policy that technology belongs to the company not the division. "We have many different ways of encouraging people to talk to one another" explained Tom Wollner, Staff Vice President, Corporate Research Laboratories. "We don't have any organized plan for networking. But we encourage it to happen as much as we can." The campus environment of 3M Center in St. Paul, Minnesota, is important. "We have definitely created something unusual here. It is not easy to repeat." In fact, 3M has found it hard to recreate the same closeness of working relationships in Japan and in Europe, and even in the new technology center in Austin, Texas. But networking is not the only way of encouraging sharing. 3M has an extensive library system recording all the new product development programs both past and present. Technology fairs are held annually in which each laboratory displays its wares, and marketing and production people are invited to browse the stalls. These systems encourage information flow and make it easy for technical directors to access work going on in other laboratories.

In other companies, many of the features of 3M's technical function—technical forums, peer audits, networking, and strong cultures—lead to bureaucracy and time wasting. In 3M, these processes are highly positive and fit well within a corporate strategy that stresses decentralization, new product development, and a performance orientation, and which concentrates on businesses in which these characteristics pay off best. Thus, 3M's technical function plays an important role within its overall corporate strategy.

3M: CORPORATE STRATEGY.   Exhibit 8–2 is a parenting advantage statement for 3M.The company's *value creation insights* have been built up over its 90-year history. They have their roots in the early days, when 3M had to find a way of succeeding against stronger, established competitors. The key to success in 3M's businesses has been to insist on superior products, based on technically unique qualities that can be defended against competitors. To achieve this, 3M's parenting emphasizes the role of the technical function in promoting creativity and innovation. This is about the quality of the technical function in each division; it is about the way the technical functions in different divisions coordinate and network together; and it is about the way central technical units nurture common technologies and provide support in specialist areas to help divisions bring products to market quickly. It is also about

EXHIBIT 8–2   3M parenting advantage statement

Value Creation Insights	Innovative new products and whole new businesses can be developed by effective parenting of the technical function, within a structure of small decentralized divisions that encourage close relationships between sales and technical people and share common technologies.
'Distinctive Parenting Characteristics	Decentralized management philosophy: • The division is the building block. • Financial performance is the main measure of success; but divisions cannot cut back on investment in research. • Close relationships between sales and technical staff. Technology and innovation-led culture: • Commitment to innovation. • Commitment to the innovator. • Status of the technical function. Long tenure, cooperative, consensus-seeking cadre of senior managers: • Few outsiders. • Supportive culture. • Trust relationships.
Heartland Businesses	Businesses developed from 3M's core coating technology, particularly those that sell products to the automotive industry and the office products industry, have clear technical leadership, and can earn the return on sales needed to support a high research expenditure.

an approach to sales and marketing that creates a close link between the customer and the rest of the business. This approach was originated by William McKnight in 3M's earliest history. Describing events in 1913, 3M's *Our Story So Far*[7] explains McKnight's early influence: "McKnight trained his salesmen to do what he had learned could be done, get into work areas, find what kind of abrasive materials were best suited for customer needs, demonstrate 3M's products and report problems precisely to the factory with samples of poor quality sandpaper." The link between sales, marketing, production, and technical staffs is still as close as it was in these early days, and 3M managers believe that it is central to their ability to innovate and get new products accepted by customers. The closeness of the relationship between the technical staffs and salespeople is a particularly unusual feature of the 3M approach.

In implementing 3M's insights, several *distinctive parenting characteristics* justify special mention. First, 3M is a highly decentralized company, but care is taken to decentralize to units that are large enough to be self-standing and, therefore, capable of funding their own research. Equally, 3M attempts to prevent divisions from getting so large that individual innovations no longer have any impact. "Over the years, we've discovered that when a division reaches a certain size, it has a tendency to spend too much of its time on established products and markets, and a lesser amount on new products and businesses." The size of divisions varies according to the size of the market being addressed. But most divisions have at least $100 million in sales. Divisions are measured against profit targets, with return on investment and return on sales as vital performance ratios. Divisions are expected to earn enough to fund their own growth and are encouraged to grow as fast as resources allow.

Decentralization is prized. McKnight is often quoted as having said, "The mistakes . . . (of individuals) . . . are not as serious in the long run as the mistakes management will make if it is dictatorial." However, divisions operate within a web of functional guidance and are closely monitored by line management to ensure that the decentralized divisions are managed in the 3M way. For example, spending on research is closely monitored and attempts to increase profits by cutting back on research investment would be quickly picked up.

The second distinctive characteristic is the careful nurturing of 3M's technology and innovation-led culture. 3M is a company that talks more about innovation and innovators than almost any other company and is used worldwide as an exemplar of innovation. 3M's commitment to innovation is symbolized by its long-standing public target of having 25 percent of sales from new products launched in the past 5 years, which has recently been upgraded to 30 percent of sales from new products launched in the past 4 years. Another public target is its commitment to spend around 7 percent of sales on research. 3M is also unusual in its commitment to and support for the individual innovator and has many ways of recognizing exceptional technical efforts. Its Golden Step awards (for U.S. employees) and Pathfinder awards (for international employees) are given to individuals and teams who achieve important product developments. Individuals with unusual technical records are elected to the "Carlton Society," named after one of 3M's most prominent technical leaders. 3M believes in the individual as the driver and champion of new ideas.

Supporting 3M's commitment to innovation and to the innovators are two other distinctive features of the parenting approach—the status of the technical function and the technical background of many of 3M's senior managers. The technical function in 3M is "first among equals." Managers are at pains to point out that success depends on good technology, good production, and good marketing. But, within this triad, the technical people feel special. "The great weight of the long-term commercial responsibility falls on the technical director in the 3M system. My role is to make sure we have the technologies that will enable us to have a long-term business position," explained one divisional technical director. The status of the technical function encourages an unusually commercial attitude, which has been carefully fostered from the earliest days and ensures the close working relationships of the three functions. Technical directors are continually trying to get a customer's perspective on development projects. They encourage technicians to visit customers, spend time with marketing people, and work with production.

This highly cooperative, technically-led culture is supported by a third distinctive characteristic: the long tenure, consensus-seeking cadre of senior managers. Many of 3M's top managers have worked together for 20 years or more, and they have developed networks and relationships that make for unusually close and supportive working relationships. This both helps to maintain the 3M way of doing things and encourages the exchange of technical information and ideas that is so essential to success.

The final distinctive parenting characteristic, which we have already discussed, is the way 3M parents the technical function.

3M's *heartland businesses* draw off a common set of related technologies: More than 80 percent of 3M's 60,000-item product portfolio is linked to the technologies that have developed from the need to understand how to coat substrates with materials. "Over 80 percent of our business is involved in precision coating and probably more than 90 percent works with polymers." Within this technological heartland, the ideal 3M business fits a particular mold. It is based on technology that is patentable or sufficiently protectable so that 3M can gain reasonable returns for its technical investments. The product area is a niche, differentiated from a mass-market positioning. The product area is small enough that 3M can gain a number one or number two position and large enough to make its investment in technology worthwhile. "Obviously we are not in heavy machinery or any low profit business environments. If the average profit is only 5 percent, we would steer away from the business." Internally, managers look for a return on sales of 25 percent in new product or business areas. Returns at this level are only possible in markets where the product can achieve a clear technical advantage.

Another feature of an ideal 3M business is a focus on the early stage of a technology life cycle. "When we get into mature product areas, we don't seem to do so well," explained one manager. More recently, however, 3M has attempted to extend its heartland to these maturer areas. "Since the mid-1970s there are fewer opportunities for us, so we can no longer afford to reduce emphasis on a business that has become more competitive. We now have to be prepared to fight competitors with our manufacturing skills and learn how to compete in the mature stages of the market."

A final feature of an ideal 3M business is that a high percentage of its products should be sold to the office products, the automobile, or the metalworking markets. "We are probably now number one in companies that serve the office market. Our office market division probably understands the customer and distribution channels better than anyone else," commented one manager. The same depth of sales knowledge exists in the automobile and metalworking industries, where 3M had most of its earliest successes. Businesses have frequently grown out of sales or technical relationships that identified a customer need and developed a solution to it. "We were selling abrasives to the auto industry. Because of contact with the factory floor, we noticed that they were having problems with paintwork. They would glue newspaper over the parts they did not want to paint. But then they would have problems removing the glue." From this recognition of customer need and a 2-year research effort, 3M developed masking tape and its product portfolio of pressure-sensitive tapes.

3M's long-term performance has been the envy of many of its competitors. A pretax return on sales averaging over 16 percent has been combined with a return on equity around 20 percent and a compound growth rate of 7.5 percent. But, as 3M has grown, its rate of growth has inevitably slowed. In 1980, the compound growth rate was 13 percent, but in 1990 the company was more than twice as large as it had been in 1980 and growth in percentage terms became harder. In the future, 3M faces the challenge of learning how to compete effectively in more mature market sectors, where manufacturing costs, volumes, and prices are the keys to success, rather than technology. In the past, growth from new products has made it possible for 3M to deemphasize markets as they matured and the products became commodity items. But in tapes, and more recently in computer diskettes, 3M has decided to stand and fight. It is an alien strategic battle, one that does not play to 3M's historic parenting strengths. It will be interesting to see whether 3M will succeed in these businesses.

Shell

The Royal Dutch/Shell Group (Shell) is 60 percent owned by Royal Dutch Petroleum, a Netherlands company, and 40 percent by Shell Transport and Trading, a U.K. plc (public limited company). In 1993, Shell had sales of £63 billion, operating profits before interest and tax of £6 billion, and a cash flow from operations of £8 billion. It is active in all phases of the oil industry, and in most countries of the world. Shell has enjoyed remarkable success in the oil industry in the past two decades. In a comment on a recent set of results, the *Financial Times* stated: "In the oil sector at least, Shell is not so much ahead of the pack as in a class of its own."[8] An important component in Shell's success has been the role played by its strong central functions and services, which have helped it to transfer technical and functional expertise around the world in support of its many local operating companies.

SHELL: CENTRAL FUNCTIONS. Each manager in Shell is attached to a particular function, which manages his or her career within Shell and sees that he or she receives appropriate training and experience. The functions are custodians of Shell's professionalism in the different aspects of its businesses and are responsible for seeing that strong functional and technical staff are available wherever they are needed. The functions range from finance, legal, human resources, and planning to technical functions such as exploration and production, manufacturing, and research. They have the job of keeping up to date with professional and technical knowledge and disseminating it throughout the Group. They also provide technical and professional audits, which are subsequently used in performance appraisals and guidance to the operating companies. The functions advise the regional organizations on the functional soundness of operating company capital expenditure proposals and plans. In addition, they give advice on the development of new technology and the selection of research programs. Overall, the functions are involved in the setting of required standards, guidelines, and procedures, and, in particular, in coordinating and stimulating the recruitment and development of people. In 1993, Shell had a total of about 700 people, divided between its head offices in London and the Hague, in its central functions.

Shell has seen that, in the oil industry, a parent providing top-quality technical expertise in different countries around the world both receives, and can take advantage of, more opportunities. It has therefore invested heavily to ensure that its technical skills are at the leading edge, and to see that they can be brought to bear throughout the world. Among the payoffs have been the creation of a major new business in LNG, which presented considerable technical challenges, both in production in countries such as Brunei, Malaysia, and Australia and in transportation to end markets such as Japan; and a leadership position during the 1970s and 1980s in upgrading refineries to produce lighter, more profitable products. Shell's technical functions have contributed strongly to the development of its businesses around the world and represent a distinctive source of strength.

Shell's commercial functions also keep abreast of, and develop, the state of the art in their respective fields. In planning, for example, Shell pioneered the scenario approach to planning that has been widely written about and commented on, and which has now been adopted by many other companies.[9] Scenario planning has helped the company to be more responsive to changes in its competitive environment, and to be more open-minded in its strategic thinking. Shell believes, for example, that it was able to respond more rapidly to both the 1973 and 1979 oil shocks due to previous discussions of the possibility of an oil crisis that had been stimulated by scenario planning. Shell's functional staff in the human resource and organizational development areas are also important in creating the internationally mobile cadre of professional managers, which, as we shall see, are integral to the success of Shell's corporate strategy.

SHELL: CORPORATE STRATEGY. Exhibit 8–3 is a parenting advantage statement for Shell. Shell's *value creation insights* bring out the importance of being able to transfer technical and functional expertise around the world, and of being able to support good local investment opportunities. Shell's corporate staff groups are vital to the implementation of this insight.

A further value creation insight is Shell's recognition that good relationships with local governments, communities, and partners—often in difficult parts of the world where other companies are less welcome—can provide Shell with access to opportunities that other companies may not enjoy. Shell, therefore, pays particular attention to its local country relationships and has seen this pay off in a variety of countries. For example, in Brunei it has developed major oil and LNG fields; in Japan, it has achieved a larger presence than any of the other oil majors; in Singapore, it has a particularly strong position in refining and marketing; and in The Netherlands, it has been able to take the lead in developing the vast natural gas resources, in a joint venture with Exxon.

Shell's corporate staffs are by no means the only *distinctive parenting characteristics* that support its value creation insights. Other important characteristics are Shell's large cadre of mobile, professional, international managers, its distinctive organizational structure and decision-making process, its strong commitment to high business principles, its long-term business horizons and strong financial resources, and its corporate brand.

Shell has a group of 10,000 managers on its international staff, representing some 70 different nationalities.[10] International staff are expected to be willing to relocate to any of Shell's over 100 operating

EXHIBIT 8–3   Shell parenting advantage statement

Value Creation Insights	A parent that can transfer relevant technical and functional expertise around the world, fund good investments that others might not get access to or support, and maintain good relations with local governments, communities, and partners can enhance the performance of operating companies in the oil industry and related businesses.
Distinctive Parenting Characteristics	Strong functional staffs, especially in technical departments.
	World's largest cadre of mobile, international, professional managers.
	Local country autonomy, within a consensus-seeking global matrix organizational structure and decision making process.
	Commitment to high Shell business principles.
	Financial strength.
	Long-time horizons.
	Strong Shell brand.
Heartland Businesses	Major, long-term, technically complex, natural resource businesses, especially in hydrocarbons, in a variety of different countries, and large associated downstream businesses in manufacturing and marketing.

companies around the world, for tours of duty ranging from a few months to several years. As a result, Shell can both reinforce local managements with international experts when needed and offer genuine international career opportunities to locals of any country in the world. There are few, if any, other companies whose management is as truly multinational as Shell's.[11] Shell's internationalism can be traced back to its origins, with a parent organization split between The Netherlands and the United Kingdom, and with activities in oil production and trading that have historically been far from these home countries.

Shell's organizational structure and decision-making process is designed to draw out the views of local managers around the world, and to hammer out a consensus between all interested parties. The structure involves a complex, three-dimensional matrix, covering geography, business sectors, and functions. Decisions require the agreement of managers from all these areas. As one manager put it: "Shell is the largest consensus hunting organization in the world." While this has costs in terms of the speed of decisions, it ensures that all managers feel consulted and that decisions take account of local knowledge, corporate expertise, global priorities, and business sector strategies.[12]

Primary responsibility for strategy and for operations lies with local operating companies, and Shell stresses the importance of preserving initiative and accountability at this level in order to respond to local needs and opportunities. However local companies report to regional organizations and are expected to consult and receive advice and support from the functions and business sectors. The nature of this support will differ, depending on the nature of the business sector. For example, the Group's upstream sector, which comprises exploration and production, takes direct responsibility for exploration in new areas where this can only be centrally initiated. Once oil or gas has been found, however, control is gradually delegated to a newly formed production company in the country concerned. The downstream sector is much more decentralized in its activities, as many of the operating companies have mature marketing and refining operations. In the case of chemicals, a more central focus is taken as the Group faces regional and global competitors, and many operating companies require more professional backup and support. On any given decision—for example, a new refinery investment—the local operating company (or companies) concerned would discuss the issues fully with their regional management, and with relevant functional and sector management before a final consensus was reached. The extensive consultation reinforces Shell's professionalism and underlines its commitment to taking a truly multinational view of initiatives and priorities.

Shell believes that a common culture and common principles are essential to hold such a far flung and diverse company together. Accordingly it has laid down a statement of business principles[13] that guides its dealings throughout the world. As Lo van Wachem, until recently chairman of Shell, states: "Bearing in mind the variation in ethical values around the world, it is vital that some form of code of conduct is agreed . . . so that the outside world recognizes the standards to which we aspire, can comment on them, and judge us by them."[14] It is evident that the principles not only express Shell's belief about how it should operate but are an important part of building and maintaining Shell's good reputation with local communities.

Shell's financial muscle and its long-term outlook have meant that the company can afford to fund operating company investments that other parents might not be able to support. The company accepts that oil industry investments tend to involve very large sums of money, long time horizons, and significant risks. A well-financed parent with expertise in oil-related businesses can create value by recognizing the merit of investments that others might see as too large, too risky, or too complex.

Operating companies can also benefit from the use of the Shell brand on their products and services. However, Shell guards the use of its brand name carefully and has established detailed policies and constraints concerning its use by operating companies. The reputation of the brand is a major commercial asset that carries weight with customers, staff, suppliers, governments, and partners.

Shell's *heartland* is in the oil industry and associated businesses. The great majority of the company's senior managers have spent their careers in the oil industry, for the most part with Shell, and they have a corresponding depth of understanding for the sorts of decisions that arise in it. They are comfortable evaluating the advantages and disadvantages of major, long-term, often technically complex exploration and production projects. They have a feel for the downstream businesses in refining, marketing, petrochemicals, and trading. And they have experience and expertise in these businesses in most countries throughout the world. All levels of management in Shell are steeped in the opportunities, issues, and problems presented by oil-related businesses.

Due to fears about the prospects in oil, and in common with all the other oil majors, Shell embarked on a diversification drive in the 1970s and 1980s. Different local companies pursued a variety of diversification opportunities, but among the major corporate moves were the acquisition of Billiton, a metals and minerals company, and the establishment of Temana, which was developed into a consumer products group. Shell Coal was established as an international coal trading company, and a joint venture with Gulf in the nuclear industry was set up. There was also rapid expansion in gas exploration and production and in speciality chemicals, and, more recently, heavy investment in some countries in forestry.

Of these new businesses, only gas, which shares many common features with oil, has so far proved an unqualified success. Shell has exited from the nuclear business and from consumer products, and has scaled down the expansion of the other new businesses since the late 1980s. Even coal and metals, which are natural resource based businesses, have proved significantly different from oil and have required much more time and money to establish as profitable businesses than was initially expected. Billiton was the subject of a bid from Gencor in 1993, and there is now much less enthusiasm for diversification than 10 years ago.

In part, the reduced enthusiasm for diversification reflects a more optimistic view of opportunities in oil compared with newer businesses. But there is also a recognition that the diversifications have taken Shell into businesses in which the key success factors differ from oil, and for which senior Shell management have a less sure intuitive feel. Comments from two Shell managers are relevant: "The difference you have if you are not familiar with the business is in not having a sense of the risks deep in your brain somewhere. You lack the 'Fingerspitzgefühle'; if you have little experience in a business, you can have disproportionate surprises." And a former executive of the consumer products business explained the difficulties he faced as follows: "Although we were set up in separate offices and with new staffs, we still had to put investment decisions up to the Shell board, who were all oil men. When I needed new money I had to justify it in their terms." It is for reasons of this sort that Shell's portfolio thinking is now reemphasizing its heartland oil-related businesses.

While Shell's record in its heartland businesses has been strong, it has therefore been less successful in its diversifications and has been pulling back from them since the late 1980s. Characteristics that led to parenting advantage in the heartland, such as functional expertise and deep knowledge of the oil industry and the workings of the global matrix, have proved to be less suitable qualities, and in some cases actual disadvantages, elsewhere. Despite Shell's long time horizons, and its emphasis on organization learning,[15] it has not proved possible to become a successful parent for most of the diversifications.

The contrast between Shell's success in its heartland and its difficulties in diversifications is mirrored in almost all the other oil companies, including Exxon and BP. Indeed, Shell probably has a better record in its new businesses than most of its oil industry rivals. However, the experience of these companies does bring out how difficult it is for a hands-on, Strategic Planning style parent to acquire a sufficient feel for unfamiliar businesses and to alter deeply ingrained parenting characteristics that have been developed for, and are primarily suitable within, the heartland.

CONDITIONS FOR VALUE CREATION AND PARENTING ADVANTAGE

Despite the general skepticism about the value created by functional and services influence, we have encountered several companies in which central staffs play an important role within the corporate strategy. The three companies described in this chapter, and several others including Banc One, RTZ, Unilever, and numerous Japanese companies such as Canon, all have powerful specialist staff groups that are major contributors to their corporate strategies. Based on our work with these companies, we can assess the conditions for value creation from central functions and services.

Opportunities for Functional and Services Value Creation

In our discussions of stand-alone and linkage influence in Chapters 6 and 7, we isolated some underlying circumstances under which parenting opportunities arise. These circumstances remain relevant for identifying opportunities for central staffs to contribute to stand-alone or linkage value creation. There are, however, some particular issues concerning the circumstances in which opportunities arise for functional or services influence to create value.

At one level, the existence of economies of scale and specialization provide the basis for central staff opportunities. Often a business's own department in an area such as manufacturing services may not have the specialist expertise or scale to be as effective as a central department. But a similar argument can justify specialist third-party suppliers setting themselves up to work with a variety of different companies. Under what circumstances is there an opportunity for a central department to be more effective than a specialized third party?

In-house departments obviously have a role when there are no effective third-party suppliers. In the early days of IT, there was a much less extensive range of consultants, advisers, and specialists offering their services to companies. As a result, in-house IT departments grew up. But, as the external market matured, the justification for internal staff reduced. A similar development has occurred in a variety of functional and services areas. Unilever, for example, used to have an in-house market research department. Now the company buys these services from independent specialists, retaining only a small staff group in-house to advise businesses on the selection of outside suppliers and on the techniques they use.

If an active third-party market exists, central staffs are only likely to be superior in cost-effectiveness if they have some proprietary skills or know-how. Most often, this is based on the continuing working relationships that they establish with the particular businesses in the company's portfolio. Cooper's central manufacturing skills have been fine-tuned by working with the range of manufacturing businesses in its portfolio; 3M's corporate technical skills have been honed as a result of experience with more than 100 3M laboratories; Shell's exploration skills have been developed through repeated application in assisting different operating companies around the world. No external supplier is likely to be able to draw on the range of specifically relevant experience in these skill areas that has been available to the parent company, or to have the depth of understanding for the corporate culture.[16] Thus Cooper businesses are better off looking to Cooper's Manufacturing Services department than they would be if they tried to build a comparable resource within the business or attempted to buy it in from an outside consultant, since the department has unique skills based on experience gained with Cooper's particular range of businesses.[17]

Sometimes a parent possesses unique skills that do not depend on its experience over time with its portfolio of businesses. For example, a company like 3M is able to draw on the skills of a few key scientists in its central research labs. Some of these individuals possess personal skills that are in very short supply, and a 3M business could not expect to be able to hire comparable people or to buy-in their services from a consultant. Rare skills or resources possessed by the parent can enhance the performance of any business to which they are relevant.[18]

An in-house department can also be better attuned to working within the corporate culture, and can establish better long-term personal relationships with managers in the businesses, than outside contractors who come and go.[19] A further reason for using in-house departments is to protect proprietary business information or know-how from competitors; there is a risk that third-party suppliers that gain access to confidential information or skills may allow it to leak out to others.

If none of these reasons for establishing or maintaining an in-house department apply, serious consideration should be given to outsourcing. Parenting opportunities only exist if there are reasons why central functions and services can have expertise or resources that are not matched by outside suppliers.

Parenting Characteristics That Fit the Opportunities

To succeed in creating value, the actual characteristics of the functions and services must match the needs and opportunities in the businesses. The central department must indeed possess superior expertise, and must achieve economies of scale from centralizing its provision. As a check on this requirement, benchmarking central staffs against other companies and against third-party providers is always worthwhile, and far too seldom done in any systematic fashion. In many ways, the most effective means of testing the quality of an internal staff department is to allow the businesses freedom to buy externally if they choose, and to encourage them to shop around.

The quality of the relationship between a central department and the businesses is also vital to the creation of value. Businesses need to feel that their needs are being taken into account by central staffs, and that the functional leadership and services provided are appropriate to those needs. Any sense that central staffs are ignoring the real needs of the business, or are impervious to criticism, damages the relationship of mutual trust and respect, on which so much depends.

The most obvious way of creating a good relationship between a central department and the businesses is by emphasizing that the department should see the businesses as its clients. The businesses, as clients, should be fully consulted on the nature and quantity of the service provided, and on its cost. Their feedback on the performance of the department should be sought, and the possibility of going to outside suppliers should remain real. This ensures that the department is responsive to the businesses' needs and attentive to interpersonal relationships. Staff departments that feel under no obligation to "sell" themselves to their users typically do not have attitudes that lead to value-creating relationships.

But a purely third-party type of relationship may also be subopti-mal. By working more closely with the businesses, the in-house depart-ment can be closer to their problems and may therefore give a better service and improve relationships. Also, the corporate parent may wish to intervene in the specification of the service to be provided, or in the charges to be made for it, and may refuse to allow businesses to deal with outside suppliers, in order to reap economies of scale and linkage benefits that would not otherwise be achieved, ensure that quality standards are met, and so forth. However, any interference with the standard client-contractor model should be handled with care, since the benefits claimed are often illusory, and since such interference can eas-ily damage relationships.

Avoidance of Value Destruction

As with all forms of parental influence, value destruction by central functions and services can follow from a lack of feel for the needs and opportunities in the businesses.[20] One aspect of Shell's move away from its diversifications was the discovery that its central functions and serv-ices were less suitable for the needs of some of its newer businesses.

Value destruction can also follow from a lack of professionalism in the departments concerned. The finance staff need to be on top of cur-rent best practice in treasury, tax, and financial control; the PR depart-ment needs to draw on state-of-the-art communication techniques; the technical experts must be competent in their respective disciplines. Furthermore, the staff departments must avoid gaffes in their handling of the personal relationships with their contacts in the businesses. In addition to a feel for the issues faced by the businesses, professionalism is necessary for avoiding value destruction by central functions and services.

The corporate parent may also destroy value through its influence on the central staff departments themselves. Some central departments can be seen as quasi-businesses in their own right. By establishing them as such, and allowing businesses to choose whether to buy from them, the parent has a practical means of testing whether they are competi-tive and value creating. A further step along this path is to encourage the departments to compete for external business. Open market compe-tition may not always be feasible or desirable, especially if there is pro-prietary know-how in the department that the parent does not wish to make available to third parties. Nevertheless, open market competition is obviously an effective way of testing a department's competitiveness, particularly in more standard administrative areas.

Viewing staff departments as quasi-businesses, whether or not they compete externally, brings out a further condition for avoiding value destruction: The corporate parent should have a sufficient feel for the function-as-a-business. Otherwise, it is likely to exercise negative influence, appointing the wrong people to the department, pressing for the wrong objectives and initiatives, and so forth. This is a particular problem if the function or service is not similar in its characteristics to the bulk of the other businesses in the portfolio, and explains, for example, why so many manufacturing companies have had difficulty establishing an effective information technology department. If the corporate parent does not have the experience and feel to make good decisions about the staffing, resourcing, and policies of the department, it may be better to outsource it.

Functional and Services Value Creation and Parenting Advantage

While functional and services influence can contribute significantly to value creation, it cannot, alone, create parenting advantage. For parenting advantage, functional and services influence needs to form part of an overall corporate strategy, including stand-alone and linkage influence, that is superior to that of rivals.

Nevertheless, we have seen that in Cooper, 3M, and Shell, the value creation insights and distinctive parenting characteristics are integrally linked to the roles played by corporate functions and services, and that the heartland business criteria take account of the contribution that they can make. The unusual skills and expertise located in the corporate staff groups are therefore important ingredients in building parenting advantage for these companies.

SUMMARY

While there are many pitfalls and dangers of value destruction in functional and services influence, well-run, expert central staffs can be a source of parental value creation. Parents that aspire to create value through functional and services influence need, however, to address the following questions:

- Why should central departments be able to be more cost-effective than an external supplier, or than businesses' own departments? Have the skills of the central departments been benchmarked against external suppliers, and has outsourcing been seriously considered? Do the central departments have proprietary know-how or special relationships with the businesses that external suppliers would lack?
- Are the relationships between the central departments and the businesses likely to lead to cost-effective service provision? If they

depart from standard client-contractor relationships, why is this justified?

- Is the corporate team able to parent the function or service effectively? If not, should it remain within the company?

Provided these questions can be answered positively, central functions and services can play an important role within the overall corporate strategy for building parenting advantage.

NOTES

1. See David Young and Michael Goold, *Effective Headquarters Staffs*, Ashridge Strategic Management Centre, 1993, which is based on a survey of the headquarters staffs of over 100 U.K. companies. The survey provides data on the size, composition, and role of the corporate staffs in these companies.

2. No doubt, hypothetical examples can be constructed in which the catering department has an impact on some aspects of businesses' policies, but except in exceptional circumstances, these will be of minor significance to the overall performance of the businesses.

3. If central staffs are imposed by the parent, these difficulties can be compounded by the perceptions of business managers. Even a highly effective department may be resented and criticized if it has not been freely chosen by its users.

4. See Carol Kennedy, "ABB: Model Merger for the New Europe," *Long Range Planning*, vol. 25, no. 5, 1992, pp. 10–17.

5. Coppola left Cooper in 1993 to become chairman and chief executive of Giddings and Lewis Inc. He was replace by Nishan Teshoian.

6. "Cooper Industries Management Philosophy: The Nature of Cooper's Businesses" (company publication, p. 3).

7. *Our Story So Far,* St. Paul, Minnesota: 3M, 1977.

8. Lex Column, *Financial Times,* May 15, 1992.

9. See P. Wack, "Scenarios: Uncharted Waters Ahead," *Harvard Business Review,* September–October 1985, and "Scenarios: Shooting the Rapids," *Harvard Business Review,* November–December 1985; P. Schwartz, *The Art of the Long View: Scenario Planning–Protecting Your Company against an Uncertain Future,* London: Century Business, 1992. Shell's most recent set of global scenarios are described in a company publication, *Global Scenarios 1992–2020,* Shell International Petroleum Company, 1992.

10. In 1990, the expatriate staff on overseas duty consisted of 1,913 British, 1,760 Dutch, 109 Australian, 142 German, 186 French, and 876 from 65 other countries. The pool of managers available for international assignments is, of course, substantially larger.

11. A small illustration of this point was provided by a dinner in London to discuss our research, which was attended by two managers from Holland, and one each from the United States, Australia, Colombia, Ireland, and the United Kingdom.

12. In this respect, Shell's structure resembles ABB's (see Chapter 7). Shell, however, has a much larger central staff than ABB, and a much longer history of working within a matrix structure.

13. *Statement of General Business Principles,* Royal Dutch/Shell Group of Companies, 1984 (revised 1988).

14. L. C. van Wachem, *Unity in Diversity—Organisation and People in Multinational Enterprises.* Address to the 46th German Society for Business Economics Conference, Berlin, 1992.

15. See A. de Geus, "Planning as Learning," *Harvard Business Review,* March–April 1988.

16. The counterargument is that the in-house department cannot have the breadth of experience across different companies of the third-party supplier, who can therefore be closer to the relevant "state-of-the-art." The issue is whether the special needs of, and experience gained from, the companies' businesses are of more consequence than the general experience of the outside supplier.

17. Recent developments in strategic management theory stress the so-called resource-based theory of the firm. The essence of this theory is that companies often cannot acquire resources and capabilities rapidly, but must build them up gradually over time. The resources that a company possesses are a function of its particular past history and experience. Thus a company's resources and skills may be unique, or at least very hard to replicate, since its previous history is unique. A parent that systematically builds a portfolio of businesses that use and develop certain skills may well therefore possess skills that could not be available to its businesses in any other way. See, for example, G. Dosi, D. J. Teece, and S. Winter, "Understanding Corporate Coherence: Theory and Evidence," *Journal of Economic Behaviour and Organization,* 1994 (forthcoming). See also Chapter 4, footnote 42.

18. One question that arises with unique resources of this sort is why their owners do not set themselves up in business to provide the resource in question to the highest bidders on the open market. Why are the 3M scientists not established as a highly specialized scientific consultancy? Why are these unique skills exploited within the structure of a corporate parent? Once again, transaction cost economics provides a basic theoretical answer to these questions. The corporate parent structure is the best way of exploiting resources that are integrally linked to the businesses. If investment in the resources would be less profitable without a guarantee that the businesses would use them, or if the businesses in question could be damaged by the use of the resources by other third parties, the corporate parent structure is best. The technical term for such situations in transaction cost economics is

"specialized assets." See David J. Teece, "Towards an Economic Theory of the Multiproduct Firm," *Journal of Economic Behaviour and Organisations,* vol. 3, 1982; Joseph T. Mahoney, "The Choice of Organisational Form: Vertical Financial Ownership versus Other Methods of Vertical Integration," *Strategic Management Journal,* vol. 13, 1992.

19. Long-term relational contracting can, however, allow the outside supplier a similar status to the in-house provider, while retaining the discipline of being an external contractor. See, for example, Hans Thorelli, "Networks: Between Markets and Hierarchies," *Strategic Management Journal,* January–February 1986; Raymond Miles and Charles Snow, "Network Organizations: New Concepts for New Forms," *California Management Review,* Spring 1986; Charles Handy, *The Age of Unreason,* Boston, MA: Harvard Business School Press, 1990.

20. See Chapters 6 and 7.

9 CORPORATE DEVELOPMENT

In Chapters 6, 7, and 8, we described ways in which the parent can influence the businesses in its portfolio. In this chapter, we shall discuss the decisions that the parent makes that affect the composition of the portfolio. We shall refer to these decisions as corporate development.

Corporate development decisions alter the definition, nature, and number of businesses in the portfolio. Decisions to amalgamate (or separate out) businesses are regarded by most parents as key corporate strategy choices. Acquisitions and divestments are often important in corporate development; and many parents stress their role in major deals. Corporate venturing can also influence portfolio composition; and several parents insist that their initiatives in corporate renewal and the creation of new businesses are vital for the long-term health and survival of the corporation. Corporate development decisions are therefore seen by most parents as essential components of corporate strategy, and as important potential sources of value creation.[1]

Corporate development differs from the sorts of parental influence described in earlier chapters because it concerns decisions where the parent is the prime mover and the source of initiative. It is for the parent to decide what businesses to have in its portfolio, and how they should be defined and structured. As such, these decisions differ from other areas of parental influence, where the primary initiative lies with the management teams responsible for the businesses.

Value creation from corporate development, however, is often hard to separate from value created by the parenting influence a business receives once it has been brought into the portfolio or restructured. While, therefore, the distinction between corporate development decisions and other areas of parenting influence is clear in principle, in practice there can be overlaps. Acquisitions, for example, are often justified both in terms of what the parent expects to do with the business once it has been acquired and in terms of the impact that the deal itself will have on portfolio composition and value creation. But the importance of corporate development decisions, and the primary responsibility of the parent for them, mean that they merit separate treatment. We shall also find that they raise some particular issues concerning value creation and destruction by the parent.

As in earlier chapters, we shall begin by identifying some of the characteristic risks of value destruction associated with corporate development activities. We will go on to discuss companies such as TI and Hanson that have succeeded in creating value through different sorts of corporate development. We will conclude by drawing out the conditions under which corporate development does create value.

VALUE DESTRUCTION

Although many corporate parents believe that they can create value through astute corporate development decisions, the evidence suggests that they are often wrong. For example, companies frequently overpay for acquisitions and establish new ventures that never prosper.

Acquisitions

One of the most common and most important sources of value destruction in corporate development is paying too much for acquisitions. Corporate histories are littered with stories of businesses acquired for $100 million in year 1 and sold in year 3 for $50 million or even $10 million. In many cases, poor subsequent parenting has contributed to the value destruction. But the main problem is often the price paid in the first place. The new acquisition proves to be much less attractive than it seemed from the outside.

An extreme example concerns Ferranti, a medium-sized electronics company. During the 1980s, Ferranti performed well, developing a variety of sound businesses in defense electronics and other areas. However, in 1987, Ferranti decided to acquire the U.S. International Signal and Communication (ISC) Group, with a view to becoming a major player in international defense markets. In 1989, it was discovered that ISC had entered into various fraudulent contracts, and Ferranti took a £215 million loss on these contracts. As a result, Ferranti was severely weakened and eventually forced into receivership in 1993. A single acquisition brought the company to its knees and wiped out all of the value created by the parent during the previous decades.

The difficulty of judging the true value of an acquisition from the outside, even if no fraudulent contracts exist, is always a problem for the acquiring company, particularly in a contested bid where due diligence inquiries are not possible before the deal is finalized. It is easy to misperceive the underlying position and prospects of the bid target, to overestimate the extent to which its performance can be enhanced, and to be drawn into negotiations that lead to paying an excessive price. These difficulties are compounded by the excitement of the chase, in which enthusiasm, optimism, and the desire to close the deal become increasingly likely to prevail over more cautious judgments.[2] The nature and dynamics of the acquisition process tilt the scales in favor of overpayment. As a result, acquisitions are often made that destroy value for the acquiring company.[3]

Corporate Ventures

The record of corporate ventures is also strewn with failures.[4] New businesses, whether based on corporate research, the exploitation of otherwise fallow assets, or new ideas that do not fall naturally into the territory of existing businesses, have a way of looking far more attractive at the planning stage than in their subsequent development. As with acquisitions, corporate entrepreneurs, excited by the prospect of getting into new and unfamiliar businesses, convince themselves that the grass on the other side of the hill is far greener than it really is.

During the 1970s and early 1980s, there was, for example, something of a fashion for large industrial companies to launch new businesses in fish farming. In one company, we were told that the rationale was that the fish thrived in the warm waste water discharged by one of the coastal plants owned by the company, and that there seemed to be an opportunity to capitalize on this chance discovery to create a new environmentally friendly, ecologically beneficial business with longterm potential. In the event, competition in fish farming turned out to be much more intense than expected, and the parent company found it difficult to get to grips with the critical success factors in the new business. In common with most of the other aspiring corporate fish farmers, the business was sold a few years later after recurrent losses.

As with acquisitions, there is always a danger that the new venture will turn out to be more difficult than anticipated from the outside. This is particularly true if the business is very different from those currently in the company's portfolio. Renewal argues for bold thrusts into new areas; realism suggests that such thrusts will often prove misjudged.

Reasons for Value Destruction

As with other sorts of parenting influence, we can identify underlying reasons that explain the widespread value destruction through corporate development. Acquisition prices are set in a market for corporate control that is, in most instances, competitive and efficient. Rather as with stock market investment decisions, it is intrinsically difficult to beat the market and strike a favorable deal without superior information. Moreover, the chances are that the buyer's information will be inferior, not superior, to that possessed by the seller. Hence we should not be surprised that many acquisitions are made at prices that destroy value for the buyer. Divestments, on the other hand, are more likely to be value creating; and we would observe that most parents look back with more pride on their divestment decisions than on their acquisitions.

Furthermore, both acquisitions and corporate ventures involve entry to new businesses, frequently in unfamiliar areas. Often there are established competitors, the new entrant must struggle to gain a position, and the chances of success are low. Without a detailed knowledge of the market and the competitors, it is easy for the corporate parent to underestimate the difficulties that will be faced.

A healthy scepticism is therefore in order when assessing the corporate development decisions of the parent. Research, experience, and economic logic all suggest that it is difficult for the parent to beat the odds stacked against it and create value through corporate development. We refer to this difficulty as the "beating the odds" paradox. Nevertheless, in the right circumstances, there are opportunities for value creation in corporate development activities.

VALUE CREATION

We shall discuss four different ways in which value can be created through corporate development: (1) amalgamating or separating out businesses to enhance their competitiveness, (2) creating viable and successful new businesses, (3) striking deals to buy businesses cheaply, and (4) realigning the portfolio to fit better with the company's parenting. Our intention will be to describe companies that have succeeded in creating value in each area, and to understand how they have done so.

Amalgamating or Separating Out Businesses

Parents can create value by consolidating businesses, or by splitting them apart, if the resulting businesses become competitively stronger and perform better. This may be due to the economies of scale or scope that accrue to the larger, integrated businesses, or to the advantages of focus that follow from the smaller, more tightly defined business units. Often, acquisitions provide the opportunity for parents to amalgamate or separate out businesses in this way.[5]

Corporate decisions to redefine the scope and responsibilities of businesses, however, can be fraught with difficulties. Indeed, there is now widespread cynicism about the effects of such moves. Business managers fear the tendency of their corporate parents to meddle with structures that are working adequately, since the costs of "yet another reorganization" are by no means always justified by better results subsequently. The suspicion is that parents feel the need to impose their stamp on the businesses, without taking account of the damage that such shake-ups cause. Value has undoubtedly been created for the many consulting firms that have been retained to assist with these reorganizations. But the difficulty of finding satisfied clients to testify to the benefits of the reorganizations five years on raises questions about how much value has been created in the businesses that have been redefined.

Nevertheless, many companies have succeeded in creating value through business redefinitions. BTR and ABB have both improved the performance of acquired businesses by breaking them down into smaller, separate profit centers, whose performance was more visible and whose management felt more directly responsible for results.[6] Cooper, by contrast, has put together divisional clusters of businesses in areas such as hand tools and automotive components, to bring about economies of scale in product development and, in particular, in selling and distribution.[7] TI, as we shall see later in this chapter, has adopted a similar approach with its international, specialized engineering businesses. GE is renowned for its commitment to make all of its businesses number one or two in their respective markets, and it has pushed through a series of acquisitions and business amalgamations to achieve this objective.[8]

The common factor in these successful business redefinitions was that the businesses concerned became genuinely more competitive, and that this would not have happened without the parent taking the initiative. Hawker Siddeley's businesses are performing better within the more decentralized, profit-focused BTR structure, but they would not have spontaneously made these changes without BTR's postacquisition restructuring. GE has built strong businesses in a variety of areas, including medical equipment, defense and financial services, by consolidating businesses together in pursuit of a more ambitious market share goal than the individual businesses themselves would have proposed. In such cases, the radical nature of the changes mean that the businesses concerned would have been unlikely to put forward the proposals themselves, and that a parent with a sound insight into the sort of business scope and definition needed for success[9] can bring about changes that create value.

Creating New Businesses

Corporate venturing creates value if successful and profitable new businesses are launched at the initiative of the parent.[10] We have found examples of value-creating corporate ventures in three different sorts of circumstances: (1) new businesses based on products or services emerging from corporate staff groups (corporate NPD), (2) new businesses created by combining activities or resources from a number of existing businesses in the portfolio, and (3) new businesses that capitalize on underutilized resources at the center or in the businesses.

Corporate New Product Development.   Companies that have extensive corporate R&D or product development staffs usually aim to use these staffs, at least in part, to seed new business developments. Both Canon and 3M are good examples of this type of corporate venturing. As argued in Chapters 7 and 8, the success of Canon and 3M in developing new products and new businesses can be attributed to the special technical expertise that their corporate staffs possess, which provides a genuine source of competitive advantage in new businesses. Motorola and Sharp are also companies that have been successful corporate venturers.[11] These special skills are what distinguish the successful NPD activities at these companies from other less successful corporate venturers.

New Combination Businesses.   In Chapter 7, we also discussed the possibility that new business opportunities can emerge that require different businesses to work together to address them. At the extreme, a parent such as Canon may choose a structure and a management approach that deliberately prevents businesses from defining too precisely their product-market territories, in order to remain open to such opportunities. Canon's successful businesses in micrographics, facsimiles, and laser printers are testimony to the value that can be created. Other companies that have succeeded in creating new combination businesses include NEC, Sharp, and American Express.[12]

The essence of value creation through new combination businesses is for the parent to perceive and push through combination opportunities that the businesses concerned have overlooked or felt unable to pursue. Many of the issues concerned with the parent's role in removing blockages to businesses working together are therefore relevant. In corporate development mode, however, the parent goes further, taking the initiative in investments or acquisitions that are needed to complete the jigsaw and sponsoring the establishment of new business entities. The success of such initiatives depends on the viability of the opportunity and on the competitive position of the resulting combination business.[13]

Underutilized Resources.   Corporate parents often perceive opportunities to create new businesses based on resources that are not fully utilized. Empty factory space can be used to produce a new product range; underutilized retail selling space can be used to start a new department; an existing sales force can be used to sell more products or services; the corporate brand can provide the leverage to launch a new business idea; and so on.

While making better use of resources is obviously a sensible, value-creating activity, it is worth asking whether the underutilized resources are best employed in starting a new business or in some other way. Our research suggests that it is often preferable to extract the value by selling or franchising the resources to a third party. Thus, the spare factory space can be sublet, the empty retail space can be run by a concession, the sales force can represent other companies' products, and even the corporate brand can be franchised on a royalty basis. The advantage of these arrangements is that value is realized without the need for setting up a new business that may not fit with the company's parenting skills and characteristics. If the new business does not fit, it can result in the parent destroying more value through negative parenting influences than it creates through modest advantages from better resource utilization. The idea, for example, that it is sensible for industrial companies to establish and run computer services businesses in order to make use of spare skills and people in their information technology departments has in most cases proved to be a serious mistake.

There are therefore few examples of successful corporate venturing based on underutilized resources. One exception is the successful exploitation in the United Kingdom of Whitbread's pub properties through setting up a restaurant business. In the 1970s, Whitbread recognized that many pubs were underutilized, and set up a separate restaurant business, which was allowed to choose the sites it wanted from the Whitbread pub portfolio. Whitbread might have been able to realize the value of its pub sites by licensing, if there had been a number of independent professional restaurateurs competing for the space. But, because many of the independents were insufficiently professional and the better restaurateurs were owned by competitors, Whitbread decided that the most value would be created by entering the restaurant business as a corporate development initiative. As a result of the initiative, Whitbread has created a strong and profitable restaurants division.[14]

Underutilized assets are only likely to be best exploited internally where three conditions are met: (1) a thin external market exists for the asset; (2) the parent has or can acquire the skills needed to start the new business; (3) the parent does not continue owning the new business as it matures, if it lacks the relevant ongoing parenting skills. All these conditions need to be met for the value created by establishing new businesses based on underutilized resources to be successfully banked. In many cases, the parent's desire to hold onto a successful new business development beyond the appropriate stage has resulted in undoing all the initial success.

Buying Businesses Cheaply

To create value through acquisitions and divestments, the businesses in question must ultimately perform better under their new owner than they did previously. This is necessary for fundamental value creation.

Our concern here, however, is with value creation associated with doing the deal at a favorable price.

It can be argued that striking the deal does not create real value. However, the prices at which deals are struck can and do represent transfers of wealth from one set of owners to another, and viewed from the perspective of either parent's shareholders, the deal itself can have a significant impact on the overall value realized from acquisitions or divestments. Exhibit 9–1 lays out the possibilities schematically, from the point of view of the buyer's shareholders. The fundamental value creation potential is the difference between A (the value under the old owner) and B (the value under the new owner as a result of superior parenting influence on the business).[15] The price at which a deal is struck determines how much of this value is available to the buyer and the seller. At price C, the buyer's shareholders capture all the value, and some more. This deal price is value creating for the buyer's shareholders, since it is below the current value of the business even under its existing management. Price C, however, is most unlikely since it provides a net loss to the seller, who gets no benefit from the deal.[16] At price D, the buyer's shareholders capture none of the value creation, since the price is higher than the value of the business under its new owners. In this case, the deal price is value destroying for the buyer's shareholders. Overenthusiasm and lack of information, as argued earlier, mean that prices set at this level are not uncommon.

At price E, the value creation is shared between the buyer and the seller, and it is less obvious whether the deal price is itself a source of value creation or destruction for the buyer's shareholders. If, however, we recognize that there are likely to be other actual or potential bidders

EXHIBIT 9–1 Acquisitions and divestments: Impact of price paid on value captured by buyer's shareholders

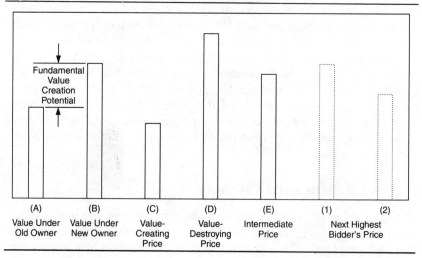

(A)	(B)	(C)	(D)	(E)	(1)	(2)
Value Under Old Owner	Value Under New Owner	Value-Creating Price	Value-Destroying Price	Intermediate Price	Next Highest Bidder's Price	

for the business, we can make a better assessment. If the next highest bidder's price (Price 1) would have been above the price paid, the deal price is value creating; indeed the buyer could, in theory, realize the value without further ado by selling on the business to the next highest bidder. If, on the other hand, the next highest bidder's price (Price 2) would have been below the price paid, the deal price is value destroying, since a tougher negotiation could have forced the price down closer to the next highest bidder's level.

This schematic brings out how difficult it is for the buyer to create value through the deal itself. It must persuade the seller to part with the business for less than it could be sold to other bidders. Given that sellers (and their advisers) are normally out for the best price they can get, this is a tall order. In the vast majority of successful acquisitions, the value creation does not come from the price at which the deal is struck.

Nevertheless, there are companies that have succeeded in buying businesses for less than they would have been worth to other owners. Hanson is a company that can sustain such a claim.

HANSON: ACQUISITION AND DIVESTMENT DEALS. In Chapter 2, we described the evolution of Hanson's corporate strategy. A feature of this strategy for many years has been a high rate of acquisitions and divestments. A number of these acquisitions and divestments have been struck at prices that represented value-capturing deals in their own right, irrespective of any subsequent performance improvement brought about by Hanson's parenting influence. Two particularly good examples are Hanson's 1986 acquisitions of the Imperial Group in the United Kingdom and of SCM in the United States. Hanson paid £2.6 billion to acquire Imperial and, within 3 years, sold on most of Imperial's businesses to other owners for a total of £2.3 billion. This left Hanson with ownership of Imperial's main tobacco business, which had an estimated net asset value of £1.3 billion, for a net cost of £300 million. A similar story with SCM allowed Hanson to pay $930 million for the company, realize $1.6 billion from sales of SCM businesses by the end of the 1980s, and retain its major titanium dioxide and other chemical businesses, as well as a 48 percent interest in Smith Corona, for a negative net cost (see Exhibit 9–2).[17]

With the Imperial and SCM acquisitions, Hanson took advantage of the fact that relatively few parents were willing to undertake major breakup bids at the time. Because the combination of businesses in Imperial and SCM made little sense and was not attractive to alternative owners, the companies' overall values to other bidders were depressed. Hanson's willingness to broker the sale of the separate parts to different owners released value that had previously been trapped. In addition, Hanson's renowned deal-making skills meant that they struck some hard bargains in the process, thereby capturing extra value for Hanson shareholders at the expense of other companies involved in the transactions.

EXHIBIT 9–2 Hanson's acquisitions and subsequent disposals with Imperial and SCM

Imperial		£ (mn)
Purchase price (April 1986)		2,600
Subsequent disposals (1986–1989);		
—Anchor Hotels, Imperial Inns,		
Happy Eater (hotels and restaurants)	186	
—Courage (brewing)	1,400	
—Golden Wonder (snacks)	87	
—Ross Young (frozen food)	337	
—HP Foods	199	
—Other	88	2,297
Net Acquisition Cost		303

SCM		$ (mn)
Purchase price (January 1986)		930
Subsequent disposals (1986–1989);		
—Paper operations	160	
—Glidden (paints)	650	
—Durkee (foods)	305	
—Allied Paper	56	
—Smith Corona (typewriters)	374	
—Other	97	1,642
Net Acquisition Cost		(712)

Other companies that appear to have created value for their shareholders through paying less for acquisitions than they would have been worth to other owners include Dover and Electrolux. Dover's informal management processes have been attractive to many entrepreneurs who wished to sell a majority stake in their companies, while retaining a management interest. They preferred to sell to Dover rather than to other corporate owners for reasons concerned with corporate culture, not price. This has allowed Dover to make some keenly priced acquisitions.[18]

Electrolux was an active acquirer in Sweden during the 1980s, picking up a variety of companies such as Husqvarna and Granges, in businesses as diverse as chain saws, motorcycles, and aluminum. Electrolux was able to buy these companies at favorable prices because they were in trouble, and the Swedish financial and government establishment were keen to find a Swedish solution to their ills, rather than allowing ownership to pass into foreign hands.[19]

Value can therefore be created by acquiring companies at favorable prices, but only if there are identifiable reasons why the parent in question can beat the market for corporate control. Sometimes these reasons relate to pure deal-making skills. More often they depend on the acquirer's bringing something to the deal that other possible bidders lack. Hanson's willingness to broker a breakup, Dover's attractions for entrepreneurs that wish to sell, and Electrolux's Swedish domicile provided the basis for value creation from striking favorably priced deals in the acquisitions described. Such acquisitions, however, need to be set within, and form part of, an overall corporate strategy.

HANSON: CORPORATE STRATEGY. Exhibit 9–3 is a parenting advantage statement for Hanson. The *value creation insights* emphasize the opportunities to broker the breakup of overly diversified groups. Such groups were often put together by companies such as Imperial to diversify away from their mature, "cash cow" core businesses. Their attempts to diversify led them into a mix of businesses outside their heartlands. As a result, a parent such as Hanson has been able to create value by aggressive acquisitions, coupled with a willingness to sell on

EXHIBIT 9–3   Hanson parenting advantage statement

Value Creation Insights	Companies that seek growth from mature businesses tend to destabilize competitive conditions, indulge in unnecessary investments, and take on excessive costs. This gives an opportunity for a parent that stresses tight profitability controls to create value.
	In acquisitions of diversified companies with mixed portfolios of businesses, value can be created by a parent that is willing to sell on different businesses to other owners to whom they are worth more.
Distinctive Parenting Characteristics	Acquisition screening and deal-making skills.
	Tried and tested process for integrating new acquisitions into Hanson's management process.
	Decentralized responsibilities for running businesses, coupled with strong personal profitability incentives.
	Emphasis on financial control processes and culture.
	Willingness to sell any business that is "worth more to others than we think it's worth to us."
Heartland Businesses	Mature businesses that are not facing rapid technological change and where there is a basic and continuing demand for the product. Ideally, they should neither require long payback investments, nor globally integrated strategies, and they should hold strong, preferably branded, positions in their markets. Manufacturing and natural resource businesses are preferred.

businesses to other owners who were prepared to pay more for them. But Hanson's corporate strategy does not rest only on its deal-making activities. Hanson has also recognized that many companies in mature industries feel compelled to seek growth at rates faster than the markets in which they are competing. This growth treadmill leads them to destabilize competitive conditions by aggressive attempts to gain market share, to indulge in unnecessary investments, and to take on excessive costs. Rather than capitalizing on the profit opportunities in businesses such as Peabody Coal, SCM Chemicals, Imperial Tobacco, and London Brick, their previous parents were emphasizing other goals, such as growth or diversification. In such situations, Hanson's parenting approach, which stresses tough profitability controls, has been able to create value.

Hanson has a number of *distinctive parenting characteristics* that are important in implementing its corporate strategy, several of which were mentioned in Chapter 2. Given the importance of acquisitions and divestments in Hanson's corporate strategy, its acquisition screening and deal-making skills are vital. These skills have been fine-tuned through experience, and the company has won a reputation for driving a hard bargain. The mergers and acquisitions (M&A) team itself is small[20] but highly professional, consisting of only three or four managers split between the United Kingdom and the United States. But all the directors of Hanson contribute their judgment and experience on the big deals, and the final decisions rest with Lords Hanson and White. Hanson reckons to consider as many as 100 possible targets for each one that it actually moves against. There are no formal guidelines for assessing acquisition prospects, but the heartland criteria are understood and accepted by all the senior managers. Assessing the major downside risks is seen as vital because "any acquisition is always something of a shot in the dark, since it won't be based on inside information about the company."

Postacquisition integration of acquired companies that are retained is a second vital area of Hanson parenting. Hanson has a number of senior managers with experience of this process and has developed approaches to it that have stood the test of repeated use. Typically, a senior Hanson manager will be appointed chairman of the acquired company, with overall responsibility for the integration process. The integration team will also include two or three seasoned Hanson line managers from other businesses, each supported by a young finance staffer, usually drawn from the corporate parent's finance department. The first step is a roadshow to meet the managers of the new acquisition, "to show them that we don't have horns" and to communicate the new Hanson regime. Within a couple of months, every significant site in the company is visited. The roadshow covers a description of Hanson and its philosophy, of the new reporting relationships, and of the Hanson reporting and control processes. Usually, however, no immediate decisions are taken during this early phase.

During the next 6 to 9 months, the basic decisions about restructuring the company and about its management are taken. Hanson maintains morale during this period of uncertainty by stressing that decisions about each business depend largely on the advice the integration team receives from the company's management about "what they can do for us," and by encouraging managers to take the initiative in proposing what should be done and what can be achieved. While the board members of the acquired company usually depart, middle managers frequently find the new, results-oriented culture of Hanson liberating and thrive on the new challenges. Hanson believes that the process gives particular opportunities for able managers below board level to move up to new responsibilities and to propose changes that they often see as overdue. In parallel, there will usually be an investigation of prospects by Hanson's external accountants or other consultants. "The essence of integration is challenge and response, not directives," says Tony Alexander, U.K. chief operating officer. "But you are in a position to make decisions because you are not responsible for any of the past cock-ups."

Once the initial phases of the transition are complete, the integration team withdraws and a new management is installed. Usually the top team comes from Hanson, to ensure that momentum is maintained during the next couple of years. After that, the new acquisition is regarded as an established part of the portfolio, and a management team from within the acquisition often takes over. Thus, full integration can take up to 3 years. "You don't want to prolong the uncertainty, but it's a delicate exercise that has to be done properly and can't be rushed."

Hanson's philosophy stresses the decentralized responsibility of each business general manager, coupled with personal accountability for results. Managers have substantial bonus incentives for achieving their targets, and Hanson preaches a message of severe sanctions for nonperformance. The budget is the crucial management process, with Hanson pushing managers to go for stretching targets and year-on-year improvements in profitability ratios. On the other hand, budgets are fundamentally bottom up. "The day we tell people what numbers they have to put into their budget, we're dead," states Martin Taylor, vice chairman.

The finance function within Hanson is powerful. There are dotted-line relationships between all the businesses' finance staff and the corporate finance director. Finance specialists are guardians of the integrity of the financial numbers and ensure that Hanson's financial control processes are adhered to. The culture is epitomized by Hanson's long-standing capital expenditure limits of £500 in the United Kingdom and $1,000 in the United States; beyond this level, business managers must, in principle, seek corporate approval. This does not mean that every personal computer becomes the subject of a major capital expenditure review with Lord Hanson, but acts as a signal to the businesses to recognize that cash belongs to the shareholders, not the business, and that all investments, however small, need to be justifiable in terms of the returns they will bring.

Lastly, Hanson remains prepared to sell any of its businesses if it receives an offer that values the business at a level greater than Hanson believes could be justified by continuing to manage it within the Hanson portfolio. Hanson's new chief executive, Derek Bonham, has talked of its "core" businesses; but, for Hanson, a core business is simply a major contributor to overall corporate results. The "core" label neither precludes selling a business if the price is right nor prevents Hanson from entering new business areas if attractive acquisitions become available, as was evidenced by the $3.2 billion acquisition of Quantum Chemical Corporation, which took Hanson into petrochemicals in 1993.

Hanson's portfolio now covers a wide range of different business sectors, including tobacco, aggregates, coal mining, construction, chemicals, materials handling equipment, forestry and lumber, bricks, and a number of other industrial and consumer products. At first sight, these businesses seem highly diverse. They share a number of common characteristics, however, which represent Hanson's *heartland criteria.* Hanson has always concentrated on mature businesses that are not facing rapid technological change and where there is a basic and continuing demand for the product or service. Lord Hanson has been sceptical about businesses that required heavy R&D expenditures, "with a prospect of a payback sometime or never." He has also preferred to avoid businesses that involved major, long-term capital investments, except where the investments were in assets with a realizable market value, such as coal reserves, forestry land, and aggregates quarries. Hanson has concentrated on the United Kingdom and the United States, and has generally avoided more global businesses, especially if they faced stiff international competition and needed complex coordination between different local companies. Particularly in consumer products, Hanson has aimed for businesses with strong market shares and recognized brands, such as Embassy cigarettes and Jacuzzi whirlpools. Recently, the portfolio has focused more on natural resource businesses and manufactured products. Hanson believes that all these businesses are amenable to the tight financial control disciplines for which Hanson has become renowned. A concentration on budgeted profitability and cash flow, a strict rein on capital spending, and a high level of autonomy for the individual business units are important for success across all these businesses and can create value if the businesses were previously being managed less tightly.

Hanson has been a remarkably successful corporate parent during the past 25 years. Rivalry from other parents, may, however, as described in Chapter 2, have narrowed Hanson's parenting advantage in recent years. Furthermore, the ability to make acquisitions, and indeed overall corporate results, were hit by the early 1990s recession in the United States and the United Kingdom. Between 1988 and 1992, earnings per share were essentially flat, and declined by over 30 percent in 1993. More generally, as Hanson has grown, it has become harder to find acquisitions that would have a material impact on its results. Faced with the prospect of both Lord Hanson and Lord White retiring within a few years, it is possible that new directions in corporate strategy will begin to emerge.[21]

Hanson's parenting characteristics fit together so well, however, that modifications run the risk of subverting the whole, interlinked approach. Deal making and restructuring are essential features of the company, and any attempts to stabilize the portfolio or concentrate on organic growth are liable to undermine the key sources of parenting advantage. The existence of more rivals makes life harder for Hanson, but a response that runs counter to the established parenting characteristics is unlikely to prove successful.

Aligning the Portfolio with the Parenting Approach

As pointed out in earlier chapters, corporate parents need to develop a clear set of heartland business criteria, which will allow them to shift the composition of their portfolios toward the sorts of businesses in which they can create the most net value. Nearly all the successful corporate parents that we have researched have made moves to alter the composition of their portfolios in this way. Moreover, the acquisition screening activities of companies such as BTR, Emerson, RTZ, Banc One, Cooper, and Hanson are devoted to identifying such opportunities. By establishing a systematic screening process, with well-defined criteria, and by sticking to targets in the types of business that meet their heartland criteria, these companies have been able to find a steady stream of acquisition candidates with genuine value creation potential.[22] They have also been able to remove businesses from the portfolio that did not fit their parenting. Corporate development moves of this sort are necessary as a precondition for other forms of parental value creation.

The British TI Group (TI) is a company that has made particularly substantial moves to realign its portfolio in accordance with a new view of the types of value creation on which it intended to build its corporate strategy.

TI: REALIGNING THE PORTFOLIO TO FIT WITH A NEW CORPORATE STRATEGY. The TI Group (originally Tube Investments) represents an interesting example of the power of a fundamental change in corporate strategy and portfolio composition. When Christopher Lewinton took over as chief executive in 1986, TI appeared to be in near terminal decline. Like so many other once proud U.K. engineering companies, it had relied for too long on its home market, had failed to keep pace, either technically or in the marketplace, with its international competitors, and had diversified into unfamiliar businesses. It was hit hard by the recession of the early 1980s, making a loss in 1981 and suffering depressed profitability for the next four years. Lewinton was recruited to reverse this trend and rapidly saw the need for a complete change of corporate strategy. The new strategy involved a clearer view of how the parent could create value and a realignment of the portfolio around businesses in which value could be created.

TI's new corporate strategy, which is summarized in Exhibit 9–4, was built on the belief that, in many specialized engineering businesses, competition is becoming increasingly international. International competitors are able to share product development and applications work across national markets, to rationalize manufacturing and transfer manufacturing skills, and to provide better service to multinational customers. However, the competitive structure in most of these businesses remains fragmented between national or regional players, each with its own local focus. An opportunity therefore exists to identify local companies that can be acquired, with a view to developing a fully international network. The local companies then perform better as part of the international network so that the acquisition premiums paid can be justified. This was TI's basic *value creation insight.* The role of TI as parent has been to identify base companies on which to build, find add-on acquisition candidates and push through deals with them, establish management teams and structures to develop the

EXHIBIT 9–4   TI parenting advantage statement

Value Creation Insights	In many specialized engineering businesses, a parent that can see opportunities to create international businesses out of previously separate national entities, and is willing to make acquisitions and divestments to do so, will create high value.
Distinctive Parenting Characteristics	Corporate mission that places a priority on international development of its businesses.
	Management style that decentralizes responsibilities to the international business heads within the corporate mission framework, but maintains pressure for short-term profitability.
	Attracting, retaining, and motivating managers with international experience and ambitions.
	Skills in identifying and carrying through acquisitions, including, where necessary, selling on parts of acquisitions that do not fit the TI mission.
Heartland Businesses	Businesses with international opportunities that make specialized, higher added value, safety critical, engineering components and subsystems, in which applications work and service support are vital for customers.

businesses internationally, and push for strategies to achieve international leadership.

Lewinton also believed that specialized engineering businesses should be TI's *heartland,* since they played to the underlying strengths of TI's management: "It was clear to me that TI did not understand the consumer goods business and the company did not have a consumer culture. TI's basic culture was engineering." As a result, major businesses in domestic appliances and bicycles were sold. TI also concentrated on businesses that manufactured "safety critical" subsystems rather than basic components or final products. Such businesses provide relatively high added-value products, often with opportunities to tailor the product for specific customer requirements, and with a need for rapid and efficient product service and backup. Lewinton and his team were comfortable parenting businesses of this type and felt that they understood the strategies that led to competitive advantage and superior profitability in them.[23] For example, managers that proposed launching new products at low prices to penetrate the market were liable to have their proposals rejected, on the basis that successful new products in these businesses gain acceptance based on product features, service performance, and customer responsiveness rather than on price. Consequently, businesses in standard, commodity tubes and automotive components were also sold, since they did not fit with the heartland criteria.

In pursuing this strategy over the period from 1986 through 1992, TI has brought about a fundamental restructuring of its portfolio with considerable success. It has sold 80 percent of the businesses in the portfolio in 1985. A few businesses in engineered seals, specialized tube and aerospace components have been identified for development in accordance with the strategy. In these businesses, a number of corporately sponsored acquisitions have been made to create international positions out of previously separate national units, and a management structure has been put in place to run the international divisions that have been created. Corporate earnings have grown by over 700 percent, from £17.6 million in 1985 to £125.2 million in 1993, while sales have increased by only 40 percent, from £997 million to £1,393 million (see Exhibit 9–5).

In the small-diameter tube (SDT) business, for example, TI's initial base in 1985 consisted of only a 50 percent interest in a small U.K. company called Fulton, with sales of £10 million. The corporate team at TI, however, identified this business as a nugget that could be developed. As a result, TI acquired Armco's European SDT operations in 1987, followed by Bundy Corporation, the U.S. market leader, in 1988. Since that time, further acquisitions have been made, in particular buying out minorities in Bundy's local manufacturing and distribution companies in different countries around the world. An international divisional structure has been created, under the name Bundy International, with a new managing director brought in from outside TI.

EXHIBIT 9–5   TI's portfolio change 1985—1993

	1985 Sales (£mn)	1992 Sales (£mn)
Engineered seals	42	448
Specialized tubes	74	571
Specialized engineering and aerospace	83	304
Automotive	166	—
Domestic appliances, cycles, and other	632	69[a]
	997	1393
Corporate profits before tax and exceptional items (£mn)	17.6	125.2

[a] *Now discontinued.*

In 1991, TI acquired Huron Products, the leading U.S. manufacturer of fuel lines and connectors. Similar corporate initiatives have been taken in seals and aerospace, and have led to the creation of the three successful international businesses that now form the heart of TI's portfolio.

TI's corporate development moves have therefore played a key part in the new corporate strategy. Businesses have been amalgamated together into more competitive international divisions, and a clear set of heartland criteria have been used to guide a radical shift in the composition of the portfolio. Aggressive portfolio restructuring of this sort can create value, provided it forms part of a valid corporate strategy and is supported by suitable parenting characteristics.

The *distinctive parenting characteristics* that have allowed TI to carry through its strategy have included a strong corporate mission; a management style that decentralizes responsibilities to the international business heads within the framework of the corporate mission; an ability to attract, retain, and motivate managers with international experience and ambitions; and skills in identifying and carrying through acquisitions.

In 1986, shortly after Lewinton's arrival, TI adopted a new mission statement, which stated that the company would focus on "specialized engineering businesses, operating in selected niches on a global basis." This mission statement, and its implications, have been hammered home on every possible occasion subsequently, through the annual report and company literature, in planning debates and investment reviews, and as a criterion against which to test all major strategic decisions that were proposed. Managers in TI's businesses quickly became aware that the mission statement was more than a set of words on paper and really would guide priorities for TI in future. As one divisional head put it to us: "What has been unusual about TI is not that it has had a mission statement, but that it has really stuck to it." Without this strong guiding framework, the transformation of TI during recent years would not have been possible.

While insisting on the importance of the corporate mission, Lewinton has emphasized the decentralized responsibilities of the managers running the individual businesses. Thus, within 6 months of his arrival, TI's imposing head office in Birmingham, a symbol of the old TI, had been closed ("always the most significant way to get people's attention and bring about a basic culture change," in Lewinton's view). TI's corporate offices are now located in a new business park near Oxford, with a total staff down from 180 in 1986 to around 50 in 1993. At the same time, the business heads have been encouraged to take more initiative and responsibility for decisions within their own areas. Lewinton expresses his views as follows: "I believe that the managers of each group are best qualified and positioned to structure and manage their own operations. I view myself as a catalyst. It is quite clear that a small headquarters group cannot manage all the businesses and, furthermore, I have no desire to manage the businesses. However, in my role as a catalyst and a creator of change, I tend to offer up to operating management a number of ideas and leave them to accept the ideas or not as they see fit. The only proviso is that if they find my ideas unacceptable, they would be wise to have some better ideas of their own because I am in the business of making things happen."

TI also emphasizes a disciplined approach to financial control, which ensures that a focus on maintaining reported profitability is retained. For example, TI closely controls the pursuit of synergies between its divisions. Advantage has been obtained from highly focused leverage of specific technology, market, and customer links, but not at the expense of divisional performance. "We don't want to allow people to take their eye off the ball and to give them excuses for not delivering their own performance targets."

A further component of the new parenting approach concerns people, rewards, and motivation. Lewinton has insisted that his senior managers should have an international outlook and has placed much more stress on marketing and professional management skills than is common in British engineering companies. This has involved bringing in several experienced executives from outside the company and weeding out members of the old management who were not able to make the necessary transition in approach. To attract the right people, the reward package for key managers has been made internationally competitive and has a large stock option component. As one member of the corporate office told us: "I now have a substantial portion of my personal net worth tied up with the company." Lewinton believes that this creates the right sort of motivation for his top team and is attractive to mobile, international executives. A recent senior recruit commented: "The attractive thing about TI is working in the sort of culture and environment that Lewinton has been trying to create. He understands the issues involved in hiring international managers, and his style and ambitions for the company are very important to me."

Another important role of the corporate parent has been in acquisitions. TI's skills in identifying and pursuing candidates, in structuring and completing deals on the right terms, and in selling on parts of acquisitions that did not fit the mission have been essential. For example, in order to acquire John Crane USA in 1987, TI had to bid for the whole of a company called Houdaille Industries, which, at the time, was owned by KKR. After the deal, TI sold back to KKR six other Houdaille businesses, which did not fit within the corporate strategy. More recently, in the 1992 bid for Dowty, TI pitched its initial offer price at a level that was generally regarded as just sufficient to prevent other contenders from entering the field. In major acquisitions, TI's corporate center takes primary responsibility for the acquisition process leaving the businesses free to concentrate on their strategies for developing and integrating the resulting international operations.

The most impressive aspect of TI's corporate strategy since 1986 has been the degree of change that has been brought about. Both the portfolio of businesses and the corporate culture have been transformed, under the influence of a new approach to parenting. Through its corporate development activities, TI has now achieved a good fit between its approach to parenting and its main businesses. Inevitably, given the rate of change, there have been some mistakes. The Thermal Technology businesses, for example, were initially built up with acquisitions but have now been divested as incompatible with the basic strategy: as capital goods businesses, they did not share enough common critical success factors with the heartland businesses. Critics also argue that, despite the opportunities it offered to build a third global leadership business, the Dowty acquisition took TI heavily into the aerospace market at a time when it was facing a cyclical decline, and that the long-term nature of the aerospace components business means it is significantly different from engineered seals and specialized tubes. TI, however, can counter these charges by comparing the health and prospects for the company in 1986 with the position in 1994. It is obvious that the transformation has been beneficial and would not have been achieved without the new parenting approach and the realignment of the portfolio that went with it.

CONDITIONS FOR VALUE CREATION AND PARENTING ADVANTAGE

Despite the difficulty of "beating the odds" against creating value in corporate development, some companies have succeeded in doing so. Often, the value creation from corporate development is bound up with value creation from parenting influence that follows the corporate development decisions. The conditions for value creation identified in Chapters 6 through 8 are, therefore, also relevant for corporate development decisions. There are, however, some conditions for value creation that relate directly to corporate development decisions.

Opportunities for Value Creation in Corporate Development

For a parent to create value through corporate development, shifts in portfolio composition must lead to improved corporate performance. The circumstances under which opportunities occur are different for each of the types of corporate development we have discussed.

The opportunities for value creation from amalgamating or separating out businesses depend on the impact that such moves have on the competitiveness of the resulting businesses. If redefinitions of businesses' scopes can lead to greater competitiveness,[24] and if the businesses have overlooked these possibilities, perhaps because they involve radical moves that the businesses may fail to see or feel uncomfortable proposing, opportunities for a parent to create value arise. Such redefinitions are often needed most when the sources of competitive advantage are shifting. The role for the parent is opened up by the difficulty for the business in conceiving of and embracing the need for radical change from established ways of competing.

The opportunities for value creation from establishing new businesses depend mainly on the possession of special expertise or resources by the parent, which lead the new business to enjoy an advantage over its established competitors. Opportunities for a parent to sponsor successful new combination businesses depend on the removal of blockages that would otherwise prevent the creation of such businesses. Opportunities for a parent to create value by setting up new businesses based on underutilized resources arise only if there are no other ways of realizing more value from the resources in question, for example by selling, licensing, or franchising them to other companies that are likely to be better ongoing parents for the business. In all these cases, the corporate development opportunities are closely related to the subsequent parenting of the new business ventures that are created.[25]

The opportunities for value creation from buying businesses cheaply depend on finding other parents that are willing to sell businesses for less than they are worth on the open market. Though comparatively rare, such opportunities can arise for parents with special skills or characteristics, which give them a favored or unusual position in the deal.

The opportunities for value creation from aligning the portfolio and the parenting approach come from improving the fit between parents and the businesses in their portfolios. If it is possible to eliminate misfits, or to bring new businesses into the portfolio that fit well, changes in portfolio composition, including acquisitions or divestments, can create value. Without such moves, the parent's value creation will always be at a lower level as a result of having fewer businesses that fit well with its corporate strategy and parenting characteristics.[26]

Successful corporate parents need to base their corporate development activities around one or more of the sorts of opportunities we have identified. Otherwise, they are liable to find that their acquisitions, divestments, new ventures, and business redefinitions will be disappointing.

Parenting Characteristics That Fit the Opportunities

Special parenting skills or characteristics are needed to capitalize on corporate development opportunities.[27] The parent's understanding of the critical success factors in its businesses must be good enough to allow it to identify and push through business redefinition opportunities that might be missed or resisted by the businesses themselves. The skill of the parent is in distinguishing these opportunities from other situations where changes imposed on the businesses will simply be disruptive, and acting on them in ways that retain the support and motivation of the businesses. For successful new ventures, the parent must genuinely possess unusual expertise or resources and must be in a position to see that the new business that is created is well parented subsequently. To take advantage of opportunities for favorable acquisition deals, the parent needs characteristics that are suitable to the situation. It must be willing to undertake deals that others avoid, or be in possession of knowledge or contacts that others lack, or have an inside track with the seller that gives a favored status, or have exceptional negotiation and bid management skills. Otherwise, competitive forces in the market for corporate control, and the superior information available to sellers in comparison to buyers, will usually lead to acquisition prices in which most of the value created accrues to the seller rather than the buyer. For successful realignments between the parent and the businesses in its portfolio, the parent's appreciation of its heartland business criteria must be clear enough, and its screening skills sufficiently developed, to find suitable acquisition, divestment, and new business candidates.

From time to time, "good deals" may arise where the parent has no special skills or characteristics. Incompetent sellers, a thin market for buyers, or pure luck may account for this. But such opportunities are rare and unpredictable. Chief executives are always tempted to believe that they have identified the one deal that will really pay off for their company; they need to ask themselves what special skills or characteristics they have that mean they can beat the generally dismal record in this area.

Avoidance of Value Destruction

With all forms of corporate development, there is a basic need to be able to exercise positive parenting influence on the continuing businesses that make up the portfolio, and to avoid value destruction in them. However justified the business redefinition, the resulting businesses must not be seriously damaged by subsequent parenting influence. However good the deal, acquisitions may end up by destroying value if ongoing parenting influence on the acquired business is inappropriate: either the new owner must be (or become) a good parent for the business, or à la Hanson, it must be willing to sell on the business to another owner.[28] However well conceived, corporate ventures will not continue to prosper if the parent that gave them birth cannot nurture them thereafter. This is a particular drawback when special skills and resources lead a parent into a new business for which, overall, it lacks sufficient feel. Such ventures are only likely to create value in the longer term if the parent is able to acquire a feel for them. Furthermore, the original new business conception is more likely to prove valid if the parent has some feel for the business in question. It can be argued that the parent's role is to challenge the conventional wisdom of those who are closest to the businesses and to come up with new ideas that would not occur to managers with a better feel for the business. While there may be some examples of successful creative leaps of this kind, we are more struck by the disasters to which they typically lead.

The avoidance of value destruction provides a further link between our discussion of parenting influence in Chapters 6, 7, and 8 and of corporate development in this chapter. While corporate development activities can be an important part of parenting, we need to remember that they are unlikely to lead to net value creation unless the company can avoid value destruction through its ongoing influence on the businesses that remain in the portfolio.[29]

Corporate Development and Parenting Advantage

Corporate development activities can play an important part in achieving parenting advantage. Without decisive moves to establish the right definitions for the businesses in the portfolio, performance will be suboptimal. Without a clear sense of heartland business criteria, and consistent efforts to align the portfolio as closely as possible with them, parenting advantage is most unlikely to be achieved. Successful corporate venturing and astute deal making, though not essential for the achievement of parenting advantage, can also play an important role in the corporate strategies of companies, such as 3M and Hanson, that have strengths in these areas. For most companies with successful corporate strategies for achieving parenting advantage, corporate development activities are important sources of value creation.

But, for sustainable parenting advantage, corporate development activities must form part of a corporate strategy that also creates value from ongoing parenting. A corporate strategy based only on shifts in the composition of the portfolio neglects the essential area of ongoing parenting, and so cannot be sufficient to achieve parenting advantage.

SUMMARY

In this chapter, we have brought out how difficult it is to beat the odds against creating value in corporate development. But we have also described some companies that succeed in doing so, and we have drawn conclusions about the conditions under which corporate development activities create value.

Questions that any corporate parent needs to address concerning its corporate development activities are:

- Are there opportunities to create value by redefining businesses in our portfolio, and if so, why have the businesses themselves not proposed them?

- Do we have unusual resources on which we can build new business ventures? If not, why do we expect our newly created businesses to be successful in their markets against established competitors?

- Do we have special skills or characteristics that will allow us to see good acquisition and divestment opportunities and negotiate favorable deals? If not, why do we expect to beat the highly competitive market for corporate control and succeed in creating value where so many others have failed?

- Are there opportunities to improve the alignment between our parenting and the businesses in our portfolio? Are our heartland business criteria clear enough for us to perceive these opportunities accurately?

- For new businesses that are brought into the portfolio through corporate development, are we confident that we can parent them well subsequently?

Parents need to confront all these questions about their corporate development activities. Given affirmative answers, however, corporate development can provide the basis for value creation and contribute to parenting advantage.

NOTES

1. Alliances and joint ventures have become increasingly popular means of pursuing corporate development. The parenting of alliances and joint ventures is discussed in Appendix D.

2. See, for example, David B. Jemison and Sim B. Sitkin, "Acquisitions: The Process Can Be a Problem," *Harvard Business Review*, March–April 1986.

3. See, for example, Julian R. Franks and Robert S. Harris, "Wealth Effects of Takeovers in the UK," *Journal of Financial Economics*, August 1989, and Michael C. Jensen and Richard S. Rubeck, "The Market for Corporate Control," *Journal of Financial Economics*, vol. 11, 1983. Both articles lead to the conclusion that the bulk of gains from acquisitions accrue to the sellers, not the buyers; in many cases, buyers end up worse off. See also Michael Porter, "From Competitive Advantage to Corporate Strategy," *Harvard Business Review*, May–June 1987; John Hunt, Stan Lees, John Grumbar, and Philip Vivian, *Acquisitions: The Human Factor*, London: Egon Zehnder International, 1987; Philippe Haspeslagh and David B. Jemison, *Managing Acquisitions*, New York: Free Press, 1991.

4. See, for example, E. Ralph Biggadike, "Corporate Diversification," Division of Research, Harvard Business School, 1979, and "The Risky Business of Diversification," *Harvard Business Review*, vol. 56, May–June 1979; Z. Block and P. N. Subbanarasimha, *Corporate Venturing: Practices and Performance in the U.S. and Japan*, Working Paper, Center for Entrepreneurial Studies, Stern School of Business, New York University, 1989. But, though average success rates for new businesses are low, some will beat the odds. Indeed, Michael Hay, Paul Verdin, and Peter Williamson ("Successful New Ventures: Lessons for Entrepreneurs and Investors," *Long Range Planning*, 1993, vol. 26, no. 5) suggest that the chances of survival for corporate ventures are more favorable than for independent new businesses. In "Start-up Businesses: A Comparison of Performances," (*Sloan Management Review*, Fall 1981), Leo Weiss, however, finds that new businesses started by established corporations performed significantly worse than those started by individuals. This suggests that the greater longevity of corporate ventures is mainly a matter of cross-subsidy.

5. In business redefinitions of this sort, corporate development overlaps with the sorts of parenting influence described in Chapters 6 and 7. It is worth reiterating that our focus in this chapter is on major moves initiated by the parent, and that this is the principle we use to distinguish between corporate development business redefinitions and other changes in the scope, positioning, or strategy of businesses that the parent may wish to influence.

6. See Chapters 6 and 7 for more details.

7. See Chapter 8 for more details.

8. See Chapter 10 for more details.

9. See Appendix A for further discussion of how to assess what sort of business definition is likely to be most competitively suitable.

10. There is an extensive literature on corporate venturing and "intrapreneurship," focusing on both the need for organizations to become more

innovative and the need to assess new ventures better. A recent book by Zenas Block and Ian C. MacMillan, (*Corporate Venturing: Creating New Businesses within the Firm,* Boston: Harvard Business School Press, 1993), argues that senior corporate managers need a good knowledge of customers and markets to make sound judgments about new ventures and that the critical role of a corporate parent is to manage the venturing process, not the new business itself. Their study includes a review of some of the research on corporate venturing. Robert A. Burgelman and Leonard R. Sayles, *Inside Corporate Innovation,* New York: Free Press, 1986, investigated in detail the process of innovation and new business development in a large corporation. Gifford Pinchot III, *Intrapreneuring,* New York: Harper & Row, 1985, advises entrepreneurial individuals on how to succeed in large corporations, and senior managers on how to foster a corporate culture and environment that supports innovation and new business development. Rosabeth Moss Kanter has investigated innovation in large corporations, and how corporations develop new businesses, *The Change Masters: Corporate Entrepreneurs at Work,* London: George Allen and Unwin, 1984, *When Giants Learn to Dance,* New York: Simon & Schuster, 1989. The literature on corporate entrepreneurship up to the mid-1980s is extensively reviewed by Paul M. Connolly, *Entrepreneurs in Corporations: Highlights of the Literature,* Work in America Institute Studies in Productivity, 47, Pergamon Press, 1985. *Entrepreneurship in Action: Successful European Company Practices,* by Gay Haskins and Roy Williams, The Economist Intelligence Unit, Special Report No. 1099, 1987, surveys innovative European companies and programs. See also Ralph Alterowitz with John Zonderman, *New Corporate Ventures: How to Make Them Work,* New York: John Wiley & Sons, 1988; Hollister B. Sykes, "Lessons from a New Ventures Program," *Harvard Business Review,* May–June 1986, pp. 69–74; Norman D. Fast, *Rise and Fall of Corporate New Venture Divisions,* Ann Arbor, MI: UMI Research Press, 1977; G. Felda Hardymon, Mark J. DeNino, and Malcolm S. Salter, "When Corporate Venture Capital Doesn't Work," *Harvard Business Review,* May–June 1983, pp. 114–120; Glenn DeSouza, "The Best Strategies for Corporate Venturing," *Planning Review,* vol. 14, no. 2, March 1986, pp. 12–14; Patrick J. Davey, *Corporate Venturing,* The Conference Board, Research Bulletin no. 214, 1987, R. Garud and A. H. Van de Ven, "An Empirical Evaluation of the Internal Corporate Venturing Process," *Strategic Management Journal,* Special Issue, Summer 1992; I. C. MacMillan, *Progress in Research on Corporate Venturing, 1985,* Center for Entrepreneurial Studies, New York University, New York, January 1985.

11. See *Motorola's Corporate Strategy,* and *Sharp's Corporate Strategy,* unpublished working papers, Ashridge Strategic Management Centre, 1994.

12. The best example of a combination business created by American Express is First Data Corporation. See *American Express's Corporate Strategy,* unpublished working paper, Ashridge Strategic Management Centre, 1994; and Koji Kobayashi, *The Rise of NEC: How the World's Greatest C and C Company Is Managed,* Oxford: Basil Blackwell, 1991.

13. See Appendix A.

14. See "Linkages and Synergy: Retailing in Whitbread," unpublished working paper, Ashridge Strategic Management Centre, 1990.

15. We assume that the valuations are based on discounted net present worth calculations for the expected future cash flows of the business.

16. Misperceptions or disagreements about the expected future cash flows from the business can, however, lead to this outcome.

17. Accurate "net cost" figures are hard to determine, given the existence of a plethora of small subsidiaries within both Imperial and SCM, on which limited information is available, and postacquistion investment prior to disposals. However, the overall picture is clear.

18. See Chapter 6 for more details.

19. For further details on Electrolux's strategy, see "The Development of Corporate Strategy at Electrolux," unpublished working paper, Ashridge Strategic Management Centre, 1994.

20. We were told that a large M&A team was avoided, "because they can always find reasons for not doing things."

21. See Michael Goold, Andrew Campbell, and Kathleen Luchs, "Strategies and Styles Revisited: Strategic Planning and Financial Control," *Long Range Planning*, vol. 26, no. 5, 1993, pp. 49–60.

22. See earlier chapters for more details of these companies' screening processes.

23. Although Lewinton's immediate past experience was in consumer products, his background was in engineering.

24. See Appendix A.

25. The discussions of specialist expertise in Chapters 6 through 8, of the removal of blockages in Chapter 7, and of the ability both to create value and avoid value destruction in ongoing parenting throughout Part Two are relevant.

26. Portfolio decisions of this sort, which are fundamental to the implementation of strategy, are discussed further in Chapter 14.

27. Footnotes 16 and 17 to Chapter 8 and footnote 42 to Chapter 4, concerning the "resource-based theory of the firm" and "specialized assets" are relevant to this condition.

28. Judgments about the right price to pay for an acquisition are much more likely to be correctly made by companies that understand the business well enough to be able to parent it well. See David B. Jemison and Sim B. Sitkin, "Acquisitions: The Process Can Be a Problem," *Harvard Business Review*, March–April 1986.

29. Strictly speaking, the requirement is that the value created by corporate development should not be more than offset by value destruction from subsequent ongoing parenting.

10 THE EVOLUTION OF CORPORATE STRATEGIES

Over a period of time, most companies' corporate strategies need to evolve and change. A company's parenting approach should be fine-tuned to increase net parenting value creation, and its portfolio composition should be shifted to take advantage of value creation opportunities and to improve the alignment with the parenting approach. Furthermore, changes in business characteristics, rival parents, and environmental conditions may open up new parenting requirements. Such modifications need not involve changes to the heartland business criteria, but in some circumstances it is also desirable to attempt to test and extend the boundaries around the heartland. Less commonly, a more radical change in the underlying corporate strategy may be necessary or desirable.

Changes in corporate strategy, particularly if they involve learning to parent new sorts of businesses or altering the whole basis of value creation, are not easy to bring about successfully. But companies that are unable to introduce modifications and changes to their corporate strategies are liable to find that historic patterns of success are sooner or later overtaken by events and cease to yield parenting advantage. This chapter, therefore, analyzes the evolution of corporate strategies in the companies we have researched.

MODIFICATIONS TO THE CORPORATE STRATEGY

Refining the Corporate Strategy

From time to time, almost all parent companies must expect to make refinements to their corporate strategies. The value creation insights remain unchanged, but the parenting characteristics are amended, either

246

to increase the amount of value that is created, or to respond to changes in the characteristics of the businesses being parented.

Companies that have introduced changes in parenting characteristics to improve the implementation of their corporate strategies include Emerson, RTZ, ABB, and Hanson. Emerson continuously fine-tunes its planning processes. RTZ has brought in a process of technical audits, carried out by the central technical staff, to help its subsidiaries to raise the cost-effectiveness of their mining operations. ABB has been working to improve the functioning of its global matrix structure by reallocating senior management responsibilities and shifting the balance of power between Regional and Business Area teams. The evolution and refinement of Hanson's corporate strategy were traced in Chapter 2. Such changes do not alter the main thrusts of these companies' parenting characteristics, but are intended to see that they deliver as much value as possible.

There may also be opportunities to bring new businesses into the portfolio to provide an enlarged scope for value creation and to divest businesses that do not fit. Changes to the portfolio that are largely consistent with a company's heartland criteria do not, however, represent substantial changes to the corporate strategy; rather, they aim to maximize value creation through refinements in the portfolio. Indeed, in earlier chapters, we have observed that successful corporate parents constantly strive to obtain the best possible alignment between their parenting approach and their portfolio of businesses.

Other companies have found it necessary to amend their parenting to deal with changes taking place in the nature of their businesses. BTR and Emerson, for example, have always been strong believers in structures that stress the stand-alone responsibility for performance of each business, and have therefore deemphasized linkages between their businesses. Both companies, however, have recognized that, in some of their businesses, the opportunities for sharing product development ideas and technology are increasing, especially between businesses with similar products in different countries. Their parenting structures have therefore recently been changed to place more emphasis on the role of a group or sector level in encouraging some focused linkages. These changes are being grafted onto the companies' well-established parenting approaches for stand-alone influence, to respond to changes that they see in the nature of some of their businesses. Perceiving and responding to changes in the parenting needs or opportunities in a company's businesses is seldom easy. Strongly held beliefs about how to create value may preclude a company from seeing the need for change; and well-established patterns of parenting may be hard to alter, especially if they have been gradually learned and developed by the senior managers in the parent. But successful parents must remain alert to the changes they need to make to respond to changes in the circumstances of their businesses.

Refinements to corporate strategy are, therefore, taking place all the time in successful parent companies. They do not entail new value creation insights, or significant changes in the company's parenting characteristics or heartland business criteria. But they are necessary to maintain freshness, to ensure that the fit between the parenting characteristics and the portfolio remains as strong as possible, and to prevent the erosion of parenting advantage as other companies also refine and improve their parenting. General Electric (GE) is a company that has made a variety of refinements to its corporate strategy in recent years.

GENERAL ELECTRIC: REFINEMENTS TO THE CORPORATE STRATEGY. Since 1981, under the leadership of Jack Welch, GE has undergone a series of changes and refinements to its corporate strategy. The main themes of the strategy have, however, remained constant and were clearly stated by Welch within weeks of his appointment as chief executive.[1] These themes have been the pursuit of number one or two market position in all the businesses in the portfolio; the sharing of skills and know-how between GE's businesses; and the release of employee energy and commitment through culture change and debureaucratization.

The "number one or number two" criterion is the simple rule that all GE's businesses should either become leaders (or number twos) in their respective markets, or else GE should exit. Since the early 1980s, this criterion has been applied with single-mindedness and has led to numerous changes in portfolio composition. Thus GE has made major acquisitions or joint venture deals in fields such as medical equipment, financial services, defense electronics, lighting, and broadcasting. For example, in 1993, GE's Aerospace business was combined with that of Martin Marietta to create the world's number one aerospace electronics company, and a deal was struck with the Irish headquartered GPA that should give GE international leadership in aircraft leasing. Divestments have included Utah International, the natural resource business, and the consumer electronics business. Through these portfolio changes, GE has attained number one or two status in nearly all its businesses,[2] and improved the alignment of its portfolio with its parenting approach.

GE has sometimes used the puzzling phrase "integrated diversity" to describe itself. The essence of this concept is the transfer of ideas and best practice between different businesses. "Integrated diversity means the drawing together of our different businesses by sharing ideas, by finding multiple applications for technological advancements, and by moving people across businesses to provide fresh perspectives and to develop broad-based experience," states Jack Welch.[3] "GE's diversity creates a huge laboratory of innovation and ideas that reside in each of the businesses, and mining them is both our challenge and an awesome opportunity."[4] In 1985, the company was restructured into 13 separate business areas, such as aircraft engines, lighting, and major appliances.[5] These business areas were primarily focused on their own strategies, but Welch also began to encourage best practice sharing between businesses. At the top level, the business area heads and the corporate function heads now meet quarterly in the Corporate Executive Council (CEC) for 1½ days, which provides a forum for discussion of issues of common interest. But the main emphasis has been placed on increased informal networking at lower levels. "You can read about these things in books, but you get more of the reality of it from working with another GE company," maintained one GE manager. "Then you know what can be achieved, and you know it can be made to work within the GE culture."

The importance of dismantling bureaucratic decision-making structures and processes has been a third major theme for GE. In the early 1980s, the focus was on the corporate planning and control systems, which were made much less formal.[6] The move to a more informal process was intended to lead to a faster, more flexible response to opportunities, and to reduce the time and effort devoted to bureaucratic meetings and reports. The process now provides for intensive debates of strategy, within a context of tough financial and strategic targets, and receives high marks from the businesses that participate in it. Since the late 1980s, the strongest corporate emphasis has, however, been placed on introducing the so-called "Work-Out" process to all of GE's businesses.

Work-Out is a process that brings together groups of employees from different levels and positions within GE's businesses to discuss ideas and decide on initiatives for improving GE's performance. At first, Work-Out concentrated on identifying and removing bureaucratic impediments, such as unnecessary reports, meetings, or procedures: "An intense and continuing program to liberate employees from the cramping artifacts that pile up in the dusty attics of century-old companies: the reports, meetings, rituals, approvals, controls, and forests of paper that often seem necessary until they are removed." Subsequently, the process has broadened in scope to encourage all employees to put forward their own ideas on any ways in which GE's businesses could perform better. The senior managers in each Work-Out meeting are required either to accept proposals that are put forward on the spot or to state clearly how they will be investigated and when a decision will be taken. The objective is to encourage all GE employees to think of ways of doing things better, to show that their ideas are being taken seriously and implemented, and to move away from "the polite deference to small ideas that too often comes from big offices in big companies."[7] Ultimately, Work-Out is intended to create "boundaryless" behavior, in which all of GE's 230,000 employees are capable of working together, irrespective of traditional functional, hierarchical, or business boundaries.

The impetus for Work-Out and boundarylessness has been provided by Welch's personal belief that there are vast untapped reservoirs of energy, creativity, and enthusiasm in large companies, and that any parent that can unlock this potential will have an overwhelming advantage. Welch credits Work-Out with raising GE's rate of productivity growth by a factor of two or more and feels that it is now improving GE's customer responsiveness as well. The process is still in its early days, and GE recognizes that it will be many years before it will come close to achieving its full objectives. Nevertheless, as tangible results have begun to be produced, much of the early scepticism about Work-Out is being overcome. The process has survived the rigors of the early 1990s recession, suggesting that it has now taken root firmly in the company.

While maintaining the essential value creation insights on which the corporate strategy depends, GE has therefore introduced a variety of modifications to its portfolio composition and parenting approach since 1981. These changes have fine-tuned the corporate strategy and allowed GE to become a successful parent across a remarkably wide range of different businesses.

GE: CORPORATE STRATEGY IN THE 1990s. Exhibit 10–1 is a parenting advantage statement for GE, which brings out the main *value creation insights* and the *distinctive parenting characteristics* that have

EXHIBIT 10–1 GE parenting advantage statement

Value Creation Insights	In many businesses, a parent can create value by: • Enforcing a market leadership criterion for portfolio composition ("Number one or two"). • Facilitating the sharing of best management practices ("integrated diversity"). • Releasing employee energy, ideas, and enthusiasm ("debureaucratization").
Distinctive Parenting Characteristics	Willing and able to implement number one or two philosophy. CEC and other forums and networks for sharing best practice. State-of-the-art planning and control processes. "Work-out" process that leads to debureaucratization. Attracting, developing, and retaining high quality, professional management. Personal characteristics of corporate parenting team.
Heartland Businesses	Diverse in terms of critical success factors. In most businesses, however, leading market share is key to competitive advantage, and there are opportunities for sharing best management practices and "debureaucratizing" management processes.

been built to support them. We have already commented on most of these, with the exception of GE's people and their skills.

For many years, GE has had a reputation as a leading exponent of modern management techniques. As such, it has attracted some of the ablest professional managers in the United States, and has developed their skills through the experience and training it has given them. Under Jack Welch, it appears to provide the stimulus and challenge that appeal to ambitious young managers, and there is an in-depth strength of professional management that is the envy of the vast majority of other companies. Indeed, GE has become a sort of training ground for the senior managements of many other U.S. companies; a spell with GE is seen as a strength on any curriculum vitae.

The personal characteristics of GE's top team, in particular Jack Welch, are specially important. Welch inspires remarkable affection, respect, and enthusiasm among GE's managers. "He is incredibly smart. He can think strategically, but he is also good with people, with deals, with organization, with politics. He can make the sort of inputs to guys running the businesses that only an outsider who has a really informed view can make," was a typical comment from one GE business head. His personal energy has driven the company forward, and his grasp of the issues in the various businesses is remarkable. But one man alone cannot discharge all the parenting tasks in a company as large and diverse as GE, and Welch depends on the skills and experience of the other key managers in the parenting team, particularly his colleagues in the Corporate Executive Office. It has been by putting together a balanced team with a variety of skills, backgrounds, and experience that GE has been able to manage a level of diversity that few other companies can cope with.

GE is active in a variety of business areas, ranging from aircraft engines, through broadcasting and medical equipment, to domestic appliances and capital services. Each of these business areas itself consists of several different subbusinesses: GE Capital Services, for example, includes more than 20 separate businesses, such as aircraft leasing, mortgage guarantee insurance, reinsurance, credit card processing, and securities brokerage. Given this degree of portfolio diversity, it is impossible to argue that all of GE's businesses conform to tightly defined *heartland criteria.* The key success factors, the nature of risks and investments, and the profile of successful managers differ substantially between different GE businesses. Indeed, the contrast between the determinants of competitive success in lighting, aircraft engines, Kidder Peabody (investment banking and brokerage), and NBC (broadcasting) could hardly be greater.

Despite this diversity, GE has made relatively few of the mistakes that are common among parents that lack a feel for their businesses. Almost without exception, the GE business managers that we met were full of praise for the way in which Jack Welch and the parenting team at the center in GE were able to zero in on important issues and exert a positive influence on decisions. Admittedly, this was particularly evident in businesses where one of the members of the Corporate Executive Office had personal experience, but even the less familiar businesses such as Capital Services had few complaints.

GE's record is not without blemishes, particularly in some of the more recent diversifications. But it is not obvious that these problems have been caused by diversification beyond the boundaries within which GE could be an effective parent. GE may have been overoptimistic about what it could achieve in factory automation; but this has been a rapidly changing and loosely grouped set of markets and technologies in which few companies have been certain about how to move forward. Kidder Peabody has encountered some problems since its acquisition by GE in 1986; but the general problems of Wall Street securities firms in the late 1980s and specific problems related to insider trading and "phantom trading" can be blamed for many of these difficulties. Even NBC, perhaps furthest from GE's traditional base in electrical engineering, performed well for several years after its acquisition in 1986, as part of RCA; though there are some signs that GE is less comfortable with this business and less sure about how to deal with the decline in ratings and in profitability it has faced in the early 1990s. In general, however, GE has coped well with parenting its wide range of different sorts of businesses.

In searching for common characteristics between the businesses, it is the ability to benefit from GE's value creation insights that sets some limits on the apparent diversity of GE's portfolio, and gives a sense of where a widely defined heartland lies. For example, GE tends to be in businesses in which market share matters and is important for competitive success. Thus an emphasis on building number one or two positions in the relevant markets creates value. Conversely, GE is less at home in, and has tended to avoid, businesses where market leadership provides few advantages, or where rapid swings in market tastes, or in product or process technologies, can undermine the advantages of an established leader. Moreover, as large, established market leaders, GE's businesses can typically benefit from an approach to parenting that stresses the elimination of bureaucracy in decision making. It is also evident that GE has embarked on no major fresh diversifications since the mid-1980s, and it is recognized within GE that the company would encounter increasing difficulty if it tried to parent a yet wider range of businesses.

GE's results under Jack Welch have been impressive. Financial performance has been strong across a remarkably varied group of businesses and GE is an admired and feared competitor in almost all the businesses where it competes. We are aware of no other company that has achieved this sort of record and reputation with such a diverse portfolio of businesses. Critics of GE claim that it has failed to take on fierce competitors from Japan in businesses such as semiconductors and consumer electronics and that, with the exception of financial services, its businesses have shown little organic growth during the 1980s and early 1990s. Furthermore, the very diversity of GE, and its lack of clear heartland business criteria, can be seen as a cause for concern. Is it really possible for the company to have a sufficient feel to parent the range of businesses in its portfolio well? We will return to the issue of corporate strategy and portfolio diversity in Chapter 11. However, it does seem that GE's corporate-level focus on value-creating activities, and the exceptional professional management skills of its parenting team, have allowed it to achieve parenting advantage across an unusually broad front during the Welch years. Whether it will be possible to maintain this success under the next generation of corporate management remains to be seen.

Extending the Heartland

Some portfolio changes involve entry to new businesses that should respond to the main value creation insights of a company but which do not meet all the established heartland criteria. For example, the new business may employ an unfamiliar technology or operate in unfamiliar markets, so that the parent may be less sure that it has a feel for the business success factors involved. In such circumstances, the company needs to recognize that the new business is testing, and may be pushing back, the boundaries around the heartland, and that it may be necessary to learn new parenting skills to deal with it. The parent company must acquire a sufficient feel for the new business to be able to pursue its value creation insights with confidence and to avoid value destruction in other areas of parenting.

Learning how to parent less familiar businesses is seldom easy. Canon, however, is a company that has systematically and successfully extended its heartland over many years.[8]

CANON: HEARTLAND EXTENSIONS. Canon was originally established in the mid-1930s to conduct research on compact cameras. Accordingly, the company has always stressed the importance of new product development and innovative technology. Its original technology base was in precision mechanics, though it soon became directly involved in fine optics, producing its first in-house lens in 1939. Using these two technologies, an indirect X-ray camera was developed in 1940. Canon's heartland, therefore, initially revolved around camera products, new product development, and the combination of two technology streams. Over the following 50 years, Canon has extended its heartland in various ways. It has moved into medical equipment, chemical products, and semiconductor production equipment. The most significant new business entry, however, was into office products.

In 1959, Canon used its technological expertise to create an office equipment product in micrographics. The product was a magnetic tape reader, called the "synchro reader." Despite being highly innovative, the synchro reader took Canon into unfamiliar markets and proved to be a commercial failure. In some respects, this episode highlights the dangers of moving into businesses outside a company's established heartland. However, Canon used the experience both to begin to learn about a new end-market, and to bolster its resources and standing. Although the synchro reader failed commercially, it was so innovative that it was written up extensively in magazines, which in turn attracted a number of creative engineers to join the company. As Canon's chairman, Ryuzaburo Kaku, later recalled: "Many students with an electric major came to Canon [in 1959] only because many magazines described the new product." As a result, Canon began to build a new third core technology in microelectronics. In due course, this led to new product developments in various fields including electronic calculators and copying machines.

The launch of electronic calculators took place in 1964. Canon initially gained a technological lead, and sales grew rapidly. By 1970, calculators accounted for 40% of Canon's total sales. However, when Casio launched a cheaper, more compact calculator in 1972, Canon was slow to respond, and lost ground. Worse still, in 1974 its new product range suffered due to defects in the critical LED (light-emitting diode) components that Canon had bought in. This led to a major profit drop in 1975, and the indignity of passing the company dividend. Despite these problems, Canon again learned from the setback and was able to build on its experience in calculators. As Kaijo Yamaji, president of Canon, put it: "The calculator group carried on to develop wordprocessors and typewriters. And we were left with our channels to the stationery stores which had stood their ground through the toughest battles." Furthermore, the experience reinforced Canon's belief in the importance of maintaining technical leadership through continuing product development and through the in-house manufacture of key components.

Canon's entry into the copier market was even more clearly based on a series of steps and experiments designed to provide learning about the new business. First, an R&D organization dedicated to electrophotography was established in 1962. It was focused on creating an indirect electrostatic process that could match Xerox without infringing its patents. The process was developed in outline by 1965, and essentially complete in 1968. Rather than wait for the new technology, however, Canon started to learn in parallel about photocopier markets and sales channels. It licensed less advanced technology from RCA, and started to sell modest quantities of copiers in Japan as early as 1965. It then licensed further technology from Australia to produce a new series of copiers in 1968. Canon established a separate company, International Image Industry, to sell these copiers in Japan. It also started to operate in the US, but only as a supplier to Scott Paper, who sold the series under the "Scott" brandname. Sales were limited to these two countries and provided Canon with relatively low risk exposure to learning prior to the roll-out of its new technology products from 1970 onwards.[9]

In entering new businesses, Canon has become well aware of the need to learn about the businesses, and to proceed cautiously during the learning process. This awareness is evident in Canon's approach to parenting new businesses. The businesses are encouraged to move forward step-by-step, often in separate or joint venture organizations. The corporate staff play an important role in getting to grips with the critical success factors in new markets and technologies, and in briefing senior corporate management. Any lack of personal familiarity or feel for these markets is also offset by an approach to decision-making that stresses the importance of wide discussion and consensus building. Senior corporate managers are less liable to insist on their own personal views, thus reducing the danger of ill-informed judgments in businesses where they lack a feel, but are able to acquire experience of the business through participation in the extensive debates leading up to decisions. Furthermore, Canon's wide use of joint ventures and alliances, both in technology and in sales and marketing, has helped the parent to learn about new business areas. Extensions to the heartland have, therefore, involved building on experience gained through a variety of technology-based new business experiments, and conscious efforts to learn new parenting skills in less familiar businesses. This approach has allowed Canon to push back and enlarge the boundaries around its heartland and to succeed in a variety of new businesses.

Currently, Canon is making further attempts to extend its heartland. It has determined that a presence in computing is important for two main reasons. Defensively, Canon believes that its existing strength in business machines will increasingly require in-house capabilities in software development and firsthand knowledge of computer products, markets, and systems. Offensively, Canon expects that its expertise in optoelectronics may become central to the design and development of computer systems. As a result, it has established a computer business, whose returns would not yet be viable as a stand-alone proposition. Over the coming decade, it will be interesting to observe how Canon learns to parent this type of business, and whether it is able to extend its heartland to include it. Past successes suggest some optimism, though the magnitude of the task should not be underestimated.

Other companies in our research that have succeeded in extending their heartlands and learning to parent new businesses include Cooper, 3M, and GE. We shall return to a discussion of the conditions under which companies are able to learn new parenting skills later in this chapter and in Chapter 15.

RADICAL CHANGES IN THE CORPORATE STRATEGY

Occasionally, parent companies choose, or are forced, to make radical changes in their corporate strategies. They may conclude that their corporate strategy is vague, weak, or ineffective as a basis for parenting advantage, or they may find that changes in their businesses or their rivals have been so great that their strategy no longer remains viable. These situations cannot be rectified by piecemeal changes in parenting characteristics or portfolio composition and require a fundamental shift in the whole focus of value creation.

Changes in corporate strategy inevitably entail major consequential changes to parenting characteristics and portfolio composition. Usually, they also call for extensive changes in management at the top level in the parent and in the businesses, since the adjustments are too great for the old team to propose and carry through effectively. There is frequently a period of uncertainty and depressed performance during the transition from the old strategy to the new, which can last for several years. As a result, successful changes in corporate strategy are difficult and comparatively rare.

In Chapter 9, we described the major portfolio restructuring that followed from Christopher Lewinton's new corporate strategy at TI. The performance crisis, and the lack of a clear previous corporate strategy, meant that these changes were accepted relatively rapidly and easily by the organization. A more long drawn-out, and in some ways more difficult, transition has taken place at Grand Metropolitan.

Grand Metropolitan: Evolution of Corporate Strategy

Grand Metropolitan dates back to 1947. It started its life as a small hotel company but has now become one of the world's largest food and drink companies, and no longer owns any hotels. The company had a turnover of £8 billion and profits before interest and tax of over £1 billion by 1993. The company's history has involved two very different corporate strategies, driven by two different parenting teams, and built on different sources of parenting advantage. By describing Grand Metropolitan's history, we can show the contrast between these eras of corporate strategy and provide an example of how corporate strategy can change radically.

GRAND METROPOLITAN: THE MAXWELL JOSEPH YEARS.   Grand Metropolitan was founded by Maxwell Joseph (later to become Sir Maxwell Joseph), a successful real estate agent. After the war, he began purchasing hotels, based on his knowledge of the property business. Joseph found that he could buy hotels with city center sites at prices that made it possible to finance the deal using the cash flow from the hotel. He believed that the hotels were good long-term investments, particularly since he could use the operating cash flow to service the debt needed to buy them. Apart from Joseph's obvious skills in property valuation and in constructing deals that were self-financing, he developed good contacts in the financial community and built up an excellent track record. As a result, he was able to raise money for deals that others might not have found so easy.

Joseph took little interest in the running of the hotels, delegating this task to Stanley Grinstead and Ernest Sharp, two accountants with managerial experience. In fact, Maxwell Joseph never formally had an office on the company's premises, preferring to orchestrate the deals from his private offices.

After the company went public in 1962, Joseph expanded beyond hotels into other businesses that had good property backing. He bought a catering business (Levy and Franks) and a dairy business (Express Dairies) because many of the sites and depots were in good city center locations. He then acquired a brewery business (Truman's) because the breweries were often in prime property locations. This led on to a much larger brewery acquisition, Watney Mann. Watney Mann cost £435 million in 1972 and was the largest industrial acquisition in Britain up to that date. It was nearly 10 times the size of any of Joseph's previous acquisitions, but the logic was the same. The properties were good and the deal could be made to "wash its face." With Watney Mann came a drinks business, IDV, which would prove to be important to Grand Metropolitan's future. Since IDV was not a property business, Joseph tried unsuccessfully to sell it.

Joseph had built a large company in only 25 years. It was in a variety of businesses, ranging from hotels to dairies, and from beer to bingo halls, but there had been a clear value creation strategy behind his success. Joseph's heartland was businesses with good quality "trading property assets," whose property value was not fully reflected in the prices at which they could be acquired. The businesses were valued for their trading performance, but they also had a property value that often exceeded their trading value. Joseph's corporate strategy was not to sell the properties, but to keep the businesses and use the growing cash flow to buy more property assets. Meanwhile, Grinstead and Sharp adopted a performance-oriented and decentralized parenting style for the businesses, making it possible for them to parent a wide range of interests.

The 1974–1975 recession, however, hit Grand Metropolitan hard. Cash flow declined, property values fell, and the company was faced with the prospect of defaulting on its bank covenants. Joseph's creation could have collapsed due to the large debt burden taken on to finance the acquisition of Watney Mann. As part of a search for improved cash flow, Allen Sheppard, a tough British Leyland manager from the car industry, was hired to help rationalize Watney Mann. This decision sowed the seed for Grand Metropolitan's future changes of corporate strategy.

GRAND METROPOLITAN: THE ALLEN SHEPPARD YEARS.   On arrival at Watney Mann, Allen Sheppard immediately sensed the cozy overmanning and inefficiencies that had built up in a beer industry dominated by a few large companies. He began rationalizing and decentralizing, and found that it was possible to reduce manning every year without any impact on volumes or quality. Over 6 years, he halved the number of employees with a style that became know as "magic numbers management." Sheppard would define a manning number at the beginning of the year, and managers would find a way to deliver it by the end of the year. To do this, Sheppard built round him a team of hard-driving, energetic managers from outside the beer industry: Ian Martin from ITT (operations), Clive Strowger from British Leyland (finance), and David Tagg also from the car industry (personnel).

With the improved productivity from Sheppard's efforts, the benefit of a rising property market, and an improving economy, Grand Metropolitan emerged from the 1970s with a strong balance sheet and good cash flow. By then, Maxwell Joseph was exerting less influence and Stanley Grinstead became chairman in 1981. Grinstead decided to move into "U.S. branded services," arguing that Grand Metropolitan needed to diversify away from the U.K. economy and that service businesses were more attractive growth opportunities. He acquired an optical chain, a child-care operation, and a home healthcare business. By the mid-1980s, this diversification program was seen to be unsuccessful, Grand Metropolitan became a takeover target, and Stanley Grinstead retired.

During the early 1980s, Allen Sheppard had repeated his rationalization program in another part of the company, Express Dairies. He had been given responsibility for the business after an unexpected profit downturn, and he again applied his tough management principles, reducing manning and raising profits. He was, therefore, the prime candidate to succeed Stanley Grinstead. Sheppard's main rival for the top job was Anthony Tennant, who had been running IDV, now a profitable and fast-growing drinks business. Culturally very different from the rest of Grand Metropolitan, this business had grown dramatically through brand marketing and acquiring distributors. Sheppard's appointment as chief executive in 1986 limited the opportunities for Anthony Tennant, and shortly afterward Tennant was head-hunted to run Guinness, an international drinks company.

Sheppard soon announced a reversal of Grinstead's diversification policy under the banner of "operation declutter." He focused the portfolio on food, drink, and retailing, even selling the company's original business, hotels. He also changed most of the senior managers in the parent company and the businesses. The members of the team who had helped him turn around Watney Mann and Express Dairies were given senior posts, and he recruited a new breed of energetic, restless managers to fill other posts. His management style was known as a "light grip on the throat," as a result of a remark he made about how the center reacted to performance problems. Those businesses he kept were put through the same rejuvenation process that had succeeded at Watney and Express. The only business to remain largely unaffected was IDV. The business was performing well and Sheppard could recognize that it would not respond to his normal operational focus.

Having put in place a new parenting team, Sheppard began to look for acquisition targets, placing particular emphasis on "international added-value brands." The company screened many targets, but found that rivals such as Nestlé or Philip Morris were often pushing prices of targets up to unreasonable levels. Pillsbury, however, proved to be an ideal target because the company was poorly managed and had been underinvesting in its brands and its manufacturing. It was highly suitable for the Allen Sheppard rejuvenation formula. Ian Martin was sent to the United States, where he repeated many of the turnaround lessons learned at Watney and Express Dairies. A variety of other smaller foods businesses have also been acquired. On the other hand, the brewing and pub businesses from Watney Mann were sold in the early 1990s to concentrate on businesses with more opportunities for growth through international branding.

While Allen Sheppard was building Grand Metropolitan by acquiring Pillsbury, the IDV team, now led by George Bull, was making major acquisitions in the drinks business. The aggressive branding and acquisition strategy started by Tennant with the acquisition of the U.S. distributor, Paddington Corporation, was followed by a 25 percent stake in Cinzano; and in 1987, IDV acquired Heublein. The IDV team discovered how brands could be made into international successes and that control of distribution was necessary to exploit the international potential.

The Allen Sheppard era at Grand Metropolitan has therefore seen the company join the top league of food and drinks businesses, based on two different sources of value creation. First, Allen Sheppard and his turnaround team from Watney Mann and Express Dairies were able to repeat their formula on a wider scale during operation declutter and subsequently with Pillsbury. They knew the importance of changing senior managers as part of a rejuvenation program. They knew how to reduce manning levels without disrupting production, and how to cut overheads without raiding the advertising budget. They knew how to hire people with industry expertise who would thrive in their "restless" culture. They also created a fierce loyalty to their management approach.

Second, at IDV the senior team had developed a successful approach to building international brands. For example, they established J&B Scotch as the world's number one whisky brand, and launched other successful brands such as Bailey's and Aqua Libra. They also knew the potential for increasing sales by acquiring the distributors of their products. In 1993, George Bull was appointed chief executive of Grand Metropolitan, and appears likely to succeed Allen Sheppard as chairman in due course.

Throughout the 1980s, Grand Metropolitan was a company with two sources of value creation: the rejuvenation skills of Sheppard's team and the international branding and distribution skills of the IDV team. In the 1990s, these are beginning to blend, with IDV's cost base being improved by applying sound operating principles and Grand Metropolitan's food businesses building international brands such as Haagen-Däzs. Allen Sheppard comments that there are many companies with branding skills and many companies with operating management skills. Grand Metropolitan's advantage, he believes, is in being able to pull both levers in a balanced way—to be good at building brands *and* good at efficient operations. "After a series of debates we eventually decided our advantage was this—our ability to combine, in a single organization, both world-class operational and marketing skills. We could not claim to be the number one at marketing, nor even perhaps at operational control. But we had a very good chance of being number one at both of them simultaneously," explained Sheppard. Exhibit 10–2 is a parenting advantage statement for Grand Metropolitan that looks forward into the 1990s.

EXHIBIT 10–2   Grand Metropolitan parenting advantage statement

Value Creation Insights	Many food and drink companies can be rejuvenated through wholesale management changes and a parenting approach that combines tight operating control with a focus on building international brand positions.
Distinctive Parenting Characteristics	Cadre of Grand Metropolitan managers with rejuvenation experience.
	"Restless," action-oriented management culture, focused on continuous improvement, and a distrust of the status quo.
	Financially oriented strategic control system that provides a "light grip on the throat."
	Skills in international branding and distribution management.
Heartland Businesses	Food and drink companies with potential for international branding where efficient operations and brand management are both critical to success.

Grand Metropolitan has undergone radical change in its corporate strategy. Under Sheppard's leadership, a new corporate strategy has been established that draws on parenting characteristics that have been gradually developed in different parts of the company, but which have been molded together into an unusual blend. There has also been extensive portfolio change to realign the businesses more closely with the new strategy. During the 1980s, commentators on Grand Metropolitan questioned whether the multiple portfolio changes resulted from a hyperactive management team or from a clear underlying corporate strategy. As Grand Metropolitan has moved into the 1990s, the nature of the new corporate strategy has become clearer, and the rationale for the changes in the portfolio and the parenting approach are more evident. After a decade of uncertainty, the direction now seems firmly set.

Requirements for Radical Changes in Corporate Strategy

Grand Metropolitan's experiences epitomize the difficulty of bringing about a fundamental shift in corporate strategy. It took a financial crisis, a complete change of top management, some fortuitously developed experience at divisional level, a series of major portfolio moves, and 10 years of struggle to bring about the transition. The size of the task involved in changing corporate strategy should not be underestimated.

In several respects, Grand Metropolitan can even be regarded as facing a relatively easy task. The old guard retired naturally, the financial crisis was dealt with fairly easily through operating improvements and allowed time for the new corporate strategy to be developed, and the seeds of a new parenting approach and the businesses to build on already existed. These circumstances can be contrasted with the crisis facing IBM in 1993.

For decades, IBM was regarded by most people as an exemplar. It achieved and maintained preeminence across a wide range of fast growing and rapidly changing IT businesses. Its management practices and culture, and its parenting approach, seemed well suited to its businesses, its employees were enthusiastic and loyal, and its results were consistently strong. But, gradually, it began to encounter a new set of challenges. As the benefits from close links between its businesses diminished, the opportunities for more focused competitors were seized by a number of aggressive new companies such as Compaq, Sun Microsystems and Microsoft, and the advantages from IBM's thorough, consensus-based decision processes began to be outweighed by their cost, bureaucracy, and slowness. Furthermore, confidence in its own ability to dominate the industry blinded it to new leverage points. It gave up crucial areas of control to Intel in microprocessor chips and Microsoft in operating systems. Although the roots of IBM's problems can be traced back several years, their full significance only became apparent in dramatically worse corporate performance from 1991 onward. By 1993, it was obvious, however, that IBM needed a new corporate strategy, and needed it quickly.

But, for IBM, deciding on and implementing a new corporate strategy was fraught with difficulties. IBM's management style and culture had been painstakingly built up over many years, and its parenting characteristics fitted together into a cohesive and interwoven pattern. Changing individual elements of the approach was, therefore, hard; nothing short of a revolution was likely to allow the company to break free of the old corporate strategy. Furthermore, the senior management was made up of long-serving IBM managers, who had grown up and thrived within the traditional approach. The chances that these managers could suddenly lead a radical and revolutionary change in corporate strategy were inevitably low. As a result, an ineffective, gradualist approach to change prevailed until after a dramatic boardroom showdown in early 1993, which led to the removal of John Akers, the chief executive, and his replacement by Lou Gerstner, who was brought in from outside IBM. The historic strengths and success of IBM made it especially difficult for the company to internalize the need for change and to embark on the changes required.

The direction and shape of IBM's future corporate strategy remains unclear. It is not yet fully evident what changes Gerstner and the new parenting team wish to make, and whether they will be able to introduce them successfully. IBM is still in a state of flux, as it moves away from its historic corporate strategy and searches for a new corporate strategy. It is in the middle of a transition that was bound to be painful and problematic, and there can be no certainty that it will emerge successfully. However, the severity of the problems has now been recognized, and the necessity of radical change is accepted.

Fundamental changes in corporate strategy are therefore fraught with problems, and should not be embarked on lightly. If, however, the old corporate strategy is nonexistent or evidently not working, a search for a new strategy may be the only option. It may be that the new strategy can emerge partly through a process of trial and error, building on different initiatives in different businesses, as at Grand Met, or it may be that a powerful new vision is needed to lead the process, as at TI. But, in any case, the final objective must be a new corporate strategy, which will give coherence to the fundamental changes that will be needed.

THE LEARNING CHALLENGE

Learning new parenting skills is never easy. Many companies stumble when they try to alter their parenting characteristics or to extend their heartlands into new and unfamiliar businesses. Attempts to embark upon wholly new corporate strategies are even more difficult. From observing companies that have been successful in learning new parenting skills, we have, however, been able to draw some conclusions about the conditions under which learning does take place, and about the extent of learning that is possible.

A precondition for successful learning is a recognition of the need to learn. Parents that assume their existing skills will always be sufficient for new situations and new businesses are not open to possible changes, and, as a result, seldom learn.[10] But, for many parents, an inquiring attitude of this sort is hard. Established mental maps are difficult to discard, and can provide filters that prevent the parent from seeing the real differences in new situations and new businesses. What is more, considerations of status and hierarchy make it unnatural for many senior parent managers to admit to their business managers that they lack understanding or skills in some areas. As a result, the need to acquire new parenting skills is often not perceived. It is only when the company has run into serious performance problems that learning begins, by which time it may already be too late.[11] Recognition that parenting skills must constantly evolve and change is far preferable to waiting for a crisis before admitting that change is needed.

New parenting characteristics are usually built up gradually and refined with experience. A feel for new businesses is slowly acquired by exposure to the issues faced by the businesses. The effectiveness of new value creation insights or parenting characteristics is tested and proved by putting them into practice. Viewed from a learning perspective, almost all parenting initiatives should be regarded as potentially useful experiments, from which much can be learned about how to create more value in the future. In practice, it is as difficult to learn from experience as it is to recognize the need to learn, and for similar reasons. Nevertheless, the success of companies such as GE, Canon, and Grand Metropolitan in modifying their corporate strategies has depended on their ability to try new initiatives and to be willing to learn both from the successes and the failures. Provided the false starts are used as a basis for learning, and provided that the first steps with new approaches to parenting or new businesses are taken cautiously with the expectation of learning more as experience is gained, initial setbacks can prepare the ground for eventual successes. If, however, the parent is unwilling, or unable, to modify its parenting in the light of experience, errors can be perpetuated for long periods of time.[12]

Some sorts of parental learning are relatively easy, while others are either hard or even impossible. The learning involved in fine-tuning well-established parenting systems and processes, or in understanding the specific critical success factors in a new business that largely meets the heartland criteria, is modest. If the parent does not recognize that some learning is needed, it can still destroy substantial value. But, in principle, the learning task is relatively easy.

As the new skills move further away from the established and the familiar, the learning challenge increases. Companies such as Canon and Shell have found that it usually takes several years to acquire a feel for new businesses with substantially different critical success factors from the established heartland. Indeed, several experienced chief executives believe that it is realistic to allow a decade or more to build the right instincts in situations of this sort, and to recognize that there is no guarantee of success at the end of the road.[13] Major modifications to management processes and structures can take almost as long to work smoothly, as companies that have introduced basically new approaches to planning or radical changes in reporting relationships will testify.

The greatest learning difficulties are presented by situations that require parenting that is incompatible with deeply held beliefs that are ingrained throughout the company's parenting. Parents, such as BTR or Emerson, that have always believed in clear individual business responsibility and accountability, find it very hard to learn to operate with an ABB matrix structure or with extensive shared resources at the center, as in Canon. Parents, such as RTZ or Shell, that naturally see their role in terms of supporting businesses' long-term investment plans through thick and thin, have great difficulty applying Hanson-type strict short-term budgetary control. There are basic conflicts between these different approaches to parenting, and no program of learning is likely to succeed in grafting them onto each other.[14] If BTR or Emerson were to find themselves in businesses that needed complex linkage management from the parent, they would have to change their whole corporate strategies to parent the businesses well. If RTZ or Shell were to enter businesses that needed an exclusive focus on short-term operating profits, they would confront a similarly fundamental need for change. Given the predispositions and skills of the existing parenting teams, and the pervasive influence of their deeply held beliefs about how to exercise their influence, such changes are most unlikely to occur. Rather than believing that they can learn to parent any sort of business, parents should recognize that there are certain sorts of parenting approach that will almost certainly be impossible for them to learn, and, hence, certain sorts of businesses that should always be avoided.

SUMMARY

The parenting advantage framework, reproduced in Exhibit 10–3, brings out the influence on corporate strategy of a company's parenting characteristics, its business characteristics, its rival parents, and the environment in which it operates. Corporate strategies need constant adjustment to reflect changes in all these areas. It is necessary to see that parenting characteristics remain well matched with the value creation opportunities in the businesses, that changes in the environment are

EXHIBIT 10–3   Corporate strategy framework

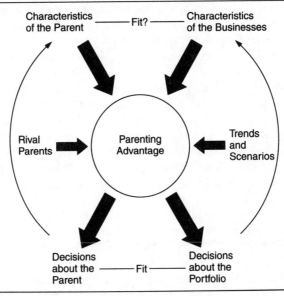

reflected in changes in parenting or the portfolio, and that parenting advantage is maintained despite changes in rival parents. Corporate strategy is about the fit between a company's parenting and its portfolio. But the fit needs to be dynamic, continually shifting to take account of changes that open up new parenting opportunities and threats.

NOTES

1. See, for example, *John F. Welch: The First Three Weeks*, Harvard Business School Videotape (9-882-004), 1981.

2. See Richard Pascale, *Managing on the Edge*, New York: Simon and Schuster, 1990, p. 216.

3. 1990 Annual Report, p. 2.

4. 1991 Annual Report, p. 3.

5. The number of business areas was reduced to 12 in 1993, with the setting up of a separate joint venture company in aerospace.

6. See Michael Goold with John J. Quinn, *Strategic Control—Milestones for Long-Term Performance*, London: Financial Times/Pitman Publishing, reissued 1993, Chapter 7.

7. 1992 Annual Report, p. 2.

8. For a fuller discussion of Canon's corporate strategy, see Chapter 7.

9. For a more detailed description of the phasing of Canon's entry into photocopying, see Canon, Inc. (B), Harvard Business School Case 9-384-151.

10. Many academics have written about the difficulty managers have in recognizing the need to learn. They find it hard to "unfreeze" from existing

attitudes, to free themselves from their prevailing mental maps, and to admit openly the need for new skills and ways of working. See, for example, Kurt Lewin, "Group Decision and Social Change," in T. M. Newcombe and E. L. Hartley (eds.), *Readings in Social Psychology*, New York: Holt, Rinehart and Winston, 1958; Bo Hedberg, "How Organizations Learn and Unlearn" in Paul C. Nystrom and William H. Starbuck (eds.), *Handbook of Organizational Design, Volume 1*, New York: Oxford University Press, 1981; Chris Argyris, *Strategy, Change and Defensive Routines*, Marshfield, MA: Pitman, 1985; Peter Senge, *The Fifth Discipline*, New York: Doubleday, 1990; Arie de Geus, "Planning as Learning," *Harvard Business Review*, March–April 1988; Edgar H. Schein, "How Can Organizations Learn Faster? The Challenge of Entering the Green Room," *Sloan Management Review*, Winter 1993.

11. Academics have shown that manifest crises are the most powerful, and sometimes the only, way to bring about organizational learning. See for example, T. K. Lant, F. J. Milliken, and B. Batra "The Role of Managerial Learning and Interpretation in Strategic Persistence and Reorientation: An Empirical Exploration," *Strategic Management Journal*, vol. 13, 1992; D. Miller and P. H. Friesen, "Momentum and Revolution in Organization Adaptation," *Academy of Management Journal*, vol. 23, no. 4, December 1980, pp. 591–614; D. Miller, *The Icarus Paradox*, New York: Harper Business, 1990.

12. The need to use experience gained to test and refine managers' mental maps and strategies has been brought out by many writers who have concerned themselves with the so-called learning organization. See, for example, Peter Senge, *The Fifth Discipline*, New York: Doubleday, 1990; David A. Garvin, "Building a Learning Organization," *Harvard Business Review*, July–August 1993; C. F. Fiol and M. A. Lyles, "Organizational Learning," *Academy of Management Review*, 1985; R. K. Kazanjian and R. Drazin, "Implementing Internal Diversification: Contingency Factors for Organisation Design Choices," *Academy of Management Review*, 1987, vol. 12, no. 2, pp. 342–354; C. Argyris and D. A. Schon, *Organisational Learning: A Theory of Action Perspective*, Reading, MA: Addison-Wesley, 1978; Charles Handy, *The Age of Unreason*, London: Business Books Limited, 1989; Rosabeth Moss Kanter, *The Change Masters: Corporate Entrepreneurs at Work*, London: Unwin Hyman, 1985.

13. The difficulties encountered in diversifying into new businesses have been particularly well-documented for companies in the tobacco, oil, and financial services industries. See, for example, Robert H. Miles, *Coffin Nails and Corporate Strategies*, Englewood Cliffs, NJ: Prentice-Hall, 1982; Robert Grant, "Diversification in the Financial Services Industry," in Andrew Campbell and Kathleen Sommers Luchs (eds.), *Strategic Synergy*, Oxford: Butterworth-Heinemann, 1992; Robert Grant, *The Oil Companies in Transition 1970–87*, Milan: Franco Angeli, 1991.

14. See Appendix C, which describes the tensions that lie behind the three parenting styles, and the incompatibility between them. This type of incompatibility exists between any approaches to parenting that are based around fundamentally opposed mental maps or other parenting characteristics.

11

SUCCESSFUL CORPORATE STRATEGIES

In Part One of this book, we introduced the parenting advantage concept, showed why we believed it was so important for corporate strategy, and illustrated the concept with parenting advantage statements for a few companies. In Part Two, we have looked in much more depth at different sorts of value creation by corporate parents, and have analyzed the corporate strategies of 15 successful companies. In this chapter, we will draw together the detailed conclusions that we have reached concerning value creation insights, distinctive parenting characteristics, and heartland businesses, which we believe are the foundation of successful corporate strategies to achieve parenting advantage.[1]

VALUE CREATION INSIGHTS

The most essential common feature of successful corporate parents is that their corporate strategies are based on insights into how they can create value in their portfolios of businesses. These value creation insights provide the foundation for all their parenting decisions and their portfolio decisions. The possession of unusually clear and powerful value creation insights is a vital difference between companies that achieve parenting advantage and those that do not.

Nature of Value Creation Insights

Value creation insights identify substantial and specific opportunities for the parent to improve performance in its businesses. By improving the service orientation and operating systems of its affiliate banks,

Banc One expects to more than double the return on assets of businesses it acquires. Through closer control of product profitability and higher productivity standards, BTR helps its businesses to achieve return on sales figures of 15 percent or better in businesses where the norm is closer to 5 percent. By supporting risky but justified mining investments that other parents or investors might reject, RTZ has helped its operating companies participate in an unusually high proportion of the major, low-cost mine developments of the past three decades. These are all important performance improvement opportunities that have provided the basis for corporate strategies to achieve parenting advantage.

To have a value creation insight, however, the parent must also perceive the role that it can play in releasing the opportunities that have been identified. Banc One has recognized how its "uncommon partnerships" approach to parenting can encourage the spread of best practice between its affiliate banks and bring about the other improvements it seeks. BTR has seen how its profit planning disciplines can help to raise the standards of financial management and operating control, and the expectations of performance, throughout its portfolio. RTZ has a view of the sort of parenting relationship that will lead to good judgments about mining investment proposals and provide suitable support in their implementation. Successful parents are unusually clear, not only about the opportunities that they are targeting but also about the type of parenting that is needed to address the opportunities.

Value creation insights are typically linked to specific sorts of businesses. They are expressed in terms such as "In businesses that make higher added value, safety-critical engineering components and systems, a parent can create value by putting together international businesses out of previously separate national entities" (TI); or "In long-term, technically complex natural resource businesses, a parent can create value by transferring technical and functional expertise around the world" (Shell). Thus the general form of a value creation insight is "In certain sorts of businesses, a parent can create value by . . . (value creation influence or activity)." The value creation insight identifies both the businesses in which the parent can create value, and the means by which it does so. If the value creation insight is applied to the wrong sorts of businesses, it will fail to create, and may well destroy, value. If Shell were to invest heavily in transferring its technical and functional expertise to businesses that were not long-term, technically complex, or concerned with natural resources, it could distract those businesses from more important priorities and, hence, destroy value. A fit between the value creation insights and the needs and opportunities in the businesses is essential.

In successful corporate parents, the value creation insights can usually be distilled down to a few main themes. For Cooper, it is manufacturing improvements, coupled with linkage benefits within divisional clusters. For 3M, it is primarily about creating and maintaining an innovative, technology-led culture. For Grand Metropolitan, it is balancing support for investments to strengthen international brands with tighter operating control. Successful parents seem to focus their value creation around a few main themes, rather than to create a little value in many disparate areas.

Furthermore, successful corporate parents seem to apply the same value creation insights across the whole portfolio, rather than alter their approach to employ different value creation insights in different businesses. Even GE, which has an exceptionally wide range of different businesses, presses all its businesses to become number one or two in their markets, to share best management practices with other GE businesses, and to release employee energy and ideas through the Work-Out process. We shall discuss the reasons for, and the implications of, the across-the-board nature of parenting later in this chapter.

In some cases, the value creation insights are explicitly promulgated. Jack Welch at GE has hammered home his messages about market leadership, integrated diversity, and the Work-Out process in annual reports, articles, books, and videos. Bob Cizik at Cooper and Alan Jackson at BTR have also stated clearly in published company literature how they believe they add most value as parents. In other companies, the value creation insights are more embedded in the corporate culture and way of managing. Canon, Shell, and Unilever are all successful parents in which the value creation insights must be inferred from corporate policies, structures, and behaviors rather than from explicit corporate strategy statements. But whether the value creation insights are explicit and public, or implicit and cultural, they are a vital ingredient in achieving parenting advantage.

In contrast, less successful multibusiness companies lack value creation insights. They may aspire to add some value to their businesses, and they may point to interesting debates that take place around planning meetings, or to a successful corporate venture in some new field, or to a conference that has brought together different businesses that serve common customers. They may be able to formulate some broad common feature ("good with marketing-oriented businesses," "understand industrial customers") that runs through their corporate strategy.[2] But their parenting activities are not targeted on identified opportunities that will make a major impact on performance. In our terminology, they do not have convincing value creation insights.

The Variety and Uniqueness of Value Creation Insights

The value creation insights of successful corporate parents are very varied. There is no similarity between 3M's strategy for promoting technical innovation and new product development, RTZ's ability to identify and support high risk but worthwhile mining investments, and Dover's approach to attracting entrepreneurial managers. Each company's value creation insights are, in principle, *sui generis* and different. Some companies, however, do have some similarity of value creation insights. We have observed some similarity between BTR's and Emerson's pressure to raise the profitability of companies they acquire through detailed planning processes; ABB and TI are both aiming to create value by building international networks in their businesses; Canon and 3M are driven by opportunities to develop and utilize core technical resources.[3] But the specific insights, and the ways in which they are implemented, differ considerably, even where the basic opportunities are similar.

The variety of value creation insights should not surprise us. Indeed, to achieve parenting advantage, corporate strategies need, ideally, to be built on unique insights, which have not been seen by other parents. Hanson's early successes were based on perceiving opportunities in poorly run, overdiversified companies that others regarded as moribund. Grand Metropolitan's new corporate strategy has potential precisely because it is rare for parents to combine a sympathy for brand development opportunities with a recognition of the payoff from tough operating controls. If value creation insights are not shared by rival parents, they can more easily lead to parenting advantage.

Value creation insights do not, however, typically remain proprietary indefinitely. Other corporate parents notice the successes of their rivals, and value creation insights are not patentable. The early pioneers of a successful new sort of corporate strategy can expect followers. Thus Hanson now has a number of rivals whose corporate strategies are founded on similar value creation insights. And the popularization of the core competences concept means that the basic opportunity that companies such as 3M and Canon have targeted so successfully is now more widely recognized. While each company's specific insights tend to be different, they are unlikely, if they do have real value creation potential, to remain unique for long.

Value Creation Insights and the Four Sorts of Value Creation

In earlier chapters, we have shown how the corporate strategies of different companies emphasize different sorts of value creation. Dover and BTR, for example, concentrate on stand-alone value creation, while Unilever and ABB stress linkage value creation. But the specificity of value creation insights means that classification of them in terms of the four sorts of value creation has only limited usefulness. It is interesting to note that Dover and BTR focus on stand-alone influence, and that linkage influence is important for Unilever and ABB. But Dover's corporate strategy is vastly different from BTR's, as Unilever's is from

ABB's. What matters most is the particular value creation insights on which a company builds, not their generic classification. The four sorts of value represent a useful checklist of ways in which a parent can create value, but the main question to ask about a corporate strategy is specifically how and in what businesses it has the potential to create unusually high value.

The value creation insights of successful corporate parents often combine value creation from stand-alone influence, linkage influence, functional and services influence, and corporate development activities. Some companies, however, build parenting advantage largely on stand-alone influence and corporate development, and exert very little linkage or functional and services influence. In contrast, companies that major on linkage or functional and services value creation cannot avoid being drawn into a range of minimum stand-alone parenting issues. To achieve parenting advantage, they must be able to exert a positive influence on these stand-alone issues, as well as on more discretionary linkage and functional and services issues. In this sense, positive stand-alone influence is a *sine qua non* of a successful corporate strategy in a way that the other three sorts of value creation are not.

Where the corporate strategy is based on stand-alone influence associated with rectifying weak business management, it can be argued that, over time, the opportunities for value creation will reduce. Once the parent has brought a weak management up to the right level, it may have relatively little more to contribute.[4] Conversely, specialist expertise and the ability to help units work better together, essential conditions for exerting positive linkage and functional and services influence, may remain valuable indefinitely. Value creation insights that involve bringing specialist expertise to bear, or facilitating complex linkages between businesses, are often important to sustaining parenting advantage over long periods of time, as we have seen in companies such as Unilever, Canon, 3M, and Shell.

Sources of Value Creation Insights

Given the prominence of value creation insights in corporate strategy, it is important to understand where they come from and how they are developed. We have found that value creation insights spring from some combination of the corporate culture and the experience and personal vision of the chief executive and the parenting team.

In some companies, such as Dover, Unilever, Shell, and 3M, the roots of the value creation insights lie deep in the corporate history and culture. Early experiences, attitudes, and values shaped the ways these companies manage themselves, and continue to influence the role and behavior of the parent today. The current generation of management is carrying on a tradition that may go back 40 years or more and has become deeply embedded. While refinements may be introduced from time to time, there is a continuity in the corporate strategy that transcends the influence of any individual or group of individuals.

In other companies, such as Banc One, BTR, Emerson, and Hanson, the value creation insights have been shaped by the personal experience of current (or recent) generations of senior management. Owen Green at BTR, Chuck Knight at Emerson, and Lord Hanson at Hanson discovered by personal experience the sorts of parental interventions that create the most value, and these value creation insights were tempered, tested, and refined by their long experience as parents. Although companies may institutionalize and refine such insights over time, they were initially derived from the personal experience of successful and long-serving chief executives.

Some chief executives stamp their own personal vision on their companies, and their value creation insights derive from this vision. Percy Barnevik's view of how ABB could prosper, Jack Welch's strategies at GE, and Christopher Lewinton's restructuring and redirection of TI were all driven more by personal belief than by corporate culture or even personal experience; although in each case experience has shaped and refined the original vision. The ultimate success of these personal creeds remains, in some instances, to be demonstrated, but it is clear that the value creation insights in these companies are closely bound up with the personal visions of their chief executives.

In most companies, corporate culture, personal experience, and vision all contribute in some measure to shaping the value creation insights. The antecedents of successful corporate strategies are therefore hard to disentangle. Exhibit 11–1 summarizes the genesis of the value creation insights for the companies described in Chapters 6 through 10. It can be seen that, in most cases, they date back many years.

The successful introduction of radically new value creation insights is rare. In most cases, there is continuity in the value creation insights on which the corporate strategy is based: Value creation insights, and the distinctive parenting characteristics that support them, are constantly refined with experience but are seldom fundamentally changed. However, in a few companies, such as Grand Metropolitan and TI, wholly new value creation insights have been successfully brought in.

Where wholly new value creation insights have been introduced, they almost always reflect a change in parenting regime. Allen Sheppard's accession at Grand Metropolitan and Christopher Lewinton's at TI both heralded a completely new approach to parenting. These chief executives stamped their own views about corporate strategy on their organizations, and put forward essentially new value creation insights.

Radical changes in value creation insights entail major consequential changes. At Grand Metropolitan and TI, the new value creation insights led to radical portfolio shifts, major senior management changes, and the need to dismantle old parenting characteristics and replace

EXHIBIT 11-1   Sources of value creation insights

Company	Corporate Culture	CEO/Top Team Experience	CEO/Top Team Vision	Date
ABB		✔	✔✔	1980s
Banc One		✔✔	✔	1970s
BTR		✔✔		1970s
Canon	✔	✔	✔✔	1960s
Cooper		✔✔	✔	1970s
Dover	✔✔	✔		1950s
Emerson	✔	✔✔		1970s
GE		✔	✔✔	1980s
Grand Met		✔✔	✔	1980s
Hanson		✔✔		1970s
RTZ	✔✔	✔		1960s
Shell	✔✔	✔		1950s
TI		✔	✔✔	1980s
Unilever	✔✔	✔		1930s
3M	✔✔	✔		1920s

them with new. Nuggets within the old portfolio may be retained and developed, some of the existing managers may prove capable of embracing and pushing through the new strategy, and some aspects of the old parenting approach may be worth keeping. But wholesale changes are usually required. Such changes are difficult to implement and communicate, and are fraught with risk. But, for a company such as TI, which had lost its way and lacked any real value creation insight as the basis for its corporate strategy, they can be the only alternative to eventual extinction. Equally, if the old value creation insights are no longer as potent as they were, or if the nature of the businesses in the portfolio has changed so that the old value creation insights no longer apply so well, there may be no future without radical changes. At Grand Metropolitan, the value creation insight on which the company was founded—the existence of underpriced "trading property assets"—became irrelevant following the 1970s property crash. Allen Sheppard had to find a new insight around which to build the company.

In Part Three, we shall work through an analytical framework and process for developing corporate strategy, and will return to the issue of finding and implementing new value creation insights. From the experience of the companies that we have researched, we should, however, recognize that new value creation insights are seldom generated purely from such a process. Rather, the analytical process can help to test, refine, and draw out the implications of value creation insights that emerge, often serendipitously, from other sources.[5]

DISTINCTIVE PARENTING CHARACTERISTICS

Successful corporate parents not only have insights about how to create value in their businesses, they have unusual or distinctive parenting characteristics that help them to bring about the value creation. In each of the companies we researched, a few parenting characteristics were specially important to the implementation of their corporate strategies.

Nature of Distinctive Parenting Characteristics

In Chapters 6 through 10, we described in some detail the parenting characteristics that allowed different companies to create high value. Examples of distinctive parenting characteristics include ABB's approaches to managing its matrix structure, which are necessary for the balance it seeks between global scale and local focus; Banc One's uniquely detailed MICS financial management and information system, which provides the basis for best practice sharing among its different community banks; Dover's lack of required formal management systems and processes, which is essential to creating the atmosphere and culture that attracts entrepreneurs into joining the company; and RTZ's reputation for successful investment and for completing mining projects on time and within budget, which leads the company to receive more approaches to participate in potentially interesting projects than other companies. The individual skills of key managers within the parent are often the most essential ingredients in distinctive parenting characteristics. All successful corporate parents need parenting characteristics that lead to the realization of the parenting opportunities they are targeting.

Suitable parenting characteristics are as vital for parenting advantage as value creation insights. Indeed they are the other side of the same coin. A parent with an exciting value creation insight but no practical means of putting it into effect will fail to create value. For example, many parents have been attracted by the idea of building their corporate strategies around the sharing of core competences between their businesses. But those that lack the unusual technical skills and organizational mechanisms built up gradually by companies like Canon and 3M have not found a core competences strategy easy to implement.[6] Value creation insights that are not supported by suitable parenting characteristics do not lead to parenting advantage.

What is more, a parent with a value creation insight that is similar to other rival parents' may still achieve parenting advantage, if it has distinctive parenting characteristics that lead to superior implementation of the insight. The basic idea that thorough, stretching budget reviews can enhance performance is widely accepted and can certainly not be regarded as a unique value creation insight. But BTR has refined its profit planning process to such an extent, and brings to it such skills of interpretation and judgment, that it creates much more value through budget reviews than the vast majority of other parents. Indeed, our research suggests that parenting advantage more often rests on parenting characteristics that provide unusually effective means of implementing an insight than on insights that are themselves unique. A key question for all corporate parents, therefore, is whether they have parenting characteristics that will support their value creation insights, and whether those characteristics are sufficiently distinctive to lead to parenting advantage.

It is possible for parents with similar value creation insights to have different and successful corporate strategies, based on differences in their distinctive parenting characteristics. Thus, it is interesting to compare the corporate strategies of Canon and 3M. There is evident similarity in the value creation insights of these companies, which both depend on the development of corporate technical competences. But, in each company, we have highlighted rather different processes and mechanisms as the distinctive parenting characteristics that support the strategy. Canon has created a flexible matrix structure and makes extensive use of ad hoc task forces for combining and deploying its technical resources into the most promising markets, whereas 3M has a decentralized structure with simple reporting lines and a culture that encourages individuals to champion their own initiatives, within a context that is strongly influenced by the policies, guidelines, and suggestions of its technical staffs. Canon and 3M's parenting characteristics overlap to some extent, but the specifics are different in each company.[7] As a result, each company pursues parenting advantage in different ways, despite the resemblance of their value creation insights. Canon and 3M have somewhat different heartland businesses and technologies, so that they are not direct rivals. But even if they were, the differences in their distinctive parenting characteristics suggest that they could each succeed in their own ways and that neither company would necessarily emerge as clearly the more successful.[8] The range and variety of distinctive parenting characteristics that we have found in our research shows why the quest for parenting advantage is most unlikely to lead to the emergence of a single dominant parent in each industrial sector, or even for each value creation insight.

The distinctive parenting characteristics of successful parents normally fit together and reinforce each other. For example, the links between Shell's distinctive parenting characteristics are shown in Exhibit 11–2. Local country autonomy helps in the recruitment of international managers. The consensus-based decision process encourages local country managers and central functional and technical experts to all participate in balanced decisions. The mobile, international cadre of managers is vital in building up the professionalism of Shell's technical and functional staffs, and in fostering cohesion among the different local operating companies. The company's financial strength allows it to adopt long-term business horizons. Its high principles support the corporate brand and are attractive to professional managers. And so on. A similar

EXHIBIT 11–2 Shell's distinctive parenting characteristics

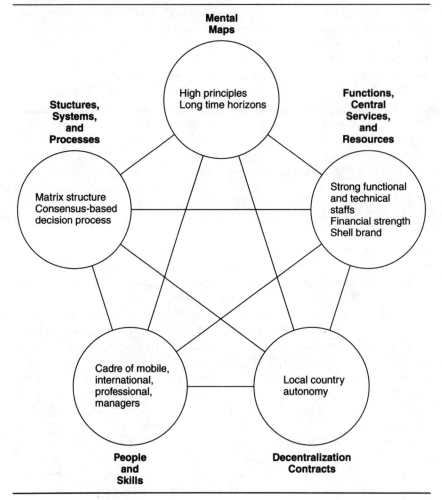

diagram can be developed for each of the successful companies we have researched, bringing out the internal consistency and connectedness of their distinctive parenting characteristics. As a result, companies' main distinctive parenting characteristics, such as BTR's profit planning process or ABB's matrix structure, permeate all aspects of the parent's behavior. They determine the initiatives that the parent takes, and rule out other behavior that is incompatible. The more the distinctive parenting characteristics fit together and reinforce each other, the more powerful they are.

Distinctive parenting characteristics tend to apply across all of a company's businesses. There may be some differences of emphasis within different divisions or businesses, but fundamentally the same parenting structures, processes, policies, and staffs apply. Given that the parenting characteristics fit together as mutually compatible and reinforcing elements of the overall parenting approach, it is difficult to adjust individual elements without affecting others, and hence to change the approach for different businesses. If, for example, a Shell business was taken out of the global matrix structure, it might well be less easy to develop and retain professional international managers to work in it, especially in technical or functional areas. As a result, while Shell recognizes that strategy needs to be driven on a more centralized basis in its exploration business sector than in its downstream gasoline sector, and the balance of responsibilities is subtly different between these sectors, all Shell's main businesses work within the basic matrix structure. In many companies, distinctive parenting characteristics also stem from strongly held beliefs of senior managers in the parent about the best ways to exercise parental influence. Even when chief executives recognize that businesses in their portfolios require different treatment, they can find it difficult to move far away from the approach to parenting with which they are personally most comfortable: Consequently, adjustments between businesses tend to be minor, if they occur at all.[9] Lastly, there are pressures for uniformity of treatment of businesses across the whole portfolio on the grounds of equity and fairness. For all these reasons, we have found that parents have only limited flexibility in treating different businesses in their portfolios differently.[10]

Sources of Distinctive Parenting Characteristics

Parenting characteristics that are distinctive and important are normally built up and refined gradually over long periods of time. Banc One has been fine-tuning its structures, systems, and processes for parenting community banks since its founding in 1968. BTR's profit-planning process dates back 25 years and has undergone constant improvement. Emerson's strategic planning process has a similar history. Unilever's processes for encouraging horizontal links between its businesses have evolved over several generations. Chuck Knight's observation that "building a smooth-running operation entails years of effort and piece-by-piece construction," sums up the slow, step-by-step way in which most genuinely distinctive parenting characteristics are honed by experience.

Sometimes, corporate initiatives may lead more rapidly to the establishment of new and distinctive parenting characteristics. General Electric's Work-Out process was launched relatively suddenly, at the behest of a chief executive who saw an urgent need for change. But even here, the basic initiative has been refined and improved subsequently, as experience has been gained. Distinctive and value-creating parenting characteristics can seldom be brought into being quickly, even if the chief executive is pushing hard for their establishment.

The length of time it takes to build distinctive parenting characteristics reflects their dependence on personal skills, attitudes, and ways of working. It is not so much the formal structures and systems that matter as the ways in which people work within them. Thus, the basic design of BTR's profit planning process, or of Emerson's strategic planning process, count less than the skills of the parent in using these processes, and the culture and atmosphere around them. It is not the schedule, attendance, and agenda of GE's Work-Out meetings that determine their success, but the way people behave in the meetings and the impact that they have on them. BTR's, Emerson's, and GE's management processes have all been written up extensively, and there are no great secrets about what they are intended to achieve and how they are designed. But very few companies have been successful in duplicating these processes, and none have been able to do so quickly. Even with a clear blueprint for the type of parenting processes and systems that are required, it will almost always take several years, and sometimes much longer, for managers in a company to acquire the personal skills and behaviors to make them work well. And many companies will never succeed in reaching this goal.

As a result, parenting advantage based on distinctive parenting characteristics is usually sustainable over long periods of time. Many of the successful parents we have researched, such as 3M, Canon, Shell, and Unilever, have been preeminent for decades. Their distinctive parenting characteristics have not basically changed, but rivals have found it difficult to copy them and become equally effective. Conversely, it takes time to build the sort of distinctive parenting characteristics required to support new value creation insights, as was evident at Grand Metropolitan and TI. Companies like IBM, that need to embark on radical changes in corporate strategy almost always take several years to implement them successfully, due to the slow process of establishing new distinctive parenting characteristics.

Frequently, it is through the gradual development, refinement, and application of distinctive parenting characteristics, rather than through sudden, blinding new insights, that corporate strategy moves forward. The impact and power of the distinctive parenting characteristics build up slowly, and it emerges, over a period of time, that cumulatively they are creating a great deal of value in identifiable ways. In these circumstances, the corporate strategy follows from, and is based on, the distinctive parenting characteristics rather than the reverse. Recognizing that the impact of distinctive parenting characteristics adds up to a value creation insight is much easier than developing distinctive parenting characteristics that will support a new value creation insight.[11]

HEARTLAND BUSINESSES

In successful corporate parents, we found that parent company managers had a particularly clear sense of what sort of businesses fall within their heartlands. In these businesses, their corporate strategies lead to high value creation, and are not offset by value destruction caused by other aspects of their parenting. Over time, the parent is able to attune its parenting characteristics to fit better and better with the needs and opportunities of the businesses in the heartland. A firm grasp of the heartland business criteria and a progressive focusing of the portfolio on heartland businesses are important for achieving parenting advantage.

Nature of Heartland Criteria

Companies describe their heartlands in terms of the nature of the parenting opportunities; and in terms of industry sectors or technologies, and the critical success factors for which they believe they have a sufficient feel. For example, Cooper's heartland, laid out in detail in Exhibit 11–3, has a number of key features. These include cell-based manufacturing businesses that have fallen behind in their manufacturing skills and lost focus on their profit opportunities; businesses with mature technologies, and leading positions and brand recognition in their markets; and businesses where consumer marketing is not key to success, and preferably where individual customers do not have high bargaining power. The heartland criteria specify the types of businesses in which the parent is likely to create high net value, and the types of businesses that should be avoided.

EXHIBIT 11–3 Cooper's heartland business criteria

Manufacturing businesses that have fallen behind in their manufacturing skills and lost focus on their profit opportunities in manufactured products.

Potential for linkage benefits through "clustering" into divisions.

Cell-based manufacturing; not continuous process or assembly.

Not consumer marketing businesses.

Stable, mature demand.

Stable technology.

Manufacturing key to success: marketing and distribution costs less than manufacturing costs.

Strong brand or leading company.

Unique technology or proprietary products.

Management of distribution channels matters (managing distributors, dealers, and retailers important to success).

Low customer power; not selling mainly to government or original equipment manufacturers (OEMs).

Manageable unions and labor contracts.

Low product liability and few environmental issues.

Large enough to support Cooper overhead.

Parents with more hands-on decentralization contracts, such as Shell or Banc One, need a deep feel for their businesses and tend to have heartlands that are more narrowly defined in terms of industries, markets, or technologies. Because they involve themselves closely in setting the strategies for their businesses, they need a feel not only for broad, high-level success factors, but also for more detailed aspects of the business. If operating companies in Shell are going to have a productive discussion with the corporate office on the detailed design, location, and capacity of a planned refinery investment, the parent must be able to grapple with the technical and market issues that may arise. We have found that hands-on parents usually encounter problems when they venture outside a few familiar markets and technologies.

Parents with a more hands-off style, such as Hanson or Dover, can have heartlands that cover a variety of different industries, markets, and technologies, provided they limit the issues on which they intervene. Parents with a decentralized style can, however, easily be tempted to diversify too widely. All parents are inevitably drawn into influencing certain minimum parenting decisions, and many go further, either from choice or as a reaction to unforeseen changes in businesses' circumstances. They are liable to destroy value through these interventions if they lack a sufficient feel for the businesses. Even a highly decentralized company such as BTR recognizes that it is much less likely to add value as it moves away from its heartland in industrial manufacturing.[12]

Several of the companies in the research, including Cooper, Dover, Hanson, and TI, have made explicit statements about their heartland criteria. In other companies, it is more a matter of a shared understanding between senior managers of the types of business that fit best within the portfolio. In general, we believe that an explicit statement of the heartland criteria is beneficial, particularly in guiding resource allocation and acquisition activities.

As companies become clearer about their heartland businesses, they are able to shift the balance of their portfolios away from businesses in which they are liable to destroy value and toward businesses where they create value. The progressive focusing of the portfolios of almost all the companies we have described, including Emerson, Grand Metropolitan, RTZ, and Unilever, reflects both increasing understanding of the nature of their heartlands and greater determination to concentrate on businesses within the heartland. This trend has been wholly beneficial for the companies in question, since it has reduced the amount of parental value destruction, and concentrated resources on businesses in which the parent has most to contribute. It is notable that the portfolios of successful corporate parents are largely composed of businesses that conform to their heartland criteria.[13]

The heartland concept differs from other concepts such as "core businesses" or "related businesses." In recent years, many companies have been attracted by the idea of restructuring their portfolios around core businesses.[14] But often a core business is simply a business that the company has decided to commit to. A business may be deemed to be core because it is large, because it is in a sector that the company likes, or because it is currently profitable. None of these criteria have anything to do with whether the company is a good parent for these businesses. A business can be in the heartland only if the parent can add value to it. There has also been a fashion for building the portfolio around related businesses. Businesses can be related for many reasons; for example, if they share a common sales force, or if they draw on common technology, or if they address common customers. While these dimensions of relatedness may provide some opportunities for a parent to create value, in themselves they are no guarantee that the parent can or will do so or that it will not destroy much more value through its other influences on the businesses. Related businesses, therefore, also differ from heartland businesses, because relatedness does not focus on the ability of the parent to create net value.[15]

Corporate parents that lack a consensus on the heartland criteria are typically less successful. They are liable to retain businesses in the portfolio in which they destroy value and to diversify unsuccessfully into businesses for which they lack a feel. There may be conflict between different members of the parenting team about the appropriate composition of the portfolio and confusion in the businesses about corporate priorities for resource allocation. Without a common view of the heartland criteria, the quest for parenting advantage will be undermined.

Changes in the Heartland

The heartlands of several of the companies that we have researched have changed over a period of time. These companies have enlarged or changed the boundaries around their heartlands, either by gradual, evolutionary moves or by more radical initiatives. Other companies have been forced to respond to changes in the critical success factors and parenting opportunities in their businesses. The extent of change in companies' heartlands ranges from modest evolution through to complete restructuring.

A number of successful corporate parents have been able to extend their heartlands over time through evolutionary change. Canon, for example, initially focused on cameras. However, it now has more than 80 percent of its sales in office equipment. Although its entry to office products drew off the technical skills and resources that had been built up in cameras, it took the company into new markets, with different channels of distribution and different critical success factors. Canon was nevertheless able to acquire a sufficiently good feel for the office products businesses by a process of gradual learning that they now form part of the company's heartland.[16] Other companies that have successfully pushed back the boundaries around their heartlands include Cooper, General Electric, and 3M.

In most cases, these companies were able to build on value creation insights and parenting characteristics that were applicable in the original heartland, and could modify or extend them for new markets, new technologies, or new critical success factors. To succeed in extending the heartland in this way, a company needs to recognize that some aspects of the new business are unfamiliar. Frequently, these concern the specifics of new markets or technologies. The parent's task is to acquire a sufficient feel for these aspects of the business at least to avoid value-destroying interventions. An awareness of the need to learn about the new aspects of the business and a program by which to bring about the learning are both needed. The danger, however, lies in being forced to make judgments about the business, for example in appointing a new managing director or in sanctioning a major capital investment, before having developed a sufficient feel for it.

In a few cases, new businesses that had few success factors in common with the original heartland and therefore required a very different parenting approach have been successfully introduced into the portfolio. GE's expansion in financial services, for example, took it into new businesses that had little in common with its heartland in the electrical industry. Where a new business has few common critical success factors with the original heartland, the parent's task is much harder. Not only must the parent learn about the specifics of the new business, it must recognize when not to apply processes, systems, rules of thumb, and success formulas that guide its parenting in the established heartland businesses. Very often, these characteristics reflect deeply held predispositions and values that are hard to alter, and we have found that parents are seldom able to operate with basically different parenting approaches for different parts of the portfolio. Hence, there are few examples of successful diversifications of this sort. Much more often, companies that move into businesses well away from their traditional heartlands find that they do not have, and cannot easily develop, a sufficient feel and suitable parenting characteristics for the new businesses. In due course, most of these diversifications are sold or closed down, usually after a protracted period of poor parenting and unsatisfactory results.

Extending the heartland is even less feasible if the new parenting approach that needs to be developed is actually incompatible with deeply embedded ways of parenting the other businesses in the heartland. Exxon's venture into office products not only took it into a business in which it needed to learn about new critical success factors, but took it into a business in which the majority of its established value creation insights and parenting characteristics were fundamentally unsuitable. To have succeeded in office products, Exxon would have needed a completely different approach to risk, timescales, competition, and investment, as well as radically revised human resource and other management processes. It would have needed a basically different parenting role and decentralization contract for its office products businesses from the role it adopted in its heartland oil and natural resource businesses. If a new business requires value creation insights and parenting characteristics that are incompatible with the existing heartland, extending the heartland is not possible. Instead, a choice must be made between the old corporate strategy and a radically new one. Grand Metropolitan and TI have fundamentally altered their portfolios, but in both cases this was a result of a complete change in corporate strategy.

Reacting to changes in the characteristics of businesses in the portfolio presents similar issues for parents. Modest changes in markets, technologies, or the nature of competition can be handled on an evolutionary basis, provided the parent is alert to the changes and willing to modify its parenting accordingly. Fundamental changes, of the sort faced in the early 1990s by IBM, are more difficult. If they require quite different, and even incompatible, parenting approaches from those on which the previous corporate strategy was based, the business in question has effectively moved out of the parent's heartland. It may prove wrenchingly difficult—and in some cases impossible—to handle such changes without changing the company's chief executive and top team. The only alternative is to divest the businesses in question. If the basic nature of the businesses in a company's portfolio changes, the parent must either be able to change its parenting approach, and hence its heartland criteria, or else be prepared to exit from the businesses.

Over a period of time, parents can extend or change the nature of their heartlands. However, they need to be aware of the changes in parenting that are required, and they need to have a realistic program for learning the new parenting skills that are needed.[17]

Portfolio Diversity

A vital question for corporate strategy is how much diversity the portfolio should encompass. Our research casts light on this question.

We have found no successful parents that apply basically different value creation insights and parenting characteristics in different parts of their portfolios. On grounds of equity alone, managers are typically uncomfortable treating some businesses very differently from others; and even if they can overcome their feelings that fairness demands similar treatment, few managers have sufficient personal flexibility to shift rapidly from one parenting approach to another. Chameleon parents are rare. Furthermore, organizations have their own momentum and inertia: To amend the management process to work fundamentally differently for different businesses is beyond the capabilities of almost all parents. Lastly, communication problems, and corridor gossip, mean that business managers will be as likely to pick up confused signals as to recognize differentiated parenting. As a result, we do not find companies that are able to provide a BTR parenting approach for one group of businesses and a Shell parenting approach for another.[18] Even in GE, whose heartland contains a variety of businesses with different critical success factors, the value creation insights and the distinctive parenting characteristics are common. Hence, all the businesses need to be responsive to similar value creation insights and distinctive parenting characteristics; otherwise, some businesses are likely to be damaged by ingrained characteristics that are applied across the whole portfolio.[19]

Companies with portfolios that consist of businesses with different value creation opportunities that require basically different parenting should strongly consider demerger. Either the corporate parent will damage one (and maybe both) sets of businesses or else will abdicate all responsibility to the divisions. Abdication of responsibility is the equivalent of demerger, while retaining unnecessary corporate overheads.

The degree of diversity that can be effectively parented is limited still further by the requirement for parents to have an adequate feel for the businesses in their portfolios. An intellectual recognition that different businesses have different critical success factors is usually not enough, since parenting influence is often based more on instincts and rules of thumb than on case-by-case analysis of the merits of the situation. In most companies, the instincts and experience of the parenting team determine the amount of diversity that is manageable.[20] However, the ability of corporate parents to have a sufficient feel for different sorts of businesses varies. GE, whose parenting team combines personal experience in different business areas and is exceptionally talented, appears able to handle businesses with widely varied critical success factors. But most companies find it difficult to add value to businesses with significantly different critical success factors. The great majority of successful corporate parents have portfolios that are quite narrowly defined in terms of critical success factors, even if their basic value creation insights and distinctive parenting characteristics could be more broadly applicable.

SUMMARY

Our research has convinced us that value creation insights, coupled with distinctive parenting characteristics, are the essential requirements for parenting advantage. Value creation insights identify a role for the parent that has the potential to create unusually high, possibly unique, value. Distinctive parenting characteristics are necessary to convert the insights into reality, and to distinguish the parent from other rivals with similar intentions. Successful parents also need to build their portfolios out of businesses that fall within their heartlands, in which they can successfully implement their value creation insights while at the same time avoiding value-destroying interventions. Companies that achieve parenting advantage usually have a clearer view of the heartland criteria, and a tighter focus of the portfolio on heartland businesses, than other rival parents.

From this review of successful corporate strategies, several issues emerge for companies that are trying to develop new and more successful strategies:

- On what value creation insights is the corporate strategy based? If value creation insights are lacking, or insufficient to create parenting advantage, what can be done to develop new value creation insights?
- What distinctive parenting characteristics underpin the corporate strategy, and how unique are they? How can the distinctive parenting characteristics be reinforced or built up to create more parenting advantage?
- Are the heartland criteria clear, and do the businesses in the portfolio conform to them? If not, what changes should be made?
- How far and in what directions is it sensible to try to extend the heartland, and how should this be done?
- Are the characteristics of the businesses in the portfolio changing, and if so, what should be the response to these changes?
- How do we compare to rival parent companies, and how are these rivals changing? What implications does this have for the ways in which we aim to establish parenting advantage?

These topics will be taken up in Part Three, which proposes a process for developing corporate strategy based on the pursuit of parenting advantage.

NOTES

1. Our conclusions are based not only on our research with the 15 companies, but also on research and consultancy work with numerous other companies.

2. Such common features are frequently vacuous and fail to have any link to parenting value creation.

3. At a broad level, companies with the same overall parenting style tend to target similar sorts of value creation opportunities in similar sorts of ways. See Appendix C.

4. In reality, there is usually a continuing role in maintaining the quality of business management at a suitably high level. See Chapter 6 for further discussion.

5. This point is, of course, relevant for business strategy as well as for corporate strategy. See, for example, Henry Mintzberg, "Crafting Strategy," *Harvard Business Review*, July–August 1987.

6. A core competences strategy can also fail if there are few genuine competences in the businesses or few opportunities for businesses to share competences.

7. The contrast between a consensus-based, Japanese approach to technology development and an individualistic, American one is itself interesting. See Chapters 7 and 8 for more detail on Canon and 3M's corporate strategies.

8. If the distinctive parenting characteristics of either of them were evidently less suitable for implementing their insights, this conclusion would not follow. Our belief is that each set of distinctive parenting characteristics is valid in its own way.

9. Businesses that are not performing well, however, receive special attention from the parent and may be treated differently during such a period.

10. The tendency for companies to have distinctive parenting characteristics that fit together and apply across all businesses parallels, at a much more specific level, the tendency for companies to have parenting styles that are internally consistent and common across businesses. Parenting style represents an overview of a company's general parenting approach, while distinctive parenting characteristics describe the detailed and particular features that matter most for value creation. A consistent style that is suitable for the businesses in the portfolio is necessary to avoid destroying value and to have some chance of creating value. But mutually reinforcing distinctive parenting characteristics that fit the opportunities in the businesses are the factors leading to high value creation and parenting advantage.

11. Henry Mintzberg has criticized the so-called design school of strategic management as a description of how good strategies emerge. See, for example, Henry Mintzberg, "The Design School: Reconsidering the Basic Premises of Strategic Management," *Strategic Management Journal*, vol. 11, March–April 1990, and *The Rise and Fall of Strategic Planning*, New York: Prentice Hall, 1994. Similarly, our account of the development of distinctive parenting characteristics and corporate strategy recognizes that good corporate strategies may evolve from experience as much as from design.

12. Many parents that follow a Strategic Control style have become too diversified. They may not require a feel for such detailed issues as a Strategic Planning parent, but they do need to focus their portfolios on businesses that they understand well. This is one factor which distinguishes the successful Strategic Control parents in our research from the many less successful exponents of the style. See Appendix C.

13. Rubbermaid, voted the most admired company in the USA in Fortune's 1993 Survey, has a statement of its heartland in its corporate mission. "Our mission is to be the leading world-class producer of best value,

brand-name, primarily plastic products for the consumer, commercial, agricultural and industrial markets." In addition, the bulk of Rubbermaid products are sold to female, U.S. consumers through mass merchandise retailers. In these businesses, Rubbermaid has a good feel for the critical success factors. Furthermore, Rubbermaid's famed new product development processes and culture are specially valuable in these businesses. Though Rubbermaid's portfolio includes a wide range of different businesses, they therefore have a high degree of similarity in terms of their parenting needs and opportunities. Rubbermaid's success has come through a clear focus on its identified heartland businesses.

14. See Chapter 4.

15. It could be argued that heartland businesses are a special case of "relatedness"; namely, related in terms of the ability of the parent to create net value.

16. See Chapter 10 for fuller discussion.

17. We shall have more to say on how to approach decisions about changing and extending the heartland in Part Three of this book.

18. It is these factors that lead C. K. Prahalad and Richard Bettis to their conclusions concerning the pervasiveness of a company's "dominant logic" in its parenting behavior; see C. K. Prahalad and R. A. Bettis, "The Dominant Logic: A New Linkage between Diversity and Performance," *Strategic Management Journal,* vol. 7, 1986. A similar point is made by Philippe Verey, "Success in Diversification: Building on Core Competences," *Long Range Planning,* vol. 26, no. 5, 1993. By the same token, these arguments cast doubt on the ability of companies to adopt the sort of differentiated approach to parenting recommended by Christopher Bartlett and Sumantra Ghoshal in *Managing across Borders, The Transnational Solution,* Boston: Harvard Business School Press, 1989.

19. It is possible for divisional parents to have somewhat different value creation strategies and distinctive parenting characteristics from the corporate parent, with the result that businesses in different divisions receive rather different parenting. For example, the division parent may emphasize linkages within the division, while the corporate parent concentrates much more on stand-alone parenting. But the distinctive parenting characteristics of corporate-level parents almost always establish a context for divisional parenting that constrains the amount of variation that can be handled effectively.

20. See Chapter 6 for a discussion of personal and team experience.

PART THREE

DEVELOPING A CORPORATE STRATEGY

12

DEVELOPING A CORPORATE STRATEGY: OVERVIEW

The first two parts of this book describe the concepts we have developed from our research and illustrate these concepts with examples. This part focuses on how managers can use the concepts to help formulate better corporate-level strategies.

We realize that our concepts are different from those of most other theorists. They contradict much of the management thinking about corporate strategy to date and they imply major changes for many corporate parents. We therefore acknowledge the need to show managers how to turn our concepts into useful planning frameworks and processes. We want to show how our concepts can help make decisions both about the businesses that should be in the portfolio and about the parent's structure, size, systems, skills, and ways of working.

We have proposed that the prime criterion for corporate-level strategy decisions should be the impact the decision has on parenting advantage, just as the prime criterion for business-level strategy decisions is impact on competitive advantage. By providing a similarly clear criterion for corporate-level strategy decisions, we believe we can raise the quality of corporate strategies in the same way that competitive advantage thinking has raised the quality of business-level strategies.

Corporate strategy is about matching parenting characteristics with business characteristics in a way that leads to advantage now and in the future. Hence a thorough process for developing corporate strategy should involve four inputs:

- Understanding the characteristics of the parent.
- Understanding the characteristics of the businesses.
- Assessing the strengths and weaknesses of rival parents.
- Judging how all these factors may change in the future.

These four inputs are necessary for an analysis of parenting advantage on the basis of which a corporate strategy can be selected. The corporate strategy will have implications for which businesses to focus on (decisions about the portfolio) and what changes to make to the parent (decisions about the parent). Concerns about any one of these four inputs can provide both the motivation and the starting point for a review of the existing corporate strategy. (See Exhibit 12–1.)

By advocating this framework, we are not implying that corporate strategists need to do a comprehensive analysis every time they review their corporate strategies. We know that this is often unrealistic, not least because addressing all the points raised in this chapter involves a number of man-years of work. At any point in time, one of the four inputs may be the focus of attention. Sometimes, the company may be worried about a particularly threatening rival. At another time, concern may be focused on the size, cost, and bureaucratic influence of the parent. At another time, concern may be about changes in the environment of a particular business: Are the changes leading to a misfit between business characteristics and parenting characteristics? At yet another time, the focus may be on the long-term prospects for the company's existing heartland businesses. Each of the four inputs can, therefore, be the main

EXHIBIT 12–1   Corporate strategy framework

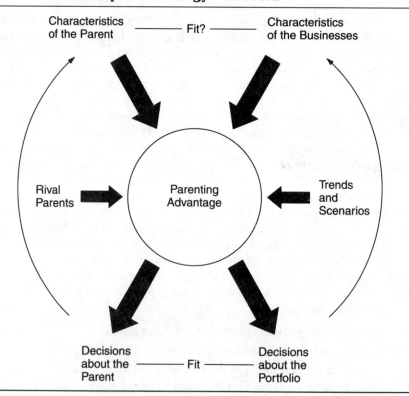

focus of attention. The value of the comprehensive framework is that it helps managers keep all four inputs in mind, so that the implications of analysis of one input can be assessed in the light of the other inputs.

In this overview chapter, we will not attempt to give detailed examples. In Chapter 13, we will describe one detailed example illustrating the thinking, analyses, and steps involved in developing a new corporate strategy. The chapter is laid out with parallel headings to this chapter. Hence the reader wishing to refer to examples can read the two chapters together. In Chapters 14 and 15, we will examine the decisions that need to be made to implement a chosen corporate strategy. These will involve decisions about which businesses to include in the portfolio and about how to design the parent organization.

CHARACTERISTICS OF THE PARENT

In Chapter 2 we described different types of parenting characteristics—the parent's mental maps; structures, systems, and processes; functions, central services, and resources; people and skills; and decentralization contracts (Exhibit 12–2). By examining the parent through each of these five lenses we can gain an understanding of its parenting characteristics. The more that is understood about the parent and how it operates, the easier it is to judge what changes might be made to improve the parent, and which businesses will gain most from being owned by the parent.

Exhibit 12–3 identifies nine areas of analysis we have found useful in helping to understand the parent. We offer this full list as a menu from which corporate strategists can select to fill a gap in their understanding. Since each analysis can in itself be a substantial piece of work, managers will want to be clear about which element of the parent they are trying to understand better and why.

EXHIBIT 12–2 Characteristics of the parent

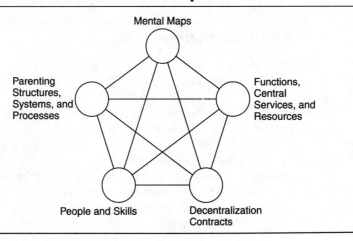

Mental Maps

Parenting Structures, Systems, and Processes

Functions, Central Services, and Resources

People and Skills

Decentralization Contracts

EXHIBIT 12–3   Types of analysis

Parenting Characteristics

Analyses	Mental maps	Structure, processes, systems	Functions, central services, and resources	People and skills	Decentralization contracts
1. Interviews/workshops	✔✔	✔	✔	✔	✔✔
2. Era analysis	✔✔	✔	✔	✔	✔
3. Values and behaviors audit	✔✔			✔	
4. Parenting roles audit		✔✔	✔	✔	✔
5. Processes and systems audit		✔✔		✔	✔
6. Linkage mechanisms audit		✔✔	✔	✔	✔
7. Function/services audit		✔	✔✔	✔	
8. Policies audit		✔	✔✔		✔
9. Decentralization contracts	✔✔	✔✔	✔	✔	✔✔

When it comes to making changes in the parenting approach, a detailed understanding of the characteristics the parent wants to change is essential. Hence time spent on detailed analysis can also be valuable in helping implement changes once a corporate strategy has been chosen. Initially, however, the strategist may want to make a rough assessment of parenting characteristics to provide an overview against which more detailed work can be targeted.

Interviews and Workshops

A critical element of any analysis of parenting characteristics is discussion with managers. Every manager in the parent company can potentially provide useful information about the skills and resources in the parent, about how the relationships with businesses operate, and about the maps and predispositions that affect the way the parent behaves. Moreover, all the business managers who have contact with the parent also have useful information on these topics.

At a minimum, there should be discussions with senior line managers in the parent to understand their parenting maps. What are their objectives? Do they have any value creation insights? What parts of the existing parenting behavior are they most committed to? What do they

think are the critical success factors of the businesses? It is also necessary to talk to some of the chief executives of the businesses to find out how they perceive the impact of the parent. What influence do they feel? What aspects of the parent do they find beneficial and what is unhelpful?

Era Analysis

Unless a company has recently been through a radical change in management or portfolio composition, the roots of its existing parenting characteristics lie in the past. Moreover, all companies are continually changing and evolving. They are moving away from some historic parenting characteristics and toward some future characteristics. To understand the current characteristics, it is valuable to understand their roots and the way they have been developing. A corporate strategy era analysis is a useful tool for capturing this information. Exhibit 12–4 is an era analysis of Grand Metropolitan, a company that we describe more fully in Chapter 10. It summarizes the history of the company into four eras of corporate strategy, recording some of the main parenting characteristics in each era.

By understanding the different eras of corporate strategy, it is possible to develop a historical perspective on the present situation that explains particular behaviors, such as why the planning process is run in a given way or why the company is committed to decentralization.

Values and Behaviors Audit

When recording parenting characteristics it is often possible to overlook the impact of culture and norms of behavior. Unless the managers in the parent are actively pushing the parent's culture onto the businesses, it is easy to assume that it is not a major source of parenting influence. But business managers, eager to be recognized by parent managers and looking for opportunities for promotion, are influenced by the culture and norms of behavior in the parent.

Many companies try actively to manage these cultural signals, even writing them down into mission and philosophy statements such as Hewlett Packard's "HP way." In these cases, so long as the espoused philosophy is the philosophy in use, much of the analysis needed to understand the culture has already been done. In other companies, the culture is more implicit. In these organizations, recording the main behavior norms and the values associated with them can help to surface the culture, adding to the understanding of parenting characteristics.[1]

Parenting Structure and Roles Audit

A parent organization structure chart is an important input to the analysis. It should identify all those organization units that are part of the

EXHIBIT 12–4 Grand Metropolitan era analysis

	1947–1973	1973–1980	1980–1986	1986–1993
Strategy	Buy property-backed assets that can produce enough cash flow to cover the cost of debt	Survive by generating the cash flow needed to cover interest	Diversify into the USA and services Rationalize Watney and Express Build IDV's brands and distribution	Declutter Acquire branded companies and revitalize Build IDV's brands and distribution
Opportunity	Many companies with valuable properties, sound cash flows, but low earnings and hence low share prices	Some of Grand Met's businesses overmanned	Some of Grand Met's businesses still overmanned IDV's brands underexploited internationally	Focus on businesses to which Grand Met can add most value Some branded companies need revitalizing Further exploit IDV brands and distribution network
Source of parenting value creation	Joseph's knowledge of property values Joseph's relationships and reputation in the city Deal-making skills	Appointment of Allen Sheppard	"Light grip on the throat" and Sheppard's team Ability to internationalize IDV's brands	Ability to combine tight operating control with effective brand development
Parenting advantage?	Yes	?	Net disadvantage due to inappropriate diversification	Yes

parent and all those units that are businesses. In large parents, particularly organizations with matrix structures, different parts of the parent are playing different roles. In ABB, the region manager is playing a shareholder, performance-focused role, and the business area manager is playing a global, strategically-focused role. In some companies, the matrix is even more complex. Exhibit 12–5 is a display of the organization matrix of Shell, probably the most complex company we researched. The matrix includes regions and functions as well as countries and business sectors. Each is playing a different role in the overall parenting of the country-based business units.

In other companies, there is a difference in roles for different layers in the hierarchy. In Cooper, a major role for the division is to create linkage value within the division, whereas the center's role is to Cooperize the division. In some companies, however, the audit reveals overlaps and duplications—situations where more than one part of the parent is seeking to do the same parenting job. Understanding the different roles is vital to understanding the parenting characteristics.[2]

Processes and Systems Audit

We have shown in Part Two that four management systems are critical to the way parents create value—the human resource process, the budget process, the planning process, and the capital approval process.

Any detailed audit of parenting characteristics should involve an examination of these processes. A flow diagram detailing each step in the process and identifying the managers involved is a useful starting

EXHIBIT 12–5   Parenting at Shell

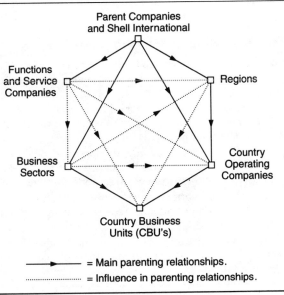

= Main parenting relationships.

.... = Influence in parenting relationships.

point. Discussions can then be held with the managers to find out how well the process operates and what influence the process has on the businesses. Each company's processes typically have strengths and weaknesses and suit one type of situation or problem better than another. An understanding of the process helps clarify which businesses benefit and which do not.

Linkage Mechanisms Audit

One of the sources of value is the way the parent influences the linkage relationships between business units. Much of the influence is informal, through line management. But there are also mechanisms such as committees, transfer pricing systems and project teams set up to increase the value gained from linkage relationships.

A detailed analysis can document each of these mechanisms and assess its impact. Exhibit 12–6 summarizes the questions that need to be asked as part of the linkage audit. The questions have been phrased as if each mechanism addressed a unique opportunity. More normally there is a cluster of reinforcing mechanisms that need to be taken together to make sense of the analysis. For example, a transfer pricing system may be part of a group of pricing mechanisms that involve a committee of marketing directors, a system of appeal and arbitration, and a whole series of exceptions and precedents that have developed informally over time.

Functions and Services Audit

Central functions and services are vital parts of the company's parenting characteristics. They can be divided into three areas: providing

---

EXHIBIT 12–6   Analyzing linkage opportunities

1. What would happen if there was no linkage mechanism and the units concerned were independent companies? This question helps to establish a base starting point for the analysis.
2. What value creation opportunities would be missed under the base starting point? This question helps to clarify the size and nature of the opportunities that the mechanism is addressing.
3. What blockages, if any, are responsible for opportunities being missed under the base starting point? Having a clear idea of the blockages that are creating the opportunity helps in selecting a mechanism.
4. How effective is this mechanism at releasing the value opportunity? The costs and benefits of the mechanism needs to be compared with the size of the opportunity.
5. Does this mechanism have any positive or negative side effects that need to be accounted for? This question is a prompt to think more widely about the impact of the mechanism.

information and support to central managers; influencing the businesses through functional guidance; and providing services to the businesses. The first part of the audit is to break the functions down into these components. In some cases, this means splitting individual jobs across the three categories. In other cases, a whole department will fit in just one category. For example, a management development function consisting of one management development manager may be involved in all three activities. The manager may have an important role in advising the chief executive on appointments and helping to develop central managers; he or she may actively influence the quality of management development in the businesses; also, he or she may do projects for business managers, such as helping them recruit a management development manager or select a management course. An audit of this function would require the management development manager to allocate his or her time among the three activities.

The second part of the audit is to understand the needs of the "customer" for each of the three activities. What service levels does the chief executive want? What are the appropriate levels of functional guidance in this area? What services do the businesses say they need?

The third part of the audit is to judge the effectiveness of the function or service. This should be based on the views of the customers, an understanding of the activities, and an estimate of costs.[3]

Policies Audit

A policies audit is a quick way of documenting some of the influences exerted by the parent. Policies can exist as part of functional influence, for example health and safety policies or human resource policies. They also exist as part of the administrative and control fabric of the organization, for example, policies about planning or capital approval. An audit of policies should first identify them from manuals and other documents and then assess the impact of the policies on the performance of the businesses.

Many policies will be largely administrative having little effect on the businesses, but some will be important, influencing the way business managers behave. Policies that require common benefit or bonus packages across the businesses, for example, can reduce the ability of some businesses to recruit appropriate staff. In a detailed analysis, each policy should be examined for its impact on each business.

Decentralization Contracts Audit

The other analyses will have helped define the parameters of the decentralization contracts as they are experienced by each business. However, it is helpful to summarize the decentralization contracts by attempting to articulate what powers are reserved for the parent and what are delegated to the businesses. Many of these will be defined in policy documents, the terms of reference for functions and committees, job descriptions, and the like. But these documents may not match well with the way in which the decentralization contracts work in practice. On what issues does the center take the prime initiative? When does the center expect to arbitrate over disagreements? What powers do the business managers have with regard to the tasks carried out by, and the staffing of, central functions? Under what circumstances does the center intervene in affairs normally delegated to the businesses? Answers to these questions help clarify the way the organization actually works.

Often it is not possible to get precise answers to these questions, both because there are too many issues to develop a complete picture and because the center normally reserves the right to become highly influential on anything that becomes critical to performance. However, broad answers to the questions, backed with a few illustrative examples, help to flesh out the decentralization contracts.

The Cost of the Parent

The final area of detailed analysis concerns costs. This is often harder to analyze than might be expected. Although it is normally possible to get a total figure for the parent, producing a breakdown by parenting activity is harder. Moreover, there is always a question of whether services paid for by the businesses should be viewed as a parent cost or a business cost.[4]

While it can be useful to have a detailed breakdown of cost by activity for the purpose of fine tuning a parent's effectiveness, we have not typically found detailed cost information to be a vital factor. This is partly because cost data does not usually throw much light on issues of fit or misfit. It is also because the indirect costs of the parent—time spent by business managers—are often much greater than the direct costs of the parent. We have plenty of examples of business managers saying that they have had to hire a planning manager or a health and safety expert to handle all the issues raised by the parent company planning team or health and safety department.

Alignment Analysis

Once the parenting characteristics have been identified, it is useful to assess the degree to which they are well aligned in support of a consistent parenting approach. We have observed that the most successful companies have parenting characteristics that reinforce each other. The structures, systems, and processes fit the mental maps; the functions and central services fit the decentralization contracts; and the people and skills provide the added ingredient that makes both the structure and the functions work well.

Frequently some parenting characteristics are out of line: The planning process may cut across the organization structure; a bonus system may undermine linkage initiatives; or a functional director may attempt to develop policies that interfere with the company's agreed decentralization contracts. In these circumstances, it is often possible to improve the corporate strategy just by improving the alignment between the parenting characteristics.

A simple way to test alignment is to use tools we have developed for classifying parenting style. Parenting style is a way of summarizing a company's parenting approach. All the parenting characteristics are relevant to a judgment about style. Once a style assessment has been made (Strategic Planning, Strategic Control, Financial Control), it is possible to identify parenting characteristics that do not fit well with the style.[5] These can then be the focus of change initiatives that will improve the alignment between parenting characteristics (see Appendix C for a fuller discussion of parenting styles).

CHARACTERISTICS OF THE BUSINESSES

The corporate strategist needs to understand the businesses in the portfolio well enough to define the parenting opportunities in each business and judge whether each business fits or does not fit with the parent.

As an initial step, the scope and definition of each business unit needs to be established. It is sensible to start with the definitions currently employed within the company. Where the existing business unit definitions are unclear, a judgment may be needed. Appendix B is designed to help with these judgments.

Once a decision has been made about unit definitions, two sets of business characteristics can be analyzed for each unit: the parenting opportunities in the business, and the critical success factors of the business. As with parenting characteristics, detailed analysis of business characteristics is a major piece of work. Initially a first cut can be made of the business characteristics and further work carried out to provide additional detail where it is needed.

Parenting Opportunities

Parenting opportunities can come from many sources. The business may be inappropriately defined, lack important skills, have an unsatisfactory strategy, or excessive overheads. The first step is to assess the performance of the business. Is the business performing as well as could be expected given its competitive position and market focus? If not, it has an improvement opportunity and may, therefore, be able to benefit from parenting influence of some sort.

The next step is to understand the nature of the parenting opportunities. This is essentially a creative analytical process. Exhibit 12–7 lists some factors we have found useful as prompts in analyzing opportunities. The exhibit draws on the discussions in Chapters 6 through 9 of the underlying conditions under which businesses are likely to have opportunities for improvement that are not being grasped by the business managers.

In some cases, there may be little improvement potential because the business is already benefiting from the parent's influence. In these situations, it is important to ask how the business would be affected if it

---

EXHIBIT 12–7 Understanding parenting opportunities

1. *Business Definition.* Is the business defined so as to maximize its sources of competitive advantage (refer to Appendix A)?

2. *Business Size.* Does the business suffer from problems related to being small (e.g., management succession, financial control skills) or big (e.g., bureaucracy, loss of motivation)?

3. *Management.* Does the business have top-quality managers relative to its competitors? Are its managers focused on the right objectives/ambitions? Is the business dependent on attracting and retaining unusual people?

4. *Temptations.* Does the nature of the business encourage managers to make mistakes (e.g., maturity often leads to excessive diversification; long product cycles can lead to excessive reliance on old products; cyclical swings can lead to too much investment during the upswing)?

5. *Linkages.* Could this business effectively link with other businesses to improve efficiency or market position? Are the linkages complex or difficult to establish between the units concerned?

6. *Common Capabilities.* Does this business have capabilities in common with other businesses that could be built, shared, and transferred between the businesses?

7. *Special Expertise.* Could this business benefit from specialist or rare expertise that the parent possesses or could possess?

8. *External Relations.* Does this business have difficult-to-manage external stakeholders (shareholders, government, unions, suppliers, etc.) that could be better managed by the parent company?

9. *Major Decisions.* Does the business face difficult and infrequent decisions in which it lacks expertise (entry into China, major acquisitions, major capacity extensions)? Would it be difficult to get funding for major investments from external capital providers?

10. *Major Change.* Is the business facing a need to make major changes for which its management has insufficient experience?

was separated from the parent. Any loss of performance that would result from separation is a form of parenting opportunity.

The difficult task in analyzing parenting opportunities is to identify those areas of improvement that would be unlikely to happen without the parent's involvement. Most businesses are planning to improve their performance, and the majority of these plans are developed by and implemented by the managers within the businesses. Only some improvement plans require the influence of the parent: Only some improvement opportunities are parenting opportunities.

The third step in assessing parenting opportunities is to attempt to put a figure on the size of each area of opportunity. What would be the performance improvement if the opportunity was successfully addressed? In crude shareholder value terms, how much would the value of the business rise if the improvement was made? This assessment of the size of opportunities helps to rank order the businesses in terms of the potential value a parent could add.[6]

Critical Success Factors

The reverse of value creation is value destruction. Understanding the potential for value destruction involves understanding the businesses' critical success factors and judging whether any of the parenting characteristics are likely to misfit with the businesses. A business's critical success factors are the critical resources and capabilities needed to be a viable competitor in the market place.

The analysis should focus on those critical success factors that are likely to be influenced by the parent. One place to start is to understand the critical success factors that relate to the minimum parenting tasks—appointing senior managers, agreeing on and monitoring performance targets, authorizing major decisions, reacting to linkage disputes. What sort of managers are needed to make a success of this business? What are the main challenges facing the business and how should performance be measured? What is the nature of the major decisions, particularly capital expenditure decisions, facing the business? What areas of linkage exist with other businesses in the portfolio? By understanding the factors critical to success in each of these areas, it will be possible to judge whether any of the parenting characteristics will misfit in such a way as to destroy value.

The analysis, however, needs to go beyond a focus on success factors that relate to minimum parenting tasks. It should also include an assessment of the success factors for all areas of the business that the parent currently influences, or is likely to influence in a future corporate strategy. If the parent has a strong engineering function, then the success factors in engineering within the businesses need to be understood. If the parent is highly influential in public relations issues, then the success factors that relate to public relations need to be understood.

The assessment of critical success factors is driven by the nature of the current and likely future parenting behavior.

Bedfellows Analysis

The purpose of this analysis is to assess whether the businesses make natural bedfellows. Do the businesses have common features that suggest they should be parented by one parent company? Do they, for example, have parenting opportunities that are similar enough to benefit from one parent company? Do they have critical success factors that are similar? In most portfolios, there is a group of businesses with similar success factors and similar parenting opportunities. But there is often a large number of other businesses with different parenting opportunities or different success factors. It is valuable to identify the natural bedfellows—the ones with similar parenting opportunities and success factors—and distinguish them from the other businesses. A future corporate strategy is likely to build a heartland round the natural bedfellows.[7]

ASSESSING FIT

The review of corporate strategy may lead to changes either in the parent or in the portfolio of businesses. The assessment of current fit gives an important pointer to where changes are likely to be needed.

Three fit tests can be used:

- Do the parent's perceptions of its opportunities to create value match the parenting opportunities in the businesses?
- Are any of the parent's characteristics particularly effective at addressing the parenting opportunities?
- Do any of the parent's characteristics fit poorly with the critical success factors?

In parents with a good fit, value is normally being created. Where the fit is poor, value is normally being destroyed. A number of different analyses can help assess the degree to which value is being created or destroyed.

- *Successes and Failures Analysis.* By identifying particular events and decisions in the company and grading them as successes or failures, it is often possible to see patterns. By assessing what contribution (if any) the parent has made to these events, it is possible to illuminate both the key parenting characteristics of the organization and the sorts of situations where value is created and destroyed. This is usually the analysis that yields most understanding of where and how the parent is creating value.

- *Performance of Businesses Relative to Direct Competitors.* Superior performance is only prima facie evidence of value creation by the parent because it may be that the performance could have been achieved by the business on its own. Some assessment of the role of the parent in creating the performance is therefore also necessary.
- *Shareholder Value Analysis.* The contribution to shareholder value, on a discounted cash flow (DCF) basis, of each business is an alternative method of measuring performance, and hence a second source of prima facie evidence of parenting added value. Once again, care must be taken, as this value may be entirely generated at the business level, with no contribution from the parent.
- *Value Gap Analysis.* An analysis of what the businesses might be worth to a predator, who would be prepared to break up the company and sell the component parts separately, can indicate businesses in which the current parent appears to be creating relatively more or less value than alternative parents.
- *Discussions and Interviews with Managers in the Parent and in the Businesses.* Managers at all levels in the company will have views on whether value is being added or subtracted, and will be able to provide examples and anecdotes to support their views. Inevitably, these views will be somewhat subjective, but they provide an essential component of the assessment.

When the answers to the three fit questions are put together with the evidence from the five ways of assessing value creation, it is normally possible to reach conclusions about which businesses are benefiting from the parent's influence and which are being harmed by it. There are always grey areas: businesses about which it is hard to make judgments one way or the other. But the assessment can help explain where and why the parent is currently succeeding and failing.

It is important to remember that the assessment is based on historic data. A parent that has recently changed its characteristics will be difficult to assess. Businesses in changing environments will also be difficult to assess. However, where there is a reasonable history of stable parenting, it is possible to do highly detailed and valuable analysis. The vice president for corporate development of Emerson, Charlie Peters, who has completed a detailed assessment of fit at Emerson, argues that analysis of parenting characteristics, business characteristics, and fit should be pushed as far as possible. "It is important to work hard at identifying the sweet spot within your portfolio: those businesses where your parenting approach creates a particularly large amount of value. Based on my experience, this requires an enormous amount of detailed and rigorous analysis, and it pays back because the results are often counterintuitive."

RIVAL PARENT ANALYSIS

Rival parent analysis involves identifying, for each business, other parent companies that might add more value. The list of rival parents should include both direct competitors and other multibusiness companies whose parenting approach might be appropriate for the relevant business. For the companies identified as rival parents, a review of parenting characteristics and potential value creation, similar in concept to the appraisal described earlier in this chapter should be carried out.

Rival parent analysis is a vital component in assessing parenting advantage, but needs to take account of the long term. A snapshot analysis of a particular business at a point in time may indicate that a rival would add more (or less) value, whereas a longer view, or a view that takes account of synergies with other businesses, might reach the opposite conclusion. Rival parent analysis will highlight businesses in the portfolio that could be sold to more appropriate parents. In other words, it provides some guidance for portfolio options. It also provides guidance for parenting by helping identify alternative parenting approaches that work.

To start rival parent analysis, it is necessary to define a group of rival parents. These are companies that could be alternative parents of the businesses in the company's portfolio. For a large diversified company, the list of possible rival parents can be very long. But we have found it valuable to generate as full a list as possible before selecting which companies to analyze. Without a fairly full list, it is easy to choose obvious rivals and miss the creative benefit of identifying rival parents that have very different parenting characteristics and portfolios of businesses. For example, an oil company, such as Shell, can easily identify another oil company, such as Exxon, as a rival parent. It is also fairly clear that a minerals company, such as RTZ, is a rival parent for Shell's minerals businesses,[8] and that Dupont is a rival for Shell's chemicals businesses. It is less obvious that a diversified company, such as Hanson, is a rival for Shell's coal or chemical businesses, even though Hanson is one of the world's largest producers of coal and base chemicals.

We suggest four ways of developing names for the list of rival parents:

1. List all the obvious rivals: companies of similar size with similar portfolios of businesses.
2. For each business in the portfolio, list all the parents that own direct competitors to the business.
3. For each business in the portfolio, list all the companies that could have beneficial linkages with the business and note the parents that own these companies. Take particular care to note parents that own similar businesses in different countries. These similar businesses often provide opportunities for skill and technology sharing.

4. For each business in the portfolio, consider the different types of value that could be added to the business (e.g., tight financial controls to improve cash flow, or linkages with sister companies in Europe), and describe the type of parents that could add this kind of value. Then identify companies that match this type.

Once the list of rival parents has been developed, the next step is to select the companies that will be analyzed in more detail. It will be impossible to do a full analysis of all the rival parents on the list. We suggest focusing on the most "obvious" rivals and then creating categories of less obvious rival parents, selecting one company to analyze from each category.

As with competitive analysis at the business level, rival parent analysis is a process of getting to know the rivals better and better, so that it is possible to use them as a benchmark of value creation. The benefits of this benchmarking are not limited to major strategy reviews. Like all benchmarking exercises, benefits can accrue in many small ways as ideas are gained for improving parenting influence. For example, one company in the electrical equipment industry noted that one of its rivals had less than a quarter of the number of managers in country head offices and yet appeared to be able to achieve as much country presence and coordination. By reverse engineering the country organization of this parent and understanding how the coordination was achieved, the first company was able to cut tens of millions of dollars from its country organizations. By decentralizing some of the functional tasks to businesses within the country and centralizing other activities to the corporate center, the country organization was able to focus on a few essential coordination activities such as liaising with the government, coordinating marketing to major customers, and coordinating graduate recruitment. Even these tasks were mainly led by the larger businesses, with the country organization providing some administrative support and impetus for action.

Most managers view rival parent analysis as a daunting task. Yet we can vouch for its value and practicality. Companies are not as secretive about their management philosophy as they are about their product technology. Normally accessible sources—company literature, ex-employees, recently sold businesses, direct contacts, studies by investment analysts, and other public sources—can provide considerable information. Moreover, it is often not necessary to devote more than a few days' work to each company to produce useful results. Exhibit 12–8 displays the rival parent analysis carried out by one manufacturing company of its two most obvious rivals. The work took two days and the results can be summarized on one page. Yet the implications are clear. Company A, a U.S.-based company, is likely to be a better parent for certain kinds of businesses—for mature, U.S.-based businesses with good cash flow potential. Company A is also likely to be better at

EXHIBIT 12-8 Rival parent analysis—manufacturing

Company A	Company B
Financially driven	Strategically driven
Quick to pull out of low profit investments	Long-term outlook
	Large "expatriate" group
Few "international" managers	International senior management group
Few nonnationals	
Authoritarian management style	Consensus management approach
Strong systems	Discussion culture
Risk averse	Willingness to joint venture
Prefer equity control	Need for operational control

rationalization opportunities. Company B, on the other hand, is likely to be a better parent for businesses with long investment lead times, such as technology-driven businesses, particularly those requiring complex global management structures and bold strategies. Even this simple analysis points to different sources of parenting advantage.

TRENDS AND SCENARIOS

All the analysis so far involves current or historic data. Yet really good corporate strategy options need to contain some vision: some view about how trends are evolving, about opportunities that will exist in 10 years' time, about how the world is going to be. The danger with all analytically based approaches to strategy is that they are overinfluenced by historic data.

One of the methods for analyzing the future that has become widely respected is the scenarios technique.[9] The technique involves developing scenarios of two or more different and yet possible future worlds. These worlds represent different ways in which current trends and influences could move. They can be used to help the process of creating ideas about future sources of parenting advantage in three ways.

First, the scenario worlds can be used to judge which rival parents are likely to do well or badly in each scenario. This can help focus attention for further analysis of rival parents and contribute to the creation of parenting options. For example, a scenario that predicts a smooth transition to a common currency in Europe and the lowering of trade barriers worldwide may favor parent companies seeking to create value through internationalizing businesses. An opposite scenario may favor parent companies seeking to create value by linking businesses within national boundaries.

The second way to use scenarios is to compare the company's list of parenting characteristics against each scenario. Each parenting characteristic can be scored as positive, negative, or neutral against each scenario, giving a deeper understanding of the match between the company's parenting characteristics and the scenarios. This analysis also provides useful insights for developing parenting options.

The third use of scenarios is to generate different ways of adding value under the different scenarios. For example, a scenario that predicts an increase in retailer brands would also predict that a number of branded manufacturers will run into trouble by attempting to resist the trend. This suggests a parenting opportunity: Buy companies with good product technology that are resisting the trend and change their strategy to be more supportive of the retailers. The insight would be the prediction that some companies will underperform because they will be locked into an outdated way of marketing. Assuming that other parents have not spotted the opportunity, the company ought to be able to buy companies with poor strategies and create value by redirecting their strategies.

Building a complete scenario is expensive and time-consuming because of the need to think through the impact of many different forces of influence. However, the alternative to scenario analysis—studying individual trends—has dangers. It can cause the analyst to overlook the impact an individual trend may have on the broader system. Frequently a seemingly obvious trend fails to emerge in the way predicted due to other factors in the system. The scenario approach attempts to look at the whole system and the total impact of all the trends. Individual trends analysis is most useful when it takes account of the likely influences of the broader system.

CHOOSING A CORPORATE STRATEGY

The previous sections of this chapter describe analyses and techniques for understanding the four inputs to corporate strategy development. This section is essentially about the creative part of corporate strategy development—the generation of options and strategies. It is also about the selection process: How to decide which strategy option is best for the company.

A useful starting point for option generation is to draw together the input analyses into an assessment of parenting advantage. In which businesses has the parent created more value than rival parents, and in which has it been inferior to rival parents? Is the company's parenting advantage in each business likely to increase or decrease in the future? These assessments will not take account of changes to the corporate strategy that may be made, but they provide the backdrop against which changes need to be considered.

The assessment of parenting advantage can be plotted on a display that also measures the potential for value creation in each business (Exhibit 12–9). A "natural owner" is a parent that is at least as good or better than rival parents: A natural owner has parenting advantage. "One of the pack" is a parent that has no obvious disadvantages, but is not clearly a "natural owner." A "value destroyer" is a parent that has clear parenting weaknesses in exploiting the sources of value creation most important for that business. Value creation potential is measured as a percentage of current value. A "low" score would be an improvement of less than 10 percent in the value of the business. A "medium" score would be an improvement of 10 percent to 50 percent. A "high" score would be an improvement over 50 percent.

A version of this matrix was first developed by the consultants McKinsey & Company, in consulting work carried out with large corporates in the late 1980s. Called the MACS framework (standing for Market Activated Corporate Strategy), it has proved a useful way of capturing both the nature of the parenting opportunities and the quality of the existing parenting.[10] It provides a good backdrop for generating options about which businesses should serve as a base for the corporate strategy and what changes to make to parenting characteristics.

Generating Corporate Strategy Options

No amount of analysis and understanding of parenting characteristics, business characteristics, rival parents, or trends in the environment

EXHIBIT 12–9   Parenting Opportunity Matrix

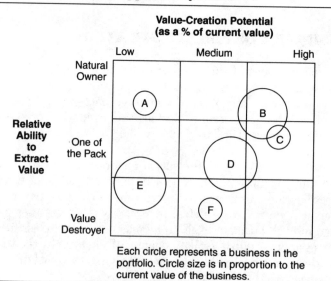

Each circle represents a business in the portfolio. Circle size is in proportion to the current value of the business.

will substitute for insight and creativity in the generation of corporate strategy options. It is a black art, and we do not wish to pretend that it is always possible to develop options that will give parenting advantage, or even options that will secure the company's future. There are situations in which we have been involved where the only solution appeared to be the dissolution of the company and the sale of the businesses to managers or rival parents. With this caveat, however, we have developed some approaches for aiding option generation and stimulating creativity. In particular, we have found it useful to generate parenting options as a separate exercise from portfolio options, and then to synthesize these two sets of options into three or four corporate strategy options.

Parenting options concern the ways in which the company aims to parent and create value in its businesses. Exhibit 12–10 summarizes a number of prompts we have found useful to the generation of parenting options. The skill in choosing options is to weave a path between being overambitious and not being ambitious enough. It is tempting to develop options modeled, for example, on ABB or BTR, when neither is a realistic ambition for the current parent. On the other hand, it is also possible to assume that all the current parent managers are immovable, making it hard to identify options that involve more than a minor change. Obviously, the parenting options must be realistic, taking account of the senior managers and their embedded values, beliefs, and ways of working. Most substantive parenting options, however, will entail some people changes.

EXHIBIT 12–10   Prompts for developing parenting options

1. *Downsize, delayer, and decentralize.* Many companies are improving their parenting by reducing value destruction.

2. *Encourage networking.* Companies such as ABB, 3M, and Unilever are demonstrating that linkage benefits can be achieved at low cost through managed networking.

3. *Clarify the dominant process.* Different options can be based on choosing different processes (e.g., budgeting, planning, or capital approval) as the dominant process.

4. *Focus on the dominant managers.* Different options can be based on the different skill combinations that could be created by choosing different combinations of the senior team.

5. *Redefine division versus center roles.* Companies frequently duplicate parenting tasks by doing them both in the division and the center.

6. *Build functional skills.* Identify core skills that could be built through functional parenting.

7. *Build corporate development skills.* Companies are frequently weak in acquisition, divestment, and venturing.

Portfolio options concern the sorts of businesses to have within the portfolio. They are often easier to develop than parenting options. The analysis of the existing parenting characteristics and business characteristics will have defined a group of businesses or a historic heartland that is likely to be the basis of most portfolio options. The challenge in option generation is to think of ways of extending, growing, or redefining the historic heartland. Exhibit 12–11 summarizes the prompts we have found useful when developing portfolio options.

The purpose of developing parenting options separate from portfolio options is to stimulate creativity. All parenting options have portfolio implications and vice versa. The process of developing the two sets of options helps break out of status quo thinking and can stimulate new combinations. Once the creative thinking is complete, the two lists need to be synthesized into three or four corporate strategy options, each of which can be described by a prospective parenting advantage statement.

The corporate strategist can also use the development of corporate strategy options to help the decision-making process. Frequently, senior management already has a strong view about a favored option, in which case additional options can be developed to provide refinement of the preferred option or a radical challenge to the current thinking. Sometimes senior managers are locked into a disagreement about the way forward, which may well have sparked the strategy review in the first place. In this case, the corporate strategy options should be chosen to illuminate the points of agreement and disagreement or establish a different logic for approaching the decision.

EXHIBIT 12–11   Prompts for developing portfolio options

1. *Mentally discard the misfits.* The first step is to mentally cleanse the portfolio of clear misfits.

2. *Assume no size constraints.* Avoid restricting options to ones that will make the company about the same size. Consider ones that will halve or double the size.

3. *Look for businesses with similar critical success factors.* It is easier to develop distinctive parenting skills and gain a "feel" for businesses if the success factors are similar.

4. *Look for linkages.* Look for businesses that share elements of the value chain, or have common skills.

5. *Be guided by scenarios.* The danger is to choose a portfolio that fits the historic analysis, not the future opportunities.

6. *Try a zero-based approach.* Assume the existing portfolio has been sold. The company now has a huge cash mountain to spend on new businesses.

7. *Consider a split or demerger.* This is particularly relevant if the existing portfolio appears to have two or more heartlands.

Selecting a Corporate Strategy

The most important criterion for selecting a corporate strategy should be the degree to which the strategy will give parenting advantage now and in the future. Comparing the degree of advantage that is likely to result from one option against another is not easy. It requires detailed knowledge of the most threatening rivals, an understanding of the value creation opportunity, and management judgment. Nevertheless, we have found that the sort of analyses used to assess historical parenting fit can be brought to bear, and that the criterion is practical and can be used to distinguish between options.

In Chapter 3 we accepted that companies can have viable corporate strategies without a clear advantage over other parent companies. A company can create wealth and avoid hostile attentions so long as it is a "good" parent. Yet we believe strongly that the parenting advantage criterion is the best guide to help managers make better corporate strategy choices. If all the options are "good parent" options rather than "best parent" options, then management should choose the "best" good parent option.

There are two other criteria that can be used to refine the judgments about which option has the most parenting advantage. These criteria are only relevant when comparing options with similar degrees of parenting advantage.

1. *The Size of the Value Creation Opportunity.* In some situations, the parenting opportunity is limited: The businesses may only need a small amount of parenting influence and only offer the potential for a small increase in performance. This is often the case where separate national businesses share skills or technology, or where vertically linked businesses coordinate product flows. It is possible for a parent to have a clear advantage over other parents and yet still have only a small opportunity to create value. The increase in skill and technology sharing that the parent can create may be small, or the improvement in the coordination of product flows due to the parent may not make a substantial difference.

2. *The Intensity of the Rivalry between Parent Companies.* In some situations, parents are locked in a fierce battle for ownership of businesses. In the late 1980s, for example, Nestlé, Grand Metropolitan, Unilever, Procter & Gamble, Philip Morris, BSN, and other large food companies were competing vigorously to acquire major brands. The prices paid for companies such as Kraft, Rowntrees, Jacobs Suchard, Nabisco's European businesses, and Perrier were high, and probably resulted in most of the value creation opportunity being realized by the selling shareholders rather than the acquiring company. Even in situations where a company has an advantage, the rivalry between parents may be so intense that the

value creation opportunity for the buying company's shareholders is small. In these circumstances, it may be better to choose an alternative corporate strategy, where the degree of parenting advantage is similar but the parenting rivalry is less intense.

Taken together, these two criteria could result in a situation where the corporate strategy option with the most value creation potential is not the one with the highest degree of parenting advantage. However, we would still advise a company to focus on the option with the most parenting advantage. To choose to be a second-best parent, even in an area where there is currently room for both good and bad parents, is locking the company into a losing position in the long term.

In addition to the parenting advantage criterion, corporate strategists should consider implementation risk: the risks entailed in implementing changes to the parent or the portfolio. If the corporate strategy calls for the development of new and different parenting characteristics, or for extensive portfolio change, it may well be far from certain that it can be successfully implemented. In our experience, managers normally overestimate their ability to change the parenting approach and to build new parenting skills and underestimate their ability to make portfolio changes.

Options with low implementation risk are preferable to ones with high risk. An option that has a lower level of parenting advantage and low risk may be preferable to one that has a high level of parenting advantage but requires developing important new parenting skills and making major portfolio changes. As we will show in the GCA Construction example in the next chapter, it can be preferable to choose a corporate strategy that builds on existing strengths rather than to reach for a bolder strategy with much higher risks.

The final criterion for choosing a strategy is the objectives and constraints of stakeholders—shareholders, customers, suppliers, employees, senior management, and others. The influence of customers and suppliers on the choice of corporate strategy is likely to be muted because their primary association with the company is through the businesses, not the parent. They therefore have less impact on the choice of parenting behavior or portfolio options. This does not mean that their objectives and constraints should be ignored, but rather that their influence is most strongly felt once the shape of the portfolio has been chosen.

Shareholders' objectives and constraints should be influential in choosing a corporate strategy. Shareholders want the value of the company to increase and hence the strategy that creates the most parenting advantage for the least risk will be the preferred option.

However, some shareholders may have specific requirements that need to be taken into account. How much risk do shareholders want to take? How important is stable earnings growth? Are shareholders prepared to support rights issues? What dividends do shareholders want?

Do shareholders see the company as an engineering company or a consumer goods company? Many companies actively survey their shareholders to find out what they think and to seek answers to these questions. But shareholders change, making it necessary to update continuously the answers to the questions. Moreover, a change in corporate strategy may precipitate a change in the composition of shareholders; as one group of shareholders sells shares due to their discomfort with the strategy or the risk involved, another group will be buying the shares because of their comfort with the company's new direction. Our advice is to assume that shareholders are interested only in maximum long-term wealth creation, unless the company's particular shareholders have made different views clear to the company.

The employees and senior managers are another important stakeholder group. The majority of employees and managers work within the business units. Their objectives and constraints affect the choice of strategy both directly and through the risk of implementation. If the senior managers in the businesses do not support the proposed parenting approach, it is unlikely to be successful. But business managers and employees will change if the businesses change. Hence their needs are most relevant once the portfolio has been chosen.

The employees and managers working in the parent have a more direct influence on the choice of strategy. If these managers want a fast-growing, deal-oriented environment, it is inappropriate to choose a "back to the core" strategy. If the managers want the company to be a member of the Fortune 500, it may be inappropriate to choose a demerge strategy. Rather surprisingly, we have found that parent company managers are often reluctant to use their personal preferences as explicit criteria. They often claim to see themselves as "servants" of the company and hence believe that their personal preferences should, in some sense, be off limits. As professional managers, they feel they ought to choose a strategy uninfluenced by inner desires, ego needs, or personal ambitions.

In practice, we find that these personal preferences do emerge. But they are attributed to one of the other stakeholder groups. Managers say, "Our shareholders would be uncomfortable if we focused only on one business," when they mean "We would be uncomfortable." Or managers say, "Our shareholders require a 15 percent per annum growth in earnings per share," when they mean, "We want to be regarded as one of the best companies in the country and this means producing regular earnings growth of 15 percent per annum, like company X."

We feel that managers' personal ambitions, desires, fears, and constraints should be an explicit part of the screening process for choosing the best option, since they will be vital to the successful implementation of the new strategy. These desires will have inevitably influenced the selection of options, but it will aid the final decision if personal aspirations are made explicit. We would discourage managers from choosing an option that only meets personal aspirations and fails to meet any of the other criteria. But equally, we would discourage managers from choosing an option that meets all the other criteria, but leaves managers feeling uninspired and disappointed. It is the managers whose skills and hard work create the value. Unless their aspirations are met, they are unlikely to create an advantage over rivals.

DEFINING THE FUTURE CORPORATE STRATEGY

The final step in the process is to define the chosen corporate strategy in a form that can aid communication, guide decision making, and help to influence the mental maps of managers in the parent and in the businesses. This involves producing a parenting advantage statement (Exhibit 12–12).

The parenting advantage statement will list the main *value creation insights* on which the corporate strategy will be built. These insights will describe the nature of the improvement opportunities the parent will focus on, and the nature of the role the parent will take up in addressing the opportunities.

The parenting advantage statement will also describe the *distinctive parenting characteristics* around which the parenting approach will be designed. These distinctive parenting characteristics will address the value creation opportunities and will reinforce each other.

EXHIBIT 12–12   Parenting advantage statement

Value Creation Insights	Insights about value creation: • Nature of the parenting opportunity. • Nature of the parent's role in addressing the opportunity.
Distinctive Parenting Characteristics	Parenting characteristics that will be at the center of the parenting approach, drawn from the following areas: • Mental maps. • Structures, systems, and processes. • Functions, central services, and resources. • People and skills. • Decentralization contracts.
Heartland Businesses	Criteria that define the type of business that is the focus of the strategy: • Industry, technology or market descriptors. • Type of parenting opportunities. • Critical success factor descriptors. • Negative descriptors.

Finally, the statement will contain, in as much detail as possible, the *heartland* criteria. These criteria will describe the nature of the businesses that fit with the corporate strategy. The criteria will include industry, technology, or market descriptors; some descriptors that refer to the type of improvement potential that exists in the businesses; and some descriptors that define the type of business the parent has a feel for and, importantly, the type of business that should be avoided, where the parent's feel is inadequate.

A clear prospective parenting advantage statement is also the best starting point for the many implementation decisions that will be needed. It will help guide decisions about the portfolio (Chapter 14) and decisions about the parenting approach (Chapter 15).

In addition to a parenting advantage statement, it is often also useful to reassess the company's objectives both in terms of its *strategic intent* (its ambitions expressed in competitive terms) and its *financial objectives*. These objectives will have been influential in the development of and selection between options. However, the objectives may have changed in the process of choosing a corporate strategy and it will be useful to revisit them to clarify what the new objectives are. Many companies use this review of objectives to develop a new mission statement. Our research into mission statements suggests that it is better to delay the production of a new mission statement until the parent has had a few years of experience with the new strategy.[11] At this stage, therefore, we believe that statements of strategic intent and financial objectives are sufficient.

SUMMARY

In this chapter, we have shown how companies can set about reviewing their existing corporate strategy or developing a new one. We have provided a framework for thinking about the corporate strategy challenge. The framework provides a structured approach to the task, and suggests analyses and judgments that can be made to arrive at a preferred option. In practice, most companies do not develop strategies in this way. Strategies emerge out of experiments and initiatives driven by senior managers. We believe that our framework adds analytical rigor and rational structure to a process that we acknowledge is essentially experimental.

Our framework is particularly useful to a company faced with major changes and the need to develop a new strategy. The old strategy may have failed, a new chief executive with different ideas may have been appointed, a hostile takeover bid may have stimulated a radical reappraisal. In the next chapter we will illustrate one such situation as a way of showing how the framework and analyses can be used in practice.

NOTES

1. A framework for understanding cultural values and their link to strategy is given in Andrew Campbell and Laura Nash, *A Sense of Mission*, Reading, MA: Addison-Wesley, 1993; Andrew Campbell, Marion Devine, and David Young, *A Sense of Mission*, London: Century Business and Economist Books, 1990.

2. See Appendix B for fuller discussion.

3. See David Young and Michael Goold, *Effective Headquarters Staff*, London: Ashridge Strategic Management Centre, 1993, Section 5, for a fuller discussion of how to review and design headquarters staffs.

4. David Young and Michael Goold, *Effective Headquarters Staff*, and *The Headquarters Fact Book*, London: Ashridge Strategic Management Centre, 1993. These volumes provide data on the size, structure, and cost of 107 U.K.-headquartered companies, and can provide some useful benchmarks.

5. A questionnaire (Style Questionnaire No. 1) has been developed to help assess the alignment of parenting characteristics. Copies can be ordered from the Ashridge Strategic Management Centre, 17 Portland Place, London W1N 3AF, England. Tel: +44-71-323-4422. Fax +44-71-323-0903.

6. It is important that the analysis of parenting opportunities focus on the improvements that are due to the influence of the parent, and distinguish these from the improvements that would occur even if the parent was not involved. While in most cases this is a matter of judgment, a more scientific way to do this was described to us by Robin Buchanan, head of Bain & Co's London office. It involves developing a "full potential assessment" for each business based on an analysis of the market, industry structure, competitive strength and development potential. The assessment identifies a range of profit, cash flow and shareholder value figures, and defines the risks that would cause the business to be at the top of the range or near the bottom. By identifying which risks the parent organization can help manage, the particular contribution of the parent can be more easily identified.

7. A questionnaire (Style Questionnaire No. 2) has been developed to help assess whether businesses will respond best to a Strategic Planning, Strategic Control or Financial Control style. When different businesses need a parent with different styles they are unlikely to be viable bedfellows. Copies of the questionnaire can be ordered from Ashridge Strategic Management Centre, 17 Portland Place, London W1N 3AF. Tel: +44-71-323-4422, Fax: +44-71-323-0903.

8. Shell was considering divesting its mineral businesses at the time of writing.

9. A good description of this technique is provided by Peter Schwartz, *The Long View*, New York: Free Press, 1992.

10. In Chapter 14 we describe another matrix for assessing businesses. The Parenting Fit Matrix evaluates the fit between businesses and a prospective corporate strategy.

11. Refer to note 1, and *Do You Need A Mission Statement?* London: Economist Publications, Report No. 1208.

13

DEVELOPING CORPORATE STRATEGY: AN EXAMPLE

GCA Construction (standing for Goold, Campbell, and Alexander) is a fictitious company, which we will use as a worked example paralleling the structure and analysis in Chapter 12. GCA has £2.7 billion in sales, mainly in Europe, with interests in construction, cement, and housing. It also has a building materials division, which includes a steel fabrication company as well as a collection of companies making materials such as tiles and roofing felt. Exhibit 13–1 shows the split in sales, profits, and assets.

The company has recently had a change in chief executive. The new chief executive was previously head of the cement business. This individual has chosen to launch a corporate strategy review. He is concerned about the maturity of some of the businesses, the cyclical nature of the building industry, and the degree of diversity of the current portfolio. He is worried by the risks being taken in the construction division, especially because he does not have the experience to judge whether these risks are acceptable. In other words, GCA Construction and its new chief executive face some tricky corporate strategy decisions.

EXHIBIT 13–1   GCA Construction (£ millions)

	Sales	Profits	Assets
Construction	1,100	40	(50)
Cement	750	94	980
Housing	500	62	390
Building materials	400	39	120
	2,700	235	1,490

The first task for GCA Construction is to develop an understanding of the characteristics of the parent company and the characteristics of the businesses in the portfolio. This provides the basis from which an assessment of fit can be made. It also provides useful data from which corporate strategy options can be developed.

THE CHARACTERISTICS OF THE PARENT

As we describe GCA's parenting characteristics, we will assume that most of the analyses outlined in Chapter 12 have been completed, and that the data from these analyses has been synthesized. To summarize the results, we will use our categorization of parenting characteristics— the parent's mental maps; its structures, systems, and processes; its functions, central services, and resources; its people and skills; and its decentralization contracts.

Despite the differences in personal style between the previous chief executive and the new appointment, there are some important common elements in the parent's *mental maps*. One predisposition is a commitment to decentralization. The importance of meeting budget is also a shared belief, based on a commitment to short-term financial performance. Integrity and fair play are deeply held values and an unexpressed, but clear, objective is to be recognized as the best company in the construction sector. Another shared predisposition is a belief that managers should not "throw good money after bad." This helps the company prune loss-making or low profit activities quickly, and causes the parent to judge investment proposals on track record rather than future promises. The parent managers also believe that attempts to promote linkages between, say, the cement businesses and the construction businesses will lead to inefficient trading relationships. As a result, all intergroup trading has been done at arm's length to ensure that a commercial judgment is being made by both parties.

The new chief executive brings to the parent company some clear ideas about value creation: a belief that companies usually allow overhead costs to get too high, so that there is normally an opportunity to reduce costs; and a belief that success in many product categories will increasingly depend on having a strong regional (e.g., European) presence. Both these ideas relate to the chief executive's experience in the cement business, where he reduced overhead costs and created a European network of cement businesses.

The previous approach to parenting was not based on any powerful value creation insights. It was a reflection of a desire to decentralize as much as possible and avoid interfering in operating issues. Previously, the center's main tasks had been to select which businesses to keep in the portfolio, prune the loss makers, and provide financial support and encouragement to the profitable units. The philosophy was one of decentralized portfolio management.

GCA Construction has a simple *structure*. The headquarters has four divisions reporting to it, each of which contains between 5 and 10 business units. Although the reporting structure is simple, it is not obvious how to define the parent. Does the parent include the division-level managers or just the headquarters managers? Analysis of the divisions using the techniques described in Appendix A resulted in concluding that the construction and housing divisions are both large single businesses. The advantages to be gained from scale outweigh the advantages from focus, making it appropriate to treat both of these divisions as single businesses. However, the other two divisions were analyzed as being made up of a number of businesses. This was not surprising for the building materials businesses; but it was an important analysis in the cement division. It was concluded that the advantages to be gained from scale were most important at the national level. This made each country operation a separate business.

The Appendix A analysis resulted in classifying the cement and building materials divisional management groups as part of the parent, but the construction and housing divisions as large strategic business units (Exhibit 13–2). The total parent organization staff are 181, after

EXHIBIT 13–2 GCA Construction—defining the parent

Division	Strategic Business Units	Parent
Cement	10 cement companies located across Europe (each cement company could be a stand-alone unit)	Headquarters and Cement Division
Housing	The Housing Division (the main sources of competitive advantage are driven from the division level for the 10 units in the United Kingdom)	Headquarters
Construction	The Construction Division (most of the business is based on major projects and it is run as one business across Europe even though there are 5 geographic profit centers)	Headquarters
Building Materials	5 business units (each business is a stand-alone unit)	Headquarters and Building Materials Division

including the staff in the cement and building materials divisions (Exhibit 13–3).

The *systems and processes* at GCA are limited, due to its historic financial orientation. People decisions are made based on line management judgment. Capital approval and decision making are decentralized to division-level boards, with large investments requiring corporate board authorization. The planning and budgeting processes are combined into a 2-year plan, the first year of which is the budget; but the unsophisticated financial and strategic analysis skills mean that the ability to analyze performance data at headquarters is limited. The cement division, however, has an elaborate and sophisticated performance review system that defines variances, measures ratios, and uses strategic measures of performance.

The *functions and central services* are limited, due to the historic parenting approach. Finance is the main function. Personnel consists of a management development manager and a secretary, who act more as personal assistants to the chief executive than as a management development function. Two functions valued by the businesses are the central analysis and library team, who respond to requests for information, and the government relations team, who help the businesses win government contracts and produce market forecasts and statistics. The other functions—pensions administration, insurance, and legal—are not seen as major value creators. These activities could be subcontracted without making any significant difference to the company. The administrative services activity includes cleaners, security, chauffeurs, and other administrative needs of the center. None of these activities are important to value creation. One important *resource* that the divisions recognize as being valuable to their performance is the company's

EXHIBIT 13–3   GCA Construction—parent staff

Headquarters Staff		Building Materials Division Staff	
Finance	31	Finance and Administration	6
Pensions Administration	21	Personnel	2
Personnel/Career		Division Management	2
Development	2		10
Legal and Secretarial	7		
Public Relations/			
Government Relations	8		
Planning, Analysis &		**Cement Division Staff**	
Library	10		
Administrative Services	26	Finance and Administration	8
Insurance*	37	Personnel	3
Central Management and		Operations	4
Support Staff	12	Division Management	2
	154		17

* *The insurance activities are run as a small insurance business.*

name. It is highly regarded in the industry and acts as a useful reassurance for customers, employees, and suppliers.

In the building materials division, the chief executive and finance director dominate a small team of 10 support staff focusing on financial performance and giving the businesses maximum autonomy. In the cement division, however, the chief executive and finance director are supported by a highly influential human resources director and a three-person operations audit team, who have a major influence on business operations. The operations audit team works closely with the financial accountants to make sure that all business units use the same accounting methods and report common statistics. This makes comparisons between operations relatively easy and aids the transfer of best practice.

The historic *decentralization contracts* have been designed to push as much responsibility down to the division levels as possible. "We believe that it is inappropriate for us, at the center, to be taking any initiatives. We try to make sure that the division managers are responsible for all of the factors that affect their divisional performance," explained the finance director. The center even delegates acquisition and disposal decisions, and decisions on the hedging of foreign exchange, to the division level.

The building materials division has a similar policy and pushes most decisions down to the business level, except for corporate development activity such as acquisitions and disposals. The cement division, on the other hand, has a more influential role, even setting policies on some operational and technical issues. The businesses within the cement division feel less autonomous than the building materials, housing, or construction businesses.

The people in the parent are all managers with long years of experience in the construction industry. There is a strong operational bias, with a number of managers coming from the house-building and building materials divisions. These are managers who prefer not to intellectualize or over analyze. Simple systems and face-to-face discussions are their preferred way of working. There are few unusual *skills* in the parent: No individuals stand out as leading functional experts in the industry.

In parenting style terms, the center and building materials division would be viewed as Financial Control parents and the cement division as a Strategic Control parent. The new chief executive has, therefore, had experience managing in a Strategic Control style. He is also more naturally a Strategic Control style manager due to his personality and intellectual approach to business. Some changes in decentralization contracts are likely with the change in leadership.

The parenting characteristics of GCA Construction are similar to those of many decentralized, diversified companies in the construction industry. The total cost of the parent company, including the building materials and cement division levels (181 people) is £10 million (0.27% of total sales).

Parenting alignment analysis shows that, historically, the GCA center's parenting was well aligned. Each of the parenting characteristics reinforced each other. An area of possible weakness was the financial controls, which could have been tightened to fit better with the Financial Control style. The parenting of the cement businesses is, however, out of step with the rest of the company, and the new chief executive's natural style will cause a misalignment between him and many of the historic parenting characteristics.

THE CHARACTERISTICS OF THE BUSINESSES

Within GCA's businesses, it is not obvious that there are many *parenting opportunities*. The housing and construction businesses are competitively strong and are each viewed as one of the best in the country. The construction business is known to be more profitable than the industry due to a culture that is focused on avoiding loss-making contracts and squeezing performance from existing contracts. The housing business is believed to be the most efficient housebuilder in the country. The cement businesses are also well placed competitively, producing profit results at least as good as competitors. In the United Kingdom, the cement business is a market leader. Only in the building materials division do clear parenting opportunities appear to exist. These businesses all have small market shares but do not perform as well as similar competitors.

Because the portfolio has been managed with a highly decentralized style, there is little reason to suppose that the businesses would perform significantly better as independent companies. On the other hand, it is not obvious that they benefit much from being part of GCA's portfolio. Many of the best competitors in housing and construction are not part of larger companies. Moreover, the best cement companies are mostly focused on cement, with only a few diversifications. So the diversified composition of GCA's portfolio is unusual.

Exhibit 13–4 is a summary of the areas of possible underperformance. The main opportunities in addition to the underperformance in the building materials division result from cyclicality, linkage opportunities in cement, external relations, management's low levels of strategic vision, and internationalization.

The *critical success factors* are different in each business. The housing business is about buying land in the right place at the right price, understanding the type of house that will appeal to the local market, developing a tightly managed building system based on a few basic house concepts, and aggressively marketing houses. The construction business, by way of comparison, is about knowing which contracts to bid for and how to price them, effectively managing subcontractors, and effectively managing the client to ensure a profit on the project. Moreover, housing and construction employ different kinds of managers. The

EXHIBIT 13–4   Areas of possible underperformance (based on Exhibit 12–7)

1. *Business Definition*	There do not appear to be any misdefinitions.
2. *Business Size*	The main businesses are all large enough to have sufficient skills and stability. Moreover, it is not apparent that they are so large that they have built excessive overheads.
3. *Management*	The business managers are mostly well regarded in their industries, with the exception of the building materials businesses. All are well focused on performance. There is some tendency, particularly in cement, to overinvest in new equipment. Most managers are operationally biased and, therefore, have low levels of strategic vision.
4. *Temptations*	The cyclicality of the businesses can lead managers to overinvest in boom years and cut back too slowly in poor years.
5. *Linkages*	There do not appear to be any linkages that cannot be handled through arm's-length arrangements, with the possible exception of the cement businesses.
6. *Common Capabilities*	The finance and purchasing functions appear to be the only areas in which there are common skills across divisions.
7. *Special Expertise*	There are no obvious areas of special expertise that the parent could develop, except possibly the ability to create a profit-focused culture in construction businesses.
8. *External Relations*	The parent could potentially develop special relations with ministers and government agencies for the benefit of businesses.
9. *Major Decisions*	No obvious parenting role on major decisions.
10. *Major Change*	If the markets become regional or global, the businesses concerned will need to become international.

housing business has many disciplined operating managers with good personnel management skills and low educational levels. The construction business has many more engineers with degrees.

Bedfellows analysis demonstrates that these businesses do not make natural bedfellows. Exhibit 13–5 summarizes the critical success factors for the main businesses, showing how different they are. The businesses need different kinds of managers, face different types of major decisions and challenges, and need to be measured using different kinds of performance targets. Even a parent that limits its influence to

EXHIBIT 13–5   Critical success factors for GCA businesses

Construction	Choosing the "right" contracts Efficient project management Profit-focused culture Effective financial accounting Low overheads
Cement	Deciding on size and location of new capacity Process technology and cost control Managing competitive rivalry: multimarket competition Profit-focused culture Coping with the down cycle
Housing	Buying good locations Knowing the local market Developing an efficient building system Marketing houses Coping with the down cycle
Bricks	Deciding on size of new/refurbished capacity Nature and quality of the clay deposit Distribution and marketing Deciding when to close capacity
Roofing Felt	Efficient purchasing of bitumen Cost-effective manufacturing Strong sales force Strong distribution
Steel Fabrication	Location of fabrication sites Management of fabrication process Service relationship with clients Low overheads Low working capital

the minimum parenting tasks will still have difficulty coping with the diversity.

To reinforce this view, a parenting style fit analysis suggests that these businesses would not all fit comfortably under either a Strategic Control or a Financial Control parent. The materials, steel fabrication, and housing businesses appear to fit best with a Financial Control parenting style, while the other businesses fit best with a Strategic Control style.

ASSESSING FIT

It is clear from the analysis so far that there are areas of fit and areas of misfit between the GCA parent and its businesses. Fit analysis involves asking three fit questions and then attempting to confirm the answers with a number of value creation analyses.

The first question concerns the degree to which any value creation insights of the parent match the parenting opportunities in the businesses. Since, historically, the parent has had no real value creation insights, there has, in the past, been no fit, except possibly in the cement division. Looking forward, the new chief executive's emphasis on low overheads and Europeanization do not appear to fit the analysis of business characteristics.

The second question concerns the degree to which the parent has distinctive skills or characteristics that address underperformance situations in the businesses. Again, with the possible exception of the parenting activities of the cement division, there is little evidence of fit.

The third question concerns whether the parent understands the businesses well enough to avoid inadvertently destroying value. Here, there is no clear evidence of misfit. Historically, the parent has had such a low profile that any lack of understanding has been difficult to spot. In the future, the lack of similar critical success factors is of particular concern, since the new chief executive is likely to be more influential than his predecessor. For example, in construction the new chief executive feels uncomfortable with the risks involved in large contracts. His inclination is to reduce the company's exposure by reducing the number of large contracts. He recognizes that this will curtail the profit potential of the business, but he believes it is inappropriate for GCA to be taking risks he does not understand. One area where there is clear misfit is between the new chief executive and the managers in charge of building materials and housing. These business heads are openly hostile to the new appointment, sensing the change in style that it implies.

To summarize the fit analyses, we conclude that the cement businesses appear to fit best with the new chief executive and his preferred style of management. The construction business seems to fit worst. The housing business and the building materials businesses are hostile to the new chief executive, making value creation in these businesses hard without management changes.

We will not go through the five types of value analysis in detail. But it is useful to give four conclusions based on the analysis.

1. The successes and failures analysis supports the fit analysis. Cement has had a greater share of successes. Construction and housing have also been successful, marred only by a failure in the housing division to anticipate a recession, resulting in large write-downs of building land that cost the company over £100 million.

2. With the exception of the write-downs in housing, all three of the main businesses have outperformed competitors and are viewed as among the best in the industry. The building materials businesses have not performed as well in their sectors and are not viewed

with the same level of respect. The success of the other three divisions does not appear to be connected with any historic parenting influence, other than in the cement division.

3. The most value creation has been in the construction business. Housing would have been the next best creator of value if it had not faced land write-downs; but even with the write-downs, housing is a value creator. In cement, significant acquisitions cloud the picture. Depending on current valuations of the businesses, the conclusion could go either way. The other businesses are either small value creators or destroyers, except for steel fabrication, which has been a big value destroyer, due to two misguided acquisitions.

4. Currently the company has a value gap. The market capitalization is £1.1 billion, and the breakup value lies somewhere between £1.4 billion and £2.0 billion.

Overall, therefore, the assessment of fit is negative. While the GCA parent does not seem to have destroyed value in the past, there is little evidence that it has created value. The failures in the building materials division are probably partly the result of poor parenting; but the successes in the other divisions are hard to connect with good parenting. In the future, the parenting approach is going to change. However, there is little evidence that these businesses could benefit from being under one ownership, and it is possible that greater strategic involvement will lead to value destruction, because the businesses have such different critical success factors.

Our summary of the position in GCA Construction may appear harsh and critical. We are concluding that the portfolio does not fit well with the parent, that the parent does not fully understand some of its businesses, and that the parent appears to have few good ideas about how to create value out of its portfolio. Many readers will say that we have created a straw man, that this is not representative of the vast majority of companies. Our experience is different. GCA is typical of many of the situations we encounter.

RIVAL PARENT ANALYSIS

GCA has many rival parents. Exhibit 13–6 summarizes a variety of different kinds of rivals that could be considered as part of a rival parent analysis. The list has been generated by taking each business in GCA's portfolio and running through the rival parent checklist (see Chapter 12).

For GCA, the future strategy already has some shape to it. Due to the personality and experience of the new chief executive, the future corporate strategy is likely to involve a Strategic Control style. It is also likely to include the cement business and to deemphasize the holdings

EXHIBIT 13–6 GCA Construction illustrative list of rival parents

Similar Businesses and Geographic Focus

Construction industry generalists
(e.g., Wimpey, Tarmac)

Construction industry focused
(e.g., Blue Circle, Redland, Trafalgar House)

Construction industry specialists
(e.g., Barratt, RMC)

Similar Businesses (more international)

Global construction companies
(e.g., Bechtel, Fluor)

European diversified construction companies
(e.g., Bouyges, Dumez)

Companies with Some Competing Businesses

Engineering consultancies
(few large ones, most are small)

Water companies
(e.g., Northumbrian Water, Wessex Water)

Companies with Possible Linkages

International linkages
(e.g., Cementation)

Raw material linkages
(e.g., British Industrial Sand)

Building materials linkages
(very broad range of companies)

Plant and equipment linkages
(e.g., plant hire companies, cement-making machinery)

Marketing information linkages
(e.g., town planning consultancies, real estate agencies)

Companies with Value-Adding Skills That Might Be Relevant

Companies skilled at cross-Europe coordination and skill sharing
(e.g., ABB, Unilever)

Companies skilled at managing cycles
(e.g., RTZ)

Financial Control conglomerates
(e.g., Hanson, BTR)

in building materials. These early indications help to focus the rival parent analysis.

Important companies to analyze are cement companies, particularly companies with broad-based portfolios, such as Blue Circle (cement, heating, and bathroom equipment) and companies with more focused portfolios, such as RMC. It will also be important to analyze housing companies, particularly companies such as Wimpey that combine housing with other non-construction businesses and focus on the U.K. market. Finally, it will be useful to look at some diversified construction companies such as Tarmac (construction, quarrying, housing), Trafalgar House (construction, property, other), and the diversified French construction companies such as Bouygues and Dumez.

Other categories of interest but of less importance are water companies (because some are aggressively diversifying into the construction sector), Financial Control companies (because their style suits some of the businesses), and companies with European integration skills (because the chief executive believes that a major opportunity is to build European businesses).

The remaining categories of rivals can be ignored, unless one of the corporate strategy options makes them relevant. Engineering consultancies are unlikely to be worth researching. Companies with possible linkages do not seem to be relevant because nearly all linkages seem to be successfully managed through arm's length relationships. Companies with skills at managing cycles could be studied later, if the management of the cycle is a critical element of one of the corporate strategy options.

Having reduced the analytical task to more manageable proportions, GCA might come to the following conclusions from an analysis of rival parents:

- Small focused cement companies appear to be at least as profitable and successful as broadly spread cement companies. Size may not be a benefit in the cement industry. Local market share and cost control may matter more.

- Diversified companies in the construction sector, whether based on cement, housing, or construction, manage in a highly decentralized way.

- The United Kingdom is the only housing market that has large housing companies and, with the exception of Tarmac and Wimpey's housing businesses, most successful housing businesses are independent focused companies.

- In continental Europe, housing is built by construction companies as part of their construction business. Many medium-size or family-controlled construction companies are likely to be for sale in Europe over the next 10 years.

- Most construction companies are not diversified. International and global construction companies are all focused on the construction business.

- International construction companies are managed in a decentralized way, with geographic businesses, specialist contracting businesses, and major projects businesses.

- None of the companies studied appear to have particularly effective systems and skills for managing the industry cycle, suggesting that this might be a potential area for creating parenting advantage.
- Some of the rivals appear to be ahead of GCA in developing the capability for managing an international, particularly European, portfolio of businesses. This relative disadvantage seems to be particularly evident in cement, suggesting that GCA's success in cement may not be dependent on its European network or linkage management skills.

TRENDS AND SCENARIOS

An analysis of the trends facing GCA businesses might have led to these further conclusions:

- Cycles in the building industry will continue every 5 to 10 years. Hence managing the cycle will continue to be important.
- The influence of the European Community will increase, and, over 10 to 20 years, more and more functional products will become standardized, providing increasing opportunities for companies with European networks. However, decorative products, building designs, and regional tastes will continue to be diverse. Hence in some businesses, a European position may be beneficial; but not in all.
- There is no reason to suppose that the house building industry in continental Europe will change. This implies a continuing difference between the U.K. industry and the rest of Europe. House building in the United Kingdom is likely to remain a specialist activity.
- There is likely to be a particularly large number of regional and small construction companies for sale due to the age profile of current proprietors, lack of family successors, and complexity of family ownership structures. Many of these companies were started after the war and are nearing the end of the second generation of family management. This may provide an opportunity to buy cheap.
- Many construction companies will continue to lack a profit-driven culture due to the lack of commercial skills of the construction engineers and desire of many owners to bid for prestigious (but often low profit) contracts. GCA's profit consciousness could be used to create value in these businesses.
- Price leadership has existed in many cement markets in the past due to the small number of large competitors in each market. As these competitors seek positions in each other's markets, the price structures are likely to erode. GCA's cement businesses may become less profitable unless a European price leader emerges.

CHOOSING A CORPORATE STRATEGY

The analysis of the four inputs to corporate strategy thinking is now complete. There are many contradictory themes, many loose ends, and many issues about which we might like to know more. However, we can be confident that GCA does not have a strong corporate strategy on which to base its future, and hence there is some urgency to develop a new strategy. Since the past corporate strategy has not been based on any clear value creation insights, it is not possible to draw together the analyses in the form of a historic parenting advantage statement; but it is possible to summarize the current position in a Parenting Opportunity Matrix (Exhibit 13–7).

The housing and construction businesses do not appear to present much value creation potential and, although GCA appears to understand the businesses, it has no special parenting characteristics. The building materials businesses are underperforming and present a value creation opportunity; but GCA does not appear to understand them and may in fact be the cause of the underperformance. Cement is the one business where GCA appears to be a natural owner, but the analysis has not pointed to any major value creation potential.

Parenting Options

By using the prompts described in Exhibit 12–10, we can identify a number of parenting options for GCA. The first prompt (downsize,

EXHIBIT 13–7   Parenting Opportunity Matrix

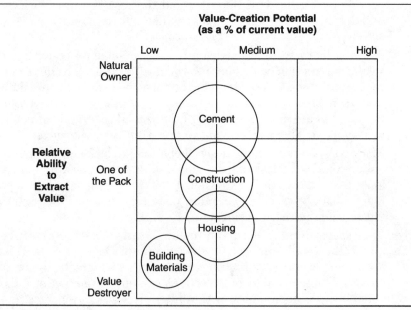

delayer, and decentralize) does not suggest any radical changes to GCA's current parenting approach. GCA has a small center, even including the managers at the cement and building materials division levels. Yet the number of people in some functions suggests room for reductions. For example, the pension work could be subcontracted to outsiders and the internal insurance activity, currently run as a central business, could be handled outside the company. Neither of these two activities are vital to parenting advantage, and since they are liable to distract management attention, one option would be to eliminate them by subcontracting the work.

The second prompt (encourage networking) suggests some changes in the finance and purchasing functions. Currently, the businesses operate largely independent of each other. The exception is the links in the cement businesses. It is possible that some networking between divisions would help in two areas—finance and purchasing. One option could be for the center to encourage more relationships between staff in these two areas.

The third prompt (clarify the dominant process) suggests reviewing the role of the main management processes. Currently, the budget process is dominant. It would be possible, although not necessarily advisable, to design the processes with a strategic plan as the dominant management vehicle.

The fourth prompt (focus on dominant managers) reinforces the importance of the new chief executive. His preferred style of Strategic Control is likely to dominate any future corporate strategy option. Only options that involve a financially oriented Strategic Control style are likely to suit GCA, due to the need to fit with the new chief executive and build on the company's history.

The fifth prompt (redefine division vs. center roles) provides a useful pointer. One area where GCA's current approach needs improvement concerns the duplication in parenting between the cement division and the center, and the building materials division and the center. One parenting option could be to redefine the roles, with the center focusing on financial budgets and the division focusing on strategic issues, or vice versa.

The sixth prompt (build functional skills) also suggests some useful options. In some areas, the parent's staffing and skills are weak. In the future, the parent may need extra resources and people in strategic planning and in financial controllership. There is also the potential to build a team of analysts and economists to monitor the construction cycle and help call the turning points in the cycle. The parent may also need additional management development skills at the center, especially if one of the options is to build a more international business. Finally, GCA does not currently have any corporate development skills. One of the parenting options could be to build skills in acquisitions, divestments, or alliances.

Portfolio Options

GCA's current portfolio does not fit well together. Some change is going to be necessary. The question facing the new chief executive is: How much change? The prompts for generating portfolio options in Exhibit 12–11 provide a useful checklist against which to generate options.

The first prompt (mentally discard misfits) would result in a much reduced portfolio. The building materials businesses are the obvious misfits. Moreover, the construction business could be regarded as a misfit (the risk of large projects), and the housing business is also likely to be a misfit unless the business head is changed.

The second prompt (assume no size constraints) helps to expand options beyond the limits of the existing portfolio. In the cement industry, for example, there are some large international acquisition possibilities. GCA could develop an option of becoming a worldwide cement company by acquiring one of the major European or American companies. It is not clear, however, that this option would create any value.

The third prompt (look for similar critical success factors) reinforces the concern with having housing, cement, and construction in one portfolio. The key factors for success of these three businesses are different. There are only two possible areas of overlap—managing the building cycle and containing overheads. One option is to create a portfolio of companies in the U.K. building industry where containing overheads is important. The parent's role would be to call the cycle based on its broad exposure to the industry and to use its financial control skills to contain overheads.

The fourth prompt (look for linkages) leads to a focus on the European and international dimensions. Both in construction and in cement there appear to be some linkage benefits from having a portfolio of companies in different countries. The rival parent analysis suggests that the benefit of these linkages is small. But the trends analysis suggests that the benefits may be increasing in some areas. Hence this prompt reinforces the option of building an international/European construction or cement company.

The fifth prompt (be guided by scenarios) also produces an interesting option. The trends analysis predicted that many construction companies will be for sale and most of these will not have a profit-oriented culture. Hence, one portfolio option would be to buy construction companies and install in them a profit orientation. GCA's construction business already has this orientation, and the parent would need to develop a way of installing or transferring a profit culture to other companies.

The sixth prompt (try a zero-based approach) surfaces the option of building a large focused cement business. If the new chief executive had not "inherited" businesses in housing and construction, he would be unlikely to buy them. He would be likely to invest surplus cash in cement businesses, or return it to the shareholders.

The seventh prompt (consider demerger or split) once again raises the question of whether cement, housing, and construction should be in the same portfolio. Housing appears to be the odd one out—no international potential because of the unusual U.K. market, and evidence that specialists do well. Moreover, it is a business the new chief executive feels uncomfortable with. Hence, one option is to split the company in three—a housing company, a construction business that could become a parent of a portfolio of construction companies, and a cement business.

Choosing Practical Corporate Strategy Options

The penultimate step in selecting a corporate strategy is to develop some practical options. In GCA's case, let us suppose that management had a clear corporate strategy preference. The preferred portfolio was housing (mainly United Kingdom), construction (Europe), cement (Europe). The preferred parenting approach was to have a financially oriented Strategic Control style, with a corporate center heavily involved in corporate development, broad strategy for each division, and linkages within countries. The division levels would be responsible for financial performance, linkages across countries, and guidance on business strategies. This approach builds on the new chief executive's belief in Europe and on the main businesses in the portfolio. Moreover, the analysis provides some support for this corporate strategy: Construction and cement provide the best opportunity for creating value out of a European strategy; and the preferred parenting approach would fit well with the company's history.

But the preferred strategy also raises concerns. Why keep housing, construction, and cement in the same portfolio? Is it realistic for the center to focus on broad strategy and delegate financial discipline to the division level? Are the linkages across countries large enough to justify paying premiums for businesses? Options need to be generated that expose these concerns. We might suppose that the following three additional options were developed:

1. Focus on businesses in the U.K. building industry that will respond to a financially oriented Strategic Control style. Create a parent company capable of assisting with strategic issues and advising on the turning point in the cycle. Focus financial controls on encouraging delivery against stretching targets and eliminating excessive overheads. Aim to be the best parent in the U.K. building industry.

2. Focus on cement and build an international portfolio of cement businesses. Parent them with a Strategic Control style, involved in managing linkages such as best practice sharing. Create parenting

advantage by having a more aggressive corporate development team, learning how to raise the profitability of new acquisitions faster than competitors, and creating more valuable linkages than competitors.

3. Focus on construction and build a portfolio of regional construction companies mainly in Europe. Parent them with a financially oriented Strategic Control style, involved in guiding them to higher profitability. Create parenting advantage by being better at installing a profit driven-culture and being better at making alliances with or acquiring family-owned companies.

The first option questions the value of a European strategy and implies that the greatest source of value may be knowledge of the U.K. construction cycle. The second and third options question the value of keeping construction, housing, and cement in the same portfolio. They illustrate the opportunities for a company prepared to commit itself to one group of businesses.

Selecting a Corporate Strategy

The purpose of option generation in this case is to challenge the preferred strategy. We might suppose that the options led to heated debate, and that the strategy chosen by management was not their original preferred strategy, but one based on being a good parent to certain kinds of construction businesses in the United Kingdom: a strategy close to the first option.

To illustrate how this might come about, we will put together a strong case for a strategy based on the first option. We will then argue against the originally preferred strategy. The arguments we present are not meant to be based on a deep understanding of the industries concerned: They are not, therefore, useful guidelines for parent companies in these industries. Instead, they illustrate the types of issue that should be discussed when choosing between options.

The case in favor of a strategy based on Option 1 is as follows:

* Many companies in the building industry lose up to 50 percent of their market capitalization during a recession and some companies fail to survive at all. Those that perform best during a recession are companies that avoid investing at the top of the boom. If a parent company could become expert at forecasting the top of the boom, it could create large amounts of value in this industry.
* No parent companies in the U.K. building industry are seeking to create parenting advantage explicitly by becoming expert at managing the construction cycle, and GCA has good reason to believe that it could become expert at this parenting task. Not only does GCA have a leading share in the cement business in the United

Kingdom, which may give it advance warning of the end of a boom, but GCA managers and board members have unusually good connections with the government and may well be able to get a better understanding of the government's real intentions than their competitors. The consumption of cement is a lead indicator of turning points because of its role in building foundations. Also government spending is one of the biggest influences in the industry.

- Because most businesses in the U.K. building industry are run by operating managers, who have worked their way to positions of responsibility due to their operating skills, these businesses often lack strategic skills and analytical capability. A Strategic Control parent can help to provide these missing skills, if it can find a way of influencing business managers. Either by applying these skills to help develop operating plans or by using sophisticated analysis to improve capital expenditure decisions, a Strategic Control parent may be able to add value to the businesses.

- The businesses in GCA's portfolio have few critical success factors in common. As a result, the parent will need to adopt a highly decentralized parenting approach. This will help avoid value destruction. By limiting parenting influence to the use of strategic tools of analysis, such as shareholder value calculations, strategic and financial controls that are negotiated with the businesses, such as overhead levels, and advice on the major turning points in the cycle, GCA ought to be able to add some value, with relatively little danger of destroying value.

The case against the originally preferred strategy (a mix of businesses, with construction and cement developing a European strategy) is as follows:

- GCA appears to be less well placed to exploit the European parenting opportunity than some rival parents. Its European experience and its knowledge of linking businesses across countries is less strong in both cement and construction than that of some direct rivals. It is not clear that GCA would be able to develop parenting characteristics that would give it parenting advantage in this area; hence the implementation risk is high.

- A number of rival parents are also beginning to explore the European option, and it is likely that the price of target acquisitions may well be bid up to unrealistic levels as both experienced and inexperienced companies compete for the opportunities.

- Despite a number of years' experience with a European strategy in the cement division, there is little evidence of the existence of a value creation opportunity. Management believe that there is an opportunity, and the industry trends suggest that the opportunity will increase; but at present there is little unequivocal evidence,

EXHIBIT 13–8   GCA Construction parenting advantage statement

Value Creation Insights	Operating managers in charge of businesses in the construction industries are liable to overinvest, particularly during the growth part of the cycle. Businesses in the construction industries frequently lose most of their net assets in the down cycle of the severe recessions that hit the U.K. industry every 5 to 10 years. This places them in a weak position to take advantage of the ensuing upswing. By "calling" the cycle, a parent company can help its businesses perform better than they would on their own and be in a position to buy assets cheaply during a recession.
	Construction and building industry businesses are normally run by operating managers with excellent hands-on managerial skills, but less strong strategic analysis and evaluation. Value can be created by applying strategic thinking and focus to these businesses, and helping them keep overheads to a minimum.
Distinctive Parenting Characteristics	A uniquely well connected and well informed "cycle monitoring" unit that funds research into the history of past cycles, maintains broad-based government contacts, and develops models of the cycle based on lead indicators and lead sectors, particularly those where the company has a presence, such as cement.
	A tight control process that is a blend of financial control and selected strategic control performance measures. A planning process oriented toward identifying and targeting strategic measures of performance:
	• Intensive strategy reviews to identify measures of performance.
	• Annual "strategic budget" to generate performance targets.
	• Particular focus on overhead levels.
	A challenging capital approval process that links capital expenditures to strategic performance measures and has a bias to risk aversion, particularly 3 or 4 years into an upswing.
Heartland Businesses	Businesses in the U.K. building industry that can be parented with a Strategic Control style and do not require international positions to sustain competitiveness (where there are no obvious international economies of scale or technology advantages).

and the opportunity may turn out to be worth less than has been predicted.

On balance, therefore, the corporate strategy of focusing on the U.K. construction industry could be the best option. It offers a better chance of GCA achieving parenting advantage. In fact, GCA may become the only parent pursuing this particular opportunity. It is, however, risky, because it is not certain that the parent can become expert at calling the cycle in a way that substantially improves the value of the businesses. If this source of value creation cannot be exploited, the other parenting activities—stressing a strategic approach to planning, budgeting and capital approval—are unlikely to be sufficient, on their own, to justify the group. The businesses in the proposed portfolio will have sufficiently different critical success factors that the benefits of good strategic control may be outweighed by the lack of feel that the parent will have for some of the businesses. Nevertheless, the chances of achieving parenting advantage under this option are higher than for the other options.

The reason GCA management would have found it difficult to accept this option is that it conflicts with one of the chief executive's personal ambitions—to build an international, particularly a European, business. Since this is a fictitious example, we can suppose that the chief executive was able to put aside this personal ambition as a result of the strong arguments in favor of a U.K.-oriented strategy. In most real situations, we find chief executives are less flexible and more committed to a particular vision.

SUMMARY

Exhibit 13–8 summarizes GCA's chosen corporate strategy in a parenting advantage statement. To implement the strategy, GCA will need to make major changes to its parenting approach and some changes to its portfolio. The following chapters on portfolio decisions and parenting decisions will explain how these decisions can be made. We will not, however, return directly to the GCA example. Instead, we will draw on a wider range of illustrations.

NOTES

1. See David Young and Michael Goold, *Effective Headquarters Staff*, London: Ashridge Strategic Management Centre, 1993 for comparative figures for similar companies.

14 DECISIONS ABOUT THE PORTFOLIO

In Chapter 12, we argued that companies should produce a parenting advantage statement to describe and communicate their future corporate strategies. This chapter helps managers turn the prospective parenting advantage statement into an implementation plan covering decisions about which business units to have as part of the portfolio. Decisions need to be made concerning what to sell, what to buy, what new ventures to launch, and what alliances to have. Each current or potential new business needs to be reviewed so that a decision can be made.

Using the prospective parenting advantage statement, we have found it useful to classify businesses into five types—heartland, edge of heartland, ballast, alien territory, and value trap, as shown on the Parenting Fit Matrix in Exhibit 14–1. The classification can be made by asking two questions:

- Do the parenting opportunities in the business *fit* with value creation insights in the prospective parenting advantage statement: Will the parent be likely to create a substantial amount of value?
- Do the critical success factors in the business have any obvious *misfit* with the prospective parenting characteristics: Will the parent be likely to influence the businesses in ways that will destroy value?

For businesses currently in the portfolio, an assessment of parenting opportunities will have been carried out as part of the analysis of each business.[1] For potential new businesses, a similar analysis is needed. Assessing the fit between the parenting opportunities and the proposed value creation insights has two parts to it: Will the parent's value creation insights address parenting opportunities in the businesses; and

340

EXHIBIT 14–1   Parenting Fit Matrix

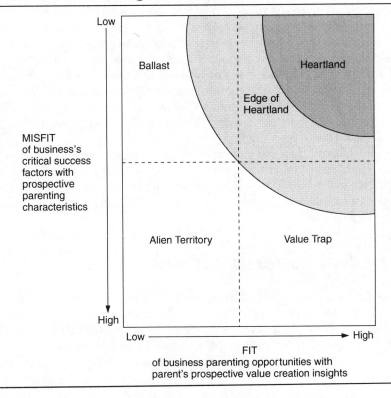

will they address the most important opportunities? The answers will fall on a scale running from high fit, where the value creation insights fit with the most important opportunities, to low fit, where the value creation insights are not focused on any of the important opportunities. If the value creation insights address all the important opportunities, there is no room for a rival parent to develop superior value creation insights. Where the value creation insights have only partial fit with the opportunities, it is possible, although not certain, that rival parents may have better insights.[2]

The second question—the misfit question—requires sufficient knowledge of the critical success factors in the businesses to be able to compare them with the prospective parenting characteristics. For businesses currently in the portfolio, the analysis of critical success factors will already have been completed. The fit assessments will, however, need to take account of planned changes in the parenting characteristics that are part of the corporate strategy. For potential new businesses, a similar analysis is again needed.

Misfit can occur for many reasons. The most usual cause of misfit is the parent's lack of "feel" for a business. Because the parent does not understand the critical success factors in the business, it inadvertently influences the business in ways that destroy value. The best way to assess likely misfits under the new corporate strategy is to list the prospective parenting characteristics and review them against each business's critical success factors. There are nearly always some parenting characteristics that will constrain or influence each business in ways that may be value destroying. The assessment is about the impact of these negative influences. Will they be likely to damage or hold back the business significantly? Or will they be minor irritants that will be more than offset by value that the parent creates? There is, therefore, a scale running from low misfit to high misfit.

Businesses that the parent does not understand well enough to judge the areas of misfit or the likely impact of misfit should be categorized as having high misfit. The parent's inability to make a judgment displays a lack of feel for the business that will almost certainly result in value destruction.

DIFFERENT BUSINESS CATEGORIES

Once the analysis of both dimensions of the matrix in Exhibit 14–1 is complete—the degree of fit between the improvement opportunities and the value creation insights and the degree of misfit between the critical success factors and the prospective parenting characteristics—current and potential new businesses can be classified into different categories.

Heartland Businesses

Businesses that fall in the top right hand corner of the matrix should be the main focus of the company's parenting. They are the prospective *heartland* of the corporate strategy: businesses where the parenting opportunity fits the value creation insights and where the net impact of the parent will be highly positive. Successful companies build portfolios in which the large majority of businesses fall within the heartland. These businesses should have priority in the company's future portfolio development.[3] The prospective heartland will consist mainly of businesses that the company already owns, but it will also include some target businesses that the company wishes to enter.

In companies where the future corporate strategy does not call for major changes in parenting characteristics, the parent can move forward in its heartland businesses with some confidence. In companies where the corporate strategy requires new distinctive parenting characteristics to be built up, or changes in current characteristics that misfit with some of the heartland businesses, there is less certainty that value will be created. The success of the new corporate strategy will depend on the extent to which the required new parenting characteristics can be established. In such situations, it is appropriate to move forward more cautiously until it has become clear that the planned changes are working out well. We return to this topic in Chapter 15.

Edge-of-Heartland Businesses

The heartland criteria lay out what sorts of businesses are most suitable for the parent's portfolio. However, they are never fully precise. Furthermore, some criteria cite characteristics that are preferable rather than essential: Cooper prefers businesses where individual customers do not have high bargaining power, but was willing to acquire Champion, which has substantial sales to the automobile manufacturers, since it met Cooper's other heartland criteria. There is therefore a grey area around the edge of the heartland: Businesses that in some respects fit well, but in others do not.

Decisions about businesses at the edge of the heartland are more difficult. For businesses already within the portfolio, a careful watch to determine whether net value is being created is necessary, with an understanding that modifications to the parenting approach may be needed to improve value creation. Potential new businesses require a cautious attitude that recognizes that entry to the business should be regarded as something of an experiment, which may not turn out well. Many less successful parents persuade themselves to continue with unsuitable businesses at the edge of the heartland for too long before acknowledging that they do not fit. However, some experiments to test the boundaries around the heartland and to learn to parent new businesses are certainly justified.

The right attitude to businesses at the edge of the heartland therefore balances realistic caution with sensible experimentation. On the one hand, caution argues for avoiding any business that does not fit at least the majority of the heartland criteria. On the other hand, too strict a limitation of the portfolio to tried, tested, and familiar businesses may miss opportunities for significant value creation and, ultimately, stultify corporate development.

Ballast Businesses

The planned portfolio should be largely composed of heartland businesses. However, the portfolio may also contain businesses in other areas of the Parenting Fit Matrix. It may, for example, include some *ballast* businesses. These are businesses in which there are no significant improvement opportunities or in which the opportunities do not fit the parent's prospective value creation insights. However, there are no obvious misfits. This situation often occurs when the parent has a feel for the business, either because it has owned the business for many years or individual parent managers have previously worked in the business. The parent may have previously added value, but there are now no further parenting opportunities that fit the corporate strategy. Most companies own a number of ballast businesses.

The instinct of most managers is to hold onto these familiar businesses. The parent knows them well and they have often been part of the portfolio for many years. But particular caution needs to be taken, because ballast businesses can slow down the progress of the parent, and sometimes they draw the parent into destroying rather than creating value. By definition, the potential to create value in these businesses is limited, due to the lack of parenting opportunities that fit the value creation insights. Hence, the time parent managers spend with these businesses is likely to be less productive than the time they spend with heartland businesses. If the time of parent managers is a scarce resource, as it normally is, ballast businesses have an opportunity cost to the parent and slow down the rate of value creation. In some situations, ballast can be a stabilizing factor, providing steady cash flow or profitability while the parent develops its prospective heartland. More normally, however, ballast businesses are a drag on performance. With ballast businesses, there is also a danger that changes in the business's characteristics or the parent's approach will increase the level of misfit, leading to serious value destruction. Consequently, disposal should be considered.

Sometimes, a strong case can nevertheless be made for retaining some ballast businesses as part of the portfolio, either because there are no clearly superior rival parents, or because there are tax disadvantages or other reasons against disposing of the business. As one planning director explained, "While selling these businesses may be technically

---

EXHIBIT 14–2 Points of guidance on ballast businesses

1. *Consider Disposal.* A ballast business may well be worth more to others, if rivals can add more value to it. It also takes up scarce parental resources that might create more value in other uses.

2. *Identify Barriers.* There may be tax issues that count against sale, or there may be a negative impact on the corporate culture if long-standing members of the corporate family are sold. But be sure to make an honest and balanced assessment of the attractions of disposal as against these barriers.

3. *Reduce Parenting.* To avoid potential value destruction, it may make sense for the parent to have a less close, and less costly, involvement with ballast businesses. Consider bringing in external partners or shareholders.

4. *Monitor Changes.* Be careful to monitor any changes that may increase parenting misfit with the business and lead to value destruction. Ballast businesses can easily become alien territory.

5. *Sell in Good Times.* Waiting to sell until the business is not performing well will be sure to depress the value that is received.

correct, it would be a very dramatic and dangerous move for us. Management loyalty and commitment is built from the family feeling of the company, and such moves would be highly disruptive." If the net impact of selling a ballast business is likely to be negative, it should be retained.

The challenges for ballast businesses are to minimize the drag effect on the rest of the portfolio and to empower the business to resist any parenting influences that may destroy value. One way to achieve both these objectives and cash in on some of the existing value is to bring in some external shareholders through a joint venture, placing of shares, or partial stock market flotation. Another solution is to reduce the parenting influence by focusing only on the minimum parenting tasks.

Frequently, managers hold onto ballast businesses for emotional reasons. They justify continued ownership by arguing, "It is foolish to sell businesses that are performing well." Our view is that the best time to sell a ballast business is when it is performing well. Any alternative view means that these businesses will only be sold when they are performing badly, at which stage they will realize a much lower price.

Ballast businesses need to be examined carefully. While there may be a place for some ballast businesses in the portfolio, there is often a temptation to be insufficiently tough-minded and objective about them. Exhibit 14–2 summarizes points of guidance on ballast businesses.

Value Trap Businesses

Value trap businesses are where parents often make their greatest mistakes. These are businesses that the parent judges as having a fit with its value creation strategy but which also have a serious misfit with some elements of the planned parenting characteristics. We have called these businesses value traps because, on the surface, they may look attractive and appear to fit the strategy, but on closer inspection, it emerges that there are important areas of misfit with the parent. As a result, net value creation will probably be negative, and rival parents that avoid the parenting misfits are likely to create more value from these businesses. We discuss a particular type of value trap business, in which the parent has linkage fit but stand-alone misfit with the business, later in this chapter.

Value traps should be avoided, unless the parent can learn, over time, to reduce or eliminate the misfits. The focus of learning needs to be on acquiring a sufficient feel for the business to avoid value destruction that more than wipes out the benefits that the parent can bring. Sometimes, the changes in parenting needed are compatible with the ways in which the heartland businesses are parented, and the value trap may eventually be integrated into an extended heartland. If, however, the changes needed conflict with established ways of parenting the heartland businesses, it will be difficult to make such changes successfully unless the value trap business is clearly separated from the rest of the portfolio.[4] We will discuss this possibility further under the heading of platform businesses.

Alien Territory Businesses

Businesses that do not fit with the prospective corporate strategy are part of *alien territory:* The parent's value creation insights are not applicable and its parenting characteristics misfit with the businesses. These businesses are alien because they need a parent with a radically different corporate strategy. For example, a business like ladies hosiery that is becoming more international and which increasingly requires global manufacturing volumes is alien to a parent like BTR that focuses primarily on improving profitability and margins. As a result, BTR sold its hosiery business to Sara Lee. Businesses that are in unfamiliar markets or technologies may also be alien. RTZ now considers any business outside mining and minerals to be part of its alien territory. Hanson avoids high-technology businesses. Alien businesses in the portfolio should almost always be earmarked for sale, and care should be taken to avoid entering new alien businesses.

Platform Businesses

It is possible that some businesses that are outside the heartland may be retained as *platforms* for a changed corporate strategy in the future. A platform business has characteristics that mean it will not respond well to the main thrusts of the company's planned corporate strategy. However, the parent may see some opportunities for value creation in the business, if it is treated differently from other businesses in the portfolio. As such, it represents an experiment with a different sort of parenting, which, if successful, may eventually lead to changing the corporate strategy. As a result, the platform businesses may, in due course, be included in a new heartland under a changed corporate strategy.

Some value traps may be retained as platform businesses, with the intention of treating them differently enough to suspend or alter the parenting characteristics that would otherwise lead to misfits. The synchro reader, as described in Chapter 10, may have been a value trap for Canon. However, Canon treated it as a platform for learning about unfamiliar office product markets and as an entrée to new technologies. In due course, it became the basis for a major extension of Canon's heartland into office equipment businesses. Some ballast or alien territory businesses may also be treated as platforms, if the parent wishes to try out new value creation insights that differ from those that apply in the heartland. When Grand Metropolitan's main emphasis was on bringing about operating improvements in its businesses, IDV could not have been regarded as falling within its heartland. However, IDV was treated differently from other businesses in the portfolio, which allowed Grand Met to experiment with parenting a business in which international branding was the key to success, and in which there was the opportunity for a parent to make a different sort of value creation contribution. Now IDV has been integrated into the mainstream of Grand Met's parenting and corporate strategy.[5] With alien businesses that are treated as platforms for a new corporate strategy, the risks of failure are higher than with ballast or value trap businesses.

At the launch of a new corporate strategy, it is somewhat unlikely that managers will want to retain any business in the portfolio as an experiment that could lead to changing the corporate strategy that has just been selected. However, as the corporate strategy matures, the parent may want to include some platform businesses, as part of a search for a new strategy. When a particular corporate strategy is maturing (the value creation potential is diminishing and the heartland is declining in size), a new corporate strategy that changes or extends the heartland may be needed.

To be successful, however, platform businesses need to be chosen with care and treated differently in order to maximize the chances of success. Exhibit 14–3 gives some points of guidance for managers who are considering platforms.

EXHIBIT 14–3   Points of guidance on platform businesses

1. *Avoid strong rivals.* A platform for one company may be a heartland business for an established rival parent. Look for businesses where there are few, strong, established rivals.

2. *Focus on Large Potential.* Platforms are difficult to parent and involve much learning by the parent. They are also a distraction from the current strategy. Unless the business is a platform that has the potential for a major extension or change in corporate strategy, it is not worth the effort.

3. *Start small.* Do the learning when the mistakes are inexpensive.

4. *Only One Platform at a Time* (At Least Only One in Each Division). If the potential is large and the learning needed is great, it is best to focus rather than fragment. Avoid a scatter approach.

5. *Isolate the Platform.* The objective is to change the parenting approach. It is hard to do this within the existing parenting structure.*

6. *Identify a Board-Level Sponsor.* If the diversification really has the potential to change the corporate strategy, it must have high-level visibility. If not, it is better to avoid the distraction.*

7. *Be Ready to Exit If Necessary.* Companies are not always honest with themselves about whether they are succeeding with platform businesses. It is important to be willing to recognize when a platform has failed and to exit in a timely manner.

See Chapter 15 for further discussion.

Divestment Candidates

There may be good reasons for retaining some edge-of-heartland, ballast, and platform businesses. Moreover, there may sometimes be difficulties in divesting value trap and alien businesses, if, for example, they operate under a common corporate brand or serve customers with which the parent's heartland businesses have important relationships. Nevertheless, the majority of businesses outside the prospective heartland should be identified as divestment candidates, since they will not represent opportunities for high value creation and parenting advantage.

Many parents are daunted by the idea of divesting large, established businesses. They feel that it is an admission of failure to withdraw from these businesses and will be badly received by most, if not all, of the companies' stakeholders. We believe, on the contrary, that decisions to divest nonheartland businesses are sound in most circumstances. We accept that stability and continuity in a company's portfolio has some value, both in communicating with shareholders and in retaining the loyalty and enthusiasm of business managers. There may also be practical barriers to divestment. We do not advocate frequent and extensive churning of the portfolio. But we do believe that, at the outset of a new corporate strategy, there is often a need for some major shifts in the composition of the portfolio. Furthermore, such changes are usually well received, both by investors and by management, provided that their justification is clearly explained and the new corporate strategy is convincing.[6]

Companies that have put off major changes in their portfolios due to concern about adverse reactions have frequently been surprised by how positively they have eventually been received. TI is now much better regarded in financial circles and has a far more motivated management cadre than in the mid-1980s, despite having changed over 80 percent of its portfolio. At the time of writing, the value of divesting inappropriate businesses was underlined with the announcement by British Aerospace of the sale of its car manufacturing business, Rover. In the week following the announcement, British Aerospace's market capitalization rose by nearly 25 percent. Markets also responded positively to the 1992 announcement by Sears, Roebuck that it would spin off or divest most of its financial service activities, and to Kodak's 1993 decision to spin off Eastman Chemical.

There are a variety of exit routes for businesses that have been earmarked for disposal. These range from sale to another parent, to a management buyout, to a separate flotation. It may also be worthwhile to consider a partial sale or flotation, though this should normally be seen as the first step in a phased withdrawal. The choice of divestment strategy is an important part of the implementation plan.

While the right divestment strategy will depend on the circumstances of each business, there are risks attached to delays. While the business is for sale, there may be problems of management motivation, since the managers in the business will know that they do not fit the portfolio. Moreover, the parenting relationship may destroy value during the period of the delay, decreasing the business's worth to a new owner.

Yet immediate sale may not be the best decision. As described in Chapter 9, Hanson has been one of the most active divesters of businesses, often creating as much value in divestment as in other aspects of the company's parenting. The timing of divestments is an important part of Hanson's skill. It can take 3 or 4 years after an acquisition to sell all the businesses Hanson does not want to keep. Some of this has to do with sequencing the workload, but part is related to timing. It is best to sell a business when the sector's price-to-earnings ratio is high, and when there are at least two eager buyers. In these circumstances, the parent can often get a price that is much higher than the business is worth to it. On occasions, it may be necessary to hold on to a business for a few years while looking for a suitable buyer. During this holding period, it is important to separate the business from the mainstream of the company's parenting activity, not only to avoid giving it inappropriate parenting influence, but also to avoid distracting the parent's management time from more valuable activities.

TYPICAL PORTFOLIO ISSUES

As managers make decisions about how to classify businesses and what implementation strategy to apply to each business, they frequently face some of the following issues.

Businesses That Need Redefining to Fit the Corporate Strategy

Some businesses need to be redefined or repositioned before a suitable portfolio decision can be taken. The business as currently defined may consist of a number of separate profit centers that need to be broken out and set up as separate units. Alternatively, the business may be too narrowly focused to be an effective competitor and may need to be combined with another unit in the portfolio or added to through acquisition.[7] While the business redefinition phase is often completed in a matter of months, it can take a year or longer to review the business's positioning and implement the appropriate restructuring or amalgamation. It is only after the business has been redefined that decisions can be made about whether to keep it in the portfolio.

Sometimes the parent may need to carry out repositioning and re-definition work on businesses it has earmarked for disposal. The restructured business may be more attractive to potential buyers than it would otherwise be. In these situations, a judgment needs to be made about the opportunity cost involved. Top management time spent on businesses earmarked for disposal distracts attention from other parenting tasks. Moreover, specialist restructurers like Hanson, some venture capital funds, and some investment banks may be prepared to acquire the business in order to restructure it and sell the pieces on to suitable parents. Unless the current parent is an experienced restructurer, it may be better to allocate its parenting time to other activities.

Businesses with Linkage Fit and Stand-Alone Misfit

A common value trap business is one that has linkages with businesses in the prospective heartland but has critical success factors that are different from those of heartland businesses. The parent can see the opportunity to create value through linkages but may not recognize the extent of the potential misfit in other areas of parenting. With these linkage fit and stand-alone misfit businesses, the parent should first look to see if the linkage benefits can be created without ownership, through a trading relationship or an alliance. If the company is a bad stand-alone parent, it will only be in exceptional circumstances that linkage influences create sufficient offsetting value. Moreover, rival parents are usually better placed to offer appropriate stand-alone parenting. If the company can find a way of releasing the linkage benefits without taking ownership of the business, it can work with a suitable rival parent to produce more value in total.[8]

If the business is retained, it should be treated as a platform, with the intention of learning enough about the business in due course to develop a sufficient feel for it, and to adjust the parenting characteristics to accommodate it in the portfolio. If successful, it will have extended the heartland. If not, it should be earmarked for disposal.

The difficulty of judging linkage fit and stand-alone misfit businesses is particularly acute when the new business is a venture based on the operating skills of heartland businesses. For example, many utility companies in Europe are diversifying away from their regulated water, electricity, and gas origins by setting up engineering and construction consultancies. These new advisory businesses are based on the engineering, construction, and project management skills in the original businesses. In other words, there is a strong skill linkage. However, consultancy businesses have very different critical success factors from utilities. Hence, it is likely that the parent will have a misfit in stand-alone parenting. It is essential that the likelihood of stand-alone misfit is recognized, if these companies are to avoid destroying value. To encourage learning that will improve stand-alone parenting, these diversifications need to be treated as platform businesses.

Declining Heartlands

A strategy based on a heartland that is declining in size poses another set of concerns and problems for management. Few companies are prepared even to contemplate such a strategy. But in some situations, the skills of the parent managers are so specialized that focusing on an existing heartland, even though the heartland may be in decline, is the only way to maximize parenting advantage. For example, many of the tobacco companies attempted to diversify, only to find that their parenting skills were not well suited to the businesses they tried. As a result, many of these companies have fallen into the hands of restructurers, leveraged buyout partnerships, and Financial Control companies: RJR Nabisco became KKR's most famous leveraged buyout and Imperial Group was one of Hanson's most successful acquisitions. These companies would have been better advised to have stuck to a portfolio of tobacco businesses. Even those tobacco companies that have diversified with greater success, such as Philip Morris and BAT, have found the process difficult and have probably destroyed value to achieve their diversifications.[9]

One model of parenting a heartland in decline is that of Crown Cork & Seal. Spotted in the 1960s as a Harvard Business School case study, the company was a small manufacturer of cans and bottle tops. Although Crown Cork & Seal could see the decline of its heartland in the face of new types of packaging, it did not follow the diversification efforts of its competitors. Instead it focused on its existing portfolio of businesses, adding others in the same canning heartland and using any spare cash to buy back shares. Its competitors found their diversifications hard to manage and each went through more than one crisis. By the end of the 1980s, the competitors had divested their canning operations. As an acquirer of one of these canning operations, Crown Cork & Seal completed an unbroken run of regular increases in earnings per share and emerged as the United States' largest canning company. As Crown Cork & Seal demonstrates, it may be better to stick to a declining heartland than to venture into territory where the company is at a parenting disadvantage.

Yet there are successes. Grand Metropolitan and other companies that have succeeded in shifting away from a declining heartland have, however, usually been able to build on parts of the portfolio and groups of managers that could form the basis of the new corporate strategy. Moving away from a heartland in decline is most successful when the seeds of the new heartland already exist within the company.

Multiple Heartlands

We have been at pains to point out in this book that successful companies tend to apply value creation insights that are similar across all the businesses in the portfolio. In other words, in terms of parenting opportunities and needs, successful companies have only one type of business in their heartlands. Some companies, however, discover that they own two or more different types of business: Each has its own separate value creation opportunities and critical success factors, and requires a parent with different parenting characteristics. Each type of business represents an essentially different heartland.

Our advice for managers in this situation is clear: Choose one of the heartlands to focus on and dispose of the others through sale or de-merger. Retaining multiple heartlands in one portfolio leads to compromises and inappropriate influences. Managers from companies such as Courtaulds, which have demerged to address this issue, are virtually always enthusiastic about the benefits that have come from separation. "We did not realize how much our culture was being compromised by efforts to work together with the other businesses," explained one manager. "Now we have de-merged, there is a new enthusiasm and energy and we are developing a very distinct culture."

On occasions, a company may decide to retain two different heartlands, because it views the second heartland as a means of hedging the company's bets and spreading its risks. Such a decision should be strongly challenged. In most cases, it weakens the company and increases, rather than reduces, risk, because it provides a target for corporate raiders.

SUMMARY

The parenting advantage statement provides the starting point for decisions about which businesses to include in the portfolio. Businesses that fit the heartland criteria should be the prime focus of the portfolio.

Companies may decide to retain some businesses in their portfolios that fall outside the heartland. They may have ballast businesses that continue to be worth more to the company than to other rivals. They may have platform businesses that are part of an ongoing dynamic to extend or change the heartland and the corporate strategy. But companies with large and growing heartlands should concentrate their efforts on the heartland businesses, where their chances of creating value are likely to be the best.

NOTES

1. See Chapter 12.

2. In selecting the new corporate strategy, the likelihood of being able to build distinctive parenting characteristics that allow the value creation insights to be effectively implemented will have been taken into account. The assumption in making these classifications is that the new strategy will be successful and that the required distinctive parenting characteristics will be developed. We shall discuss the implementation of the new corporate strategy in terms of the decisions that need to be made concerning the parenting approach in Chapter 15.

3. It is possible that some businesses that can be categorized as heartland should nevertheless be earmarked for disposal. This will be the case if it is judged that the business is better suited to another rival parent, which has more powerful value creation insights or more appropriate parenting characteristics.

4. Chapters 10 and 15 provide fuller discussions of whether and how parents can learn to change their characteristics.

5. See Chapter 10.

6. See, for example, Gordon Alexander, George Benson, and Joan Kampmeyer, "Investigating the Valuation Effects of Announcements of Voluntary Corporate Selloffs," *The Journal of Finance,* vol. XXXIX, no. 2, June 1984; and Prem Jain, "The Effect of Voluntary Sell-off Announcements on Shareholder Wealth," *The Journal of Finance,* vol. XL, no. 1, March 1985. See, also, the discussion of restructuring in Chapter 4.

7. See Chapter 9 and Appendix A for further discussion.

8. See Appendix D for further discussion.

9. Philip Morris's famed rejuvenation of Miller Beer has been argued to have cost more than the value created. Philip Morris's acquisition of General Foods was also widely viewed as unsuccessful until it was rescued by the acquisition of Kraft. BAT's diversifications have all had problems, and the company was under threat of being broken up in the mid-1980s when challenged by Sir James Goldsmith.

15 DECISIONS ABOUT THE PARENT

Implementing a new corporate strategy will nearly always involve making some changes to the parenting approach. The purpose of these changes is to improve the parent's ability to create value, either by developing parenting characteristics that better match the businesses in the portfolio, or by eliminating parenting characteristics that are destroying value. Many types of change are possible. One company may need to increase decentralization, strengthen its budgeting and planning processes, and find ways of encouraging linkages between autonomous units. Another company may be building expertise in its central technical function, raising the quality of technical debate among senior parent managers, and developing tools for analyzing technical issues. The broad changes needed will follow from the parenting advantage statement. This chapter is about converting these broad directions of change into specific decisions about the parenting approach.

We have found that corporate managements often underestimate the difficulty of making changes to the parenting approach. "If we need to change the way we are managing these businesses," they argue, "We must knuckle down and make it happen. We are all experienced professional managers. Once we have defined what needs to be done, we can make it happen." Our experience has led us to a different conclusion. We have noted that, in most cases, it is easier to restructure the portfolio to bring it into line with the prevailing parenting approach than to change the parenting approach to fit the needs of the portfolio. So we will open this chapter with a discussion of why changes to the parenting approach are hard to make. We will then examine three situations that are typical of the changes many parents make. The third section will address some guiding principles that managers can use when changing their parenting approach. The final section of the chapter will examine how companies learn to parent new businesses.

WHY CHANGES ARE HARD

Companies can and do change their parenting approach. Among the companies in our research, we have noted major changes during the past 10 years at Grand Metropolitan and TI. Also, we noted that ASEA made major changes to the way Brown Boveri's businesses were parented when the two companies were merged as ABB. In these cases, a new parenting approach was brought about by making wholesale changes to the managers in the parents and, in many cases, also to the managers in the business units. There is no question that a fresh parenting team can dramatically shift the whole parenting approach. We are not arguing that change is impossible. But, as a result of long years of research and consulting, we are all too aware of the difficulties that get in the way of change and that make it hard to achieve a desired impact.

The first reason making change hard is the importance of the mental maps in the heads of parent managers. Some parts of these mental maps are deeply embedded, reinforced by personality traits, values, and years of experience. Others are less deeply held and hence more easily changed. Unfortunately, it is often hard to know which parts are deeply embedded until an effort is made to make changes that conflict with the mental maps.

The process of reviewing the corporate strategy and developing the parenting advantage statement is one way of changing the mental maps of parent managers; but this will only change the less deeply held parts of the map. If the parent managers' mental maps are central to the parenting approach, and if some parts of these maps are deeply embedded and difficult to change, it is not surprising that it is hard to identify what to do to achieve a desired change in parenting.

A possible solution is to change the parent managers. But managers with the right mental maps and skills may not be available. One company, in the middle of a radical change in its parenting approach as a result of a new chief executive and the removal of most of the existing senior management team, was trying to recruit a chief operating officer with the following qualities:

- Business experience of two areas of the portfolio for which the new chief executive did not have a good feel.
- Strong operational control skills to help improve the parent's financial and strategic control processes.
- Experience of radically pruning overheads so that the chief executive's value creation insight (that most of his businesses had excessive overheads) could be speedily implemented.

After a long search process, one candidate with most of the requirements did consider the job, but could not be persuaded to join the company. The chief executive ended up having to rely on his own skills to implement the first and third tasks, and recruited an exconsultant with relevant business experience to improve his control systems and strengthen his strategic dialogue with the businesses. It was not possible, despite nearly a year's search, to find the right person to implement the planned parenting approach.

The second reason changes in the parenting approach are hard to orchestrate is that much of the value is created through relationships. It is the relationship between the chief executive officer and the business head that causes the business head to make valuable changes to the business's strategy. It is the relationships between the central purchasing manager and the business purchasing managers that make it possible to create value by coordinating purchasing. It is the relationships between the marketing managers in the businesses that cause them to share knowledge about customer contacts and product positioning. The relationships are often strengthened because there is a parenting opportunity, because the manager in the business can see some value from the relationship, but they do not exist *only* because of the parenting opportunity. They exist because the managers involved have taken time to learn how to get the best from each other, how to influence each other, and how far to trust each other.

When changes are made to the parenting approach, and particularly when new managers join the parent or the businesses, old relationships are broken and new relationships have to form. Often these new relationships do not develop in the way planned. For example, one parent company hired some additional planning staff to improve their planning discussions with the businesses. Early in the relationship, the business managers were offended by the attitude of the planning managers. As a result, the planning meetings became "hide and seek" sessions with the business managers deliberately smoothing away the main issues and fending off the parent managers. The result was value destruction: wasted time and expense, with no compensating benefits.

Relationships are fragile and unpredictable. They are essential to effective parenting, but they cannot be created by management fiat. Good relationships should be prized and preserved. Bad relationships should be recognized, but are difficult to rectify. Working on the decentralization contract helps to clarify roles and build relationships. But, in the end, relationships remain unpredictable, are subject to the human factor, and take time to change.

The third reason it is hard to change the parenting approach is that parenting characteristics are often interlocking and mutually reinforcing. For example, in one company it was clear that a tighter approach by the parent to short-term profitability control would be preferable for some of its businesses. However, such a change was difficult to bring about. The company's parenting characteristics reinforced each other and fitted well together (Exhibit 15–1). Its organization structure allowed and encouraged strong staff groups, at the center and in the businesses, to participate in and contribute to the decision process. Decisions were only reached after extensive discussion and review. Managers throughout the company expected to be consulted on decisions, and felt that it was their right and responsibility to bring to bear their particular knowledge and expertise. In these circumstances, it is hard to hold individual managers tightly accountable for results, since responsibility for decisions is effectively shared. A more flexible, long-term approach to control fits much better with the nature of the organization, the decision process, and the people in the company. To modify the control process for some businesses would have required consequential change in several other important aspects of parenting. It was by no means clear that these consequential changes could have been brought about without serious knock-on effects, particularly since the desired changes in control were only needed for a few of the company's businesses.

A fourth reason changes are hard is that parenting performance is difficult to measure. It is never easy to disentangle the contributions of the parent from the contributions of the business. Poor performance could be caused by the business itself or by the parent. Furthermore, the corporate hierarchy may prevent open criticism from reaching senior management in the parent. The damage brought about by the parent is much more often a subject for corridor gossip than open debate, and habits of deference may even suppress recognition of it within the business. In one company, a business's planning manager told us that, despite serious misgivings, his business had gone along with suggestions from the parent without dissent because "we thought they must know something we didn't." The parent, which had recently acquired the business, was a leading multinational with a fine reputation, and the business

EXHIBIT 15–1   Fit between parenting characteristics for a Strategic Planning company

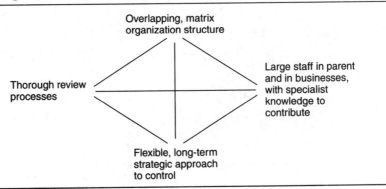

Overlapping, matrix organization structure

Large staff in parent and in businesses, with specialist knowledge to contribute

Thorough review processes

Flexible, long-term strategic approach to control

managers were too much in awe of the parent to voice their reservations—despite the fact that the parent had no previous experience in the business. Without clear performance measures and open discussion of the parent's performance, it is hard to know whether particular parenting characteristics are making a positive contribution or not.

We have dwelt on the reasons why changes in parenting approach are hard because we believe they provide an important context within which the rest of this chapter should be set. The reasons relate partly to the difficulty of deciding what to change to achieve a desired effect, and partly to the problems of making the change happen. We have seen many situations where the planned change never happened because the people involved were too locked into a previous way of operating, where the change produced an outcome quite different from the one desired, and where the change was seemingly successful but had little real impact on the influence felt by the businesses. We have also seen successful changes, where both major and minor improvements have been made to the parenting approach to make it fit better with the proposed corporate strategy.

EXAMPLES OF SUCCESSFUL CHANGE

In this section, we shall discuss some examples of typical changes facing many parent companies. Change is best understood by examining each of the five types of parenting characteristic (Exhibit 15–2)—mental maps; structures, systems, and processes; functions, central services, and resources; people and skills; and decentralization contracts. Effective change comes from thinking through the decisions that are needed in each of these five types of parenting characteristic.

EXHIBIT 15–2   The five types of parenting characteristics

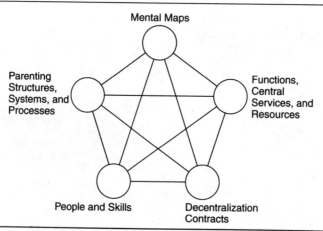

As we have pointed out, taking action that directly impacts the mental maps of parent managers is not easy. Rather, mental maps are influenced by taking action on the other four types of parenting characteristic. As we describe the examples, we will describe the impact on mental maps in the context of the other four types of parenting characteristic.

Developing New Parenting Skills

In some situations, a new chief executive or some new members of the parenting team believe that it is possible to improve substantially the amount of value the parent company is creating. These situations involve developing new parenting skills to exploit fully the existing value creation opportunities. The emphasis is on making the parent company more effective at implementing an existing corporate strategy.

In one company, this occurred as a result of the appointment of a new chief executive. He was comfortable with most of the businesses in the portfolio and with the Strategic Control parenting style. He was also generally comfortable with the historical corporate strategy. The company's heartland was food manufacturing and branding, particularly in international products such as snack foods, pasta, and cooking ingredients. The value creation strategy had two parts to it. First, the parent's knowledge of these products enabled it to squeeze extra performance out of businesses that would have been satisfied with less as independent companies. Second, the parent helped expand the products internationally. Historically, the parent's distinctive characteristics had been a dominant chief executive, the company's founder; an autocratic management style; highly informal decision-making processes; and a lean headquarters. The knowledge and experience of the founder and the relationships of loyalty he had created provided most of the added value by the parent.

The new chief executive recognized that the parenting approach would need to change after the founder's retirement. He wanted to make the parenting added value less dependent on one individual. He also felt he could further enhance the performance of the businesses by encouraging the business managers to take more responsibility for the strategy of their businesses and by creating a transfer of best practice between similar businesses in different countries. He therefore set about making the following changes:

- *Structure, Systems, and Processes.* Previously, the company had three geographic divisions—a U.S. division, a U.K. division, and an International division. To encourage cross-border linkages between businesses in the same product category, the company was restructured into global product divisions. Within each of these divisions, task forces were set up to study best practice in manufacturing, marketing, distribution, and product development.

The division managers had no staff and were expected to focus their energies on cross-border linkages. Division managers chaired all the task forces.

Another change was in the process of decision making. In the past, many of the big decisions had been made by the chief executive personally. The process had been clear, and with a few exceptions, the decisions had been good. But it was a process that had not developed the decision-making skills of the business managers. The new chief executive introduced formal capital expenditure requests and discounted cash flow calculations, disbanded the central executive committee, and personally encouraged division managers to develop their own strategies and proposals. During business planning meetings, the chief executive demonstrated that he had personally studied and analyzed the plans by asking detailed questions and expecting business managers to know the answers. He publicly humiliated one marketing director who did not know his market shares and stopped a business planning meeting after only an hour's discussion because he said that the management team was not properly prepared.

- *Functions and Central Services.* In support of the new structure and processes, two central functions were strengthened—financial analysis and strategic planning. The role of these functions was to provide a service to the businesses, global product divisions, and corporate headquarters in preparing and reviewing strategic plans, major decisions, and performance results. They were expected to take an independent position and advise on the design of planning systems and the formats for proposing and reviewing major decisions. The new chief executive believed that these central functions would help professionalize the decision-making process and provide support to business managers who wanted to propose initiatives that were not favored by their line bosses.

- *People and Skills.* To support his new, more analytical, more professional parenting approach, the new chief executive made some key appointments. He replaced the finance director and hired a business development director to take responsibility for the new planning function and for international acquisitions. He also retired the executives who had been in charge of the U.K. and International divisions.

In addition, he launched a major management development initiative, which involved three separate weeks of workshops and seminars on strategy and financial analysis, business planning, and competitor analysis. This initiative was designed to build analytical skills and help change the mental maps of many of the top managers. To help discredit the previous "seat of the pants" decision-making process, a case study was developed for use on the management development program that demonstrated how a detailed analysis of one of the company's past decisions would have resulted in choosing a different and clearly superior solution.

To help the parent managers develop their skills, he asked them to work closely with the management development consultants, both in agreeing what should be taught in the workshops and in preparing teaching sessions that the parent managers led at the workshops. In addition, he gave personal coaching to parent managers who were either taking too little or too much responsibility.

- *Decentralization Contracts.* The new chief executive recognized that the existing decentralization contracts did not place sufficient responsibility or authority on the business managers. The formal authorities were clear. But, informally, managers had been pushing decisions up to the founder and focusing their energy on trying to understand his intentions, rather than analyzing the marketplace or generating options. The new chief executive therefore increased the decision-making authority of both business heads and the heads of the product divisions. He also personally looked for opportunities to signal the nature of the new decentralization contracts he wanted to create. He advised business managers to use his planning and financial analysis staffs to help evaluate options and develop plans and capital expenditure proposals. He also picked a number of low-risk decisions around which to signal the change in responsibility. When these proposals came up for review, he limited his involvement to two questions. To the business managers, he asked, "Are you convinced that this is the best proposal?" To the staff managers, he asked, "Have the business managers considered a variety of reasonable options?" On receiving a yes answer to both questions, he approved the proposals without further discussion.

Although the corporate strategy changed little, the new chief executive set about building a variety of new parenting characteristics and changing others that were dysfunctional. The performance of the group improved dramatically, with increases in market share and margins and faster international expansion.

A Major Change in Corporate Strategy

It is not uncommon for parent companies to attempt much greater changes than the fine tuning of the first example. One company made dramatic changes to the parent organization as part of a new corporate strategy. Previously, the company had been broadly diversified with a corporate strategy only loosely connected with value creation. The company had been seeking to balance its investments in Europe with increased investments in the United States. The company had also taken the view that it needed to develop skills in service businesses and had made a number of acquisitions in service-related industries such as retailing.

The new chief executive had been appointed in part because of the lackluster performance of the group, and he set about changing the corporate strategy and the parent. He had successfully rationalized one of the company's largest businesses in the United States by focusing management attention on profitability, cutting staff levels, and eliminating bureaucracy. He perceived that this approach could be used to improve the performance of other businesses that the company already owned or that could be acquired for reasonable prices. He had earmarked a number of businesses for sale.

His first task, however, was to create a parent company capable of bringing about the performance improvements he thought were possible:

- *Structure, Systems, and Processes.* The CEO started by making a clear distinction between the parent company and the businesses. Heads of businesses were removed from the corporate board and from the parent's executive committee. He wanted the business heads to focus on running their businesses, and not be distracted with responsibilities within the parent. Two business heads left the company arguing that the change amounted to a demotion.

  The CEO set up Executive Committees for each business that contained managers from the business and two executives from the parent. He eliminated country-level managers and their staff, whose jobs had been to coordinate activities in their countries. The CEO made the business head of the largest business in each country responsible for countrywide issues, and centralized a few country-based staff activities such as tax management.

  Policy manuals were scrapped, paperwork eliminated, and all systems and processes re-engineered with a zero-based logic. A previously elaborate planning process that involved long-range planning (10 years forward) and business planning (5 years forward) was radically simplified into a 3-year business plan, produced after the budget. The budget became the central management process, and the business plan was a look into the future once the budget for the next 12 months had been agreed.

  One part of the new parenting approach was to tear down many of the linkage mechanisms that had been created to encourage synergy between businesses. The new strategy's focus was on stand-alone parenting. The linkage mechanisms were not only a distraction for business managers, they could also restrict their freedom of action. As a result, more than 30 cross-business committees, policy groups, and task forces were eliminated.

- *Functions and Central Services.* Two major central functions were eliminated—an information technology function and an engineering function. The information technology function was "sold" for a minimal sum to a large IT consultancy as part of an agreement on the provision of consultancy services. The engineering function was decentralized to the businesses, and half the staff were made redundant. In all, the size of the parent organization was reduced from 400 to 120.

- *People and Skills.* To support this radical change in parenting behavior, almost all the senior managers in the parent organization changed. The new chief executive promoted some of the team of managers he had worked with in the United States, and hired some additional individuals who had the action orientation that he required.

  The total upheaval of the parent company was further reinforced by two decisions that were explicitly designed to influence the culture and mental maps of the managers. First, he moved the head office building to a modern, practical, low-status building and insisted on an open-plan layout. Second, prior to the move, he had a public "eliminate files day." This day was preceded by a zero-based analysis of the corporate files. "If in doubt, throw it out" was the policy. Information that might be useful to the businesses was transferred to them if they wanted the files.

- *Decentralization Contracts.* The CEO made it clear to the business heads that they had full authority to run their businesses within the performance criteria agreed with the center. The center's control of capital expenditure was, however, tightened, with capital expenditure limits for some business heads reduced by half. The CEO reinforced his message by talking frequently about the "budget contract" between a business and the parent. "Budgets," he was at pains to point out, "are personal commitments made by managers to their superiors, their subordinates, their shareholders, and their self-respect. We do not accept excuses for failure to deliver on the budget contract."

The energy created by the changes, the performance improvement demanded from the businesses, and the acquisitions made by the corporate center resulted in a transformation of the company's performance.

Increasing Linkages

A common challenge facing many companies, particularly those that have focused their portfolios on a limited range of businesses, is to increase the value being created from linkages. In fact, this was one of the objectives of the chief executive in the first example we described. Many companies are reasonably satisfied with their stand-alone parenting but feel there is an opportunity to increase the sharing of assets, transfer of best practice, and coordination of strategies between their businesses.

One company had a portfolio of wholesale and retail businesses in similar product areas. In previous years, the parent managers had focused their attention on diversification, in the belief that the original businesses were mature and provided little growth opportunity. A series of unsuccessful diversifications led to a decision to refocus on a subset of the portfolio and find ways of increasing performance through linkages. The value creation strategy was to develop superior operating systems for its retailing businesses, leverage skills in space planning and direct product profitability analysis, combine the warehousing and distribution of certain products, gain price reductions from suppliers by pooling purchasing volumes, and raise the quality of marketing skills throughout the businesses. After gaining agreement to the strategy from managers in the parent and the main businesses, the chief executive set about creating some distinctive parenting characteristics to support the value creation strategy.

- *Structure, Systems, and Processes.* The chief executive set up task forces for each of the linkage initiatives. Each task force then developed different solutions. The systems task force decided that the largest retail business should take the lead in developing a system that could be used by the other businesses. The space planning task force set up a unit of two people within the parent to help implement space planning techniques in business units lacking the appropriate skills or motivation. The distribution task force gained agreement from three businesses to set up a common warehouse for one product category. Each task force evolved its own distinctive parenting solution to the opportunity it faced. One of the task forces even disbanded itself after three unsatisfactory meetings, and the initiative in its area was abandoned.

- *Functions and Central Services.* There was only a small change in the functions and services at the center. The planning function gained a small space planning team and the IT function halved in size from five to two people.

- *People and Skills.* The chief executive carefully chose five senior managers (two of which were parent managers and three of which were business managers) to chair the five task forces. These managers were given help from external consultants in how to facilitate coordination and how to analyze the potential within their remit. The task forces that made the most progress were the ones where the chief executive's appointment was an individual with the motivation, status, and knowledge to champion the initiative. The less successful task forces suffered through lack of leadership from a natural champion.

- *Decentralization Contracts.* There was little change in the overall decentralization contracts between the parent and the businesses. The parent's involvement in linkage management was limited to setting up contact between the businesses and applying pressure to resolve particular areas of disagreement. The wider decentralization contracts remained largely undisturbed.

After 3 years, the new strategy had worked in some areas, but not all. The parent had developed ways of creating valuable linkages in three out of the original five task forces.

FITTING THE PARENT TO THE CORPORATE STRATEGY

As the examples illustrate, decisions about the parent are driven by the corporate strategy as embodied in the parenting advantage statement. The value creation insights explain the nature of the improvement in business performance that the parent is trying to achieve, and the distinctive parenting characteristics describe the main ways in which the parent is going to influence the businesses. These provide the structure around which parenting decisions are made. The most obvious way of fitting the parent to the corporate strategy is, therefore, to design the structure, functions, decentralization contracts, and people to fit the value creation insights and distinctive parenting characteristics. Other parenting activities should be carefully screened to reduce the potential for value destruction. Parenting characteristics that are not related to the value creation insights are more likely to destroy value than create it.

If the value creation insights are about squeezing performance improvements from industrial manufacturing businesses through tight budgeting, the parent is likely to select a highly decentralized structure of largely stand-alone business units. The parent may limit central staff to the finance function and acquisition team, and employ parent executives with strong budgeting skills and years of experience reviewing the performance of, and setting targets for, industrial manufacturing businesses. In other words, the parent might look somewhat like BTR.

If the value creation insights are about encouraging marketing linkages between businesses and countries in fast-moving consumer goods, the parent may also have a highly decentralized structure of largely stand-alone business units, but in addition, it will have some powerful coordinating mechanisms, such as the selection, training, promotion, career development, and deployment of a cadre of product managers. In other words, the parent will have some mechanisms in common with Unilever.

If the value creation insights are about developing a manufacturing services function to help businesses catch up with modern techniques for manufacturing small volume items mainly out of metal, the parent is also likely to have a decentralized structure of largely stand-alone businesses. But the parent may contain a manufacturing staff function and parent executives with strong manufacturing backgrounds, to work with businesses reviewing their manufacturing processes and helping them redesign the workflow, the union contracts, the shift pattern, the logistics flow, and the supplier relations. In other words, the parent will have many features similar to those in Cooper Industries.

In the last two examples, where the focus is on marketing and manufacturing, it may also be possible to implement the value creation insights with a different, more centralized, approach. The cadre of product managers could be developed by centralizing the marketing activities of the business units, a policy often used in the research function. This parenting approach is only likely to succeed if the market environments and product positionings in each of the business units are highly similar. Centralizing a function inevitably leads to less local tailoring and more loyalty to the central values and policies. In the manufacturing example, the improvement in manufacturing techniques could be achieved by creating a central manufacturing function, with all factories reporting to a central manufacturing director. As before, the approach is only likely to succeed if the factories are serving similar businesses with similar processes, lead times, and market demands. More normally, the factories in each business have different pressures on them that make it important for them to report to the business chief executive rather than to a central manufacturing function.

Our point is that the parenting advantage statement provides the starting point for parenting decisions, but it does not provide a complete blueprint. The details of the management systems, central functions, decentralization contracts, and people need to be selected based on the peculiarities of the company, its history, the people, short-term pressures and challenges, and many other factors that are often unique to the situation. This does not mean that there are no rules: that parenting decisions are all unique to the situation. But it does mean that managers should think twice before accepting the more popular generalizations, such as "no manager should have more than eight people reporting to him or her," "businesses should be grouped by industry," "all companies should have a long-term strategic planning process involving the development of scenarios," "managers should be empowered by increasing decentralization," or "complex environments require matrix organization structures." We have examined these generalizations and others, and the following list of guiding principles captures some of the generalizations we have found practically useful.

Mental Maps

As we pointed out at the beginning of this chapter, mental maps are not only difficult to analyze, but also hard to address directly. Most of the change in mental maps occurs as a result of changes in the other four types of parenting characteristic. Three points about mental maps are, however, worth noting.

First, the strategy review process itself, whether at the corporate level or at the business level, is in part about exposing, testing and modifying the mental maps of the managers involved. The analysis that is carried out during the review, the questions that are asked, and the discussions that occur all influence the managers' mental maps. The review process and discussions designed to gain commitment to the implementation of the strategy are the most direct influence on mental maps.

The second point is about the degree to which the parent's mental maps should include knowledge of the businesses. The parent's knowledge of its businesses needs to increase the more the parent is involved in influencing them. This means that the parent's understanding of business characteristics needs to be much richer and deeper for businesses where the parent is highly influential. In Unilever's personal products coordination, the parent is attempting to influence decisions over a range of product categories; has developed a total quality program for the businesses; actively manages the career paths and development of product managers; and influences the businesses in many other ways. This requires a deep understanding of the critical success factors and the nature of the parenting opportunities in each business, if the parent is to avoid destroying more value than it creates. Where the parent is less influential, or influential on only a few issues, its mental maps can be less rich and less detailed.

The third point about mental maps concerns deeply embedded habits, rules of thumb or predispositions. The deeply embedded mental maps that are not likely to change over the planning period should be used to guide implementation decisions. Most parenting initiatives can be implemented in a variety of ways. If, for example, the parent wants to encourage some businesses to improve their market position by moving to up-market, added-value products, there are many ways in which this can be done:

- The parent chief executive could hold informal conversations with the business heads.
- The strategic planning process could be used to expose the issues and get agreement to an up-market strategy.
- A request could be made to each business to write down and gain central approval for a mission statement.
- A central marketing function could be set up to help businesses redesign products and reposition advertising.
- A committee of marketing directors could be set up to discuss the issues.
- A performance measure, such as percentage of products sold at prices above a certain level, could be used as part of the budgeting process.

Which method of implementation a manager should choose depends on the deeply held mental maps of the parent managers and the senior managers in the businesses. If these managers believe that formal strategic planning processes are a waste of time, then informal discussions will work better. If the company is driven by the budget, because managers believe that the budget is the only way of exerting effective control and motivation, then adding a performance measure to the budget process is likely to be more effective than focusing on mission statements. Parenting decisions need to be taken with a clear understanding of the deeply held mental maps. They provide a guideline as to which implementation tactic is likely to be most effective.

Structure, Systems, and Processes

A number of generalizations can be made about the design of the structures, systems, and processes of the parent. A common pitfall is to duplicate parenting tasks at different layers in the parent organization. For example, in some companies the division level reviews the strategy of a business and the corporate center then carries out a further review, duplicating the review process. A similar problem can occur with capital approval requests, where each layer of the parent organization may review the proposal before passing it on to the next layer. Duplication is wasteful in management time, can lead to confusing signals for the businesses, and demotivates those seeking guidance or approval. But eliminating duplication often requires major changes in the way the layers of the parent operate.[1]

A second guiding principle is to avoid mixing business and parent responsibilities. This recommendation is often referred to as "getting the barons off the board." Many companies have their most senior business managers on the corporate board. This may be to recognize their seniority or to give them additional perspective. However, the implication is that they are being asked to wear two hats: to act as part of the parent when on the board and as head of a business at other times. On the surface, this is not an impossible task; but it seldom works. Because the objective of the parent is to influence the business heads, it is awkward if the business heads are also part of the parent. It is unlikely that much beneficial influence is going to result from having a business head influence himself or herself. Moreover, implicit pacts often grow up between the barons to avoid interfering in each other's businesses.

Asking business heads to wear two hats makes sense where the creation of value depends on blending views to gain agreement, for example to a capacity rationalization or joint product offering. In these situations, the wearing of two hats can be limited to the particular issue under discussion by setting up a joint committee or task force. It is only necessary to make the business heads permanent members of the parent if there is a continual stream of linkage issues that need a blending of views to resolve.

Another guiding principle concerns the way the businesses are grouped into divisions. The parenting advantage logic implies that a business should report to whichever division is able to give it the best parenting. This means that businesses should be grouped by their parenting needs. Often businesses with strong linkages are best grouped together, but this is not always the case. Stand-alone parenting is normally more influential than linkage parenting or functional parenting. This suggests that businesses should be grouped first by the nature of their stand-alone parenting needs and only then further divided into subgroups where linkages are particularly strong.

A final guiding principle is about the importance of structures, systems, and processes relative to the other characteristics of the parent. Structures, systems, and processes are the parent's skeleton. They cannot create value unless they are staffed with the right people and brought alive by relevant skills. If the parent has the right people and skills, well-chosen structures, systems, and processes will make the people and skills more effective and influential. However, a good structure or well-designed system will not help a parent that lacks the right people and skills. People and skills are the most important ingredient. Hence structures, systems, and processes need to be built round them so as to make skillful managers even more effective.

Functions and Central Services

We pointed out in Chapter 8 that functions and central services need to be justified against the beat-the-specialists paradox: They need to demonstrate superiority over external providers. It is important to keep this paradox in mind as decisions about functions or services are being made. Two other challenges to functions and services are also useful. One challenge is to test the existence of the function or service against the value creation insights. If the function or service is not central to the value creation insights, it should be closely examined. The risk of value destruction is high. Not only do functions and services develop a bureaucratic life of their own, but they also take up valuable time of senior parent managers. This time is nearly always better used on other activities. Where the service can be largely self-managed, the benefits are easy to define, and the activity has a low risk of value destruction (such as pensions or insurance) it can, however, be justified.

Another challenge to the existence of peripheral staff functions is to assess whether their activities could be better executed by line managers with the appropriate skills. Human resource management, for example, is a staff function that does not exist in all parents. Where it is not central to the value creation insights or where the focus is on the appointment and development of only a few managers, a skilled line manager may do a better job than a staff function. Many companies are finding that they can slim down corporate staffs by allocating the task to line managers with the appropriate skills.

People and Skills

Throughout this book, we have stressed the importance of key individuals within the senior parenting team. Often, the implementation of a new corporate strategy depends on changing or reinforcing the top team.

While it can be difficult to remove established members of the team and find suitable replacements for them, much can be achieved by rebalancing the team through the addition of new members with different skills and attitudes. This may involve recruitment from outside or promotion from within. In either case, one or two new faces can bring about major shifts in the way that the top team influences its businesses.

The need to rebalance or reskill the top team explains the apparent anomaly of appointing a manager like Lou Gerstner, with a background in financial services and consumer products, to help restore the fortunes of IBM. As an addition to the top team, these transplants can bring vital new parenting skills and perspectives. When these blend with the existing skills and the knowledge of the businesses of existing team members the results can be dramatic. The danger is obvious. The new person, with no feel for the businesses, may take initiatives that destroy value rather than create it. If the transplanted individual operates as part of a parenting team, the danger of this occurring is greatly reduced.

Decentralization Contracts

The decentralization contract is part mental map, part precedent, and part policies and rules. Surfacing existing decentralization contracts is a hard task in itself (see Exhibit 15–3). Deciding on the clauses of new contracts is even harder. The following guidelines are helpful to managers designing new contracts.

The first guideline is to avoid widely different decentralization contracts for different parts of the portfolio, particularly if the businesses are similar or contiguous. Not only do parent managers find it difficult to adjust their parenting behavior from one business to the next, but unit managers are often not prepared to agree to a system that does not appear fair. "Why should his powers of authority or freedom to operate be any different from mine?" For most successful corporate strategies, the value creation insights and distinctive parenting characteristics are similar for all the businesses in the portfolio, making it appropriate to have similar decentralization contracts. Where different contracts are necessary, they need to be separated organizationally into a different division or different country.

EXHIBIT 15-3 Surfacing the existing decentralization contract

Part of Contract	Questions/Issues	Comment
Product/market scope	Product range Customer coverage Technology range Overlap with other units	Broad scope often clear. Issues at the margin normally "for negotiation"
Value chain scope	Degree of backward or forward integration Intertrading rules	Normally defined by precedent unless it involves intertrading
Objectives and values	Influence of corporate objectives Business-specific objectives Corporate values	Often written into a corporate-level or business-level mission, vision, or philosophy statement
Authority levels	Budget changes Capital approval Functional policies People decisions	Normally written into policy statements, but also include many common practices
Other policies and behaviors	Policy manuals Constraints on authority Behavior of senior parent managers	Best understood from manuals and by interviewing businesses
Decision processes	Committees and membership Appeal procedures Due process procedures	Formal system normally well defined Informal system also important, but difficult to document

The second guideline on decentralization contracts is to make sure the contract facilitates the value that the parent is trying to create. For example, many parent companies are trying to create value by promoting synergy and linkages between their businesses. Yet the heads of the businesses have not acknowledged the role that the parent has to play in this area. The parent accuses the business heads of "not-invented-here" attitudes, and the business heads accuse the parent of interference. Unless the decentralization contract makes it clear that the parent not only has a right but also a duty to promote certain kinds of synergy and linkages, there is little potential to create net value. The decentralization contract must acknowledge the powers and responsibilities of the parent in those areas where the parent is expecting to create value. This guideline provides a useful criterion for reviewing decentralization contracts. The parent should only retain an influence in areas where it is expecting to create value. Elsewhere, it is better to decentralize decision making to the businesses.[2]

The third guideline concerns the process of changing decentralization contracts. Because the contract only exists as a result of the agreement of both parties—the parent and the business—changes to contracts need to be negotiated. Ineffective parenting occurs most frequently in situations where the businesses are not only resisting the parent's influence but also challenging the parent's right to interfere. Sudden changes may be perceived as "breaking faith," and may meet with angry resistance from established general managers. More subtle changes may be gradually accepted, but they may also be perceived as disturbing trends that should be fought fiercely to avoid a damaging precedent. Such concerns about "the thin end of the wedge" often lead to unexpectedly virulent rejection of corporate initiatives, which were perceived by different parties in very different ways. For example, in one multichain retail group, the new chief executive was anxious to create greater value from linkage influence. As a result, he established various mechanisms to prompt previously separate divisions to work more closely together. Some of the divisional managers were highly resistant. They felt they were wasting their time in cross-divisional meetings or were irritated by "interference" from other divisions. They were also concerned that central staff were becoming too powerful. Although the changes were relatively small, they prompted considerable fear about "the way the wind was blowing."

Because decentralization contracts are hard to write down, parent managers frequently fail to seek formal agreement from businesses either to the existing contract or to changes they want to make. This causes confusion, resistance, and mistrust—a poor environment in which to create value. Particular problems can arise with the arrival of new business unit managers from outside the company. When such managers move from one organization to another, they may be only partly aware of differences in the unwritten decentralization contracts. For example, the new managing director of a property development business angrily challenged the interventions of the group finance director: "You don't seem to understand that I am in charge of project decisions. If you want to set an overall limit to exposure on a project, that's fine. But I don't expect to discuss the merits of a particular retail development under close questioning. If you think you can do it better than me, then you should be running the business." This confrontation was based on the past experience of both managers. The group finance director was used to being intimately involved in project decisions. The new business unit managing director was used to having significant autonomy. To mitigate problems of this sort, our advice is to make decentralization contracts clear by explicitly writing down as much as possible, and by discussing the issues and debating scenarios. The issues covered by the contract are complex, sensitive, and vital to good parenting. We therefore encourage managers to talk through areas of the contract issue by issue, and then keep a rolling dialogue on the subject to increase clarification over time.

Identifying and discussing the issues, however, is not enough. Reaching agreement is essential for an effective contract. Discussions must continue until agreement has been reached, even if this results in having to change the relevant manager. These discussions may benefit from being extended over a year or more to allow time for experience of the new strategy to build and fears about loss of autonomy to subside. Continued disagreement, however, cannot be tolerated, because it creates a blockage to the parent's value creation efforts.

The final guideline on decentralization contracts concerns individual decisions about the degree of centralization or decentralization. The parent's involvement in an issue can vary from having decision-making authority to having no influence. In between these extremes are shades of gray. The parent can comment and advise but leave the final decision to the business. The parent can vigorously challenge and continue to challenge until a decision has been made that the parent is comfortable with. The parent can encourage discussion and debate with the objective of seeking consensus. If consensus does not emerge, the parent can then arbitrate between competing views. Each of these different ways of operating involves different degrees of centralization. The decentralization contract should specify which way of operating is appropriate for each type of issue.

In general, our advice is to increase the amount of decentralization for issues that have the least commonality across the businesses. When decisions are centralized, the parent's views, values, and logic prevail over those of the businesses. For issues where the circumstances in the businesses are common, the parent can gain experience and learning as a result of exposure to a number of similar issues. The parent's views may, therefore, be better informed than the views of an individual business. Centralized decision making may result in better decisions. Where the issues and business circumstances are different, the parent has little opportunity to gain useful experience through exposure to other businesses and is likely to overlook or be ignorant about the special circumstances facing a particular business. Decentralized decision making is likely to be better because it leaves the decision in the hands of the managers closest to the detail.

PARENTING AS LEARNING

All new corporate strategies involve learning new parenting skills. In the previous sections of this chapter, we have talked about the design of the parenting approach and the importance of people and skills in bringing the parenting approach to life. New people bring with them new skills, and it is for this reason that we link people and skills together. However, new people are not the only solution. The existing parent managers can learn new skills. This section is about how parents develop new skills. It is focused around three types of learning: (1) continuous incremental improvements to parenting, (2) gaining a feel for a new business, and (3) learning to parent businesses that are incompatible with the existing heartland (platforms).

Continuous Learning

All parents should be striving to learn how to add more value. When a new corporate strategy has first been launched, the learning required to implement new distinctive parenting characteristics successfully is particularly great. The characteristics of the businesses are changing on a continuous basis, however, and parenting skills and methods need to be refined and updated all the time. In concept, the learning that parent managers need to do is no different from the continuous learning needed at any other level in the organization. Yet, due to the hierarchical nature of the relationship, parent managers are less likely to admit their learning needs, either to their colleagues or to themselves. For parent managers, the first requirement for successful continuous learning—a learning attitude that explicitly recognizes the need to learn—may be harder than for managers elsewhere in the company. But it is vitally necessary.

A number of other requirements peculiar to parent companies are worth emphasizing. One important source of learning is often overlooked—feedback from the businesses. If the parent organization thinks of the businesses as customers and thinks of its influence as a service offered to its customers, the potential for learning from the businesses becomes clear. The businesses are the recipients of the parent's influence. Hence, they are in the best position to advise the parent on how to improve its parenting. Unfortunately, too many parent managers are not listening. In one company, a business manager described in detail to us some of the many problems with the planning process. He told us that he had found the discussion useful because he would shortly be attending a meeting to review the planning process with the chief executive. We asked him whether he would make the same comments to the chief executive. "Oh no," he replied, "It's not that sort of meeting. The chief executive will not want to hear us say what is wrong with his planning process."

Another important source of learning is a regular system for reviewing the parenting approach and decentralization contracts. If these matters are openly discussed with the businesses, there is an opportunity to identify inconsistencies and invite constructive criticism. Parent managers normally assume that these discussions will focus purely on the cost of the parent and encourage the businesses to say that they want the parent to be smaller. But it is possible to have a constructive discussion of the parent's costs and benefits and learn useful lessons from it. It is common for the parent to ask the businesses to present their plans. It is not common, however, for the parent to lead by example and present its plan to the businesses.

Within this review of the parent's plan, we believe there is particular opportunity for learning from discussing the decentralization contracts. It is not necessary to surface all details of the contracts because most of them will be uncontroversial. However, it is useful to identify any disputed decentralization contract issues and discuss them with the businesses.

The process for negotiating and charging out the costs of central staffs and functions is another opportunity for parent learning. If these costs are not charged to the businesses, or if they are charged on an arbitrary basis such as sales volume, share of profit, or numbers of employees, the opportunity for learning is minimal. If, however, the costs are charged out on the basis of agreed service contracts, the potential for learning is much greater. The businesses will be continuously looking for ways of getting the benefits of central staffs at lower cost, and the central staffs will be continuously thinking of additional benefits that could help justify their costs. Negotiated agreements between central staffs and businesses are costly in management time, but they stimulate the learning process.

Developing a Feel for New Businesses

A parent is unlikely to have a feel for new businesses coming into the portfolio, unless they are very similar to businesses the parent already owns. It is, therefore, normal for parents to be faced with the problem of learning at least enough about the critical success factors of the new business to ensure that value is not destroyed.

Most managers' first instincts are to stand well back from the new business during this learning process: Avoid interfering until a better understanding is achieved. This learning strategy has two problems. First, the parent has a set of minimum parenting tasks, such as appointing senior managers and agreeing performance targets, that cannot be decentralized. The parent needs to develop a feel for these tasks as fast as possible. Hence, an active learning program is necessary. Second, by standing back, the parent may both delay learning about the critical success factors in the business and fail to address the parenting opportunities, which justified the business being acquired in the first place. We do not, therefore, recommend standing back as a learning strategy. The best way to learn is to get closely involved with the business. This means spending time with the business and its managers, monitoring the decisions it faces and the results it achieves, and obtaining a full briefing on all the relevant issues. It does not, however, imply interfering on matters that go beyond the minimum parenting tasks, unless and until the parent has learned enough to feel confident that its influence will be beneficial.

Provided the business is believed to be in the heartland, the parent can move more quickly and more boldly in addressing the parenting opportunities. The distinctive parenting characteristics are likely to fit the new business because the value creation insights are similar to those applied in the other businesses. Even here, however, the parent will need a learning program to become familiar with the business's specific critical success factors. This cannot be effectively carried out just through the normal budgeting, planning, and capital approval processes. The parent has to engage actively in a learning campaign. Visiting every site, speaking with a cross section of managers, commissioning consultants' reports, setting up task forces, and asking the new business to re-budget in the parent company's format are all ways of speeding up the learning. Corporate staff can also play a role in briefing top managers on the new business.

To acquire a real feel for a new business, however, takes time. Unless the parent's feel for existing businesses in the portfolio is transferable to the new business, it will take a number of years before a feel develops. Often it is at least one economic or investment cycle before the parent has been exposed to the full range of commercial issues in the business and begins to acquire the right sort of instincts and gut reactions for influencing the business. If the business is different from any of the other businesses in the portfolio, it can take 10 years or more for the parent to develop a feel. Many parent managers reject this observation as being unreasonable. Ten years seems an inordinately long time. Yet, our research interviews are full of remarks such as this: "When we joined the group, they were clearly perplexed by us. In the first years they kept trying to apply standard policies to us, and they didn't understand the commercial issues. We had a tremendous struggle to get the money to keep up with our competitors. In the last few years they have gained a better understanding. In fact, they are quite helpful on some of our more difficult decisions! I would say that it took about 12 years before they felt comfortable with our business." Very few stories like this have a time frame of less than 10 years.

Parenting Platform Businesses

Platform businesses present opportunities that are outside the heartland. In these businesses, the critical factors for success are different from those of the heartland businesses, and the mainstream parenting approach is likely to destroy value rather than create it: The parenting opportunities require different parenting characteristics. Platforms are experiments that can lead to a major change in the corporate strategy. The parent, therefore, needs to create a new and separate parenting approach for the business.[3]

In practice, complete separation is impossible. The business cannot be isolated from deeply embedded parenting characteristics or the basic values of the existing culture. In fact, it is appropriate that the platform business should be exposed to these deeply held parts of the existing approach. The platform is an experiment to help find a new corporate strategy. It will be more likely to achieve this objective if the new business responds well to the deeply embedded parenting characteristics and basic values of the old strategy. Without this link, the experiment is likely to be rejected by the host parent, whatever the commercial outcome.

The best platforms emerge because they are strongly championed by some senior or middle manager with the relevant experience. For example, a country manager might champion the opportunity of diversifying into other businesses, as a result of an unusual relationship with the local government or a major customer. A division manager may see the potential for creating a new business out of the distribution needs of the businesses in his or her division. A business unit manager may discover the potential for rationalizing a business and perceive the opportunity to do the same to a number of similar businesses in the same area. The best ideas for platforms come from managers who can sense the opportunity and how to exploit it. In these circumstances, the platform should be parented by the championing managers, allowing them to test out their strategy. The challenge is to defend the business from the potential negative influences of the existing parent.

Because of the awkwardness of platform businesses, because they are part of the portfolio but lie outside the normal parenting behavior, it is important to develop them quickly. There is a time limit for a platform business of probably less than 5 years. If, in this time, the parent cannot learn how to create value from the business, it is unlikely to be worth holding onto the investment. The business can only be isolated from the normal parenting approach for a limited period. This is an additional reason why platforms are normally successful only when the company has an internal champion who can accelerate the learning process.

If the learning is successful, a decision needs to be made about the parent's future corporate strategy. Should the platform be the basis of a new corporate strategy, should it remain a separate activity until it has evolved further, should it be sold or joint ventured with another parent, or can it be integrated within a modified form of the existing strategy? The parent should consider carefully what it will do if the platform is successful, before making the initial commitment to it.

The practice in many companies of acquiring platform businesses, in competing technologies or new growth markets, and adding them to the portfolio as just another business in the corporate line up is doomed to failure. Unless the company is willing to separate the business from its mainstream parenting, has a manager that can champion the parenting of the platform, and has a clear understanding of the implications of success, investment in platform businesses outside the heartland almost always destroys value.

SUMMARY

Decisions about the parent are as important to corporate strategy as decisions about the portfolio. Both should be driven by the parenting advantage statement. Because the parent's effectiveness is so influenced by people and skills, and intangibles such as the managers' mental maps and the nuances of the decentralization contract, each situation is unique and each parent organization needs to find its own solution. The company's history and culture are important, as are the personalities and predispositions of senior managers both in the parent and in the businesses. Finding a blend that works is the challenge.

Designing the parent organization to fit the planned corporate strategy involves making good initial choices and then learning faster than rivals. The prize is superior parenting and a clear advantage in the company's chosen heartland. But advantage seldom lasts forever. Good parenting is a continual process of developing strategy, designing the parent, adjusting the strategy, adjusting the parent, readjusting the strategy, and readjusting the parent. Parenting decisions need constant refinement to maintain parenting advantage as circumstances change.

NOTES

1. See Appendix B for a fuller discussion of parenting structure.

2. This principle is similar to the "loose-tight" concept described in Thomas J. Peters and Robert H. Waterman, Jr., *In Search of Excellence: Lessons from America's Best-Run Companies,* New York: Harper & Row, 1982. Parents should hold some powers (tighten control) in areas where they believe they can create value and decentralize (loosen control) elsewhere.

3. One of the reasons for separating the business from the rest of the portfolio is to avoid incompatibilities in the parenting approach. For example, if the new business requires the parent to take a long-term strategic approach whereas the current heartland performs better under a tight short-term financial approach, the new business needs to be kept separate.

16

PUTTING PARENTING ADVANTAGE INTO PRACTICE

The parenting advantage concept has the potential to transform thinking about corporate strategy and the management of multibusiness companies. It can put an end to the specious and superficial arguments that so many companies offer to justify ownership of their businesses and can force a fundamental re-assessment of why groups of businesses exist. It does not necessarily imply that companies should become less diverse in terms of the numbers of businesses they own or the range of product markets in which they compete. But it does mean that corporate parents should be able to show why the businesses they own, or propose to enter, will benefit from their parenting. As a result, decisions about acquisitions, divestments, and new business entries should improve, and there should be a better fit between parent companies and the businesses that make up their portfolios.

The logic of parenting advantage can also clarify the roles of managers in the parent and in the businesses. In particular, it can sharpen the thinking of senior managers in the parent about ways in which they can create value through their influence and activities, and facilitate more open discussion of the relationships between the center and the businesses. This leads to better decisions about how the businesses in the portfolio should be parented.

There are therefore major benefits to be gained from adopting the parenting advantage approach to corporate strategy, and we have found that most managers find the parenting advantage concept intellectually persuasive. But there is sometimes a gap between intellectual acceptance and practical application. This last chapter attempts to bridge that gap and provide guidance for managers who wish to introduce parenting advantage thinking into their organizations. We start with a brief summary of the main principles of parenting advantage. Then we offer some tips for gaining practical commitment to them as a basis for corporate decision making.

THE PRINCIPLES OF PARENTING ADVANTAGE

Like most powerful concepts, parenting advantage is, in essence, simple. Its main messages for corporate strategy can be captured in six basic principles:

1. To justify their role, corporate parents should aim to create some value and to avoid value destruction through their influence on the businesses in their portfolios.
2. To create value, the resources, skills, and other characteristics of the parent should fit with the needs and opportunities of the businesses: This fit, which needs to be dynamic and to evolve over time, is the basis for value creation.
3. To win the competition with rivals, corporate parents should aim to create more value in their portfolios than other parents could: Often they will be moving toward this aim rather than achieving it.
4. Corporate parents should search for superior insights about how to create value in their businesses: Value creation insights are an essential component of corporate strategy.
5. Corporate parents should be particularly good at realizing the parenting opportunities that they identify: They should build distinctive parenting characteristics that will allow them to implement their value creation insights more effectively than other parents.
6. Corporate parents should be aware of the dangers of destroying value and should concentrate on businesses in which they can create high net value: They should concentrate on businesses in their heartlands.

These principles, straightforward in concept but far harder to put into practice successfully, are the basis of a valid corporate strategy.

PUTTING THE PRINCIPLES INTO PRACTICE

One of the participants in a program on corporate strategy that we ran recently was excited by the parenting advantage concept. He was a young vice president of corporate planning and felt that he had finally found a powerful framework to guide his company's corporate strategy. After the course, he wrote to thank us in fulsome terms. "Either this program will fundamentally alter the way that my company is run, or else I will resign," he told us. He was gone within six months. This rather sad story illustrates how difficult it can be to introduce the parenting advantage concept to a sceptical organization, and to bring about the radical changes that it often implies.

Resistance to the parenting advantage concept is seldom based on rejection of the principles that it depends upon. We have found very few managers who reject the notion that parent companies should add value. Moreover, especially in the United States and the United Kingdom, managers recognize that corporate parents compete with each other, and that the parent that can add the most value will, in theory, be the long-term winner.

However, intellectual acceptance of the logic of parenting advantage does not always lead to action. Parent managers may continue to be influenced by other approaches to corporate strategy that can conflict with parenting advantage. They may be uncomfortable with the degree of challenge that parenting advantage presents to the current corporate strategy. They may feel no pressing need to tamper with established patterns of parenting. Under these circumstances, the campaign to introduce parenting advantage thinking will need to be carefully planned and skillfully executed. We will therefore provide some advice for those who have been converted by the concept, want to put it into practice in their organizations, but are not sure how to begin.

Winning the Support of Top Management

Without support from the top of the organization, whether at the corporate level or at the division level, little will be achieved. The top managers in the parent are normally the dominant source of value creation or destruction. So the most essential step in introducing the parenting advantage concept is to gain their commitment to it.

The right way to draw top managers into acting upon the parenting advantage concept will depend on the situation in each company and in each management group. It also depends on the role and position of the individual who is championing the parenting advantage concept. For a chief executive, it is a matter of gaining buy-in from his or her senior colleagues. For division managers, the challenge is to engage the interest of the top team in the corporate parent. For staff advisers or consultants, the need is to build support from line management, especially in the corporate parent but also in the divisions. In each case, the tactics and priorities will need to be rather different.

Sometimes winning top management support is relatively easy. If the chief executive has recently been appointed and is prepared to challenge past approaches to corporate strategy, the strength of the parenting advantage logic is usually appealing. If there are obvious tensions and frictions in the relationships between the corporate headquarters, the divisions, and the businesses, the value of clarifying the role of the parent is evident. Alternatively, if performance pressures or the threat of takeover are forcing a re-appraisal of corporate direction, parenting advantage offers a powerful means of addressing long-running problems. In these circumstances, natural triggers within the organization lead to a more ready appreciation and acceptance of the parenting advantage concept.

If, however, there is no particular reason or desire to take on new ideas, and no imminent crisis to force through a change of approach, enlisting the support of top management is harder. In such situations, persistence and persuasiveness will be needed, as well as logic. Parenting advantage will need championing; but the championing must be done with diplomacy, tact, and a sense of timing. Too much "hard sell" at the wrong time can be counterproductive. The ground in which the new ideas will be sown must be carefully prepared, and the relevance and value of parenting advantage must be clearly demonstrated.

Preparing the Ground

Parenting advantage is a new and different way of looking at corporate strategy. As a result, it needs to be explained carefully. Managers may claim to understand and accept the concept without having fully thought through or bought into it. It is necessary to take time to explain the concept fully to all the key members of the management team, and to be prepared to confront openly the sort of objections raised in Chapter 3.

It is particularly important to show how parenting advantage relates to the current logic for corporate strategy decisions. Whether the current logic is based on core competences, synergy, balance, growth, or some other rationale, it is necessary to understand the thinking that parenting advantage logic must augment or replace. Resistance to parenting advantage as a basis for corporate strategy is inevitably stronger from managers who have already attached themselves mentally to an alternative rationale. As discussed in Chapter 4, parenting advantage conflicts with much of the "conventional wisdom" about corporate strategy; it is better to address these conflicts directly rather than allow them to fester beneath the surface.

Even if managers understand the concept and claim adherence to it, we have found that it takes time to internalize it. In the same way that tennis players need long hours of practice to perfect their forehand drives and to be able to produce the shot under pressure in a match, corporate managers need repeated exposure to parenting advantage thinking before they will apply it instinctively to all the decisions and emergencies they face. It is wrong to expect the internalization process to take less than a year, and it can often require longer.

In selling the parenting advantage concept, it can be helpful to enlist the support of influential allies. Top managers in the parent will be influenced by the views of nonexecutive directors, institutional investors, and senior divisional and business managers. These constituencies are potential allies in encouraging a new approach to corporate strategy. Nonexecutives and external investors frequently recognize the absence of any clearly articulated corporate-level strategy, and welcome the parenting advantage framework because it provides a more robust basis for decisions. Senior divisional and business managers may also feel the need for clearer guidance on the role and intentions of the corporate level. As "customers" of the company's parenting efforts, they see clearly any shortcomings in the current corporate strategy, and often support the parenting advantage framework as a way of clarifying the context within which they are supposed to be working. If a consensus in favor of change needs to be built, powerful allies can help by creating pressure for change.

Demonstrating Relevance

However logical the parenting advantage concept may be, few managers feel enthusiastic about using it until they can see its practical relevance to them. It is therefore essential, as part of the process of gaining senior management support, to show what sorts of decisions are implied by the new way of thinking.

Rival parent analysis can be a useful way in. Analysis of the performance and behavior of successful rival parents almost always leads to worthwhile discussion and can start to shift perceptions. Focusing on how other companies influence their businesses often triggers ideas for specific initiatives, so that "the point" of parenting advantage thinking comes to life. Furthermore, fear of predators is a great motivator; companies under threat of a bid are often catalyzed into actions that have previously been resisted or delayed. Rival parent analysis can be used to similar ends. By identifying a particularly threatening rival and speculating about the actions this rival would take if it made a successful takeover bid, it is possible to confront managers with a parenting challenge.

It is also helpful to encourage contacts with successful parents, such as those described in this book. Discussions with senior managers in these companies can be highly influential in reinforcing the parenting advantage message. Such companies may not use the jargon, but they base their corporate strategies on parenting advantage logic. Talking to them about their corporate strategies will create a deep and practical understanding of the nature and importance of value creation insights, distinctive parenting characteristics and heartland business criteria; and the clarity and conviction of their stories will be an impressive testimony to the power and relevance of parenting advantage thinking.

Successes and failures analysis, as described in Chapter 12, can also lead rapidly to practical conclusions. Every company has some businesses that are performing well and others that are performing poorly. A focus on the role of the parent in influencing both the strong and the weak businesses often brings into sharp relief those aspects of parenting that are valuable and should be reinforced, and those that are damaging and should be changed.

The parenting advantage concept should be introduced as a way of addressing difficult, topical decisions, not as an interesting intellectual construct that leads to a different sort of corporate planning process. Attention should be focused on important issues, such as portfolio composition or parenting structure, rather than only on the concept as such.

Rough Cut View of a Possible New Corporate Strategy

At an early stage, it can be valuable to go beyond piecemeal issues and to provide a broader view of what a corporate strategy based on parenting advantage might be like. One of the barriers to the acceptance of parenting advantage is discomfort with uncertainty. Managers are not happy to assent to parenting advantage without knowing where the new logic will take them. An illustrative, rough-cut corporate strategy not only gives an example of the parenting advantage logic at work; it also provides a focus for anxiety and a specific proposal to be examined, challenged, and evaluated.

The rough-cut corporate strategy does not need to be highly detailed. On the contrary, it may even benefit from lacking detailed analysis and support, in order to emphasize that it is not a fully worked proposal. But the debate around the proposal will clarify the application of parenting advantage principles, and allow managers to express personal concerns or reservations more openly. It is easier to deal with such concerns when they are explicit rather than suppressed.

The attempt to build a rough-cut new corporate strategy will also focus attention on the search for value creation insights. For companies that currently lack any value creation insights, this can be uncomfortable. However, unless the need for value creation insights is accepted, parenting advantage will never be achieved. Brainstorming to unearth possible value creation insights often leads to real breakthroughs in understanding the parenting advantage concept and its implications.

SUMMARY

Putting parenting advantage into practice is not a simple task. The problems that are likely to be encountered in introducing the concept and following through its implications should not be underestimated. In some companies, resistance to change runs so deep that it is likely to withstand any efforts to implant the parenting advantage concept. However, it is usually possible to win acceptance for parenting advantage through a combination of logic, persistence, diplomacy, timing, and conviction. The key is to show how the parenting advantage concept can illuminate the main issues and opportunities that the company is facing.

In the longer term, increased pressure from successful rivals and more active corporate governance will provide powerful stimuli for general conversion to parenting advantage. In the shorter term, the rewards for companies that grasp the nettle of early adoption will make all their efforts worthwhile.

APPENDIXES

A   DEFINING BUSINESSES

In Part One of this book, the parent and the business units are defined organizationally. In other words, we define the businesses as being whatever the company chooses to operate as organizationally separate profit-responsible units. Such entities are often referred to as Strategic Business Units, or SBUs, for the very reason that they are organized as largely separable businesses with control over the main strategic levers that affect their performance.[1] While focusing on an organizational definition is appropriate for identifying the businesses and parent as currently structured, it does not address the issue of whether one particular organizational definition of business units is superior to another. The superiority of certain definitions, however, is alluded to in Chapter 4, and emerges more fully in Chapter 9, where we note that certain parents create value by changing business definitions and structures within their portfolios. Similarly, in Chapters 12 and 14, we discuss the importance of business unit definition in the context of opportunities for value enhancement. More broadly, appropriate business definitions can be seen as the foundations of corporate-level strategy. If the business building blocks are inappropriately defined, there will be structural tensions in the corporate strategy that is built above them.

To address this issue, we must go beyond the organizational definition of a business. In this appendix, therefore, we consider the basis for an economic definition of a business. We examine how this economic definition relates to organizational definitions. We conclude that not all organizational definitions are equally valid or appropriate. Organizational definitions should take account of underlying economics; if they do not, value will be destroyed.

THE BASIS OF AN ECONOMIC VERSUS AN ORGANIZATIONAL BUSINESS DEFINITION

At the heart of all businesses are individual product-market transactions. Something is bought and sold. Property rights are exchanged between two parties, though we tend to distinguish between one, the customer, who primarily provides money, and the other, the supplier, who primarily provides a product or service. In some transactions, the business acts as customer. For example, it provides money (among other things) in exchange for certain services from its employees. In other transactions, the business acts as supplier. It sells goods or services in exchange for money.

Each transaction is unique. However, some sets of product-market transactions seem very similar. This similarity depends on some combination of features:

- The similarity of the product or service sold.
- The similarity of the buyers.
- The similarity of the occasions of purchase.
- The similarity of the purpose of purchase.

The purchases by two 45-year-old men in the Bronx on a hot afternoon of cans of beer to quench their thirst seem to be similar transactions. The purchases of a bottle of wine or a bottle of gin by the same men later in the day, or while on holiday in Florida, are somewhat similar to the previous transactions but also notably different: The products are all alcoholic drinks, and the customers are the same, but the buying occasions and purposes are different.

Businesses are most often defined in terms of the products and services they offer.[2] The development of marketing thinking has helped to bring other features of the transaction into greater prominence. Customer segmentation,[3] analysis of customer needs and intentions, price curves, buying triggers, and so forth have drawn attention to a simple but important point: A similar article may be sold in extremely dissimilar transactions. What is bought is not so much the physical product or specific service, but a bundle of tangible and intangible benefits that the customer perceives will be acquired. The nature and magnitude of these benefits depend on the details of the situation. This explains, among other things, the ability to achieve radically different prices for the same basic product or service in different contexts. As an extreme example, a millionaire stranded in the desert would pay a large sum of money for a bottle of dirty water which, in different circumstances, he would not purchase at all.

Occasionally, businesses are set up expressly to focus on a single product-market transaction, such as the completion of a major construction project. However, most businesses engage in hundreds, thousands, or even millions of such transactions (or sales) every year. Even so, they only focus on some tiny subset of the total possible range of transactions. The more focused they are, the more specifically they can align themselves to the needs of a particular transaction type. For example, a computer software applications company focusing entirely on the needs of a particular type of customer with a particular type of hardware should be able to align its practices and capabilities very closely to the requirements of this transaction type. Its staff can build relevant expertise at a rapid rate. Its sales methods can be focused on the distinctive interests of the customer group. Its internal processes can be molded to the particular needs of its market. This gives it certain advantages over a similar business that offers applications on a much broader front. In contrast, however, economies of scale and scope can be gained by broadening the range of transactions covered. A global producer of mass-market automobiles has advantages over a rival focusing solely on a single, small country. Many elements of fixed cost, such as R&D, design, and engineering can be spread across a much larger base; purchasing economies may be achieved at a global level; and so on. Nevertheless, the more focused producer may be able to satisfy particular home market needs that the global player cannot easily understand or replicate. There is therefore a tension between the benefits of focus and the benefits of scale and scope.

Since each transaction is unique, each business is also necessarily unique. However, just as there are clusters of transactions that seem more or less similar, there are clusters of businesses that seem more or less similar.[4] Supermarket chains each focus on slightly different transactions. But there is a broad similarity in the clusters of transactions that they target. This groups supermarkets together as being distinct from convenience stores, specialist food retailers, or discount stores. The supermarket chains compete with each other more directly: They target similar clusters of transactions, and they make similar tradeoffs between different types of focus and scale.

Although there are many such clusters of transactions and businesses, two points are notable. First, some clusters of transactions are targeted by a large number of similar rivals. There are many supermarkets in the world, many nationally based airlines, many manufacturers of personal computers for global distribution. Second, only a tiny fraction of theoretically possible clusters are populated at all. There are no business units that offer computer maintenance and foreign currency exchange, or engine parts and ice cream. Such combinations seem unreasonable and faintly bizarre. But why should some clusters be commonly targeted and well populated, while other potential clusters are unknown?

The answer reverts to the tension between the benefits of focus and of scale. Some clusters of transactions are popular targets because they can be served by entities enjoying an economically attractive combination of focus and scale. The "average" management team can perform better by targeting such clusters than by building a business around alternative clusters that offer other combinations of focus and scale. Clusters that offer the best combinations are competitively superior. Businesses targeted on such clusters should perform better than businesses targeted on less favorable clusters. We call these economically superior clusters "Strategic Business Opportunities" or SBOs. An SBO is a cluster of product-market transactions able to sustain a successful focused business, that would be commercially viable as a stand-alone operation.[5] We have chosen the term SBO for this economic definition of business scope to parallel its organizational counterpart, the SBU.

But why are there boundaries around clusters of transactions that represent an SBO? Let us start with a single transaction. A business set up expressly to address this transaction will have significant focus benefits. However, it will suffer from a lack of scale benefits. To achieve greater scale, it must increase the breadth of the cluster. As the cluster is broadened, it will become more diverse, reducing the opportunity to achieve benefits of focus. The tradeoff is sometimes described in terms of "costs of complexity outweighing benefits of scale."[6] The tradeoff, however, is by no means linear or the same across any expanding group of transactions. Some combinations of transactions allow for significant scale benefits while only marginally diluting focus benefits. In other cases, the very act of building focused capabilities for one type of transaction will preclude building focused capabilities for another type of transaction. As a result, the combined benefits of focus and scale increase with broadening of the transaction cluster, but only up to a point. Beyond this point, the combined benefits once again decline. These points of inflection represent boundaries around an SBO. The boundaries may be more or less distinct depending on the rate at which aggregate benefit builds up and declines on either side. If a business only targets some of the transactions in an SBO, it loses potential benefits from scale more than it gains additional benefits from focus. If a business targets transactions that go well beyond the SBO boundary, it loses benefits from focus more than it gains additional benefits from scale.

The magnitude of benefits from scale or focus is derived from two sources: efficiency improvements that reduce cost, and customer satisfaction improvements that increase value. For example, selling high-quality perfume through supermarkets or out-of-town warehouses would be economically more efficient than selling it through department stores or specialist boutiques. Scale benefits would reduce the cost of retailing. On the other hand, most customers do not wish to buy a high-quality perfume in this way. They value other aspects of the buying occasion, such as the ambience of the purchase and the nature of other products on sale. If customer preferences change significantly, or the cost advantages of scale change significantly, the magnitude of benefits from a particular transaction cluster will also change. At a given time, however, the magnitude of combined focus and scale benefits determines the boundary around the SBO.

Some businesses misguidedly focus on clusters of transactions that are economically inferior or unviable. Concorde's attempt to create a profitable business focused on supersonic jet airliners failed because the number of transactions would not support the required infrastructure of the business. Many new retail concepts fail because they have not identified a cluster of transactions with a viable combination of focus and scale benefits.

However, some SBOs exist that are unrecognized and unpopulated. This is due to two factors. First, in setting up a business, or continuing to run a business, most people's thinking is significantly shaped by the past. Because there have been jeweler's shops for many years, setting up or maintaining a jeweler's shop is an obvious option. In contrast, it takes a leap of imagination or insight to identify previously unknown SBOs, such as fast-fit in auto repairs, or facilities management in computing. Without innovators, SBOs can remain unpopulated for indefinitely long periods. Second, the relative benefits of particular types of focus and scale change over time because of changes in technology; for example, removing certain economies of scale through the use of computers and packaged software, or through flexible manufacturing techniques. Changes also occur because of shifts in customer preference, for example increasing the value of differentiation and the benefits of focus. Such changes create new SBOs that take time to spot or discover. As new SBOs become populated, some existing SBOs may shrink or even disappear. So-called "category killers," such as Toys "R" Us, exploit newly recognized SBOs which have significant benefits over more traditional transaction clusters.

OVERLAP AND SUBSTITUTION BETWEEN SBOs

Competition occurs both within SBOs and across them. Businesses focused on the same SBO compete directly. For example, two supermarkets in the same catchment area, or two strategy consulting companies serving a similar customer base, compete directly. Each strives to build competitive advantage over its rivals. If it succeeds, it gains share or is more profitable than others targeting the same SBO. But competition also occurs across SBOs. A business may be gaining share against direct competitors but losing out against others focused on overlapping SBOs. For example, one department store may be gaining share against others, but the whole department store SBO may offer declining benefits relative to more specialist retail SBOs. If so, specialist retailers will gradually erode the opportunity for even the most successful department store. This type of competition is less direct but can still be significant. If different SBOs satisfy similar customer needs, they overlap and affect each other.

At a much broader level, there is competition across all SBOs for a share of spending. If consumers' fuel bills go up, they may decide to cut or reduce spending at the supermarket. Rather than hire strategy consultants, a company may feel it would be a better investment to send some of its managers on a development program, or it may decide that it cannot afford either expenditure because of completely different needs elsewhere.

Even if businesses are targeting the same SBO, they can differ in the way that they put together their value chains to serve the given transaction cluster. For example, the strategy consulting firm will almost certainly subcontract its office cleaning and maybe some administrative functions. But can it also opt out of more critical processes, such as recruiting, concept development, marketing, or completion of the actual assignments? At first sight, it seems unlikely, but consideration of other consulting operations may suggest a different conclusion. Some very small firms consist of little more than one or two partners who develop client contacts and then pull together teams of independent consultants, often in a loose network, to work on specific projects. The transaction with a client may be fairly similar to that of more traditional firms, but the value chain of the "network" competitor is very different from that of the mainstream firm. The two value chains attempt to realize the SBO's potential benefits of focus and scale in very different ways. In some cases, one value chain configuration is clearly competitively superior to others. Competitors with the superior value chain configuration will prevail over those with inferior ones. In other cases, different value chain configurations can each provide viable ways of addressing the SBO in question. However, because the value chains are different, they may be able to capture different combinations of benefit, particularly as the market evolves. This may lead to a growing divergence between the transaction clusters that are best served by each value chain, and possibly the emergence of two separate, though somewhat overlapping, SBOs.

SBOs therefore overlap, causing businesses focused on overlapping SBOs to compete with each other. Improved efficiency or effectiveness can be achieved by clustering transactions in different ways, by reconfiguring the value chain, or by changing the amount of subcontract, rather than in-house, production.

SPOTTING SBOs

In determining whether a given transaction cluster is a viable target, and therefore an SBO, three tests can be applied:

1. Are any successful stand-alone businesses focusing on this cluster?
2. Would a unit focused on this cluster, but currently part of a multi-business company, be viable if it was spun off or bought out by management?
3. Does economic modeling (for example, detailed value chain analysis) suggest that this cluster is competitively viable based on its particular combination of benefits of focus and scale?

The attraction of the first test is that it can provide the most tangible evidence of viability. By listing companies in the industry and then grouping together those that target similar transaction clusters, it is possible to get a reasonably clear picture of the currently populated SBOs. Caution must be exercised in checking whether apparently successful businesses really are so. If they are cross-subsidized or subject to special conditions, the viability of the SBO may be disguised. Small national airlines may fit into this category. A much greater problem with this test is that it will not detect any currently unpopulated SBOs. Prior to the development of Federal Express, for example, a number of mail and freight-related SBOs existed, but the viability of focusing a business exclusively on express delivery of small packages was yet to be discovered.

The second test is similar but can address a slightly broader range of possibilities. There may not currently be successful stand-alone entities focused on the cluster, but the existence of such a unit within a multibusiness company may suggest that an SBO exists. Examining the unit's performance may throw light on the economic viability of the cluster. However, linkages within the portfolio may obscure whether the unit could survive on its own. In assessing its potential viability as a stand-alone entity, there is a danger of either underestimating or overestimating the changes that would be required. For example, the unit may currently benefit from a number of group services. But if it were spun off, could it acquire similar services readily, or do they represent a major source of advantage that could only be accessed as part of a larger grouping? Although this test will benefit from rigorous analysis, it will necessarily involve some subjective judgment as well.

The third test, economic modeling, has the great advantage of being able to analyze transaction clusters that have not yet been targeted by a real business. Prompted by thinking about new combinations of focus and scale, the entrepreneur or strategist can explore innovative SBO ideas using economic modeling. For example, growing differences in customer needs may signal the emergence of more focused SBOs. Alternatively, growing harmonization of standards or new scale economies may signal that an SBO is expanding from national scope to regional or global scope. The disadvantage of the approach is that it is potentially time consuming and difficult to do well. As with any other theoretical modeling, it may ignore important aspects of the real world or interpret data in ways that turn out to be incorrect. The value of increased focus may be overestimated, or the benefits from scale economies misunderstood. Nevertheless, in spotting unpopulated SBOs, some mix of creative inspiration, intuition, and analytical testing is the only way to avoid a purely historical view.

SBOs AND CORPORATE-LEVEL STRATEGY

In corporate strategy, the prime significance of SBO analysis is to improve organizational business unit definition. If business units are defined to address transaction clusters that are not SBOs, they will suffer a competitive disadvantage. If their definition is too small—for example, targeting a national market within a global SBO—they will suffer scale disadvantages. If their definition is too broad—for example, providing "one-stop shopping" for an inappropriate aggregation of transactions—they will suffer focus disadvantages. If their definition targets a transaction cluster that straddles two SBOs, they will suffer from disadvantages relative to businesses built specifically around each. In such cases, parents can create value by reconfiguring the business definitions within their portfolio. Conversely, parents can destroy value by redefining business units in ways that do not address SBOs.

Parents also have an opportunity to create value where SBOs themselves are changing. For example, an industry may be moving from a series of national SBOs to a series of more narrowly defined global SBOs, based on changes in technology and customer preference. At the start of this transition, it is appropriate for business units to be defined at the national level. As the advantages of a global redefinition gradually increase, an appropriate parent can facilitate strong linkages across countries.[7] Eventually, it may redefine the units, and change the role of country managers. The parent can smooth and facilitate a transition that stand-alone businesses would find difficult to achieve.

In other situations, the definition of underlying SBOs remains unclear for some time. Parents can create value by providing a framework in which tensions or multiple definitions are held open. For example, they may define business units at a fairly local level to achieve benefits of focus but work intensely to network these units on different dimensions.[8] This captures at least some of the scale benefits offered by wider transaction clusters. Although the individual units would not be viable as entirely stand-alone operations (and are therefore not addressing SBOs in themselves), the network enables them to compete with businesses targeting larger transaction clusters. Over a period of time, one of the larger transaction clusters may emerge as the dominant SBO. However, if the time period is long, a network will reduce risk by simultaneously capturing at least some of the benefits of rival clusters. Alternatively, the parent may adopt one definition but establish a context in which the shift to a different definition can occur rapidly and easily. Many Japanese companies establish business units but make them "incomplete" or reliant on certain central resources that can be moved around.[9] This reduces the territorial dangers of becoming frozen into a set of business definitions that may lose their relevance.

SBOs change over time, but in some areas they change more rapidly than in others. Where relevant technology is undergoing significant development, or where customer needs and preferences display major shifts, understanding SBOs is a challenging, but vital, task for parents. In these areas, linkage approaches that cut across, or downplay, strict business definitions may be appropriate.[10] In more mature areas with slower rates of change, clarity of business definition and avoidance of complexity is more likely to be beneficial. This is reflected in the contrasting approaches of successful parents such as Canon and BTR, whose heartlands are subject to very different rates of SBO change.

REVIEW OF BUSINESS DEFINITION

Businesses can be defined purely on the basis of the current organization. However, not all organizational definitions are equally appropriate. The fundamental issues in business definition are straightforward and may be summarized as follows:

- Business units focus on particular types of transaction.
- It is viable to focus on some clusters of transactions, but not on others.
- Business units group around viable clusters and squeeze out other businesses that attempt to serve less appropriate clusters. We call a cluster that can support a successful stand-alone entity a Strategic Business Opportunity (SBO).
- Different businesses targeting the same SBO sometimes configure their value chains differently. It is important to select a viable configuration. Over a period of time, differences in value chain configuration may lead to the discovery of new SBOs.
- The relative attraction of clusters, and hence the definition of SBOs, changes over time, depending on technology and customer preference.
- Parents destroy value by:
  —Ignoring underlying economics in their organizational business definitions.
  —Misinterpreting SBO boundaries.
  —Creating too much, or too little, clarity in the business definitions they establish.

- Parents create value by:
  —Defining their businesses to address SBOs more accurately.
  —Spotting unpopulated SBOs.
  —Smoothing transitions in business definition that reflect shifts in SBO boundaries.
  —Holding open business definitions while SBO boundaries are unclear.

NOTES

1. Sometimes it is more difficult to define the businesses organizationally. This topic is dealt with in Appendix B.

2. For a discussion of different approaches to defining a business, see Derek F. Abell, *Defining the Business*, Englewood Cliffs, NJ: Prentice-Hall, 1980.

3. In marketing, a segment is a group of customers with similar needs that can be reached through similar channels. A good review of the marketing use of segments is contained in Philip Kotler's *Marketing Management* (5th ed.), Englewood Cliffs, NJ: Prentice-Hall, 1984.

4. The concept of "strategic groups" is widely used in the literature. Michael Porter describes and discusses this concept in *Competitive Strategy*, Chapter 7, New York: Free Press, 1980.

5. Various academics and consultants have identified such clusters in similar ways. John Kay's concept of a "strategic market" is particularly relevant. See J. A. Kay, "Identifying the strategic market," *Business Strategy Review*, pp. 2–24, Spring 1990; J. A. Kay, *Foundations of Corporate Success*, Oxford: Oxford University Press, 1993, ch. 9.

6. A recent article in the McKinsey Quarterly discusses the costs of complexity and provides many examples: Peter Cummings, David White, and Stefan Wisniowski, "Strategic Simplicity," *The McKinsey Quarterly*, no. 3, 1990, pp. 80–90.

7. See discussion of TI in Chapter 9.

8. This appears to be part of what ABB does through its matrix; see Chapter 7.

9. See, for example, the discussion of Canon in Chapter 7. See also N. Campbell and T. Kagono, *Organisational Peristroika: Intra-Company Markets in Japanese MNCs*, Manchester Business School, Working Paper No. 249, June 1993.

10. For a discussion of such approaches, see Chapter 7.

DEFINITION AND STRUCTURE OF PARENT ORGANIZATIONS

B

To simplify the exposition of our views, we frequently refer to the "parent" as if it were a single entity. In reality, many business unit managers perceive a series of different entities within the parent organization as a whole. These may include divisional or sector layers, staff groups, and regional groups, as well as the center or head office. In some cases, managers may not even be sure what constitutes the parent, and who falls within its boundaries. This appendix addresses the issue of defining the parent and considers how different parent organizations are structured.

WHAT CONSTITUTES THE PARENT?

A basic definition of the parent is that it is doing something other than directly running a business. Theoretically, therefore, it is not difficult to identify the parent. First we define the organizational business units.[1] Whatever is left outside the business units but within the company must be the parent.

In many companies, identifying the parent is straightforward. Business units are defined clearly in terms of organizational structure and management responsibility. Each unit has identifiable resource boundaries (e.g., staff and tangible assets). It has a general manager who integrates different functions, initiates strategic proposals, is held responsible for profitability, and has the sense of "running a business." In many cases, the unit could survive and prosper as a stand-alone entity if it was spun off, or was the subject of a management buyout. If business units are easy to identify, then so is the parent. The parent may consist of several levels of general management above the business units (e.g., division, group, or country levels) and it may consist of different types of personnel (e.g., line managers, functional staff, or central services). But the parent organization is easily distinguished from the business units.

In some companies, however, it is less easy to identify the organizational business units, and hence it is less easy to determine what organizational entities and individuals are part of the parent. This may occur for three reasons, illustrated in Exhibit B–1.

First, the so-called general manager of the business unit may in fact have very little initiative or control over major strategic decisions affecting the unit. This situation may occur because the management level above has centralized major decision making (illustrated in Exhibit B–1 section 1(a)). For example, a manufacturing plant may be set up as a profit center, but be obliged to make a defined range of products only for sale to a single internal customer or sales force, while product development is controlled by another unit outside the manufacturing profit

EXHIBIT B–1   Difficulties in defining organizational business units

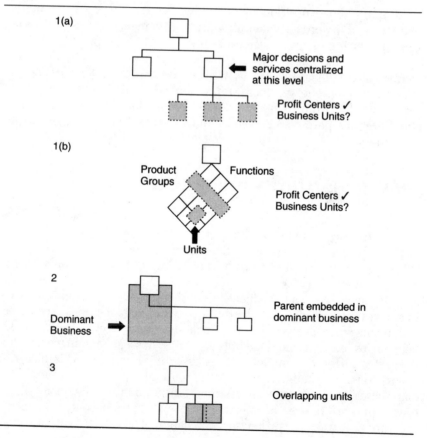

center. Equally, a unit may rely significantly on centrally controlled departments, providing services that cannot be bought-in from outside the company, and over which the unit has limited cost or quality control. In such cases, the unit in question may be a profit center, but it may have too little strategic initiative to count as a fully–fledged "business."

A similar situation also occurs in some matrix contexts (illustrated in Exhibit B–1 section 1(b)). For example, a product or brand manager who draws on resources from different functions may or may not perform a full-blooded general management task. Equally, a unit manager may be subject to so much influence and so many constraints from the product groups and the functions that they have too little discretion to be regarded as running a genuinely separate business unit.

In such cases, the appropriate definition of the business unit is at a level higher than the profit center itself. The first level of real general management is above the profit center, and the parent organization starts at a correspondingly higher level. Defining this first "real" level of general management is somewhat subjective. In practice, however, we have come across few cases where managers cannot readily reach agreement on where it is.

A second type of difficulty is illustrated in Exhibit B–1 section 2. The parent organization may be embedded within the dominant business in the company. This is particularly common where a single business company with a long history has recently developed smaller new ventures. For example, a long-standing construction company may have set up a property development business and a house-building business as separate units. But the whole group may be run predominantly by the managers and staff departments of the construction business. Their activities are therefore blurred between running the dominant business directly and parenting the fledgling units. But in such cases, although individuals may be both business managers and part of the parenting organization, the distinction between the two roles is, in concept, not difficult to make.

A third category of some ambiguity is where two or more units overlap heavily with unclear boundaries (illustrated in Exhibit B–1 section 3). For example, if two business units share a sales force that is not under the direct control of either of them, how should we define the sales force? Is it part of the parent because it is not directly within a unit, or is it a part of both units? In such cases, the answer depends on the way in which the operations are run. For example, if the sales force is jointly managed by both units and its costs are controlled and divided up between the units, it would best be defined as part of the units, and therefore outside the parent organization. If the sales force is set up as a profit center in its own right, serving the needs of both units, but independently managed, it should be defined as another organizational business unit, again outside the parent. But, if it is run as a central service, probably as a cost center or recharging on some formula to the business units, and reporting through a group or company sales director to a level of general management above the business unit heads, it should be defined as part of the parent organization.

Although in some cases identifying the parent requires careful thought, it is usually possible. Sometimes, however, perceptions regarding the role of individuals or groups remain unclear or contradictory. Underlying these more complex or ambiguous cases are two quite different causes: unintentional ambiguity and intentional ambiguity.

In some cases, the ambiguity of definition may be unintentional. For example, an organization that has been a single business company for many years may gradually evolve into multiple businesses but not establish a clear separation between the business units and the parent. Indeed, the need to distinguish between business roles and parenting roles may only arise gradually, as new businesses grow up around the original business. This situation has occurred in a number of recently privatized companies. Prior to privatization, such companies are often run in a centralized, functional way. Following privatization, they face more focused competition in specific areas. They also face pressures to outsource, to generate new business streams and to understand and manage profitability more tightly. This leads to the establishment of separate business units, though these are often overlapping and closely linked. However, the managers of the dominant business may retain overall control, effectively exerting parental influence over the other units. Due to the ambiguity this creates, tensions can develop between the "new" businesses and the managers of the dominant business, who may be confused between their two roles. In such cases, even if an individual manager does retain two roles, it is helpful to distinguish clearly between them. Failure to do so encourages inappropriate interventions in the new business units.

In contrast, some companies deliberately leave business unit definitions at least partly ambiguous. Sometimes this occurs during the transition from one organizational form to another. For example, a company may gradually integrate a series of related but separate business units in different territories. Initially, each unit may have a general manager. Over a period of time, however, as the units become more and more closely linked, the role of their managers may become increasingly circumscribed. Meanwhile, the role of the management level above, part of the parenting organization in the past, will become closer to that of the first level of true general management.[2]

Longer term ambiguity is encouraged by companies that fear the potential rigidity of clear business definitions. A structure that is appropriate for today may be ill-suited to tomorrow. Specifically defined business units may come to obstruct the ability of the company to redeploy its resources appropriately.[3] In such cases, the company itself is seen as the prime entity, holding and deploying all its resources, and directing parts of them at specific product markets as and when opportunities arise. The composition of the parent and the boundaries between units may change frequently. The parent organization is often relatively large, providing a number of services and central resources that may play a major role in business unit operations. At any given time, however, it is still usually possible to distinguish between the parent organization and the business units. In Chapter 7, we examine Canon which demonstrates a number of these characteristics. At an extreme, a parent may be so involved in business unit management that it borders on being a centralized, single-business company.

At any given time, the parent organization is therefore whatever lies outside the company's defined business units. This is true whether the business units are appropriately defined and structured or not.[4] If, however, the units are restructured, it may have an impact on what is included within the parent organization.

HOW ARE PARENT ORGANIZATIONS STRUCTURED?

In practice, there are almost as many parent structures as there are parent organizations. However, certain basic models emerge. These are not rigorously distinct, and they merge into each other. Nevertheless, it is helpful to distinguish between some different but commonly encountered positionings to illustrate the range of possible options and to identify various benefits and dangers.

We will discuss these positionings under three main headings:

1. Simple reporting.
2. Divided parenting:
   a. Contact executives.
   b. Existing businesses versus corporate development.
   c. Shared responsibilities.
   d. Matrix.
3. Duplicated parenting.

Simple Reporting

The simplest parenting structure involves a single level of line management above the individual business units. This is usually the most effective structure for smaller companies with relatively few business units. However, as the number of units increases, it becomes less satisfactory. For example, until 1985 Dover Corporation had a single parenting layer. At that point, however, the number of business units within the corporation had grown to more than 20, and the chief executive decided that it was no longer feasible for all units to receive adequate attention from a single parenting team. There is no universal law that determines the maximum span of parenting control, but at some point many companies feel that this maximum has been reached, and a new approach is required.

Theoretically, one solution is to split the company in two, give shareholders shares in both halves, and continue to use a single parenting layer for each. In reality, this approach is seldom, if ever, adopted.[5] The alternative is to create additional structures within the parent organization to expand its capacity. This expansion of parental capacity can be achieved in a variety of ways. There is a conceptual difference, however, between retaining a single parenting task, while dividing it up between different levels or groups, and duplicating parenting tasks, with different parenting levels carrying out much the same tasks. We call the former "divided parenting," as a single parenting task is divided up. We call the latter "duplicated parenting," as each level is fulfilling much the

EXHIBIT B–2   Different approaches to structuring the parent

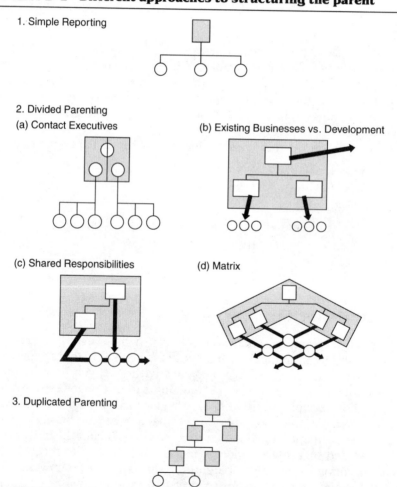

1. Simple Reporting

2. Divided Parenting
(a) Contact Executives

(b) Existing Businesses vs. Development

(c) Shared Responsibilities

(d) Matrix

3. Duplicated Parenting

same sort of parenting role. These different approaches are illustrated in Exhibit B–2.

Divided Parenting

Divided parenting increases the capacity of the parent organization by creating specialist groups within the parent. These groups may specialize in a particular part of the portfolio or in a particular aspect of parenting.

Contact Executives. The simplest form of divided parenting involves the specialization of individuals within a single parental level. Members of the executive committee, for example, may divide up the portfolio and each take special responsibility for some part of it. In effect, they become "contact executives" for a subset of the total portfolio. (This role is also referred to as "sponsoring director" in some companies.) In such cases, all business units will still come to the full executive committee for agreement on major matters, such as annual budget approval or significant capital expenditures. However, for more frequent and informal contact, the businesses will rely on their contact executives. In theory, contact executives are part of a single parent level and are not a separate layer between the businesses and the center. They act in the place of the chief executive, who would be spread too thinly to deal with all units directly on all matters.

During the mid-1980s, Sir John Harvey-Jones introduced the contact executive structure into ICI. Each main board executive director acted as contact executive for certain businesses, while the executive board as a whole retained shared responsibility for major parenting decisions. The directors were able to become more fully briefed on the affairs of their businesses, and to spend more time in informal discussions with them. But there were no personal staffs, no consolidation of results, and no formal review meetings for each director's group of businesses, and all major decisions and reviews were handled by the executive board collectively. The structure was intended to allow the corporate center to maintain sufficient contact with, and shared responsibility for, each of ICI's many businesses, but without establishing an extra parenting level. The structure was continued under Sir Denys Henderson until ICI's demerger in 1993.

The contact executive solution seems an obvious extension of simple reporting, and several companies have used it successfully to parent portfolios of businesses that had grown too extensive to be handled by a single chief executive. However, it is a structure that can encounter problems. The contact executive stands in for the chief executive, but only under certain circumstances. Beyond these, the chief executive must be directly involved. Characteristically, there is some uncertainty as to what exactly these circumstances are. Lack of clarity and consistency can undermine the contact executive's position, and business units may feel there is no point in dealing with him or her, rather than going directly to the chief executive. Contact executives may also feel uneasy about the boundaries of their roles. If they become too associated with a designated group, the chief executive may start to hold them directly responsible for "their" businesses, rather than retaining shared parenting responsibility with them. The basic uncertainties of the position, and difficulties to do with "sitting on both sides of the table," can, therefore, sometimes undermine the benefits.[6]

Existing Businesses versus Corporate Development. A different way of splitting the parenting task is to create two, or more, levels of parent that focus on different sources of value creation. One typical split involves the top layer primarily focusing on corporate development activities and external relations, while the next layer focuses primarily on parenting the existing portfolio. The top layer also defines and supervises, to a greater or lesser extent, the parenting approach to be carried out at the level below.

When Dover expanded beyond a simple reporting structure, it followed this logic. Gary Roubos, the chief executive, and a small central group continued to deal with corporate development issues (such as acquiring new companies), external relations (for example with banks and shareholders), and defining the role of the parenting groups below them. This next level down provided the type of influence on individual business units that was previously provided by the single parenting layer. The center controls this influence primarily by careful choice of the managers that will play this role. Their attitudes and capabilities replicate those of the original parenting layer, increasing its effective span of control. However, Roubos also keeps a careful watch on the way that parenting is being carried out at this next level to ensure that it remains consistent with Dover's parenting philosophy.

BTR has developed a much larger organization based on the same fundamental principles. Having grown by 1993 to encompass roughly 1,300 profit centers spread across some 40 countries, it would be impractical for all units to report to the same parenting team. BTR's parenting structure, however, expands the scope of the center by dividing the parenting task. The prime parenting task is carried out by 25 group chief executives (GCEs), each responsible for a group of business units. Many of these business units report directly to the group chief executive. Smaller units, however, are grouped together at a level below the GCEs. Above the GCEs is the chief executive and the corporate-level parenting team. This group is particularly concerned with corporate development activities, such as major acquisitions, external relations, and the performance of the GCEs. It is also sometimes involved with the GCEs in review of particular business units. This is a mechanism for maintaining alignment in the company's overall parenting approach:

The center can see that GCEs are parenting in a way that faithfully replicates the company philosophy and can also remain close to important business issues.

Although in principle the parenting task is basically divided under this type of structure, duplication can occur in some companies. First, reviews of individual businesses may sometimes involve two sets of discussions, one with the second parent level and one with the first parent level. This can shade into duplicated parenting, which we will discuss later in this appendix. Second, in supervising the parenting role of the middle layer, the top layer may become heavily involved. This reduces the span of control extension of the parent and may lead to unhelpful second guessing rather than parenting quality control.

Shared Responsibilities.   This approach also involves dividing up the parenting task between two layers but with a different split of responsibilities. Here, the higher level parent is not just concerned with corporate development and external relations. It also plays an active role in influencing businesses within the portfolio. The level below, often called a "division," typically has prime responsibility for stand-alone influence on the individual business units, and for linkages within the division. However, the higher level also has some direct influence on the business units, particularly in terms of budgetary and strategic control.[7] In addition, it exerts any influence that exists on cross-divisional linkages. Furthermore, it tends to apply influence, especially control influence, to the division itself as an entity.

Cooper Industries provides an illustration. Cooper's business units are grouped into several divisional clusters, such as the hand tools division. Parenting at this divisional level is heavily involved in the planning of each unit, and also in controlling individual business performance. There is also a focus on linkages within the cluster, aiming to create significant benefits through coordination of product ranges, shared product development, and shared sales forces. At the next level up, the corporate level, parenting is concerned with corporate development issues but plays a wider role as well. It maintains various central services, such as a specialist manufacturing group that is potentially valuable to all Cooper's businesses. It is also involved in the stand-alone parenting of individual units, especially on the control dimension. Finally, it acts partly as a parent to the divisions themselves. Some of these divisions, such as hand tools, are clusters of linked but easily identifiable units. Others are closer to being single businesses with lower level profit centers. To maintain close informal links with the divisions, Cooper also uses the "contact executive" structure described earlier. Three executive vice presidents at the center each have a particular responsibility for certain divisions. Although all the divisions meet regularly with the full executive team, these contact executives provide a focus for day-to-day contact.

This model of parenting identifies fairly distinct roles for the divisional and the central levels. However, there is a degree of overlap, particularly in the stand-alone influence on individual business units. If the distinction between roles is clear, and the degree of overlap small, each parenting level can add value. However, the greater the uncertainty of the role, the more likely that tensions will arise between levels. Furthermore, if the overlap is extensive, the model shades into duplicated parenting.

Matrix.   In a simple matrix, business units report to parenting groups on two dimensions, one typically representing a regional grouping, the other a product, brand, or service grouping. Above this parenting level is a further level that pulls together the two sides of the matrix. This higher level is concerned with arbitration in disputes between the two sides of the matrix, with corporate development, with external relations, and with guiding the parenting approach of the groups below. ABB's use of a matrix is described in Chapter 7.

In such a matrix, each business unit has a direct relationship with different parenting groups for different purposes. In this respect, it is like the previous approach, where both the division and the center may deal directly with a business. However, because the different groups within the matrix are theoretically at the same hierarchical level, additional tension is created. Whether this tension is a positive source of balance or a negative source of confusion depends on the organization.

In this sort of organization, lack of clarity or excessive overlap are potential dangers; specialization of parenting, allowing for focus and development of particular skills, are potential advantages.

Duplicated Parenting

Duplicated parenting involves repeating the same basic tasks at different levels of aggregation. A number of business units report to a division; a number of divisions report to a group; a number of groups report to a sector; and so on. Each level parents the level below, exerting stand-alone or linkage influence as it sees fit, and often providing functional influence and services. Prior to its acquisition by Hanson in 1986, Imperial Group appeared to be following this approach.[8]

The danger of such an approach is that the cash and time costs of duplication are not justified by additional value creation. In fact, the greater the number of parenting levels, the more difficult and unlikely it becomes for each level to make a distinctive and additive contribution. If it is hard to add value by parenting a business, it is even harder to do so by parenting a parent. Intermediate levels, carrying out a full parenting task in their own right, see performance data first, are liable to aggregate and massage the numbers, and resist direct access of higher levels to the business units. Alternatively, intermediate levels may act as little more than post boxes, adding scant value, but slowing up communications both upwards and downwards. Business unit managers typically have the sense that distant parenting levels have specific but unknown demands of them, which lead to delays in capital expenditure approvals, iterations of planning and budgeting processes with apparently arbitrary revisions, and surprise initiatives. A pervasive fear of second guessing can lead to excessive politics and deliberate concealment of information between parenting layers. Although in theory each layer might add value by parenting the one below, our research has not identified companies where this approach has seemed effective. As one manager summed up the review process within his own company: "We have a number of rakings over at different levels, each one too shallow to get at the real issues."

As described earlier, having more than one level within the parent organization does not necessarily lead to duplicated parenting. However, it will do so unless a single parent role is split up in some way, avoiding significant overlap.

REVIEW OF PARENTING DEFINITIONS AND STRUCTURES

We define the parent as those who are within the company but outside the business units as currently structured. The parent organization can itself be structured in different ways. As we have seen, however, different approaches blur into each other at the boundaries. For example, parents who are basically dividing up a single task will still have some areas of overlap between different groups or levels. This will blur into duplicated parenting as the higher level's guidance of the level below turns more into a review and control process.

In all such situations, it is important to consider the aggregate influence of the various parenting groups. This is what will lead to parenting advantage, or the lack of it. However, it is also worth trying to isolate the distinctive value added by each separate group. The more that there is overlap, the more likely that redundancy or unhelpful second guessing will occur. It is therefore important to ask detailed questions about the composition of the parent and the specific contribution of different parenting groups.

- Who is currently contained within the parent organization? What are the different groups within the parent?
- Are some parenting groups essentially part of a business?
- Are some parenting groups potentially stand-alone entities, which would be better defined as business units in their own right?
- What is the role of each parenting group in adding value to the businesses, and in building or maintaining parenting advantage?

- How does each group interact with other parts of the parenting structure?
- Are different parenting groups performing essentially the same role, and duplicating effort?

Such questions help in addressing the effectiveness of the existing structure and the nature of possible alternatives, and are highly relevant to the parenting decisions discussed in Chapter 15.

NOTES

1. However, not all organizational business definitions are equally appropriate. For a discussion of economic business definitions, see Appendix A.

2. For a discussion of such changes in business scope, and the implications for managerial roles in the parent, see John A. Quelch, "The New Country Managers," *McKinsey Quarterly*, no. 4, 1992, pp. 155–165. See also C. K. Prahalad and Yves L. Doz, *"The Multinational Mission,"* London: Free Press, 1987.

3. See, for example, the description of the "postentrepreneurial" corporation in Rosabeth Moss Kanter's *When Giants Learn to Dance,* New York: Simon & Schuster, 1989. See also C. K. Prahalad and Gary Hamel, "The Core Competence of the Corporation," *Harvard Business Review*, May–June 1990, pp. 79–91.

4. For a discussion of appropriate business unit definition, see Appendix A.

5. Demergers, which have this effect, are usually justified by the difficulties of parenting and developing different businesses within a single corporate entity rather than by pure span of reporting considerations. See Chapter 14 for further discussion.

6. Similar problems are caused by "putting the barons on the board," where major division heads also have responsibilities as members of the corporate parent.

7. See Michael Goold with John J. Quinn, *Strategic Control,* London: Financial Times/Pitman Publishing, 1993, Appendix 2.

8. See Michael Goold and Andrew Campbell, *Strategies and Styles,* Oxford: Basil Blackwell, 1987.

C PARENTING STYLES

In our descriptions of corporate strategies, we have made use of the concept of parenting style. This appendix will explain the concept more fully and show how a company's parenting style relates to the success of its corporate strategy.

PARENTING STYLES

In our research, we have encountered companies with many different parenting approaches; indeed, each company has its own distinctive approach to parenting. We have, however, found it possible to discern some broad patterns in parenting, which we refer to as "parenting styles."

In an earlier book, *Strategies and Styles*, we explored the broad differences in parenting style between companies.[1] The book identified three basically different parenting styles. Exhibit C–1 is a display that brings out the main differences between the styles in terms of planning influence and control influence. Planning influence refers to the approach that the parent takes to the formulation of plans, strategies, and budgets in the businesses. It varies from low influence (highly decentralized) through to high influence (much more closely involved and influential). Control influence refers to the approach of the parent to the control process. At one extreme, we found parents that emphasized strongly the achievement of short-term financial targets ("tight financial control"); at the other extreme, we found parents that were primarily concerned with strategic goals and underlying competitive position, and hence were more flexible about short-term financial targets ("flexible control"); and, in the middle, we found parents that believed in tight

411

EXHIBIT C–1 Parenting styles

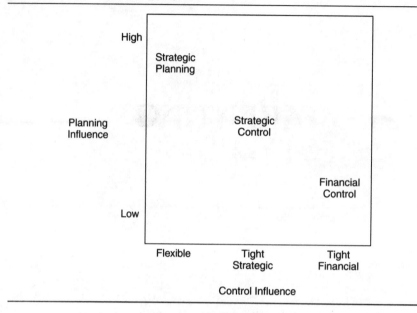

control, but endeavored to strike a balance between financial targets and strategic targets ("tight strategic control"). In effect, the control axis in Exhibit C–1 represents the degree of importance attached to the delivery of short-term budgeted financial targets.[2]

The three main parenting styles that we have identified are the Strategic Planning, the Strategic Control, and the Financial Control style.[3] As shown in Exhibit C–1, the styles lie along a spectrum. Although the basic features of each style are very different, the boundaries between them are not sharp. Thus a company such as Unilever lies at the boundary between Strategic Control and Strategic Planning and a company such as Grand Metropolitan at the boundary between Strategic Control and Financial Control. It follows that Unilever's version of Strategic Control is considerably different from Grand Metropolitan's.

The Strategic Planning Style

Strategic Planning style parents are closely involved with their businesses in the formulation of plans and decisions. They typically provide a clear overall sense of direction, within which their businesses develop their strategies, and take the lead on selected corporate development initiatives. On major decisions, they expect businesses to seek a consensus with headquarters and other interested units. They often have large or powerful functional staffs at the center, including shared resource or service departments in areas such as marketing, engineering, R&D, or personnel. Strategic planning and capital expenditure review processes are used both to check the validity of business plans and as a vehicle for corporate suggestions, and resource allocation is driven by the requirements of agreed long-term strategies. In most, but not all, cases, Strategic Planning companies are heavily involved in encouraging cooperation and coordination between businesses, and have structures that involve overlapping or matrix responsibilities and shared resources. Strategic Planning parents believe that they have an essential role to play in helping their businesses to arrive at better plans and strategies and in developing new businesses for the corporate portfolio.

The control process in Strategic Planning companies stresses the long-term health and development of the businesses as the top priority. Operating plans or budgets are seen as detailed quantifications of the first year of a business's strategic plan, and performance against short-term financial targets is regarded as part of a wider overall assessment of performance. In consequence, formal monitoring of monthly financial results is de-emphasized, provided the parent remains confident that the management of the business is pursuing the right strategy. Typically, business managers are expected to identify with the company as a whole, rather than with their specific business, and their rewards and incentives are based as much on corporate results and contribution as on business-specific performance.

Our original views on the Strategic Planning style were based mainly on research with British companies such as BP, BOC, Cadbury Schweppes, and Lex Service Group. Subsequently, we have refined our understanding of the Strategic Planning style through contacts with a wide range of companies in all the main developed countries. We have found there are relatively few companies in the United Kingdom, the United States, and other Western countries that pursue a full-fledged Strategic Planning style, and that some leading exponents of the style have recently moved away from it. IBM,[4] for example, has decided to delink its business units into a number of much more separate entities, to cut back on headquarters staff and influence, and to press more strongly for profit improvement in its businesses. BP is another company that has been attempting to push more responsibility onto its businesses, to rein back on corporate overheads and interference, and to move from Strategic Planning to Strategic Control.

Despite this trend, there are some notably successful Western Strategic Planning companies, and the Strategic Planning style is much the most popular style among leading Japanese companies. Shell's basic parenting style is Strategic Planning, with strong emphasis placed on a consensus-seeking global matrix form of organization, and an attitude to investment that stresses long-time horizons. Banc One is another successful Western company which pursues a Strategic Planning style. In Japan, most companies stress the importance of consensus decisions, regard the corporate center as having an essential contribution to make to the formulation of business strategies, and are driven by long-term goals and performance.[5] Canon, for example, is a highly successful Japanese company that follows this path.

The Strategic Control Style

Strategic Control style parents basically decentralize planning to the businesses but retain a role in checking and assessing what is proposed by the businesses. Thus, businesses are expected to take responsibility for putting forward strategies, plans, and proposals in a "bottom-up" fashion, but the parent may sponsor certain themes, initiatives, or objectives, and will only sanction proposals that meet an appropriate balance of strategic and financial criteria. Corporate staff in Strategic Control companies are usually concerned primarily with support to the parent but may also include some functional centers of excellence and some service departments, mainly available to the businesses on a voluntary use basis. The strategic planning, capital expenditure, and budgeting processes are designed to allow the parent to question the assumptions behind the businesses' plans and to test the quality of thinking and the projected financial and strategic objectives they propose. Businesses are usually encouraged to work together to achieve synergy benefits, but within organization structures and responsibilities that stress individual business unit performance. Strategic Control parents believe in the benefits of decentralization but see a role for themselves in ensuring that the businesses' plans are sound, and in complementing these plans with suitable corporate development initiatives.

Strategic Control parents place high importance on financial objectives in the control process, but they also pay attention to strategic milestones and objectives. Ideally, the planning process includes a strenuous negotiation not only of financial targets but also of explicit strategic performance targets, or milestones, that can be measured with some precision as a basis for subsequent control.[6] Results are regularly monitored, and performance against planned targets is an important determinant of personal career progression and compensation. Managers are expected to identify closely with their businesses, and their success is judged largely on the performance of the businesses in question rather than of the company as a whole. If, however, circumstances have significantly changed since the plan was made, it is accepted that business managers may not be able to deliver fully on their original targets and that a revised forecast may be needed. In this way, Strategic Control companies seek a balance between financial and strategic targets.

Among the *Strategies and Styles* companies, ICI, Courtaulds, and Vickers exemplified the Strategic Control style. Subsequent work has confirmed and extended our views on the key features of the style. We have found that the Strategic Control style is considerably the most popular style. In a survey of U.K. companies, well over half of all companies identified themselves as Strategic Control parents,[7] and the bulk of the companies we have described in this book, including 3M, ABB, Cooper, Dover, Emerson, GE, Grand Metropolitan, RTZ, TI, and Unilever basically follow a Strategic Control style. Since the Strategic Control style represents the middle of the spectrum, between the extremes of Strategic Planning and Financial Control, this is hardly surprising.

Despite its popularity, we have found that it is not easy to make the Strategic Control style work well. Among the five Strategic Control companies in our original *Strategies and Styles* group, two (Plessey and Imperial) have been taken over, two (Courtaulds and ICI) have chosen to demerge themselves, and one (Vickers) has undergone considerable portfolio restructuring.[8] Companies such as Emerson, GE, and Unilever have, however, been highly successful Strategic Control parents.

The Financial Control Style

Financial Control style parents are strongly committed to decentralization of planning. They structure their businesses as stand-alone units with as much autonomy as possible, and with full responsibility for formulating their own strategies and plans. The parent's primary roles are to insist that all decisions are "owned" by the businesses and that proposals must meet required financial criteria. There is minimal staff at the headquarters, focused on corporate management support and financial control. The planning process concentrates on annual budgets, which are seen as vital vehicles for testing and stretching the operating plans, and, especially, the financial targets of each business. In most cases, there is no formal strategic planning process. Capital investments, however, are carefully examined, with project-by-project approval dependent on expected financial returns, frequently measured in terms of speed of payback. Different businesses in the company are encouraged to deal with each other as if they were independent entities, working together only if they see mutual benefits in doing so. This approach to planning stems from the belief that the businesses are in the best position to make their own plans, and that the parent should avoid interfering, except to establish required standards of bottom-line performance. Financial Control parents are, however, active in seeking new acquisitions that will benefit from their Financial Control style of parenting.

In Financial Control companies, the control process concentrates on financial targets and results. Once agreed, the financial targets represent a vital "contract" for the business, and no excuses are acceptable for nondelivery. The parent monitors actual results closely and frequently, and exerts strong pressure on businesses that are behind budget. Business managers' careers and bonuses are strongly influenced by their ability to meet budget, and managers who miss budget are in severe danger of losing their jobs unless they can show that they are taking radical action to correct the situation. Business managers identify with their separate businesses rather than the company as a whole, and their prospects and pay are determined by the performance of their specific businesses. The control process, therefore, emphasizes the personal responsibility of each manager for delivering the financial results that he or she has promised for his or her business.

Strategies and Styles identified several prominent British Financial Control companies, including BTR, GEC, Hanson, and Tarmac. Of these, both BTR and Hanson continue to prosper with a fundamentally unaltered parenting style, whereas GEC and Tarmac have performed less well.[9] Smaller U.K. companies that have followed a Financial Control style with success in recent years include F. H. Tomkins and Williams Holdings. The Financial Control style, in its pure form, is less popular in continental Europe, though companies such as Haniel and Trelleborg have employed it, and the style is almost unknown in Japan. In the United States, the philosophy behind the Financial Control style inspired the huge growth of the LBO (leveraged buyout) partnerships during the 1980s. Companies such as KKR have prospered by creating a motivation and focus on performance for the companies in which they invest that is similar to BTR or Hanson.[10] The mechanisms are different, with the emphasis placed on personal ownership stakes and the disciplinary role of debt finance. But the outcome is similar: strongly motivated management teams with high levels of personal accountability for delivering the best possible profitability and cash flow figures for their businesses.

Parenting Styles and Value Creation

The three parenting styles that we have described each emphasize different sorts of value creation. In particular, their approaches to stand-alone, linkage, and corporate development value creation are different.

In terms of stand-alone and linkage value creation, the Financial Control style concentrates on operating improvements and financial control, and encourages the businesses to deal with each other as if they were independent third-party organizations. The Strategic Planning style is primarily concerned with the long-term strategies and goals of its businesses, and is much more inclined to facilitate sharing, coordination, and a blurring of boundaries between businesses. The Strategic Control style aims for a balance between the other two styles.

In terms of corporate development, Strategic Planning companies are usually active corporate venturers, devoting substantial resources to the creation of new businesses for long-term corporate renewal. They also create value through acquiring and integrating businesses together to create larger, more international or better resourced businesses that will have stronger underlying competitive positions. Financial Control companies very seldom go in for corporate venturing. However, they are active acquirers and divesters. They aim to create value for their shareholders through their deal-making skills and

through subsequent restructurings, which usually emphasize breaking companies up into smaller, more separate profit centers. The smaller units can then be the subject of radical cost cutting and efficiency improvement or, if appropriate, can be sold on to other more suitable owners. Strategic Control companies, again, combine elements of the Strategic Planning and the Financial Control approaches.

Tensions Implicit in the Parenting Styles

Underlying the differences in parenting style are different attitudes to certain basic tradeoffs or tensions that face all corporate parents. Should the parent establish a decision process in which all those with relevant views are encouraged to work together and share responsibility, or in which specific individuals have clear and separate roles and responsibilities? Should the parent give a clear lead on major issues and insist on being involved in a thorough planning dialogue with the businesses, or should it give as much freedom and autonomy as possible to the businesses to propose their own strategies? Should the corporate control process aim to buffer the businesses from short-term profit pressures and encourage the pursuit of flexible long-term strategies, or should it try to sharpen the motivation of business managers to deliver against stretching short-term financial goals?

The Strategic Planning style, for example, is characterized by a commitment to a collective decision process that stresses cooperation, consensus, and shared responsibility;[11] by a close relationship with the businesses in developing their strategies and plans in which the parent provides leadership and direction; and by a desire to encourage long-term strategies through a control process that buffers the businesses from short-term profit pressures. As such, Strategic Planning parents such as Shell are diametrically different from Financial Control parents such as Hanson. What is more, Strategic Planning parents must accept that they will have to forgo the more individualistic decision process, the clear and separate roles and responsibilities, the freedom and autonomy for the businesses in devising strategies, and the tight, short-term financial control processes that are the hallmarks of Financial Control companies. Strategic Planning companies have certain advantages in their relationships with their businesses, but they cannot at the same time have the advantages of a Hanson. There are, in other words, tensions or tradeoffs that cannot be avoided. The Strategic Control style attempts a balance between the extremes represented by the Strategic Planning and Financial Control styles but is consequently forced to be less fully committed to either end of the tension. It enjoys some of the advantages but also suffers some of the drawbacks of both Strategic Planning and Financial Control.[12]

There is also a sort of internal cohesion among the choices made by each style. Thus the Financial Control style's belief in leaving the businesses free to make their own plans fits well with its preference for defining clear individual responsibilities for decisions, but would be much less compatible with a more collectivist approach to decisions. Equally, clear responsibilities and a high level of freedom to discharge those responsibilities implies a need for performance measures to assess how this freedom has been used. Short-term profitability provides just such a measure, whereas a more flexible, long-term control process is less suitable.

There is a basic parenting conflict between an emphasis on working together with the businesses to come up with better plans for their long-term development, and an emphasis on tight control and delivery of promised performance targets. The parent that is closely involved and implicated in developing the strategies of the businesses cannot so readily stand back and appraise objectively the results that are subsequently achieved. The more the parent insists on exercising influence in planning, the less possible it is for it to create a truly tight control process.[13]

Changing and Adjusting Parenting Styles

The parenting style of a company follows from the basic beliefs of the parenting team about how relationships between the parent and the businesses should be handled, and about how the parent can add most value. It reflects the experience, philosophy, and values of the chief executive and his or her team. As such, it is deeply ingrained and difficult to alter. We have found that companies seldom voluntarily change their basic styles without a change in chief executive. A crisis may force a sudden change in style, and, over time, a gradual evolution of a company's style can occur. But a planned move from one style to another, without a major shift in the composition of the top team, is rare.[14]

Equally, very few companies can adjust their styles to establish basically different relationships with different businesses or divisions. Normally there is a dominant style, with, perhaps, limited variations about it for different businesses.[15] Attempts to treat different businesses fundamentally differently seldom succeed. Either the real differences in treatment are modest,[16] or the differences in treatment carry undesirable overtones with them, and so work poorly. For example, several companies have claimed to us that they are able to fine-tune their style, citing the fact that they apply much stricter financial controls to businesses that they believe are in trouble or are on the "for sale" list. But the signals that tight financial controls carry in these circumstances are that the parent perceives the business in a negative light. This is not compatible with a continuing, value-creating relationship with the business in question and does not represent a viable alternative style. To shift between basically different styles for different businesses, and to be equally effective in each style, seems to be beyond the management capabilities of all the companies we have researched.

MATCHING THE PARENTING STYLE AND THE BUSINESSES IN THE PORTFOLIO

It is important to distinguish between the different parenting styles because they are each suited to different sorts of businesses. Businesses that are well suited to a Strategic Planning style parent are likely to be damaged by a Financial Control parent, and vice versa.[17]

Businesses That Match the Strategic Planning Style

Strategic Planning parents typically aim to contribute specialist knowledge and expertise from the corporate parent and its staff resources; engender a wider, more thorough debate about major decisions; encourage coordination and sharing between businesses that might not otherwise occur; create a sense of shared purpose and commitment throughout the organization; and support a more tenacious pursuit of long-term goals. These influences stem from the collective nature of the decision process, the proactive involvement of the parent in planning, and the flexible control process. Thus, businesses that perform well with a Strategic Planning parent typically face large, risky, long-term investments in assets, technology, or market development that are critical to their futures, and for which a thorough review of options prior to a decision, with inputs from corporate staff specialists, is likely to be helpful. They have opportunities to build important sources of competitive advantage by coordinating their activities and decisions with other businesses in the corporate portfolio. And they operate in rapidly changing, fast growing, or fiercely competitive industries, with strategies that stress long-term competitive position rather than current performance, where the flexible Strategic Planning control process is likely to be beneficial.

Conversely, the Strategic Planning style is ill suited to certain businesses. In businesses where tight operations, quick decisions, and low overheads are vital, the time-consuming and costly review processes that are characteristic of Strategic Planning companies add more cost than value. In businesses that have few linkages to other units in the portfolio, the search for synergies through coordination and consensus building is likely to be counterproductive since it tends to reduce the sense of personal responsibility and "ownership" of each business's management team and to increase the cost of decision taking. And in situations where the appropriate strategy is to press for current performance and cash flow, a corporate control process that provides a buffer from short-term profitability pressures will be confusing and potentially damaging. The center relinquishes its role as the objective guardian of clear and measurable standards of profit performance and can be drawn into supporting overambitious and risky long-term strategies that never deliver the results they promise. BTR, for example, is scathing about the influence on the profitability of their businesses of Dunlop's and Hawker Siddeley's traditional beliefs in the need for a long-term view of investments and results.

Businesses That Match the Financial Control Style

Financial Control style parents typically try to foster high levels of motivation in individual business managers, who feel strong personal ownership of the strategies and results that their businesses achieve. Financial Control parents also challenge business managers to set themselves higher and clearer standards for profitability targets and for operating effectiveness than they would otherwise have proposed. A third important influence is the parent's swift reaction to deviations from budget, which prevents complacency and weeds out weaker managers quickly. In the best Financial Control companies, business unit managing directors are energized by the clarity of the success criteria, by the freedom they have to do what is necessary to reach their targets, and by the constant feedback on performance they receive.

These influences are most potent in businesses with room for improved financial performance, and where an emphasis on short-term profitability does not damage long-term prospects and can be met through a multiplicity of individually small, low-risk, quick payback decisions; and where the autonomy of each business unit managing director is not compromised by the need for a parent to intervene to realize value from potential linkages between the businesses in the portfolio. A Financial Control emphasis also fits well for businesses in mature industries and stable competitive situations that should be aiming for strong profit and cash generation, and for businesses with strategies that are intended to create a rapid, short-term turnaround in profitability or to harvest maximum cash from the business.

Conversely, the sort of businesses that benefit from a Strategic Planning parent are very liable to be damaged by the diametrically opposite priorities and emphasis of the Financial Control style. In such businesses, the concern for short-term, individual business results will distract from strategic development, reduce flexibility in pursuing opportunities that arise for long-term advantage, and discourage desirable cooperation between businesses in the portfolio. We would not expect that Canon's businesses would prosper after an acquisition by Hanson or BTR, nor would we recommend an LBO for Shell's oil businesses. Indeed, Financial Control parents are best advised to move rapidly toward an exit decision if they find themselves in businesses undergoing fast technological change, facing fierce international competition, or requiring long-term investments.

Businesses That Match the Strategic Control Style

The Strategic Control style aims to achieve a balance between the features of the Strategic Planning and the Financial Control style. It decentralizes decision making and encourages managers to feel personally responsible for their own businesses, but it also aims to raise penetrating questions about the proposals they put up and to encourage businesses to work together and cooperate if there is benefit in doing so. It allows for long-term decisions, but without sacrificing a focus on short-term results. It attempts to raise standards and enhance motivation to deliver, both in terms of profitability targets and in terms of strategic goals and milestones.

As such, the Strategic Control style has considerable flexibility, and different Strategic Control parents strike the balance in different ways. It is therefore a style that can be compatible with a wide variety of different sorts of businesses. Indeed, there are few businesses for which it is fundamentally unsuited, except those that are extreme examples of either the Strategic Planning or the Financial Control heartland. If a business needs to build a global position against strong competition through major, long-term investments in core technologies that are shared across different businesses in the portfolio, a Strategic Control style parent will probably contribute less to success than a Strategic Planning parent. Conversely, if a business is embarking on a radical turnaround from a financial crisis, the clear disciplines of a Financial Control parent may be more effective in helping to raise operating standards and profitability than a more complex Strategic Control approach. In most businesses, however, the Strategic Control style can work well.

But, because the Strategic Control style is compatible with a wide range of different sorts of businesses, it can tempt companies to diversify too far. Alternatively, it can be seen as an answer by companies that are already overdiversified. In fact, Strategic Control parents with portfolios of businesses with widely different critical success factors seldom succeed in creating value, not because their parenting style is basically unsuitable, but because they lack a feel for some or all of the different businesses. Successful Strategic Control parents tend to have portfolios that consist of businesses with similar critical success factors.

Misfits between Businesses in the Portfolio and the Parenting Style

A fit between a company's parenting style and the characteristics of the businesses in its portfolio is a necessary condition for creating value. Exhibit C–2 summarizes the types of business that fit with each style. However, while style fit is a necessary condition for adding value, it is by no means a sufficient condition, as shown in Part Two of this book.

EXHIBIT C-2 Businesses that fit best with different styles

	Nature of Decisions	Nature of Portfolio Linkages	Nature of Competitive Environment	Nature of Strategy
Strategic Planning	Big, risky, long term	Many/complex	Open or fierce	"Build"
Strategic Control		←——— "Middle Ground" ———→		
Financial Control	Small, incremental, short term	Few/simple	Stable	"Harvest" or turnaround

Misfits between a company's parenting style and the characteristics of businesses in its portfolio will, however, inevitably lead to value destruction. A misfit between the businesses in the portfolio and the parenting style will undermine the effectiveness of any corporate strategy.

A particular problem is presented by businesses whose characteristics change. The businesses in the portfolio of the U.K. GEC company, for example, have become less suitable for a Financial Control style, while IBM's businesses have become less suitable for a Strategic Planning style.[18] Both companies have suffered difficulties as a result. In terms of the family analogy, a parent's children may change their characteristics as they grow up, and come to need a different sort of parenting. Such situations cause severe problems for parents. Their tendency is to continue to provide the same sort of attention and care for each business, even when this is no longer appropriate.

There are no easy answers for a parent in these circumstances. It can make conscious efforts to modify its parenting for the businesses in question, but if the parent remains generally committed to its basic style, there are limits to what can be expected. It can embark on a corporate move toward a new style, but this may not be suitable for other businesses in its portfolio and is likely to prove difficult without major management changes. It can spin off or divest the businesses. This may appear as a painful option, especially for Strategic Planning parents, which usually encourage a deep sense of belonging to the family. But we believe it is often the most practical way of addressing the issue, especially if the changes have only affected a few of the company's businesses.

Companies whose portfolios consist of businesses that require different parenting styles also face problems. Adjusting the company's style for different sorts of businesses is extremely difficult, and it may well be preferable to spin off or demerge the different businesses rather than attempting to parent them within the same portfolio. After many years of wrestling with a portfolio that contained mature commodity chemicals on the one hand and more differentiated, research-intensive pharmaceuticals and agrochemicals on the other, ICI has recognized these fundamental differences by demerging into new ICI and Zeneca. It will be easier for new ICI and Zeneca to adopt different styles that fit their respective businesses than it was previously within the combined ICI portfolio.

MITIGATING THE TENSIONS IN EACH STYLE

By focusing the portfolio away from the sorts of businesses that are liable to be damaged by its chosen style, a parent can do much to reduce the negative impact of the tensions that are inherent in each style. Nevertheless, these tensions remain, and successful exponents of each style need to develop parenting characteristics that will offset them.

Strategic Planning Style

Characteristic criticisms of Strategic Planning companies are that central management interferes in the affairs of the businesses, that decisions get bogged down in costly and time-consuming coordination processes, that control against results is too loose, and that corporate development activities are overambitious. Successful Strategic Planning companies therefore need to be able to provide leadership from the center, but without interfering with the businesses; to facilitate linkages between their businesses, but without a costly coordination bureaucracy; to support long-terms goals, but without looseness of control; and to invest aggressively in developing strong businesses, but without overambitiousness.

If the parent provides strong leadership and advice to the businesses, the danger is that business heads will be irritated, and ultimately emasculated, by too much hands-on involvement. A mutual understanding of, and respect for, the nature of the decentralization contract prevents friction in this area. But it is also necessary for the parent, and its staffs, to possess real expertise on the issues that it chooses to influence; the dividing line between "help" and "interference" depends on the quality of the advice as much as on the nature of the issues concerned. Furthermore, the parent must avoid an autocratic, directive manner in its communications with the businesses, recognizing that it depends on enlisting the support and enthusiasm of the businesses for the ideas it puts forward.

A second key requirement is to establish decision processes, linkage mechanisms, and structures that do not lead to inflexible, costly, and bureaucratic decision making. For example, if matrix structures and coordinating committees are used, they need the sort of flexibility found in Shell to make them work well.

A third feature of successful Strategic Planning parents is an ability to establish a control process that is long term and strategic in orientation, but that avoids looseness. The complaint in many Strategic Planning companies is that "strategic," "long-term" plans and goals allow businesses to get away with mediocre short-term performance almost indefinitely. To avoid looseness, business managers must feel some pressure to perform. For example, while Canon is primarily motivated by pursuit of its long-term vision, its businesses are challenged by the highly ambitious goals derived from this vision and expressed in their 3-year, medium-term plans and their 6-month operating plans.[19] Both peer pressure and long-term career progression combine to give force to these goals.

Lastly, successful Strategic Planning companies typically support aggressive corporate development activities, intended to create competitively stronger businesses. But the danger is that these initiatives are overambitious. Too much is paid for acquisitions; unfamiliar businesses are brought into the portfolio and cause problems; too many initiatives are undertaken simultaneously. Some Strategic Planning companies, such as STC, the U.K. telecommunications group that has now been acquired by Northern Telecom, have been brought to their knees by over-ambition.[20] Successful Strategic Planning companies temper their ambitions with realism, not undertaking corporate developments that are too far beyond the capabilities and resources they possess.

Financial Control Style

Critics of Financial Control companies charge that they focus so much on short-term financial goals that their businesses are unlikely to have any long-term future; that they create an atmosphere of fear that demotivates good managers; and that their corporate strategies do not provide for long-term corporate growth and renewal. To deal with these potential weaknesses, successful Financial Control companies agree stretching targets for their businesses, but without milking the businesses. They establish a no-excuses culture, but without demotivating their managers. And they aim for growth through acquisitions and subsequent restructurings rather than through organic developments.

A real danger for Financial Control companies is that their tough budgetary processes and profitability objectives end up by milking their businesses. Over time, the competitive strength of the businesses is dissipated through lack of investment and too much focus on current profits. This charge has been leveled against most adherents of the Financial Control style at one time or another and has been behind recent skepticism about LBOs. Accordingly, an ability to judge targets that will stretch but not milk each business is a key parenting skill for Financial Control companies. The best Financial Control companies, such as BTR, have sufficient feel for their businesses to avoid targets that are too tough.

Another danger for Financial Control companies is that good managers will be demotivated, burned out, and ultimately lost to the company through the fierceness of the financial control process. The pressures of a no-excuses, constant-improvement culture will then fail to improve performance. A second key skill is therefore the ability to create a tight control culture that nevertheless motivates managers in the businesses. We have found that Financial Control companies can create a sort of "winner's" psychology in their managers. Managers know that they are expected to achieve highly testing targets; if they succeed, they derive enormous satisfaction and self-confidence from their achievement and are reinforced in their determination to do even better in the next time period. This winner's psychology depends on the clarity of the Financial Control goals, the constant feedback on results that are achieved, and the rewards, both financial and psychological, for the best performers. The atmosphere and the culture of the company are key ingredients, as much as the formal control processes. The Financial Control style depends on the motivation it creates; and it must create an atmosphere of winning and ambition, not of fear and failure.

Lastly, it is in the nature of Financial Control types of businesses that growth in their markets will be modest. Since profitability improvements and market share gains cannot be continued indefinitely, this implies that organic growth from ongoing businesses will eventually tail off. Indeed there are real dangers in seeking too much organic growth in mature markets. Tarmac's attempts to achieve growth of 15 percent per annum in the construction industry were a major factor in its crisis during the 1990s recession.[21] Furthermore, the style is not likely to create new businesses through corporate venturing. Successful Financial Control companies, such as Hanson, have however achieved spectacular corporate growth through a series of acquisitions, followed by turnarounds in performance. Their portfolios may not include many businesses in fast-growth, internationally expanding markets. But their corporate results have shown very substantial bottom line growth.

Critics nevertheless retort that the opportunities for such turnarounds are diminishing and that the size of acquisitions needed will become ever greater. They argue that companies and capital markets are growing more efficient so that there are fewer companies in need of turnarounds, that the competition for target companies is growing, and that as a company like Hanson grows, it must make larger and larger acquisitions to sustain its growth. But successful Financial Control companies reject the premises of these arguments. They are driven by value creation and profitability improvement, not by growth as such. Therefore they will only make acquisitions as and when they can do so at a price that will allow them to create value. They recognize the danger of pushing for growth as a primary objective since they are operating in mature markets, and they concentrate instead on their ability to deliver high profits, dividends, and cash flow. Sufficient opportunities for growth by acquisition have emerged for most Financial Control companies; but it is essential for Financial Control companies not to aspire to unrealistic organic growth ambitions.

Strategic Control Style

The downsides of the Strategic Control style are dangers related to falling between two stools. It can fail to promote the close linkages of the Strategic Planning style, but also miss the clear individual business performance focus of the Financial Control style. It can stress the importance of standing back from business decisions, but still insist on asking questions about businesses' strategies that are often insufficiently well-informed. It lacks an unequivocal commitment either to short-term performance or to long-term goals, and so can confuse business managers. Therefore, it is important for Strategic Control style companies to have parenting characteristics that are conducive to balance rather than confusion. They include the ability to encourage some linkages between businesses, without losing focus on each business's performance; to raise penetrating and constructive questions about businesses' strategies that are based on real knowledge of the businesses; and to achieve a balance between strategic and financial objectives that avoids ambiguity.

Successful Strategic Control parents, such as Unilever, support worthwhile links between their businesses, but wish to preserve the responsibility of each business for its own results. Often, this means promoting voluntary sharing of skills or networking about best practice, rather than imposing central policies. In this way, the ultimate responsibility for performance of the businesses is retained.

Far too often, Strategic Control parents are distant from their businesses and so go through planning processes that are superficial, adding only cost and no value. The success of Emerson's Strategic Control planning process is dependent on the top team's ability to zero in on the key issues in each business, and to engage in a constructive debate about them. This ability is based on a depth of understanding of the businesses which distinguishes Emerson from many other Strategic Control companies whose strategic planning processes work less well. A portfolio composed of businesses with common critical success factors makes this requirement much easier to satisfy.

A final common problem for Strategic Control parents is that their control processes are confusing for their business heads. Rather than striking a balance between different desirable objectives, they vacillate between them, shifting priorities as circumstances change. A classic complaint from business managers in Strategic Control companies is that the parent seems to be all in favor of long-term strategic investment during the strategy review process in the spring, but exclusively focused on next year's profit performance when it comes to budget time in the autumn. This represents ambiguity, not balance, and leads to confusion and demotivation on the part of business managers. To avoid this pitfall, successful Strategic Control companies need to maintain a consistent emphasis between different goals, which recognizes the tradeoffs that often exist between short-term performance and long-term objectives.

NOTES

1. See Michael Goold and Andrew Campbell, *Strategies and Styles,* Oxford: Basil Blackwell, 1987. In *Strategies and Styles,* we had not yet developed the concept of "parenting," and therefore simply referred to "management styles." A related classification of parenting roles is put forward by Sigurd E. Reinton and Nathaniel Foote in "Why Parents Must Be More Particular," *The McKinsey Quarterly,* Autumn 1988, pp. 46–53.

2. See Michael Goold with John J. Quinn, *Strategic Control,* London: Financial Times/Pitman Publishing, reissued 1993.

3. We refer to companies that combine low planning influence with flexible control as "Holding Companies." Such companies create little value through their parenting, and we do not regard this style as a viable parenting option. We also regard the combination of high planning influence and tight financial control as nonviable: In effect, the parent is then sharing the decision-taking responsibility with the business managers but holding the business managers tightly accountable for the results achieved. This is not a form of decentralization contract that is attractive to capable business managers.

4. In *Strategies and Styles,* IBM was identified as a Strategic Planning style company.

5. See Nigel Campbell, Michael Goold, and Kimio Kase, *The Role of the Centre in Managing Large Diversified Companies in Japan,* Ashridge Strategic Management Centre Working Paper, 1990.

6. See Goold and Quinn, *Strategic Control.*

7. See David Young and Michael Goold, *Effective Headquarters Staff,* Ashridge Strategic Management Centre, 1993.

8. See Michael Goold, Andrew Campbell, and Kathleen Luchs, "Strategies and Styles Revisited: 'Strategic Control'—Is It Tenable?" *Long Range Planning,* vol. 26, no. 6, December 1993.

9. See Michael Goold, Andrew Campbell, and Kathleen Luchs, "Strategies and Styles Revisited: Strategic Planning and Financial Control," *Long Range Planning,* vol. 26, no. 5, October 1993.

10. See *"KKR's Corporate Strategy,"* Ashridge Strategic Management Centre Working Paper, 1993.

11. In some Strategic Planning style companies, decisions are pushed through by strong autocratic central leadership rather than by consensus building.

12. Richard Pascale argues that, in successful companies, the conflicts that arise due to these tensions are productive and keep companies on their toes (see *Managing on the Edge,* New York: Viking, 1990). Charles Hampden-Turner maintains that some tensions are dilemmas that can be resolved by skillful management (see *Charting the Corporate Mind,* Oxford: Basil Blackwell, 1990). But the recognition that fundamental parenting choices must be faced by all parents remains essential.

13. In centralized companies, the center sets the strategy and then requires the businesses to implement it. In this context, there may be tight control against the detailed implementation steps, rather as with a franchisee. But the overall performance of the business, as opposed to the implementation steps, is now the primary responsibility of the center, not of the business's general manager—and, in this sense, the unit is not a fully fledged business. The parenting tensions we have been discussing concern the relationship between a parent and a fully fledged business. See Appendix B for further discussion.

14. See Goold and Campbell, *Strategies and Styles,* and Goold, Campbell, and Luchs, "Strategies and Styles Revisited: 'Strategic Control'—Is It Tenable?"

15. The real range of behavior that most chief executives are capable of is relatively limited; the meaning of "tight financial control" is very different for a died-in-the-wool Strategic Planning chief executive as compared with a hard-nosed Financial Controller.

16. Or, at least, are perceived by the businesses to be modest. Chief executives often complain that they are prisoners of their own reputations, and that businesses seem unwilling to recognize intended changes in treatment, assuming that the established style remains in force despite attempts by the center to signal changes in it.

17. See Goold and Campbell, *Strategies and Styles.* See also Alfred J. Chandler, Jr., "The Functions of the HQ Unit in the Multibusiness Firm," *Strategic Management Journal,* vol. 12, 1991, pp. 31–50; David J. Collis, "The Organisation of Multibusiness Corporations: Four Roles of the Corporate Office." Unpublished working paper, Harvard Business School, 1994; Vijay Govindarajan, "A Contingency Approach to Strategy Implementation at the Business-Unit Level: Integrating Administrative Mechanisms with Strategy," *Academy of Management Journal,* 1988, vol. 31, no. 4, pp. 828–853; V. Govindarajan and Joseph Fisher, "Strategy, Control Systems, and Resource Sharing: Effects on Business Unit Performance," *Academy of Management Journal,* vol. 33, no. 2, 1990, pp. 259–285; Charles W. L. Hill, Michael A. Hitt, and Robert E. Hoskisson, "Cooperative versus Competitive Structures in Related and Unrelated Diversified Firms," *Organization Science,* vol. 3, no. 4, November 1992; Charles W. L. Hill, "The Functions of the Headquarters Unit in Multibusiness Firms," in R. Rumelt, D. Teece, and D. Schendel (eds.), *Fundamental Issues in Strategy Research,* Cambridge: Harvard University Press, 1994.

18. See Goold, Campbell, and Luchs, "Strategies and Styles Revisited: Strategic Planning and Financial Control," and Chapter 10.

19. We are indebted to Professor Tadao Kagono of Kobe University for bringing out what he calls the "pressure kettle" nature of many Japanese companies' control processes. Kagono suggests that a key role for senior managers in the parent organization is to establish and use sufficiently stretching goals to challenge the business managers to fresh efforts and creative ideas for achieving them. Thus, he reported to us a conversation in which a Japanese CEO claimed that to set a goal of achieving a 3 percent cost reduction might be very hard, while to set a goal of a 30 percent cost reduction might be much more helpful.

20. See Goold, Campbell, and Luchs, "Strategies and Styles Revisited: Strategic Planning and Financial Control."

21. See Goold, Campbell, and Luchs, "Strategies and Styles Revisited: Strategic Planning and Financial Control."

D ALLIANCES

Alliances of one type or another have always formed part of corporate life. In recent years, however, there has been growing interest in alliances, particularly as an alternative to acquisition.[1] Between 1976 and 1987, there was a sixfold increase in the rate of U.S. alliance formation,[2] and by the early 1990s, U.S. corporations averaged four cooperative agreements for every one foreign subsidiary.[3] In Japan, alliances have been even more common. Japanese firms are estimated to obtain only 5 percent of supplies through noncooperative relationships; 40 percent come from the internal network, and 55 percent from cooperative networks.[4] Some industries, such as semiconductors, involve a complex web of global alliances, where each major player may be part of four or five overlapping groups that span the world.[5]

Alliances can be important in a corporate strategy, because the parent often plays a major role both in initiating them and in helping to parent new entities that emerge from them. In this appendix, therefore, we will start by distinguishing between different forms of alliance, and considering what rationales underlie them. We will then examine the role of the parent in alliance formation. Finally, we will focus on a subset of alliances of particular interest to the parent: those that involve more than one parent company influencing a single business.

DIFFERENT FORMS OF ALLIANCE

The term "alliance" suggests a relationship that is based on more than short-term arm's length dealings. There is an intention to cooperate in some way, with a view to mutual benefits that would not be achieved by

430

a string of purely "spot market" transactions. But the term also suggests a relationship between parties of similar status. One party may be larger or stronger than others, but it is not hierarchically distinguished from them. Alliances are between "partners." Alliances therefore occupy the middle ground on a spectrum between purely arm's length markets at one extreme, and full ownership by the same parent at the other.[6] This middle ground covers a broad range of relationships, and the term "alliance" can be used to cover quite different subsets of these relationships.[7] Given the practical difficulties of achieving an agreed definition, we will identify some different types of relationship that are sometimes grouped under the alliance label.

Licensing agreements fall close to the "market" end of the spectrum. Frequently, they do little more than reduce contracting costs by stringing together a series of similar transactions over time. Instead of agreeing a contract for each transaction, a single contract covers the basic terms under which each of the transactions will be concluded. However, by committing both parties to a longer term relationship, it is more likely that unforeseen circumstances will arise than in a spot market transaction. As a result, each party is potentially more vulnerable to the behavior and attitudes of the other. This introduces the need for trust. Although the conditions of the licensing agreement may be largely explicit, both parties know that they cannot legislate in advance for all possible outcomes. There is therefore benefit in working with a partner who is trusted.

Franchise agreements could be regarded as a complex form of license. The franchisor licenses the use of a concept, brand name, and other supporting elements (such as documented procedures or specified equipment) in exchange for payments that are partly contingent on performance. In some senses, the franchise embodies a form of quasi-parenting. What the franchisee acquires is a package of stand-alone, linkage, and functional influence, largely expressed in contractual clauses and procedures. The commitment to spend a certain percentage of revenues on brand advertising, for example, could be regarded as a linkage mechanism binding together the various separate franchised businesses. Similarly, the setting and policing of quality standards may embody stand-alone and functional influence in largely contractual terms. In this sense, a franchise is an unusually explicit form of decentralization contract. Despite its contractual nature, the complexity of the agreement and the opportunity for both parties to damage the other through failing to honor commitments typically increase the requirement for trust relative to a straight licensing agreement.

The importance of trust, and an underlying relationship that is not merely contractual, increases with increased uncertainty as to future outcomes. *Relational contracting*[8] describes situations where significant elements of future outcomes cannot be legislated for in advance. In other words, the explicit element of the contract is no more important than the underlying relationship that will determine future behavior by each party. This sort of loose or open contract, based on tacit understandings involving mutual good will, enables parties to work together in ways that would be impossible without trust.

Relationship management focuses on benefits that can be achieved not just from greater trust, but from greater understanding and involvement. For example, a supplier may have a relationship with its customer that goes beyond simple one-off transactions. By understanding more about the customer's needs and preferences, the supplier can tailor its offerings more appropriately and may also identify new commercial opportunities. The improved commitment and service to the customer can also lead to loyalty, and the establishment of trust as an output of the relationship as well as an input to it.[9]

Consortia focus less on the relationship between buyer and supplier than on the relationship between complementary suppliers. By pooling skills or coordinating approaches, each member increases its chances of gaining access to a transaction. Once again, the terms of the consortium may be largely explicit, but the costs of fully detailed contracting are high. Some level of trust and an underlying noncontractually based relationship will therefore be an advantage in establishing and running a consortium.

Virtual corporations and *virtual functions*[10] extend the concept of the consortium in much the same way that relational contracting extends the concept of fully explicit contracting or licensing. Rather than form a dedicated consortium for a specified purpose, organizations work together more flexibly in a network. For example, the many small pottery firms in the Sassuolo region of Italy work together in shifting patterns that align to meet the best opportunities that any one of them creates.[11] The opportunity is therefore addressed by a "virtual corporation," in that there is no long-term organizational structure that maintains the short-term pattern of alignment.

In all these cases, some type of alliance is formed. The greater the level of trust involved, the more readily the term "alliance" is applied. Trust can be developed in different ways that extend the relationship beyond the purely contractual. An obvious way is to tie the fortunes of the parties together in some wider sense. Cross-holdings are typically used for this purpose. In Japanese horizontal *keiretsus* or business groupings, 26 percent of the stock of each member is typically held by other members.[12] This underlines the concept of mutual support without dependence. Cross-holdings imply an intent to cooperate on a range of projects or issues over a prolonged time span.

An extension of cross-holdings is a full-blown *joint venture*.[13] Rather than creating links across existing units, parents can pool interests and resources in a new entity in which they share ownership. Instead of focusing on the value of individual inputs, as in a market transaction, a joint venture shifts the emphasis towards maximizing the value of outputs. This is particularly relevant if the inputs are difficult to value accurately, such as skills, access to customer networks, or technologies that are rapidly spawning new applications. Although these inputs must still be valued approximately to determine a fair ownership structure, valuation of inputs is deemphasized relative to achieving success for the new entity, in which all parties share.

Cross-holdings and joint ventures are therefore important types of alliance, but are by no means the only ways in which alliances can be formed.

RATIONALES FOR ALLIANCE

There are two basic rationales for an alliance:[14]

1. An alliance can provide benefits that could not be achieved either by arm's length transactions or by full ownership.
2. Full ownership would be desirable to at least one party but is blocked by another party or by external constraints.

As we observed in the preceding section, alliances are attractive relative to a string of arm's length transactions when fully explicit contracting is impossible or very costly. By creating or extending trust, alliances enable partners to reduce the cost of arm's length contracting. This is particularly useful when the future outcomes are extremely unclear or when the parties are potentially vulnerable to predatory action by each other. For example, two businesses may wish to share assets, such as a production facility, distribution center, or computer installation, which are only economically efficient in larger blocks than required by either party. It may be possible for one party to own the asset and to sell excess resource to the other. However, this is sometimes difficult in practice. The two parties may be competing, causing each to mistrust the other. If one acts as supplier, it could use its ownership of the asset to disadvantage its competitor. Alternatively, it may be difficult to determine in advance exactly how the capacity will be divided up, under what circumstances one party will receive priority over the other, what will happen if quality standards are not met, and so on. To increase trust and reduce the complexity and cost of explicit contracting for all possible future outcomes, an alliance may prove economically attractive. By setting up a joint venture, for example, both parties may feel less exposed to damaging behavior by the other.

Similarly, it will sometimes be difficult to make explicit contracts for sharing complementary business skills. For example, if one company has a potentially valuable technology and another company has relevant expertise in production and marketing, it may be more efficient to bring these together than for each company to develop the skills it currently lacks. It may be possible for one company to sell its skills to the other under a straight contract. The technology patents of one company or the marketing database of the other might be sold outright. However, such transactions may once again be hard to conclude. The technology company may feel it has no way of valuing its new breakthrough without a better market understanding. The production company may feel it cannot transfer its capabilities without selling its actual people. Given the uncertainties of the situation, explicit contracting may also be costly. In such a case, some form of alliance will be attractive. The specific type will depend on the nature of contracting difficulties. A contingent licensing agreement will resolve some difficulties in valuing the technology. But if the technology itself is not easily transferred from one organization to another, some more integrated form of joint venture will be required.

Gaining access to parenting skills, rather than business skills, may also be valuable. A company may perceive that a business which it currently owns or wishes to develop would greatly benefit from the parenting of a different company. To gain access to beneficial stand-alone or linkage influence, some form of alliance will be required. For example, a parent may wish to establish a new unit in a territory that is significantly outside the parent's past experience. Linkage with other businesses in the country may be very useful, as well as external contacts and stand-alone advice on different local issues. Sometimes these benefits can be bought in through local staff and advisers, but they may well be provided more effectively by an appropriate local parent. In such cases, a joint venture may be the price required by the local parent, rather than charging a fee for its services.[15]

A rather different alliance rationale depends not so much on sharing assets or skills, but on sharing risk. In a highly volatile environment, individual players may pursue alliances in order to hedge their bets. With finite resources, they may wish to have a 25 percent share in four emergent technologies, for example, rather than a 100 percent share in one, which may prove irrelevant or a failure. Once again, if the risk can be hedged with a straightforward contract, no complex alliance is required. For example, rather than form an alliance with a French company to limit its French currency exposure, a U.S. corporation can simply buy a currency hedging contract. But sometimes the market is not able to provide an appropriate mechanism. In developing new media, for example, it is not simply a question of buying into the right technology. It is also a question of being involved with a number of technologies that may shape, and be shaped by, those who join together in exploiting them. The boundary between risk sharing and skill sharing is therefore blurred.[16]

In situations prompting alliance rather than market transactions, buying the entire company with which the alliance is made sometimes provides a theoretical solution. Although such purchases do occur (e.g., the purchase of small high-technology companies by larger companies with greater marketing clout), they may be less attractive than an alliance for various reasons. Most obviously, if the area of alliance represents only a fraction of the activities of the partners, the benefits of integration may be outweighed by wider disadvantages. Antitrust considerations may also be important. In the case of risk sharing, full acquisition of the partner would be self-defeating. A parent who is capable of buying a partner may also be concerned that its own parenting will be inappropriate. By bringing the partner too much under its own influence, the parent may destroy the very things it wishes to access. This is one of the problems that large companies have faced in buying small businesses with desirable skills and intellectual property.[17]

Even if full acquisition or merger is seen as an attractive long-term outcome, an alliance may provide the opportunity to build trust and mutual understanding in advance. By providing a courtship period, both parties can find out more about each other's aims and characteristics. If merger becomes appropriate, this should improve the chances of eventual integration. It may also lead both sides to conclude that an apparently attractive merger would not be viable in practice.

On other occasions, hierarchical integration may be economically attractive but blocked for other reasons. In many countries, full ownership of businesses by foreign parents is either discouraged or illegal. If a company wishes to operate in these markets, some alternative means of access will therefore be required. Similarly, owners of certain businesses or technologies may refuse to consider outright sale, while being prepared to form an alliance. Such views are not always economically based. A would-be acquiror may decide that alliance is not the optimal way forward, but is preferable to allowing a competitor to form a similar alliance.

For various reasons, alliances have become increasingly popular in the late 1980s and early 1990s. First, the level of technology, market, and capital risk has risen dramatically in many industries. Second, increasing globalization and major shifts in world demographics have taken many companies from the developed world into countries with which they were previously unfamiliar, and in which local ownership is difficult. Third, given the poor track record of acquisitions,[18] interest has focused on alternative ways of achieving potential benefits of linkage, synergy, or scale. In particular, the desire to avoid inappropriate stand-alone influence while capturing linkage benefits has highlighted the attraction of networks or keiretsu rather than full ownership.[19] Fourth, concern over the capital costs of direct investment or acquisition has prompted many companies to explore less capital-intensive expansion routes, especially following the stock market slump of 1987.[20] Finally, along with many other factors, fashion has played a role; it has spawned a large number of conferences, books, and articles on the topic, and possibly has encouraged over-optimistic claims for the future role of alliances in corporate-level strategy.

Alliances are evidently attractive in many situations. However, it remains important to weigh up carefully the benefits of an alliance as against full ownership or merger. In this context, the comments of Percy Barnevik, chief executive of ABB, are interesting to note. "There have been plenty of articles in the last few years about all the cross-border mergers in Europe. In fact, the more interesting issue is why there have been so *few*. There should be *hundreds* of them, involving *tens of billions* of dollars, in industry after industry. But we're not seeing it. What we're seeing instead are strategic alliances and minority investments. Companies buy 15 percent of each other's shares. Or two rivals agree to cooperate in third markets but not merge their home-market organizations. I worry that many European alliances are poor substitutes for doing what we try to do—complete mergers and cross-border rationalization."[21]

THE PARENT'S ROLE IN FORMING ALLIANCES

If a business unit within a company sees good reasons for an alliance, the parent's role may be simply to authorize, or block, the proposed move. At a minimum, deals over a certain size will require parental approval, based on a more or less formal evaluation process. The parent will therefore adopt a role that parallels acquisition approval or capital expenditure appraisal. The parent's ability to create or destroy value in this process closely parallels the discussion of such processes in Chapter 6.

Frequently, however, parents take a more active role in alliance formation. First, as part of their stand-alone influence, they may encourage businesses to seek alliances in certain situations with specific partners. For example, if the relative size and risk of new developments in a business area is increasing rapidly and involves moves into new markets, the parent may press the relevant division to seek external partners, both to reduce its capital exposure on individual projects and to harness the assessment skills of local companies.

Second, as part of their linkage influence, parents may seek to coordinate the alliances of their individual businesses. For example, they may steer businesses away from alliances that would come into conflict with each other or that would involve different, and directly competing, rivals. Similarly they may steer businesses toward alliances with partners who have good relationships elsewhere in the company. By coordinating alliances, a better or deeper overall relationship may be fostered.

Third, acting as a function or central service, the parent may provide relevant specialist expertise. For example, a central legal department that has experience in joint venture contracting, or a personnel function that has dealt with alliance staffing issues, may help a business in negotiations or deal structure.

Fourth, as part of its corporate development activity, the parent may itself structure alliances as an alternative to acquisition or disposal. For example, it may choose to establish a joint venture for any of the reasons described in the preceding section.

In each of these areas, the parent's ability to create value is subject to the paradoxes discussed in Part Two of this book. If the parent cannot overcome the basic paradoxes associated with each sort of value creation, it is as likely to cause damage with its alliance interventions as it is on any other topic. Parents often destroy value by acting as a drag on the process, or constituting a major impediment to useful alliances. Insistence on inappropriate clauses, delays in decision making, criteria emphasizing personal contacts rather than business needs are some of the typical complaints aired by unit heads. One business head explained to us that 2 years of work establishing links with a potential Japanese partner were effectively ruined by one meeting with senior managers in the parent company. The attitudes conveyed by the parent undermined the positioning of the business unit, and partnership relations were terminally damaged. Similarly, parents may press their businesses to become involved in alliances that are distracting or even damaging to the basic competitive position of the unit.

However, parents can also smooth the way to alliances, particularly through good relations with their counterparts in other multibusiness companies. Through a mixture of skills in management assessment, influencing, and communications, they can create a favorable context for business-level alliances. Similarly, if they have specialist experience in structuring alliance deals, they can play a helpful role.

MULTIPARENTED ALLIANCES

We have seen that the term alliance can be applied to a wide range of relationships that go beyond strict market transactions, but fall short of full ownership by the same parent. Within this broad grouping, certain types of alliance, most notably joint ventures, involve multiple parenting of a single business. In other words, more than one parent is in a position to exert influence on the same business. These situations are of particular interest from a parenting perspective, and form the focus of this section.

Whatever the parent's role in their development, the existence of multiparented units creates a quasi-extension of the portfolio with which the parent is concerned. In many cases, business units themselves become the parents of a new joint venture. But whether the relationship is managed through a business, a division, a group, or directly by the head office, a potentially complex parenting role is established. For a parent to create value in this role, many of the conditions and observations from our main text apply. However, there are three related and distinguishing features of parenting in such circumstances: (1) A number of normal influencing mechanisms are not fully accessible to the parent; (2) by definition, there is at least one other parenting group outside any overarching hierarchical structure; (3) alliances usually represent an arena for learning, in which the partners compete as well as collaborate.

The first distinguishing feature is important because parenting characteristics that are effective within the fully owned portfolio may be inapplicable to a multiparented alliance. For example, while particular skills in best practice sharing or in developing networks through managing career paths may be important to a parent's linkage influence inside its own portfolio, they may be difficult to replicate in a joint venture. Similarly, if tight management of financial controls or the appointment of senior business managers are the main vehicles of a parent's stand-alone influence, their operation in a multiparented alliance may be limited for reasons of shared governance.

The second feature creates a need to clarify the roles of the different parents. Within a company, multiple parenting is not unknown.[22] For example, the business units in a matrix have at least two parents of notionally equal standing but with different perspectives. This creates a tension that can either be healthy or damaging.[23] However, the existence of an overarching structure and single chief executive usually provides an ultimate mechanism for resolution of deadlocks.[24] Even if the lower parenting groups seldom resort to this mechanism, its existence has an important effect. In multiparented alliances, however, there may be no such mechanism. This can affect the way that different parents attempt, or are able, to influence a unit. In extreme cases, the unit may play off one parent against another with even greater ease than in a matrix. Even without such intent, concerns about creating or resolving parental differences may reduce the ability of either parent to play a normal role. It is often noted that parents must share objectives and risks if alliances are to work.[25] However, it is also important that they share perceptions as to how the business will be parented. For example, an apparently fair decision to have equal representation on the board often results instead in unhelpful ambiguity. Parents must think through what mechanisms or vehicles will be needed to help the business, and structure their parenting roles accordingly. A division of parenting tasks and roles that is appropriate for one context may be inappropriate for another. Successful alliances involve clear agreement about these roles and about how difficult issues can and must be raised with the other side.[26] They also depend on regular contact (often informal) between the higher level parent organizations, so that disputes can be resolved in an atmosphere of trust rather than suspicion.[27]

The third distinctive feature concerns competition between parents. Many companies seek out alliances with overlapping competitors or even direct rivals. By engaging in joint activities, they effectively open a "second front" of competition. Instead of competing directly in the marketplace, they compete in their ability to outlearn their existing or potential competitors.[28] Parents can play a crucial role in either enhancing or blocking the rate of this learning and in transferring it to other parts of their portfolio. If a joint venture is treated as a "dead end," visited by few parent managers, staffed by executives who stay in place or are never reintegrated, and uncoupled from the fully owned portfolio, the value of corporate learning is unlikely to be high. Conversely, active parenting of the learning opportunity can both accelerate and spread intangible benefits. The Japanese are often considered particularly adept at this form of competition through collaboration,[29] which lies at the heart of many successful alliance strategies.[30] Just as it provides value creation opportunities for a suitable parent with the right characteristics, it poses a severe threat to inappropriate parents who undermine the competitive advantage of their businesses. The ability to learn, and the parent's role in accelerating learning, are central to the success of multiparented alliances.[31] The concept of "parenting advantage" is brought into unusually high relief, as parents are competing directly to create value in their different portfolios from the same basic material: the businesses that they jointly parent.

Multiparented alliances therefore involve pitfalls even for companies that create significant value in their wholly owned portfolios. In contrast, some parents prove particularly adept in these situations.[32] They reveal skills in handling other parents and are able to create value from businesses to which they cannot apply the normal range of influencing mechanisms.

Alliances may indeed provide a useful vehicle for addressing the related problems of risk, and of gaining access to skills, markets, and growth opportunities, but the difficulties of parenting them and the dangers of falling prey to parents with learning advantage, should encourage some caution in their use.[33]

NOTES

1. See, for example, Brian Bollen, "A Growing Trend towards Alliances," *Financial Times*, July 20, 1992; Tim Dickson, "An Emerging Taste for Strategic Alliances," *Financial Times*, May 27, 1993. For a broader view of this trend, see M. Hergert and D. Morris, "Trends in International Collaborative Agreements," F. Contractor and P. Lorange (eds.), *Cooperative Strategies in International Business, Joint Ventures and Technology Partnerships between Firms*, New York: Lexington Books, 1988.

2. Karen J. Hladik and Lawrence H. Linden, "Is an International Joint Venture in R&D for You?" *Research Technology Management*, vol. 32, no. 4, pp. 11–13, July–August 1989.

3. Contractor and Lorange, *Cooperative Strategies in International Business*.

4. Frank Hull, Gene Slowinski, Robert Wharton, and Koya Azumi, "Strategic Partnerships between Technological Entrepreneurs in the United States and Large Corporations in Japan and the United States," in Contractor and Lorange (eds.), *Cooperative Strategies in International Business*.

5. See Philippe Gugler, "Building Transnational Alliances to Create Competitive Advantage," *Long Range Planning*, vol. 25, no. 1, pp. 90–99, 1992.

6. As such, alliances are often analyzed as a hybrid between the polar "markets" and "hierarchies" that dominate so-called transaction cost literature. This literature is highly relevant to an understanding of different types of alliance. See, for example, O. E. Williamson, *Markets and Hierarchies*, New York: Free Press, 1975; David J. Teece, "Economies of Scope and the Scope of the Enterprise," *Journal of Economic Behaviour and Organization*, 1, 1980, pp. 223–247; Keith MacMillan and David Farmer, "Redefining the Boundaries of the Firm," *The Journal of Industrial Economics*, XXVII, March 1979, pp. 277–284; P. Mariti and R. H. Smiley, "Co-operative Agreements and the Organization of Industry," *The Journal of Industrial Economics*, XXXI, June 1982, pp. 435–451; Hans B. Thorelli, "Networks: Between Markets and Hierarchies," *Strategic Management Journal*, 7, 1986, pp. 37–51.

7. The term "network" is also used in this context, with a wide variety of meanings, spanning relationships both within an organization and outside it. See Nitin Nohria and Robert G. Eccles (eds.), *Networks and Organizations*, Boston: Harvard Business School Press, 1993; J. Carlos Jarillo, "On Strategic Networks," *Strategic Management Journal*, 9, 1988, pp. 31–41.

8. See Peter Smith Ring and Andrew H. Van de Ven, "Structuring Cooperative Relationships between Organizations," *Strategic Management Journal*, vol. 13, 1992, pp. 483–498.

9. Trust may also be important in gaining sufficient access to the customer to understand its needs.

10. See, for example, Arnoud De Meyer, "Creating the Virtual Factory," INSEAD Working Paper.

11. Approximately 300 small firms in a tight geographical grouping work together in a constantly shifting pattern. This blends a high degree of flexibility with economies of scale in distribution, labor utilization, specialist skills, and even some aspects of branding.

12. Roy L. Simerly, "Should U.S. Companies Establish Keiretsus?" *Journal of Business Strategy*, vol. 13, no. 6, November–December 1992, pp. 58–61; see also Philippe Lasserre, "The Management of Large Groups: Asia and Europe Compared," *European Management Journal*, vol. 10, no. 2, June 1992, pp. 157–162.

13. See, for example, Kathryn Harrigan, "Joint Ventures and Global Strategies," *Columbia Journal of World Business*, Summer 1984, pp. 7–16;

Kathryn Rudie Harrigan, *Managing for Joint Venture Success*, Lexington, MA: Lexington Books, 1986.

14. In practice, it should be recognized that many alliances are formed for reasons that defy economic logic. Personal relationships, chance meetings, and internal political considerations all play a role. As a result, some alliances exist for no better reason than that they are difficult to untangle. However, we will focus on the economic justification for alliances rather than on their historical causes.

15. The latter approach might anyway lead to a different type of relationship, which would not achieve the desired objectives.

16. Fumio Sato, President and Chief Executive of Toshiba Corporation, illustrated this point in his comments in a *Financial Times* advertorial: "With today's rapid advances in high technology, product development costs in the electronics industry, not to mention the risks involved, have grown enormously. To reduce these, shorten development times and to develop advanced technologies, Toshiba is actively involved in international alliances."

17. This has led to a wide range of alliance forms between production and distribution entities, for example, in the movie and music industries.

18. See, for example, Michael E. Porter, "From Competitive Advantage to Corporate Strategy," *Harvard Business Review*, May–June 1987, pp. 43–59; William W. Bain, Jr., "Shopping for Companies," *Across the Board*, July–August 1986.

19. See Chapters 7 and 14.

20. Although financial theory suggests that capital is always available for suitable projects, managers' perceptions of capital availability may be different. See, for example, "An Emerging Taste for Strategic Alliances" *Financial Times*, May 27, 1993.

21. William Taylor, "The Logic of Global Business: An Interview with ABB's Percy Barnevik," *Harvard Business Review*, March–April 1991, pp. 90–105.

22. See Appendix B on parent definition and structure.

23. See the discussion of matrices in Chapter 7.

24. Shell and Unilever do maintain two boards at the highest level, but both companies have clear mechanisms for resolving any deadlocks.

25. E.g., Peter Lorange, Johan Roos, *Strategic Alliances: Formation, Implementation and Evolution*, Oxford: Basil Blackwell, 1992; J. D. Lewis, *Partnerships for Profit: Structuring and Managing Strategic Alliances*, New York: Free Press, 1990.

26. See Lewis, *Partnerships for Profit*; William H. Newman, "Launching a Viable Joint Venture," *California Management Review*, Fall 1992, pp. 68–80; also *Birth of a Successful Joint Venture*, Lanham, MD: University Press of America, 1992.

27. For a discussion of the situations and alliance structures that are inherently more likely than others to be associated with high opportunity to cheat; high behavioral uncertainty; and poor stability, longevity, and performance, see Amind Parkhe, "Strategic Alliance Structuring: A Game Theoretic and Transaction Cost Examination of Interfirm Cooperation," *Academy of Management Journal,* vol. 36, no. 4, 1993; see also C. Koenig and G. van Wijk, "Interfirm Alliances: The Role of Trust," in J. Thepot and R. A. Thietarat (eds.), *Microeconomic Contributions to Strategic Management,* New York: North Holland, 1991.

28. David Lei and John W. Slocum, Jr., "Global Strategy, Competence-Building and Strategic Alliances," *California Management Review,* Fall 1992, pp. 81–97; see also R. A. Bettis, S. P. Bradley, and G. Hamel, "Outsourcing and Industrial Decline," *Academy of Management Executive,* vol. 6, February 1992, pp. 7–22.

29. In an article in the *Financial Times,* May 7, 1993, Christopher Lorenz reported on research into learning in collaborations between U.S. and Japanese firms. This research, by Mary Crossan of Western Business School, Ontario, and Andrew Inkpen of Temple University, in Philadelphia, highlighted the relative weakness of the U.S. companies in managing the learning process. See also K. K. Jones and W. E. Shill, "Allying for Advantage," *McKinsey Quarterly,* 3, 1990.

30. In "Strategic Alliances with Japanese Firms: Myths and Realities," *Long Range Planning,* vol. 26, no. 4, Dominique Turpin argues that the reasons for success or failure in joint ventures in Japan are not very different from those outside Japan.

31. For further discussion of parental learning, see Chapters 10 and 15.

32. Many books and articles provide useful advice on how to increase the chances of success, though seldom from the particular perspective of how parents can add value. See, for example, Lewis, *Partnerships for Profit;* Lorange and Roos, *Strategic Alliances;* Stephen Gates, *Strategic Alliances: Guidelines for Successful Management,* The Conference Board Europe, Report No. 1028; Contractor and Lorange, *Cooperative Strategies in International Business;* Nohria and Eccles, *Networks and Organizations.*

33. See D. Lei and J. W. Slocum, Jr., "Global Strategic Alliances: Payoffs and Pitfalls," *Organizational Dynamics,* vol. 1, 1991, pp. 44–62.

Author Index

Subject Index

446